The Walking Qur'an

ISLAMIC CIVILIZATION AND MUSLIM NETWORKS

Carl W. Ernst and Bruce B. Lawrence, editors

A complete list of titles published in this series appears at the end of the book.

The Walking Qurʾan

ISLAMIC EDUCATION, EMBODIED KNOWLEDGE, AND HISTORY IN WEST AFRICA

RUDOLPH T. WARE III

THE UNIVERSITY OF
NORTH CAROLINA PRESS
CHAPEL HILL

This book was published with the assistance of the Authors Fund of the University of North Carolina Press.

Manufactured in the United States of America
Set in Minion by Tseng Information Systems, Inc.

The University of North Carolina Press has been a member of the Green Press Initiative since 2003.

Library of Congress Cataloging-in-Publication Data
Ware, Rudolph T., III
The walking Qur'an : Islamic education, embodied knowledge, and history in West Africa / Rudolph T. Ware III.
pages cm — (Islamic civilization and Muslim networks)
Includes bibliographical references and index.
ISBN 978-1-4696-1431-1 (paperback) —
ISBN 978-1-4696-1432-8 (ebook)
1. Islamic religious education—Africa, West. 2. Qur'an—Study and teaching—Africa, West. I. Title.
BP43.A358W37 2014
297.7′70966—dc23 2013051122

18 17 16 15 14 5 4 3 2 1

Tom Pow, untitled poem, 2007, translated into Arabic in the cover illustration by Everitte Barbee by permission of the author:

> A man and a woman once sat down
> at a bare table and looked out
> at the sky. What needs to be done?
>
> they asked, so that, in later years,
> their children or their grandchildren
> might ask, What shall we do today?

بسم الله الرحمن الرحيم

Lovingly dedicated to the women who have filled my life with joy and wonder: my mother, Christine; my wife, Kaaronica; and my daughters, Samonia, Shamarra, Ismaʿilia, and Rabiʿa

My servant draws not near to Me with anything more beloved by Me than the worship I have enjoined upon him, and My servant draws ever closer to Me with voluntary devotions so that I shall love him. When I love him I am the ear with which he hears, the eye with which he sees, the hand with which he strikes and the foot with which he walks.

—Ḥadīth Qudsī, or Holy Saying, God's speech as paraphrased by the Prophet Muḥammad

صلى الله عليه وسلم

CONTENTS

MAPS AND ILLUSTRATIONS

Maps

Illustrations

ACKNOWLEDGMENTS

Gratitude wells within me as I write these lines that are both a beginning and an end. Though they are the first words for the reader, they are the last for the writer, and thus they are filled with emotion. This book has been an odyssey, a journey to fulfill a mission that has occupied me for much of the past twelve years. In my bodily, spiritual, and intellectual travels, I have accumulated debts of gratitude that can never be repaid. Nonetheless, I offer my inadequate thanks to some of the many people who made this book possible. I humbly ask forgiveness of all those who can be only too briefly mentioned here as well as the many whose names must be omitted for reasons of space. I can only sincerely pray, as people so often do in Senegambia, that God reward all of you for all you've given to me: *Yàll naa leen Yàlla fey.*

There is no way of enumerating all of the people who have helped move this book forward during my years in Senegal. I must thank by name, however, Ababacar Fall, Souleymane Bachir Diagne, Mamoudou Sy, Ibrahima Thioub, Ibra Sene, Moulaye Ismaël Keita, Cheikh Tidiane Fall, Fatou Niang, and Ahmad Fall. I must also thank Mamadou Ndiaye (of the Islamic Institute), Thierno Ka, Djibril Samb, Papa Ndiaye, Khadim Mbacké, and Ibrahima Thiaw of the Institut Fondamental d'Afrique Noire. At the West African Research Center, Wendy Wilson-Fall, Leo Villalon, Fiona McLaughlin, Leigh Swigart, Ousmane Sene, and many others have helped advance this project. I also thank Saliou Mbaye and Mamadou Ndiaye from the Senegalese National Archives. The people that I need to thank in Fouta Toro, Tivaouane, Kaolack, and Touba are too many to list here, but in Fouta, I thank Thierno Seydou Nourou Ba, Mokhtar Kebé, Hachirou and Madani Tall, Oumar Issa Sow, Thierno Mody Bokar Diallo, and Ahmad Sow. In Tivaouane, I owe unpayable debts to Amadou and Ramatoulaye Fall, Mansour Thiam, and Ibrahima Badiane. In Medina-Baye Kaolock, I would be remiss not to most warmly thank Cheikh Tidiane Cissé and his brother, Cheikh Mahi. Finally, I express my heartfelt gratitude to the many people in the heartlands of the Muridiyya who added to this study in countless ways: El-Hadj Ndiaye Ndindy, Moustapha Diattara, and especially Cheikhouna Lo and his entire family in Ngabou and Touba.

I wholeheartedly thank all my colleagues and friends from my formative years at the University of Pennsylvania, especially Steve Feierman, Luther Adams, Lee Cassanelli, Barbara Savage, Barbara von Schlegell, Nancy Farriss, Cheikh Babou, Mamadou Sow, El-Hadj Ndiaye, Deborah Broadnax, Joan Plonski, and the late Valerie Riley. I also thank Jean Allman, Victoria Coifman, Allen Isaacman, and Keletso Atkins, who helped me during my stints of study and teaching at the University of Minnesota. I was also blessed with wonderful friends, colleagues, and mentors during my time at Northwestern University, and many of them read and commented on early drafts of parts of this book. I offer special thanks to Ruediger Seesemann, Zachary Wright, Sherwin Bryant, David Schoenbrun, Robert Launay, Jonathon Glassman, Darlene Clark-Hine, Carl Petry, Rebecca Shereikis, Muhammad Sani Umar, Jock McLane, Regina Graffe, Henri Lauzière, Paula Blaskovits, Susan Hall, Susan Delrahim, and Richard Joseph.

Finally, my time at Michigan has brought wonderful people into my life, and many of them have made valuable contributions to this book. I extend special thanks to Rebecca Scott, Peg Lourie, Derek Peterson, Gabrielle Hecht, Jean Hébrard, Juan Cole, Kali Israel, Nancy Hunt, Joshua Cole, Geoff Eley, Sherman Jackson, Kathleen King, Diana Denney, Dawn Kapalla, Sheila Coley, Diane Wyatt, Connie Hamlin, and Amir Syed. Among the many other colleagues who have contributed in ways great and small to this work, I thank Mamadou Diouf, Andrea Brigaglia, Boubacar Barry, Karima Direche, David Robinson, Ousmane Kane, Bruce Hall, Pier Larson, Carolyn Brown, Ousseina Alidou, Joseph Miller, Benjamin Soares, Charles Stewart, Kim Searcy, Aly Dramé, Abdoulaye Niang, Bocar Kane, Denis Gril, Saïd Bousbina, Emmanuel Girard-Reydet, and Blandine Pont.

The University of Pennsylvania, Northwestern University, and the University of Michigan have all provided funding for parts of the research I present here. Fulbright-Hays, the Ford Foundation, the Woodrow Wilson Fellowship Organization, and the Reseau Français des Instituts des Études Avancées have also provided support for portions of this work. I sincerely thank all those who have given material and moral support to help bring this book to completion.

No one has sacrificed more to see this book to completion than my family and friends, and my warmest thanks are reserved for them. My mother-in-law, Judith Evans, has helped lighten my burden in more ways than I can count. Timely support from my oldest friends—Shawn Young, Delonté Moore, and Martin Proctor—has meant very much to me. I thank my oldest and dearest friend, my brother, James Ware, for everything he has contributed to my life. I am also grateful that my father, Rudolph Ware Jr., was able to spend time with me while this book was being completed. There is no repaying my mother, Christine Treanor, for the endless support that she has given to me and my work. To my daughters, Samonia, Shamarra, Ismaʿilia, and Rabiʿa, and to my son, Idris, please try to forgive me for all of the hours I stole from you and gave to this book. I pray that one day you will read it and believe, as I do, that it was time well spent. To my wife, Kaaronica, as a fellow writer and loving companion, I know you understand better than anyone the sacrifices that I have made for the sake of this book; I pray that God will reward you beyond all your expectations for all that *you* have sacrificed.

My deepest gratitude, heartfelt praise, and final thanks are for God Most High, the most nurturing Lord and best of teachers. Any good in this book is by His will alone, and all the mistakes are mine. I thank Him for choosing me for this work in spite of my many inadequacies and for blessing me with so many wonderful people as sources of aid and inspiration. Foremost among these is His final Envoy, the best of guides, the champion of Truth by Truth, upon him God's blessing and peace.

ORTHOGRAPHIC NOTES

In this work, all translations from Arabic, Wolof, French, Fula, and any other language are mine unless otherwise noted. The three main languages transcribed here form plurals in radically different ways, so I will generally form plurals by adding a terminal "s," though occasionally I will use plural forms from these languages for expository reasons or because the foreign term ends in an "s" in its singular form. I have tried to render placenames in the spelling that will be most familiar to most readers—usually the official English or French orthography of the countries in question.

With the exception of authors who have published in European languages, whose names will appear in their published forms, African Muslim names are transcribed according to the ordinary orthographic conventions of local languages—for example, Hammet for Ḥamad in Ḥasāniyya Arabic, Hamadi and Amari instead of Ḥamadī in Fula and Wolof, respectively. I have standardized and simplified very common compound names that mean "servant of" followed by one of the names of God: ʿAbdul-Qādir instead of ʿAbd al-Qādir. All dates are C.E. unless otherwise noted. All translations from the Qurʾan are italicized and are my own.

Arabic

All foreign words except proper nouns in this study are italicized, but certain Arabic terms, such as "jihad" and "hadith" have become so familiar in English that their anglicized forms are used here. In the case of Islam's Holy Book, however, I have opted for Qurʾan, a modified spelling that I prefer to both the phonetic "Qurʾān" and the anglicized "Koran." The Arabic alphabet is transcribed here according to the following *abjad* schema:

ء ا ب ج د ه و ز ح ط ي ك ل م ن ص ع ف ض ق ر س ت ث خ ذ ظ غ ش

sh gh ẓ dh kh th t s r q ḍ f ʿ ṣ n m lk ī(y) ṭ ḥ z ū(w) h d j b ā ʾ

Short vowels are transcribed as "a," "u," and "i." Consonants are doubled by the *shadda*; I have not doubled initial consonants following a definite article (al-Tijānī instead of at-Tijānī). The *tāʾ marbūṭa* (ة) in final position is transcribed as "at" only as part of an *iḍāfa* structure, as in *dāʾirat al-mustarshidīn*. Otherwise it is spelled only with an "a," as in *dāʾira*. The other common forms of *ʾalif* (*maqṣūra*, *khanjariyya*, *madda*) are transcribed as "ā." I will use diacriticals on Arabic words throughout the work, in part because it helps to visually distinguish Arabic vocabulary from African-language materials.

African Languages

This study uses many terms from Wolof and a few from Fula, mostly drawn from the Senegalese dialect known as Pulaar, though some terms are drawn from the Fulfulde dialect and several terms are common to both. Fula speakers throughout West Africa have complex ways of categorizing linguistic and ethnic belonging; for the sake of simplicity, I will refer to Fula as the language and Fulɓe as an ethnonym. With the exception of the proper names of published authors and well-known cities, all words, places, and names appearing in this work are spelled according to the Republic of Senegal's officially sanctioned system of Latin transcription for its national languages. Whenever available, I have employed the orthographies appearing in the *Dictionnaire wolof-français*, edited by Jean-Léopold Diouf (Paris: Karthala, 2003), and Christiane Seydou's *Dictionnaire pluridialectale des racines verbales du peul* (Paris: Karthala, 1998).

These languages can be read fairly easily by Anglophones, but the following consonants in Wolof and/or Fula have values that may not be intuitive for readers:

ɓ—implosive, unaspirated "b"
c—English "ch" as in chair
ɗ—implosive, unaspirated "d"
ñ—identical to the Spanish letter
ŋ—"ng" as in king ("ng" in Wolof is pronounced with a fully articulated "g")
q—hard, guttural "k" sound, Arabic letter ق
r—rolled Spanish or Arabic ر
x—Spanish "j," German "ch," or Arabic خ
ƴ—implosive "y"

The doubling of consonants lengthens the articulation of the letter, producing an effect very similar to a *shadda* in Arabic, although in Wolof, doubled consonants often sound slightly aspirated. The initial nasal consonant clusters "mb," "nd," "ng," "nj" are pronounced without any preceding vowel sounds.

Most vowels in Wolof and Fula have very close analogs in European languages, though their transcription may not be immediately apparent:

a—partially closed "a" in the English word "what," more open than "ë"
à—open "a" sound, the British and French pronunciation of the letter "a"
e—identical to the "e" sound in "bet" or the French "è" in "*père*"
é—French "é"
ë—French "eu" in "*fleur,*" close to the "u" in the English word "flurry"
i—identical to the "i" in the English word "bin"
o—open "o" in the French word "*pomme*"
ó—closed "o" in the English word "go"
u—vowel in the English word "who," represented in French by "ou"

The doubling of vowels indicates an elongated pronunciation rather than a change in the quality of the vowel. In the place-name "Kebemeer," the sounds of the vowels are identical, but the final syllable is elongated. The doubled vowel "ii" corresponds to the vowel heard in the English word "seen."

The Walking Qur'an

INTRODUCTION

ISLAM, THE QUR'AN SCHOOL, AND THE AFRICANS

Emulate the blacks, for among them are three lords of the people of Paradise: Luqmān the Sage, the Negus, and Bilāl the Muezzin.
—Saying attributed to the Prophet Muḥammad

The Qur'an School

Believing Muslims hold that more than fourteen hundred years ago, a chain of recitation was initiated in a cave on Mt. Ḥirā', just outside of Mecca. The Angel Gabriel (Jibrīl) began reciting the Word of God to a man who had been chosen to bear the burden of prophethood. Muḥammad ibn ʿAbdullah heard the command to recite and obeyed. He listened intently to the words that followed and repeated them faithfully as he had heard them. He taught this recitation (Qur'ān) first to his wife, Khadīja, and then to a close circle of people whose hearts were touched by the reading and submitted (*islām*) themselves to the service of the One God. Central to that service was the ritual prayer (*ṣalāt*), which soon became the principal way of giving the faith concrete form. This act engaged not only the tongue, the heart, and the intellect but the limbs as well. Muḥammad learned the movements by copying Jibrīl, who sometimes appeared to him in human form.[1] He passed this prayer on to those who had submitted to God (Muslims) by reenacting the motions and reciting the words. Nearly a millennium and a half later, small children in West Africa are forged into new living links in this chain of recitation every day. Many suffer hunger, thirst, and corporal punishment to make their fragile young bodies into worthy vessels for God's verbatim speech. They then mimic their teachers, bending and prostrating those bodies to reproduce the movements of the angel who Muslims believe taught humanity the Word of God and the most perfect form of worship.

This book explores one of the institutions most responsible for the transmission of the Qur'an and its embodiment in lived practice—the Qur'an school. In Qur'an schools, children memorize and recite the Holy Book of Islam and learn to read and write the Arabic script. They are also introduced to the basic precepts and practices of the religion. Formal schools of this kind

A Qur'an school in Dakar, Senegal, from an early twentieth-century French postcard.

may date to the time of Islam's second caliph, ʿUmar b. al-Khaṭṭāb (r. 634–44), who is sometimes credited with instituting the school's traditional weekend, which begins on Wednesday after the noon prayer and ends after the noon congregational prayer on Friday. Other reports suggest that children (like adults) memorized verses of the Qur'an during the lifetime of the Prophet himself (570–632) perhaps with the aid of inscriptions on wooden tablets (*alwāḥ*) and the wide flat shoulder blades of camels and cattle.[2] It is not clear when the Qur'an school first came to sub-Saharan West Africa, though it likely arrived with the early Muslims who crossed the Sahara in the eighth century. Qur'an schooling has played a foundational role in building the Muslim societies of the African West for at least a thousand years. Nevertheless, it has been little studied and is often fundamentally misunderstood.

When they have drawn attention at all, West African Qur'an schools have often been maligned. In the past century and a half Muslims and non-Muslims alike have increasingly found fault with them. Qur'an teachers rarely explain the meaning of verses to children, focusing instead on recitation and memorization, and leading many observers to conclude that such schools are pedagogically backward. In most of these schools, however, instruction has extended beyond the rote memorization of Qur'an. Practical instruction in prayer, ablution, and the other daily elements of the faith has figured prominently. And though reading comprehension was almost never emphasized, developing literacy skills was. Students learn to read and write the Arabic script, even though the vocabulary of Qur'anic Arabic is foreign to them (as it is even for native speakers of Arabic). Some discursive teaching also takes place in Qur'an schools, though usually outside of formal hours of study. The Book has long been the sole object of formal study, with other kinds of teaching inscribed in the margins, so to speak.

Educational methods throughout the Muslim world have changed much over the past 150 years. In spite of (or perhaps because of) its antiquity, many societies have abandoned this style of learning and teaching the Qur'an. Secular education and new kinds of Islamic schools have come to prominence. Many—both within and without Islam—have come to look at Qur'an schools across a vast epistemological divide. They are separated less by *what* they think than by *how* they think. Seen from that distance they often appear strange, controversial, even *nonsensical*. A seemingly narrow focus on memorization is only the beginning; one finds in the schools of the African West a whole range of practices that depart from the modern educational ethos: Qur'an verses are absorbed into the body through osmosis; personal service, gifts, and veneration are lavished on teachers. Children are often subject to corporal punishment, and some work or beg for alms to contribute to their maintenance. These practices have led many to conclude that the schools are at best retrograde and at worst sites of child endangerment and abuse. The way that they "know" seems not to be "knowing" at all, and the way they teach seems literally to make no sense. This book seeks to make sense of Qur'an schooling and the philosophy of knowledge it represents and reproduces.

Understanding traditional Qur'an schooling on its own terms should hold inherent value. There are, after all, few more fundamental questions in religious studies than how the core scripture of a religion is learned and taught.[3] But this book is more than an institutional history of Qur'an schools in a particular time and place. One of its major premises is that Qur'an schooling can also serve as a window onto an Islamic way of knowing. After all, much can be learned about what people believe knowledge *is* by paying close attention to how they attempt to transmit it to one another.

Bodies of Islamic Scholarship

The major argument of this book is that classical Qur'an schooling and its contemporary manifestations in West Africa are based on what were once broadly held Islamic ideals about educating the whole of a human being rather than the narrow transmission of discursive knowledge. Islamic knowledge is embodied knowledge. In these pages, I focus on the human body and the ways Muslims have used it to archive, transmit, decode, and actualize religious knowledge. Islamic studies has always been interested in *bodies of knowledge*, but the ones under consideration here are not only texts, libraries, and archives but also the physical forms of human beings.

Anthropologists and some historians have recently written much about "the body," but little of this literature thinks with—or thinks through—Islamic conceptions of it. In scholarly studies of Islam, *the text* still hangs over *the body* like a veil, hiding its role in shaping Islam. This is beginning to change; a recent special edition of a prominent French Islamic studies journal focused on the "the body and the sacred" in the Near East and featured a number of valuable contributions, not least a pathbreaking conceptual essay by Catherine Mayeur-Jaouen.[4] But even in this volume, none of the essays uses embodiment as a paradigm to understand *Islamic scholarship* in Africa or elsewhere. I use "scholarship" here to refer to the closely related phenomena of schooling and scholarly production. There are notable exceptions to this pattern of inattention: anthropologist Corrine Fortier has written a handful of extraordinary articles on knowledge transmission and the body in Mauritania.[5] Louis Brenner alluded to embodiment in captivating early works but moved toward the concept of an "esoteric episteme" to characterize knowledge in precolonial Islamic Africa.[6] And finally, Michael Lambek's work on the Comoros offered stunning explorations of Islamic knowledge and corporeality but tended to compare "the objectified textual knowledge characteristic of Islam . . . with the embodied knowledge of spirit possession."[7]

GENDER, POSSESSION, AND THE BODY

A number of recent studies have expanded such discussions of the body in Muslim societies by employing a gendered analysis of spirit possession cults (*zār*, *bori*, *holey*).[8] There is much to commend in such studies. They have opened up predominantly female spheres of social and ritual authority, given voice to women, and recovered precious histories of female resistance. What is problematic, however, is that they, too, construct a conceptual divide between textual Islam and corporeal spiritism. More troubling still is that most of these works carry powerful subtexts of African resistance to supposedly alien Islamic cultural intrusions, resulting in an inordinate focus on syncretism.[9] Robert Launay has cogently traced this focus on syncretism to

Africanist anthropology's unspoken discomfort with Islam as breaching the "authenticity" of its subjects.[10] *The field has been constructed as though one cannot be authentically African and authentically Muslim at the same time.*

This viewpoint is a problem, especially in overwhelmingly Muslim African societies where such cults are often largely derived from practices of jinn propitiation in the broader Islamic tradition.[11] The existence and characteristics of jinn are, after all, discussed quite prominently in the Qur'an. Practitioners and anthropologists alike are often unaware of the deep Islamic roots and classical textual precedents for some kinds of interactions with jinn. They usually have become part of recent struggles over authority, gender, and authenticity and come to be marked as "African" even when they came from Arabia centuries ago. Some things that look (to insiders and outsiders alike) like feminine forms of African animist beliefs were described in detail in texts written by medieval Arab men.[12] In other cases, specific spirits—or, less commonly, whole systems of ordering interactions with them—can be clearly identified with pre-Islamic African ritual practices but no longer belong to any coherent religious system. In this context, formal syncretism, which presupposes two distinct religions in interaction, is unhelpful.[13] Moreover, glossing such practices as "religion" in the first place does not quite fit. They are frequently better understood as forms of healing or practical reason.[14]

All of this has profound implications for how we understand embodiment in African Muslim societies. The composite picture looks like this:

Islam = Arab, masculine, public, textual, disembodied
Spirit possession = African, feminine, private, oral, embodied

In this catalog of Cartesian dichotomies laid atop each other, Islam is the realm of the mind (masculine, rational, and Semitic), while spirit possession is the realm of the body (feminine, emotional, and African). A handful of scholars have lamented the way this emergent cliché—African women's Islam—has overshadowed the struggles and achievements of women such as the nineteenth-century African scholar Nana Asma'u and others who have asserted their piety and religious authority through learning, teaching, and producing Islamic scholarship.[15] This volume highlights the achievements of a handful of such female scholars in Senegambia but also argues that ordinary Qur'an schooling—long available to most girls in West Africa—was designed to produce specific sorts of bodily sensibilities toward Islamic scholarship, some of them universal, others explicitly gendered.

SUFISM AND EMBODIMENT

Beyond the context of spirit possession, embodiment has begun to be pursued in more generative ways. Scott Kugle's recent study, *Sufis and Saints' Bodies*, asks fundamental questions about embodiment's role in Sufism, Islam's major mystical tradition. This provocative work charges western scholars and "Wahhabi" Muslims with a kind of collusion in defining Islam "as a uniquely 'disembodied' religion."[16] To redress this misrepresentation, he attends to specific limbs of the body—and the body as a whole—in Sufi literature. It is a welcome step, but the book treats corporeality in Islam as though it were associated narrowly with Sufism rather than with Islam (much less Islamic knowledge) more broadly. Another important recent work is Shahzad Bashir's *Sufi Bodies*, which uses medieval literature and art to explore the theme, but it too examines Sufism in isolation. Such recent works build on *Embodying Charisma*, a compilation with an insightful interpretive essay by editors Pnina Werbner and Helene Basu. These pioneering works produce much insight but focus tightly on Sufism, to the point of suggesting that Sufism is the realm of the body in an otherwise textual tradition. None of these authors considers embodiment as a central aspect of Islamic knowledge as a whole or looks at the body as a means of transmitting knowledge.

My approach is distinct. I see Sufism as only one (very important) discipline among others in the curriculum of advanced religious study. From the ninth to the nineteenth centuries, many—probably most—Muslim scholars took this view. I find that Sufism draws its bodily approach to knowledge from the broader Islamic ethic, not the other way around. The relationship between the spiritual guide (*murshid*) and the aspirant (*murīd*) is but one face of a broader master/disciple relationship in Islamic schooling. The bond between the transmitter of the Qur'an and the receiver is the archetype of all such relationships.[17] Thus, my aim here is not to erase salient distinctions among, for example, Qur'an schooling, Sufi experiences of gnosis, and spirit possession cults. I want to suggest instead that they are not distinguished but rather united by explicit attention to the body. Distinctions have to be sought in different styles of corporeality and the different meanings they index and produce.

BODIES OF KNOWLEDGE

One final body of scholarship is relevant to further situate my approach to embodiment. Works on memorization and textuality, mimesis and service, and sensibilities toward reading and listening have moved the study of traditional Islamic schooling and scholarship in exciting directions, lacking only a systematic exploration of the unifying framework, the approach to knowledge, that connects—or even produces—such practices.[18] Attention to an ancient—and once widely shared—Islamic epistemology of embodiment helps to bring together these seemingly disparate threads. We have been missing a basic fact: the human being as a material reality and practices of corporeal remolding are essential for the classical epistemology of Islam to work.[19]

There is one final distinction I wish to make between *The Walking Qur'an* and the works discussed above: this book seeks less to employ theories drawn from academic scholarship to understand Qur'an schooling and more to uncover the *implicit theory of knowledge* in Qur'an schooling and see the past from within it. The resultant story is grounded in all of the conventions of academic history documentation and citation but attempts to see through the looking glass of epistemological history.[20] I am not so much writing an *analysis* of an African and Islamic approach to knowledge as I am writing a *history* through it.

The Walking Qur'an

It is reported that ʿĀ'isha, wife of the Prophet and one of the early Muslim community's most important intellectuals, was asked to describe the character of her deceased husband to a man who had not known Muḥammad in life. No stranger to the arts of rhetoric, she answered the man's question with a question: "Have you recited the Qur'an?" The man affirmed that he had. "Then you know his character," she replied; "his character was the Qur'an."

This hadith is often mentioned in sermons and speeches in contemporary Muslim societies. The manifest meaning is that the Prophet's comportment and behavior matched the revelation he had been chosen to bear. Often uttered in moralizing contexts, this hadith seems to be invoked to enjoin its hearers simply to study the Qur'an and emulate the normative Prophetic example (*sunna*). Beyond this, however, the hadith might be understood as an ontological statement about the Prophet himself. In this reading, the implication is not that the Prophet was merely the vessel for revelation or simply that his character reflected it but that God's Word had filled his inner being to the point that he physically embodied the Word. In a report sometimes cited alongside this one, ʿĀ'isha leaves little doubt that she wishes to evoke this more concrete form of embodying the Book, saying of her late husband, "He was the Qur'an walking on the earth."[21]

Remaking the children of Adam as living exemplars of the Qur'an was the basic aim behind Qur'an schooling. Human forms must be disciplined, shaped, and trained to become appropriate vessels for God's Word. Approaching Islamic knowledge as embodied—captured in the image of the walking Qur'an—focuses our attention on all the ways in which knowledge practices in the classical tradition were and are corporeal. Corporeal knowledge practices such as the internalization and recitation of texts, or imitating and serving masters, helped bridge the gap between shaykh and disciple, inscribing Islam onto the bodies and comportment of believers. This kind of embodiment goes beyond the metaphorical meanings of the term in English—as exemplar or practical application—and encompasses meanings closer to incarnation, instantiation, and manifestation.

Human "bodies of knowledge" are made, not born. Islamic learning is brought into the world through concrete practices of corporal discipline, corporeal knowledge transmission, and the deeds of embodied agents. Knowledge in Islam does not abide in texts; it lives in people.[22] From this viewpoint, some of the *non-sense* of the Qur'an school may make sense after all. If the goal was not so much to impart discursive knowledge as to transform a vile lump of flesh into God's living Word, then remolding the body was essential.[23] Disciplining the limbs and the appetites created certain kinds of bodies and sensibilities. Hunger and thirst, corporal punishment and mimesis, love and service helped inscribe the Book onto the body and being of a child. The usual Arabic noun for one who has memorized the Qur'an is *ḥāfiẓ*, which communicates a sense of carrying the Book within the self. The *ḥāfiẓ* is the guardian, protector, and *keeper* of the word of God. This sense of physical porterage that is implicit in *ḥifẓ* is explicit in *ḥaml* (carrying), another word used to refer to bearing the Qur'an in classical texts. Those who internalize the Qur'an carry and safeguard the Revelation inside their very being.[24] In my research with Senegambian men and women who had memorized the Book in Qur'an schools, they spoke of it in these terms, often using the Wolof verb *yor* (to hold or possess). They possessed the Qur'an within themselves, as a kind of inalienable spiritual good.

People who spent years learning the Book in this way frequently tied their educational experience to a propensity for the rigorous and natural practice of Islam. This intimate relationship with the Book facilitated living the religion on a daily basis. This idea elucidates another shade of meaning in embodiment: to embody Islamic knowledge is to actualize it, to make it concrete through deeds. Classical texts typically insist on the inseparability of *ʿilm* (knowledge) and *ʿamal* (deeds, practice, action). Knowledge needs to be materialized in concrete form in the world to be of any value. The goal of Qur'an schooling is not just to teach the Book but also to fill children with the Word of God, allowing them to embody the Prophetic example.

That one could embody the Book is a notion deeply rooted in the Muslim societies of West Africa. This understanding is properly epistemological rather than ideological and thus is not often explicitly discussed, but subtle traces of it are everywhere. According to the family histories of southwestern Saharan clerical lineages, one famous precolonial female scholar made the equation explicit, saying, "I am the ninth of the nine Books of my family; meaning—and God is best informed of the truth—that she was the ninth, among the people of her family, knowing [by heart] the Qur'an."[25] And among the famous late-eighteenth-century clerics of the Senegal River Valley was "Ceerno Siise Salamata, who was called Ceerno Siise 'Deereeji.' Deereeji means 'the papers of the Book.'"[26]

Settings, Stakes, and Sources

A major premise of this book is that much of the West African past can be understood as the historical expression of an epistemology—a way of conceiving, composing, and constituting knowledge. The West Africa to which I refer here is a space with rough edges. For Africanist historians, this usually means sub-Saharan Africa, west of Lake Chad and extending to the south to encompass Cameroon. I use it in this sense, though for me, West Africa explicitly includes the southwestern Sahara as well. I attend to this broader West Africa mostly as a way of crafting a regional macrohistory of Islamic learning and embodiment, but the primary historical setting I explore is a smaller subregion within this broader area: Senegambia.

The area roughly bounded by the Senegal and Gambia River Valleys (Senegal, Gambia, and Mauritania as well as parts of Guinea and Mali) shares in a broader regional tradition of Qur'an schooling that continues to thrive over truly vast areas of the African continent. Throughout West Africa, many (perhaps most) children who learn the Qur'an still do so seated on the ground, with their legs folded under them in the seated position (*jalsa*) of the ritual prayer. They receive their lessons on wooden tablets (*alwāḥ*) laid across their laps and run their fingers across the boards to help them recall the words. Most rock rhythmically as they recite, using their bodies as a pianist would use a metronome. Teachers or older students inscribe the verses on the children's tablets using reed pens and ink made from charcoal or the soot from cooking pots. Then they watch and listen carefully, frequently brandishing short lashes or canes to remind the learners to pay attention and avoid mistakes in recitation.

The physical material in the Qur'an school is full of symbolic meaning. The first verses that Muḥammad learned from Jibrīl that day on Mt. Ḥirāʾ

spoke of God teaching humanity "*that which it knew not*" by means of "*the Pen*" (Q 96:1–5). The reed pen of the Qur'an school stands in for the Pen of Power. The wooden tablets are explicitly likened to the tablets on which Mūsā (Moses) received the commandments that he carried to the children of Israel. And when the lesson is memorized, students often wash the boards and then drink the water, bringing the Word into their bodies as the Qur'an was poured into Muḥammad, the Walking Qur'an.

This kind of schooling, which I detail in chapter 1, can be found in strikingly similar forms from Senegal to the Sudan, from Dakar to Darfur, a distance from east to west of three thousand miles.[27] This schooling tradition also extends from the Saharan fringes to the equatorial forests of the Ivory Coast and Cameroon, spanning between five hundred and seven hundred miles north to south. Until the early years of the twentieth century, it was clearly the paradigmatic approach to schooling in Northwest Africa (Morocco, Algeria, and Tunisia), and there are compelling reasons to believe that Egypt, especially southern Egypt, also shared in this approach to schooling.[28] That tradition is not thriving today north of the Sahara; however, for nearly a millennium, Muslim societies on both sides of the desert as well as those within it were part of a single shared space of Islamic learning. I use the term "African West" to evoke this broader ecumen of Islamic learning that once traversed racial and spatial boundaries separating "White Africa" from "Black Africa," boundaries that scholars are now loath to cross.

STAKES AND SOURCES

This study is an interdisciplinary inquiry into the epistemology and history of Senegambian Qur'an schooling written by a historian of Africa. I argue that a focus on the body was characteristic of the approach to Islamic knowledge in this region, and I link this to a more ambitious claim, one that no single study could definitively *prove*. I argue that while specific materials and techniques of instruction may have differed in other parts of the Muslim world, this embodied approach to knowledge was once paradigmatic throughout the Muslim world.

This book results from more than a decade of historical research and has been strongly shaped by engagements with anthropological approaches to Africa and Islam, on the one hand, and the textualist tradition of Islamic studies, on the other. The book began with eighteen months of field research in Senegal in 2001–2 that included significant oral and archival components. The archival research was conducted primarily at the National Archives of Senegal as well as in collections at the Institut Fondamental d'Afrique Noire

(IFAN). The former offered a wealth of documentation on Islamic education of various sorts, while the latter provided a number of valuable sources, but none more important than the Cahiers William Ponty, take-home examination notebooks containing essays written by students at the École Normale William Ponty in the 1930s and early 1940s.[29] The Ponty collection includes more than a dozen autobiographical accounts of personal experiences written by former students in the Qur'an schools. The essays range between twenty and one hundred pages in length and total more than five hundred pages of firsthand accounts of life in Senegambian Qur'an schools in the late 1920s and 1930s.[30] An unexpected but priceless find, the Cahiers offer a rare resource for understanding the practical mechanics, social history, and struggles over the meanings of Qur'an schooling in colonial French West Africa during the interwar period.

Much of that initial research was focused on oral history. In 2001–2 I conducted formal interviews with more than forty former Qur'an school students (listed in the bibliography).[31] I conducted those interviews without an interpreter or an assistant. All were in Wolof, except for three interviews with interlocutors who were more comfortable in French. Two interviews took place in Dakar, while the rest were conducted in Tivaouane and Touba, either within the city limits or in their immediate hinterlands. Both are major centers of spiritual authority in Senegal's two largest Sufi orders, the Tijāniyya and the Murīdiyya, respectively. My interlocutors spoke of experiences of Islamic education in the Wolof heartlands from the 1930s until 2002, though most had begun their Qur'an studies between 1950 and 1970.

I supplemented these sources with other kinds of first-person accounts of life inside the schools in the colonial and postcolonial periods, including transcribed field notes from French social scientists as well as published and unpublished autobiographical narratives. I also considered a handful of fictional sources, especially biographical and autobiographical novels, on Islamic schooling. Like the oral history interviews and take-home exam essays, these accounts were useful for understanding representations of Qur'an schooling. Unlike these other sources, they are not necessarily meant to represent things that actually happened. But sometimes—especially in Cheikh Hamidou Kane's extraordinary novel, *Ambiguous Adventure*—they conveyed *truths* deeper than mere *facts*.

After that initial historical research on Senegal in the twentieth century, I expanded my approach over the ensuing decade. I began putting my materials in dialogue with a range of classical and medieval textual sources on Islamic education as well as new French and British archival sources, travelers' accounts, and other sources on the deeper past and on a broader West Africa. At the same time, I also began to take a more explicitly anthropological approach to my topic. Hours of informal discussions about Islamic education with friends, colleagues, and neighbors had informed my early publications, but over the years, participant observation in Senegalese Muslim social and intellectual life has become increasingly central to many of the arguments in this book.

In a sense this was perhaps inevitable: I am a practicing African American Muslim; I have spoken fluent French since 1996 and Wolof since 1999; and I have lived, researched, and raised my children in Senegambia for extended periods of time. I do not claim to be a practicing ethnographer. My graduate training was primarily in African history, though I received formal training in the literature and methods of anthropology. But in this work I do occasionally make claims based on my direct observations and personal experiences either during my intensive research in 2001–2 or in fifteen additional months of research trips to Fuuta Tooro, Kaolack, Banjul, Dakar, and elsewhere during shorter trips to Senegal, Mauritania, and Gambia in 1996, 1999, 2005, 2007, 2008, 2010, and 2013.

Sayings, Hadith, and Sunna

Each chapter of this book begins with an epigraph containing a *saying* attributed to the Prophet Muḥammad. Though this book centers on embodiment, I do not ignore the power of discourse. For Muslims, the Prophet was not only the Walking Qur'an but a walking exegesis (*tafsīr*).[32] His normative example (*sunna*)—comprised of both his deeds and his words—explained the Book and how to live it. So it is fitting to use sayings attributed to him as a source of insight and as a way of summarizing crucial points, and they are used this way in much Muslim life and scholarship. For many (perhaps most) modern Muslims, "sunna" refers exclusively to the normative example of the Prophet. But many West African intellectuals continue to use the more expansive notion of sunna that obtained in early Islam; they also take the *ʿamal* (deeds) of the Prophet's companions as a guide to living Islam. A new kind of scripturalism, usually associated with Salafism and Wahhabism (but also Orientalism), appears to trust the *salaf* (forebears) as little more than reporters. Though some reformists have taken their name (*salafī*), few have taken their practice as a normative source for living Islam, even though they knew the Prophet much more intimately than later generations and could model themselves on his example.

My experience with West African scholars and my historian's training have made me wary of this kind of scripturalism. It usually narrows discussion of Islamic values to texts and validates reformist claims to "true Islam."[33] This can be seen even at the level of names. *Salafī* is arguably used less frequently by scripturalists than it once was. Now, many often claim only to be Sunni, as if they are the only followers of the sunna. This usage defies that word's history, since it conventionally came to refer to followers of the four Sunni legal schools (*madhāhib*). New "Sunnis" usually rigidly oppose the classical legal schools. Despite their suspicion of the *madhāhib*, these "Sunnis" often either implicitly or explicitly associate themselves with the Ḥanbalī *madhhab*, ostensibly because it was a formative legal influence on Muḥammad b. ʿAbdul-Wahhāb, the founder of Wahhabism. Some, however, seem to admire it because they describe it as more strict and, in a puzzling leap of fundamentalist logic, therefore more orthodox.

Some Salafis now call themselves *Ahl al-sunna wa-l-jamāʿa*, People of the Sunna and the Community, appropriating the term used in early Islam to distinguish the Sunni community from Shiites and others. Some "People of the Sunna" literally refer to themselves as *Ahl al-ḥadīth*, People of Hadith, even though the two are radically different things. Hadith is only a single—albeit very important—source for knowing the sunna. Reformists usually access hadith only in the form of texts reduced to writing, as opposed to oral transmissions from teachers with accompanying explanations and demonstrations. Many early Muslim scholars did not accept hadith transmitted only in writing as authoritative at all. Person-to-person transmission was required. In written form, hadith is an impoverished and incomplete source of knowledge of sunna. The latter is best understood as an abstract concept, not knowable in its entirety. Hadith reports, conversely, are—at least in principle—finite and knowable. Many Muslims today (and some in the past) treat hadith as scripture, but they are best understood as historical traces of normative practice that can also be known through chains of embodied transmission. In chapter 1, I return to the important implications of this distinction for understanding classical ways of knowing in Islam.

"EMULATE THE BLACKS"

This chapter's Prophetic dictum is "Emulate the blacks, for among them are three lords of the people of Paradise, Luqmān the Sage, the Negus [Emperor of Abyssinia], and Bilāl the Muezzin." The first layer of meaning I wish to evoke here is simple. If the Prophet characterized black people as exemplars of knowledge, justice, and piety in Islam, then it is about time for Western scholarship to do so as well. More precisely, I mean to suggest that

Islamic and African studies need to take African Muslims seriously as bearers and interpreters of forms of Islamic knowledge and embodied practice with powerful claims to scriptural authority and Prophetic precedent.

West Africa has drawn relatively little attention from scholars interested in the history of Islamic knowledge. Scholarly studies of Islam here—as elsewhere in sub-Saharan Africa—turn on binary oppositions of syncretism and orthodoxy: "African Islam" or "Islam in Africa."[34] The former consists of a complex including Sufism, divination, spirit possession, and talismanic uses of the Qur'an. Though controversial to some observers, all of these practices are ancient in Islam and are present in every Muslim society in the world. "Islam in Africa," conversely, is often synonymous with Salafi, Wahhabi, and Islamist influences. It consists of "reform," which entails the promotion of modernized schooling, literalist approaches to texts, Arab cultural mores, and a distrust of all forms of esotericism. Western scholars and many modern Muslims often uncritically accord Islamic orthodoxy and textual legitimacy to these "reformists," who, paradoxically given their reverence for scripture, have often opposed traditional Qur'an schooling.

Since the nineteenth century, increasing numbers of Muslims and non-Muslims have come to portray the Qur'an school and its epistemology as backward. In itself this is misleading but not surprising: modernist discourse often disparages "traditional" thought in such terms. The epistemology explored in this book, I maintain, did seek to create agents of change, and it achieved this goal through a focus on reproducing the Word of God in living human beings. Though much attention was paid to fidelity, pedigree, and authority, the goal of what I call the "classical" approach to Islamic education was always dynamic. The careful, painstaking, and even tedious transmission of the Qur'an as a line of recitation and interpretation was not intended simply to preserve the text and its integrity—any written copy would have done this. It was designed instead to inculcate Islamic sensibilities in human beings, to instill the character of the Qur'an within living agents. It sought to cultivate embodied human beings who would be able to draw on their intimate knowledge of the Qur'an and its intrinsic power as God's verbatim speech to shape and reshape the world around them in the face of any contingency. *The Walking Qur'an is not only the Qur'an embodied but also the Qur'an in action.*

Since the second half of the nineteenth century, text-minded scholars—particularly Salafi intellectuals, colonial administrators, and even many academic scholars of Islam—have caricatured this traditional approach. They have represented it as obscurantist, superstitious, and intellectually stultifying. Many observers saw the supposed decline of Islamic civilization and the ascent of the West as rooted in the failure of old-fashioned Islamic education. They suggested—implicitly or explicitly—that to reach (or regain) the heights of progress, Muslims ought to reform or discard their ways of learning and teaching in favor of others. These new pedagogies and the epistemology that girds them swept across the Muslim world, transforming knowledge practices. Most of this change in Muslim ways of knowing occurred only in the past century. This book will not explicitly focus much on those changes; countless studies already do so. Proponents of these Islamic novelties receive far more attention than the traditional Islam they strenuously claim to replace. This book aspires to redress that imbalance.

Politics, Ideology, and Epistemology

Confrontations between Salafis and more traditionally inclined Muslims are often analyzed as political—struggles over power, authority, and access to material resources. They are also frequently studied as ideological quarrels. In such studies, intellectual and doctrinal disputes lie at the heart of debates over the correct content of Muslim identity and Islamic practice. Power and ideology are certainly at play in all such conflicts, but they may not explain them as well as we think. Inasmuch as this study attends to reformism at all, I analyze such clashes as primarily epistemological in nature—rooted in basic, usually unarticulated, differences in how such groups define what it means to know.[35]

Attending to epistemology as a root cause of conflict highlights the importance of schooling, and attention to modern Muslim schools immediately reveals how closely they are based on European models. Curiously, in spite of the novelty and extrinsic origins of such schools, many scholars now see these schools' approaches to knowledge as emerging from pristine Islamic sources in the distant past; they light the road to the true religion of the *salaf al-ṣāliḥ* (righteous forebears). But how meaning is made in contemporary Salafism, Wahhabism, and Islamism owes as much to Enlightenment rationalism as to the scholarly tradition of Islam. Proclaiming Islamic purity is essential to their ideologies, but their understandings of what knowledge *is* are plainly hybrid constructs, born of colonial encounter. Much contemporary Islamic discourse, however interested in classical texts, conceives, constitutes, and transmits knowledge in ways that differ radically from those known by earlier Muslim intellectuals.

Contemporary Salafis, Wahhabis, and Islamists often espouse a confrontational and oppositional stance vis-à-vis the West, but Western rationalisms and positivisms are inscribed at every level of their approaches to knowledge. Cheikh Hamidou Kane's exquisite novel on the colonial clash between occidental modernity and the traditions of Muslim Africans had a poetic way of expressing this. The protagonist in *Ambiguous Adventure*, Samba Diallo, is a former Qur'an school student who leaves the old ways of knowing, goes to a state school, and finally pursues advanced studies at a European university. The new knowledge changes him irrevocably, and he cannot go back to the old ways. He loves the West, but the West does not love him. He becomes embittered, and in one of the novel's most memorable passages, Diallo says, "The most poisonous hatreds are those which are born out of old loves."[36]

ISLAM INSTRUMENTALIZED?

In many parts of the Muslim world, modern state schools were the first wave of a sea change that slowly washed away the classical style of Qur'an schooling. Islamic education was incorporated into the bureaucratic structures of ambitiously intrusive modern states.[37] In Gregory Starrett's *Putting Islam to Work*, both the title and the key analytical term—"functionalization"—capture the ways in which institutions of Islamic education in Egypt were instrumentalized over the course of the twentieth century: "The importation to Egypt of European-style mass schooling . . . took place in part through the appropriation of indigenous Qur'anic schools for public use. This is where we can see how the process of functionalization, first aimed at the physical institutions in which formal religious socialization occurred, began to transform people's ideas about the subject matter itself."[38] In most such schools—and in the private schools that mirrored them—Islam became one subject among many, an objectified, depersonalized topic of study. Post-Enlightenment ideas about education and knowledge transmission dramatically altered the face of Islamic schooling in many parts of the Muslim world. This was most dramatically the case in many of the predominantly Arab countries, places often presumed by a sort of racial alchemy to preserve the essence of Islam.

For a variety of reasons that I explore mainly in chapters 4 and 5, Qur'an schooling was never functionalized in quite this way in francophone West Africa. This is but one of the reasons that West Africa continues to preserve the original form of Qur'an schooling and its attendant corporeal dispositions toward knowledge. Other reasons are rooted in deeper pasts. Chapter 2 shows that in many ways, Qur'an schooling was the key public symbol of Muslim identity in West Africa from at least the fourteenth century. Moreover, the specific social and (a)political position of the West African clerisy (which developed by about 1000) made their embodying of Islam particularly salient. The fact that clerical communities were seen as safe havens during the Atlantic era (explored in chapter 3) reinforced their societal import. In short, the roots of Senegambian attachments to Qurʾan schooling run deep. Though it has faced many challenges since the 1850s, Qurʾan schooling has survived into the twenty-first century as the basic institution of religious socialization for millions of West African children. In the pages of this book, I explore and historicize an argument that was expressed to me in dozens of ways during my research in Senegambia: We in West Africa have held on to something worth keeping, something that many in the Muslim world have abandoned, the classical Qurʾan school.[39]

Invisible Muslims

This book seeks to engage with and foster dialogue between two main interdisciplinary audiences: Islamic and African studies. For demographic reasons alone, such a dialogue should be an urgent matter, yet the study of Islamic religious culture in Africa is strangely marginal to both fields. Africa's population is, by conservative estimates, well over 40 percent Muslim, and some observers maintain that Africa is likely the only continent with a Muslim majority. According to recent figures published by the Pew Research Center, at least 27 percent of the world's 1.6 billion Muslims live in Africa, and, contrary to what one might imagine, far more of these people live south of the desert than north of it. Roughly one-tenth of the world's Muslims (164 million) live in North Africa, while more than one-sixth of the world's Muslim population (273 million) lives south of the Sahara. The proportion of sub-Saharan Muslims is expected to grow dramatically in the next twenty years, both in comparison to the non-Muslim population of Africa and as a percentage of the global Muslim population. "Black Africa"—as it is still sometimes called—already has more Muslims than does Pakistan or Indonesia, the countries that currently have the world's largest Muslim populations.[40]

Because of the close association between Arabs and Islam, casual observers may not be aware that there are far more sub-Saharan African Muslims than Arabs, who make up a relatively small proportion of the population of the Muslim world. For example, Sudan has as many Muslims as do Syria, Jordan, and Palestine combined. Defining Arabs geographically, there are just over 60 million Muslims living in Arabia proper; in contrast, Nigeria alone has at least 75 million Muslims. In fact, Nigeria is probably home to more Muslims than Iran, and Ethiopia has at least as many Muslims as Iraq does.[41]

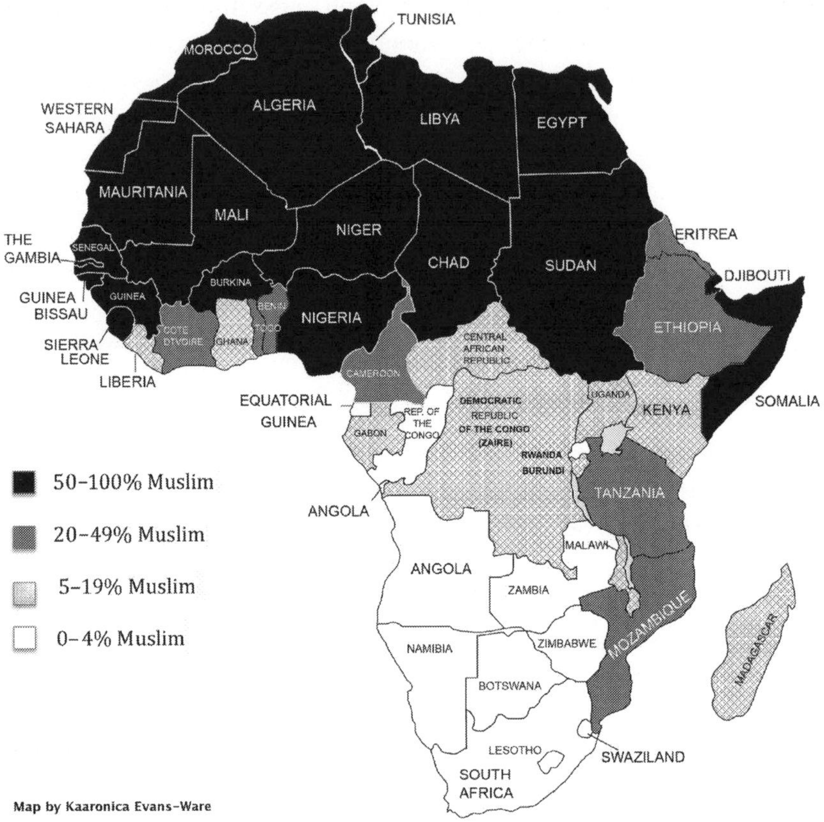

Map by Kaaronica Evans-Ware

Islam in Africa, ca. 2010. Countries are shaded if they meet 5%, 20%, or 50% thresholds in either Pew Research's published study of the global Muslim population or the CIA World Factbook for 2013.

In Nigeria, Muslims are probably a slight majority—and certainly a plurality—in a population that includes many Christians and a smaller number of practitioners of traditional African religions. Similarly, in Ethiopia, Muslims are (at the very least) a large minority in a religiously diverse population. But these 273 million African Muslims are not always—or even usually—islands of Islam in seas of religious pluralism. Muslims comprise more than 98 percent of the population in such widely separated countries as Niger and Somalia, narrowly outpacing both Saudi Arabia and Pakistan (each with 97 percent) in this regard. Senegal has a higher percentage of Muslims (96 percent) than either Egypt or Syria (95 percent and 93 percent, respectively).

Examples could be multiplied. Even cursory attention to the magnitude of the Muslim presence in Africa is revealing, indicating that those of us interested in Islam ought to be paying more attention to sub-Saharan Africa than we usually do. If one were to walk from Africa's westernmost point in Senegal to its easternmost point in Somalia, one would cut across a swath of predominantly—almost entirely—Muslim societies that have been part of the global community of Islam for roughly one thousand years. Going down the East African coast, African Muslims have lived on the coasts and offshore islands of Kenya, Tanzania, and Mozambique for at least twelve centuries.[42] From these ancient centers of Muslim civilization in sub-Saharan Africa, the religion has spread—especially in the past two centuries—implanting significant Muslim minority populations in virtually every nation on the continent.

ISLAM NOIR

Those of us interested in Islam ignore Africa at our own risk, and vice versa. By reason of their sheer demographic weight, African Muslims need to figure more prominently in both African and Islamic studies. But beyond the mere numbers, Islamicists can learn lessons from the particular forms of Muslim thought and practice found in Africa. This perspective has gained little ground as a consequence of the ways in which Islamic religious culture in Africa has been understood. Again, the study of sub-Saharan African Muslims has usually been framed either as "Islam in Africa," a narrative in which Islam is an alien, external force, or as "African Islam," which posits that Islamic practices in "Black African" societies are by definition exotic and heterodox.

Historians of Africa as well as other parts of the Muslim world will hear echoes of colonial racial assumptions in this discourse. Many late-nineteenth- and early-twentieth-century colonial authorities and "Orientalists" (often one and the same) thought of Islam as the property and proper expression of the Arab genius. Paul Marty, director of the Office of Muslim Affairs in early-twentieth-century French West Africa, exemplified both the tendency to conflate administrative and intellectual functions and the habit of equating race with religion. In the francophone world, he was the individual most responsible for shaping the governance of African Muslims and their academic representation. He was not kind to non-Arabs: "As Islam distances itself from its cradle it becomes increasingly deformed. Islamic confessions, be they Malaysian or Chinese, Berber or Negro, are no more than vulgar forgeries of the religion and state of the sublime Qur'an."[43] Serving from 1912 to 1921 as the director of the Office of Muslim Affairs, he published no fewer than twenty-five hundred pages of studies, casting a long shadow of racialized analysis over the field.[44] In less than a decade, Marty worked his way through all of French West Africa documenting Islam Noir, a recently arrived, second-rate, poorly understood, syncretistic, and therefore nonthreatening brand of Islam.

Some of the scholarship was of objectively poor caliber. In an influential report on Qur'an schooling, for example, Marty claimed that the alphabet was taught "in the following order which is classic and invariable, *alif*, *baa*, *taa*, *tha*."[45] In fact this manner of teaching the alphabet, which is an ordering system based on the shapes of the letters, was rarely if ever used in Senegalese schools of the time. Marty seems to have thought this alphabet, used in dictionaries and in his training as an Arabic interpreter, was the only way of learning the Arabic letters. The *abjad*, which is the oldest way of ordering the Arabic alphabet (as well as the other Semitic alphabets), was much more widely known in Senegal. More common still was teaching children the letters of the alphabet in the order in which they were encountered during memorization.[46]

Paul Marty did not know the alphabet, but he quickly gained recognition as an academic authority on Muslim schooling and every other aspect of West African Islam. His ascent was rapid but not smooth. In 1913, the *Revue du Monde Musulman* was urged by no less a figure than William Ponty, the governor-general of French West Africa, to publish Marty's first study, on Senegal's Murīdiyya Sufi order. Marty was a high-ranking official but not a trained scholar. The editors of the journal disavowed some of his findings, especially Marty's conclusion that the Murīdiyya "must be considered a sort of new religion born from Islam."[47] In their foreword, they questioned his scholarly credentials: "This is an administrative report, addressed to the colonial authority. . . . It was thus necessary that M. Marty deal with subjects which, although well known to specialists in Islamology, might be less so to functionaries specializing in other competencies."[48] These early reservations were eventually overcome, however, and Marty's later work was frequently published in the *Revue*. Marty's work appeared during the heyday of European scientific racism, and he overcame his lack of credentials by routinely appealing to the logic of race. He was an artful and humorous racist, shrewdly tapping deeply held stereotypes of black civilizational and intellectual inferiority to make his administrative reports more persuasive. His ideas about the religious deficiencies of African Muslims and his relentless presentation of their biological (or perhaps bodily) predisposition to animism have cast a long shadow over the study of Islam in Africa.

Àlluwas by Shaykhuna Mbakke. From right to left, the first board shows the first verses taught to children, _al-Fātiḥa_ (The Opening), _al-Ikhlāṣ_ (Sincerity), _al-Falaq_ (Daybreak), and _al-Nās_ (Humanity). The second board shows the _abjad_ alphabet, along with a beginning lesson on the vowels needed to recite the Qur'an according to the reading of Warsh (728–813). Photograph by Kaaronica Evans-Ware.

SYNCRETISM AND ISLAMS

Marty attacked the orthodoxy of black Muslims in ways that were extreme but were hardly isolated. By the time he left French West Africa in 1921, the die was cast. Islam Noir (which I revisit in Chapter 4) had become a matter of administrative and intellectual orthodoxy in francophone circles. Colonial administrators and scholars in British Africa thought and acted along similar lines, and together their racialized framing of African Islam has had lasting consequences, outlined here by Rüdiger Seesemann: "In the works of French and British 'scholar-administrators' such as Paul Marty and Harold Ingrams, and of later academics, occasionally with a missionary background, such as Vincent Monteil and John Spencer Trimingham, there is an obvious conflation of the categories religion and race. 'African Islam,' or Islam Noir in the French parlance, has since become the common denominator in both academic and nonacademic discourse about Islam in Africa, conveying the image of an essentially syncretistic and superstitious, and in any case adulterated, version of Islam."[49]

In another important corrective, David Robinson has sought to transcend the ideological limits of the Islam in Africa/African Islam dyad with a discussion of the contingent processes through which African societies adopted Islam (the Islamization of Africa) and made it their own (Africanization of Islam). He adds that these processes do not differ from similar processes elsewhere in the Muslim world: "There is *nothing* pejorative about the africanization of Islam. . . . There *is* something pejorative about the way that European and many Mediterranean-based Muslims have perceived 'African Islam' and the africanization of Islam."[50] Robinson productively situates the negotiation of Islamic religious culture in a narrative of adoption and adaptation.[51]

We can all agree that processes of negotiation take place within all Muslim societies between local cultic and cultural legacies and a broader Islamic religious culture. I would, however, amplify his point about the way that Islamic Africa is exoticized and marginalized. For many observers, the following equations seem to be implicitly accepted:

African religious culture + Islam = syncretism
Arab religious culture + Islam = Islam

Robinson's intervention is valuable, but exploring the dynamics of "Africanization" and "Islamization" is still a discussion of syncretism and assimilation. Such framings have subtle spatial and normative assumptions hidden within them and may not take us so far away from imperialist Orientalism after all. They emerge from sturdy old civilizational models of diffusion and reception. When applied to Islam, they tend to carry the implicit (or explicit) notion that the center's claims on normative authority are spatially and structurally immutable.[52] In other words, Arab Muslims are in positions of perpetual tutelage over non-Arabs. From within a framework of syncretism and assimilation, it is difficult for the "periphery" to provide meaningful insights on the "center."

Framed somewhat differently, this is the discourse of islams wherein there are manifold local forms that constitute the organic traditions of Muslim life. These are the sites within which *Islam* (with a capital "I") is negotiated and domesticated.[53] Again, such a discourse allows little room for places beyond the so-called Islamic heartlands to contribute much to *Islam*. At its best, the story of *islams* functions as an antiessentialist and empowering narrative of cultural relativity and contextual specificity, but embedded within it are powerful notions of center and periphery. Stories of *islams* all too often become the story of *Islam* with local color. Africa, India, Indonesia, Malaysia—these are places that receive *Islam* and transmute it into *islams*. They adopt and adapt Islamic religious culture. From within this metanarrative, it is very difficult (perhaps impossible) to claim that a history of Muslim religious culture in West Africa could provide revealing insights about the history of knowledge in *Islam*. Yet a main goal of this book is to do just that; *its core contribution to Islamic studies is to highlight and historicize an embodied approach to knowledge that was once paradigmatic but now thrives in few Muslim societies*. It is ironic—considering the racial and spatial logics at work—that many of these societies are far from Arabia in the African West.

"LOOK AFTER THE BLACKS?"

This brings us back to this introduction's epigraph. Robinson's reference to the pejorative perceptions of Africans held by "Mediterranean-based Muslims" offers an important reminder: white colonialists were not alone in carrying condescending ideas about blacks. The treatment of this hadith in medieval and early modern Arabic-language works on slavery, blackness, or "the curse of Ham" reflects this phenomenon. In some of these writings, the word *ittakhādhū*, which I have translated as "emulate," received quite a different meaning. Some authors argued that what the Prophet meant by this word was "look after" the blacks, a paternalistic gloss also used by a prominent Western scholar to translate this hadith.[54] Zachary Wright, in his exemplary dissertation on the community of West African Sufi Shaykh Ibrāhīm Niass, caught this mistranslation and noted that "Hans Wehr's *Dictionary of Modern Written Arabic* contains no such meaning for the verb in question, but rather includes: 'to take on, to assume, to adopt, to imitate, to affect,' etc."[55]

This is just another small reminder that antiblack racism has its own history within Muslim societies. Bernard Lewis's treatment, *Race and Slavery in the Middle East*, is riddled with problems of poor documentation, blatant Islamophobia, and a naked attempt to draw parallels between the "Occidental" and "Oriental" slave trades. It treats the history of Eastern racism with the clear aim of establishing moral equivalencies with the racism of the West.[56] It also suggests, like many studies, that slavery was an indelible part of Islam. In all these respects, Lewis's work participates in an Orientalist tradition going back to the nineteenth century.[57] Such reactionary efforts are intellectually impoverished and cannot be maintained; they were developed to alleviate European guilt over the Atlantic slave trade, demonize Islam, and justify colonial conquests in Asia and Africa. But no postmodern critique of Orientalism is capable of erasing the objective fact that many Muslims have held Africans in contempt. Nor can any revisionist history erase the fact of extensive slaving and slave trade in the lands of the caliphate. The conquests of the first Muslim century brought people of all colors and national origins into slavery at the hands of Muslims, and Arab ethnic chauvinism reached heights that are hard to fully grasp today.

This book is not the place to treat the problem of "race" and slavery in Islam exhaustively, but unresolved issues of skin color and slavery in Islamic societies have played a major role in assaults on the orthodoxy and intellectual achievements of African Muslims.[58] Many Senegalese Muslims consider Arab racism more virulent than its European cousin, claiming that "white" Mauritians (*bayḍān*) are more likely to use *ʿabd* (slave) to refer to a black person than a French person is to use the word *nègre*. The French term for "Negro" is a precise equivalent for *ʿabd* because it collapses "black" and "slave" into a single term.[59] The Senegalese Muslims with whom I spent time were well aware of the stereotypical perceptions of their supposedly syncretistic religiosity, both among Arab Muslims and among some presumptuously judgmental European and American non-Muslims. I raise these reflections on racialized perceptions of African Muslims only to historicize and transcend them.[60] To that end, I propose three partly rhetorical questions: What possible reason would the Prophet Muḥammad have had to see blacks in a condescending and paternalistic way? What evidence do we have that he did see blacks in this fashion? And finally, if "look after" the blacks was the meaning he wished to convey, then why use a word that usually means "emulate"?

During my research stays in Senegambia, members of the Murīdiyya Sufi order sometimes pointed out that both the Qur'an and the Prophet Muḥammad were highly critical of Arabs. Within the circles of the Murīdiyya, a particular pride is attached to the idea that the founder of the order, Amadu Bamba Mbakke (d. 1927), was a black man. He did not derive his Sufi legitimacy from the Qādiriyya or the Tijāniyya, the two other major orders in

Senegambia, which are named for a medieval saint from Baghdad and an eighteenth-century North African saint, respectively. Members of the Murīdiyya Sufi order represent Bamba as a proud and cultured man of his people who spoke excellent Wolof but wrote only in Arabic and whose primary commitment was to Islam.

In this respect, as in many others, characterizations of Bamba portray him as a mirror image of the Prophet Muḥammad. I was sometimes reminded that the Prophet, while a cultivated expert in Arab culture, was also an astute and often biting critic.[61] There is no denying that the Book that the Prophet had written on his heart reproached the Arabs for their ignorance and haughtiness. Though his intentions obviously cannot be known across fourteen centuries of history, I doubt that if he did say the words "*ittakhādhū al-sūdān*," he did so with the conceits of pride and conquest that later Arab authors felt when they tried to explain them away. Because it was a central concern of many of my interlocutors (not just Murids) and because it is an important part of repositioning Africans at the center of discourses of Islamic knowledge, I briefly explore some of the relevant context that he may have had in mind if and when he uttered those words.

THE WALKING QURʾAN AND THE AFRICANS

I maintain that when Muḥammad heard the angel Jibrīl speaking to him and listened intently to memorize the following words, the Prophet took them quite seriously: "*O people, indeed We have created you male and female and made you into nations and tribes so that you may know one another. Indeed the most honored among you is the most God-conscious. And indeed God is the Knowing, the Cognizant*" (Q 49:13). This verse contains a powerful meditation on equality and the meaning and purpose of human bodily difference. Distinction is caused by remembering God, not by gender, national, or ethnic differences. And if we remember God, we can learn much from one another: our diversity becomes a source of wisdom. Another verse expands on this point, specifically mentioning the diversity of colors in the human family as being a "sign of God," the same way that verses of the Qur'an themselves are signs (*ayāt*): "*And among His signs is the creation of the heavens and the earth and the diversity of your tongues and colors and surely in this there are signs for the learned*" (Q 30:22).

The three persons mentioned in the saying "emulate the blacks" are all among the learned: Luqmān the Sage, the Negus of Abyssinia, and Bilāl the Muezzin. Their stories amplify the point made in these Qur'an verses. A brief word on each helps contextualize the intended meaning of the saying and helps situate an outlook underlying many African Muslim claims on knowledge. The Revelation Muḥammad carried within him had a thirty-verse chapter, Luqmān. It takes its name from a pre-Islamic African sage whom the Book represents as a model of piety and a teacher of the doctrine of *tawhīd* (God's radical oneness). Strikingly, the sura is about both the endless knowledge of God and the unity of mankind:

> *And if all the earth's trees were pens and the sea its ink, with seven more seas to flood it, the Word of God would not be ended. Truly God is Mighty, Wise.*
> *The creation of all of you and your resurrection are only like that of a single soul. Truly God is the Hearing and the Seeing.* (Q 31:27–28)

Later exegetes would maintain that Luqmān was not a prophet but a sage, in spite of his prominent and auspicious mention in the Book. They would also, perhaps not coincidentally, claim that Luqmān was a slave, though the Qur'an itself makes no such statement.

Muḥammad grew up in an Arabia that knew Africans more as conquerors than as slaves, even if the bulk of later Arabic scholarship often seemed to forget this. As a reminder, one need only recall another verse that the original Walking Qur'an carried inside him. The Chapter of the Elephant (Q 105) makes unambiguous reference to the war elephants that conquering Abyssinian armies rode in southern and western Arabia in the sixth century and before. The African Christian kingdom of Aksum frequently ruled over portions of the Arabian Peninsula, and this sura is usually understood to refer to the final defeat of those Abyssinian conquerors and their expulsion from the Ḥijāz (western Arabia), an event conventionally dated to 570, also recorded as the year of the Prophet's birth. But the Prophet's reference to the Negus was not a general allusion to the power of an African king; it was a specific reference to the grace and piety of a black Christian who saved the early Muslims from possible extinction.

No longer African overlords in Arabia, the Ethiopians nonetheless remained a major power in the Red Sea region. When the Muslim community was threatened with extinction in Mecca, the Prophet Muḥammad appealed to the Negus or Najāshī of Abyssinia for help. The beginning of the Islamic calendar is the *hijra* (migration) to Medina in 622, which allowed the Muslim community to establish itself free from the oppression of the Quraysh, the Prophet's blood kin but bitter enemies of his radical vision of monotheism. It is often forgotten that there were two earlier *hijras* to sub-Saharan Africa. Fearing for the lives of his still very small group of followers, Muḥammad sent at least one hundred of the first Muslims, including ʿUthmān, Islam's third caliph, to seek asylum in the Christian kingdom of Aksum (Abyssinia or Ethiopia) in 615 and 616. Islam reached sub-Saharan Africa literally before Islamic time began.

When the Quraysh came and demanded extradition of these one hundred refugees—certainly a prelude to a massacre and the end of Islam—the Negus refused. In the accounts of the early Muslim historians, the Quraysh then claimed that the new faith slandered Jesus. The Negus asked one of the Muslims to recite what the Qurʾan says of Jesus (ʿĪsā), and the Muslim recited one of the Qurʾan verses referring to ʿĪsā as the "Spirit of God." Muslim historians maintain that this recitation, along with the example of the Muslims, so moved the king of Aksum that he converted to Islam but hid his new faith from his royal court.

Bilāl (580–642), the final black exemplar of justice, wisdom, and piety mentioned in the hadith, has been a particularly cherished figure for West African Muslims. He enters Muslim sacred histories as the slave of a powerful Meccan family that was enraged when he became one of the first people (perhaps the second adult male after Abū Bakr) to accept the new religion of Islam.[62] For this crime, Bilāl was brutally punished—laid out to roast on the hot desert sand with heavy stones on his chest. When his tormentor would come to ask if he would recant, he would only repeatedly moan the word *aḥad* (one). Bilāl's affirmation of *tawhīd* in the face of torture appears to have inspired the Prophet to arrange for Abū Bakr, who would later become the first caliph, to purchase the enslaved man's liberty.

Later, after the Angel Jibrīl had taught the Prophet the gestures of the prayer, the Muslims had to decide how they would call the faithful to congregational worship. Would they call the people with church bells, like the followers of Jesus? Would they be assembled—as if a prelude to the last day—with the sound of a horn, like the followers of Moses? What instrument should the Muslims use? Characteristic of his foundational emphasis on anchoring Islam in the human body as the Qurʾan was anchored in his own, *the Prophet chose the human voice*. Bilāl's strong and beautiful voice is usually cited as the reason he was selected to make the call. Perhaps the Prophet believed that in addition to his beautiful voice, Bilāl's sincere belief in God's oneness, which could not be cowed by a slavemaster, burned with sun or sand, or crushed by heavy stones, made him uniquely qualified for the job.

In 630, Muḥammad returned to Mecca as the victorious commander of the faithful. His party made its way to the Kaʿba, the structure built for the worship of the One God. According to many accounts, Muḥammad watched

Bilāl's victory *adhān*. From the illustrated version of al-Darīr's *Siyer-i Nebi* (History of the Prophet), produced for the Ottoman Sultan Murād III, completed in 1595. Courtesy of Topkapi Palace Museum, Istanbul, Turkey/The Bridgeman Art Library.

Bilāl climb to the top of the House of God and make the call to prayer. The sound of his voice at that iconic moment echoes through the ages. It has been memorialized in art, literature, and oral performance. After Muḥammad's passing, some maintain that Bilāl only made the call to prayer on very special occasions and that when he did, those who had known the Prophet were moved to tears. This story speaks to a very close association between Muḥammad and Bilāl, for the presence of one called hearts to lament the absence of the other. Is it too much to suggest that the men were close friends who had suffered much together and relied on one another? Perhaps simple friendship and love was the reason that Muḥammad made Bilāl Islam's first muezzin. Did the Prophet have paternalistic contempt in his heart at this moment?

When Muḥammad entered Mecca as a victorious general, he did not enslave his defeated enemies. That so many (though by no means all) Muslim scholars from the subsequent era of conquest accepted aggressive jihad, wholesale enslavement of the prisoners of war (and their dependents), and skin-color prejudice only shows us that they were not immune to the effects of a world awash in slaves and dripping with ethnic chauvinism. The Prophet Muḥammad did not live long enough to walk in such a world, and so I doubt that he had paternalism or condescension on his tongue or in his heart if and when he uttered the words, "Emulate the blacks, for among them are three lords of the people of Paradise."

■ Under the Ummayads, the descendants of the Quraysh, some of Muḥammad's bitterest enemies, the worldly conquests of the Arabs unfolded. By the seventeenth century, blacks were probably a majority of the slaves in the lands of Islam. By the nineteenth, they were nearly the only slaves left, and they were more numerous than ever before. Blackness and slavery, slavery and unbelief were now all collapsed together in unprecedented ways. This development had important implications for Muslim perceptions of the religiosity of blacks: unbelief—or at least religious inferiority—was increasingly read onto black bodies.

The scale of the slave trade from sub-Saharan Africa to the lands of Islam before the sixteenth century has been vastly exaggerated, anachronistically racialized, and callously politicized. But it did happen. Its resultant anti-black racism, in the East as in the West, is a simple fact of life. But it is also a quintessentially modern phenomenon. "As the Atlantic world developed its modern racism through slaving, so too did the Mediterranean world of Islam; indeed, the two are probably best understood together as the growth of a single racism as an aspect of modernity."[63] In the Muslim world, the enslavement of Africans and its attendant racism reached its nadir in the nineteenth century, just as modern Orientalism—and Islamic reformism as well—were being born. Africans had never been so despised and marginal in the so-called heartlands of Islam.

This study seeks neither to minimize nor sensationalize the slavery and racism practiced by Muslims in the Mediterranean world (and the Indian subcontinent, which received a large volume of the East African slave trade). Rather, it seeks to tell a different story about Africans and Islamic knowledge. A story about Islamic knowledge cannot linger too long on ideas of race, but they so deeply permeate colonial documents, secondary literatures, and the views of contemporary Muslims that any scholarship that ignores this history is doomed to repeat it. Staring Eastern and Western racisms in the face is uncomfortable, but if we refuse to look away, we eventually see beyond the surface and recent centuries of bigotry. A careful look allows us to glimpse a time before such chauvinisms were fixed. Envisioning a time when an African could stand atop the House of God and call the world to Islam helps us to imagine the past on its own terms, not those of a racially divided modern world.

Writing Islamic Knowledge into African History

We must see beyond race and put Africans back at the center of Islamic studies, where they belong, and so, too, must we put Islam at the center of African studies. To be fair, West African Muslims have drawn their fair share of attention, but the inner workings of Islam as a system of religious meaning in their lives has not. Redressing this oversight is imperative, in part because of the huge (and growing) demographic weight of Islamic Africa. Reckoning with the role of religious meaning in the past, present, and future of hundreds of millions of African Muslims requires that we pay attention to their engagements with Islamic knowledge.

The first generations of postcolonial scholars in Islamic West Africa were mainly political scientists and sociologists who tended toward materialist analysis. They did not usually carefully attend to the contents of religious culture. Anthropologists, otherwise central to Africanist research, tended to overlook Islamic Africa altogether. Robert Launay explored the reasons for—and consequences of—this phenomenon in an extraordinary survey of the field, "Invisible Religion?: Anthropology's Avoidance of Islam in Africa." Among his many valuable insights is his attention to the problem of authenticity: "Arguably, there existed a tacit partition of African realities among academics, with anthropologists appropriating the study of '*authentic*' Africans with genuinely 'traditional' religions while the study of African Muslims, those whose pristine authenticity had apparently been violated, was left to historians if not to 'Orientalists.'"[64]

If historians and "Orientalists" were expected to pick up the slack for reluctant anthropologists, the results have been uneven. In short, the presumption of mutually exclusive African and Islamic authenticities that dogged West African anthropology was by no means absent from historical or Orientalist writing. The Orientalist avoidance of Islamic Africa probably rivaled that of the anthropologists. For historians, conversely, it expressed itself less in an absolute avoidance of Islam and more in a reticence to take on Islam as a system of religious meaning and in a focus on materialist analyses instead. When historians did attend to the contents of religion, they added a temporal dimension to the story of syncretism. This tended to produce a linear narrative of progressive advances in the "orthodoxy" of "African Muslims." Anthropologists focused on Africanized Islam, and historians built a linear narrative of the progress of "Islam in Africa."

This process was supposed to have taken place under constant pressure from the weight of the textual tradition, waves of immigration by Arab Muslims, and particularly in West Africa, the state-building efforts of Muslim clerics who led jihads in the nineteenth century. ʿUthmān b. Fūdī (Usman dan Fodio, d. 1817) and ʿUmar b. Saʿīd al-Fūtī (al-Ḥājj Umar Taal, d. 1864), for example, were studied by historians primarily as state builders. Yet both men taught Qurʾan for much of their lives and produced countless pages of scholarly works before ever becoming involved in politics.[65] Only a fraction of their works have been treated systematically in publication or translated into European languages. If "Orientalism" in Launay's formulation refers to translation, annotation, and textual analysis of the Arabic or *ʿajamī* literary production of West Africans, then the field remains underdeveloped. Moreover, the famous "West African jihads" themselves have been fundamentally misunderstood. In chapter 3, "The Book in Chains," I show that these movements were more a struggle against the Atlantic slave trade and the enslavement of Muslims (especially those who had memorized the Qurʾan) than a fight against syncretism.

The composite macrohistory portrays African engagements with Islamic knowledge as unintellectual, superficial, and syncretistic. The story is rife with colonial tropes. Africans stay faithful to ancestral custom, adopting Islam—represented as an imported, imperialist, and culturally alienating tradition—only superficially. They finally yield to Muslim identity only when it is brought at the point of the sword or during the twentieth century, when it allows them access to an alternative universalist identity that shields them from European cultural imperialism. The internal moral, historical, and social dynamics that drove African engagements with Islamic knowledge are flattened in the face of this essentially colonialist narrative tinged with hints of African nationalism.

A reassessment of the role of Islamic knowledge in the historiography of Africa is due. The story of Qurʾan schooling and epistemology that I tell here aims to spark such a reassessment. It highlights the role of Qurʾan schools and Islamic knowledge in building the societies of the African West. No external conquest brought Islam to sub-Saharan Africa. Reed pens and wooden tablets were the preferred weapons of the warriors of the faith. The work of spreading Islam—the subject of chapter 2—was carried out by teachers and scholars who embodied Islamic knowledge and inscribed it onto disparate communities across West Africa. This is story of the Walking Qurʾan not only in action but also quite literally in motion.

PRECOLONIAL AFRICA

Approaching this story of schooling and epistemology in the longue durée may help provide a way out of an interpretive morass for African studies more broadly. In the past decade or so, leading Africanists such as Steven Feierman and David Schoenbrun have put forth an urgent call to put *precolonial* African systems of meaning into more fruitful dialogue with the forces of colonial and postcolonial modernity. A focus on colonial questions and imported idioms is producing a general interpretive malaise that this book seeks to help redress.

Feierman, a distinguished anthropologist and historian of East Africa, first began to light the road forward in a watershed 1999 essay, "Colonizers, Scholars, and the Creation of Invisible Histories." He posited that the development of long-term regional historical narratives rooted in Africa was the way out. He stressed, however, that the obstacles to producing such "macro-histories" were daunting at the level of sources, narrative conventions, and especially power relations. He cautioned that creating such regional histories while remaining sensitive to "the global flows of styles, discourses, and practices" was a "paradoxical task" conditioned by a deep structural dilemma: "There are so many local histories that, taken in the aggregate, they dissolve. . . . What is left in the shared memory . . . is the history of forces which affect all localities. . . . The power of ideas about the postcolony, about global flows, leads once again to the erasure of regional specificities, even when these latter are the focus of intense scholarly attention. *They survive merely as local color.*"[66]

Feierman went on to note that more recent works by "historians and ethnographers of hybridity" had produced "brilliant cultural histories" in African contexts that had the troubling tendency to leave intact Eurocentric metanarratives. The problem he identified was not necessarily at the level of these studies individually; rather, they could not be pulled together as a regional metanarrative. This issue, when paired with the fundamental incommensurability—present both at the level of underlying logics and specific narratives—between African and European givens was erasing African knowledge and epistemology and making it impossible to write *African* history: "The studies of commodities (or of Christian sin) in one place, and then another, and then another can be aggregated only on the basis of their shared relationship to the relevant European category: they cannot be placed within a larger or more general African narrative. What is African inevitably appears in a form which is local and fragmented, *and which has no greater depth than the time of colonial conquest, or the moment just before it.*"[67]

Schoenbrun, a specialist in comparative historical linguistics (particularly within the Bantu language family of Central Africa) and a historian of the deep precolonial past, built explicitly on Feierman's framework while accentuating the problems posed by Africanist historiography's increasingly short time depths: "The valuable emphasis on modernity in colonial and postcolonial African studies has profoundly divided precolonial African history from what comes after. But the depth and complexity of African aspirations for moral community and the forms of collective action they inspire . . . exceed the explanatory power of narratives of modernity oriented toward the history of capital, colony, and commerce. Long-term regional histories of *durable bundles of meaning and practice* grounded in Africa address these matters in part by *working across tight spaces of ethnicity and beyond shallow chronologies.*"[68]

Schoenbrun emphasized that we need to understand those "durable bundles of meaning and practice" on their own terms and within their precolonial contexts to make their engagements with colonial and postcolonial modernity meaningful. Only exploring them from within their own categories and tracking them over the longue durée could restore the internal coherences—and struggles for control—of African ways of knowing and being.

Schoenbrun's linking of these "tight spaces of ethnicity" and "shallow chronologies" has profound importance. Colonial and postcolonial histories that do not engage deeper pasts tend to naturalize contemporary identities, ethnic and otherwise. Even when examined critically, shallow time examinations of belonging are structurally inclined to trace the roots of recent identities instead of opening up the past to earlier configurations of society, polity, and identity. In East Africa, this phenomenon expresses itself in studies that unwittingly reinforce ethnic particularism. In Islamic West Africa, these tight spaces of identity often enclose single Sufi orders, making it difficult to conceive studies that cross the lines of Sufi affiliation.

"African Islam" has become almost coterminous with Sufism in much scholarship, but Sufi orders have "shallow chronologies" in most of Africa; they became powerful forces only in the nineteenth and twentieth centuries. Excellent recent studies that historicize the success of Sufi shaykhs such as Amadu Bamba or Ibrāhīm Niass in attracting massive followings, for example, almost always begin by tracing how such leaders transformed Sufi ideas and practices in unique and attractive ways.[69] But this approach forecloses on the exploration of deep time constitutions of—and transformations in—Muslim identity.[70] The popular response to their models for Sufi society—and even those scholarly models themselves—were rooted as much in long-term patterns of Islamic schooling and regional legacies of clericalism as in the internal contours of a given order or even Sufism as a whole. Making such an argument requires not just regional scope but *more time*.

"Tight spaces" of "race" and their equally shallow chronologies are a more troubling element of the same problem. Recent layered racializations of Saharan and sub-Saharan societies have pulled Islamic West Africa apart. Saharans claiming Berber and/or Arab descent, known today collectively as *bayḍān*, are often seen as quite distinct from *sūdān* (blacks). Whatever conceptions of skin color, genealogy, and belonging were in place in the deeper past were dramatically transformed by successive expansions of Saharan slaving in the seventeenth and nineteenth centuries. Such differences became rigid colonial constructs of "race" and "ethnicity" in the twentieth.[71] Colonial and postcolonial states could surveil, police, and incentivize such identities in unprecedented ways, fixing them as immutable. Historicizing such transformations is only part of the solution to this problem. Another part is to attempt to discern earlier configurations of identity—roads of belonging that have not been much traveled in the more recent past but that were well trod centuries ago and may yet be reopened.[72] The story I tell in this book reaches back to a time before popular Sufi orders, to a time before "race," to tell a story about schooling and knowledge that puts back together recently fractured pasts.

The opportunity is special. If Islam can finally come to be understood as an integral and authentic part of the African historical experience, then Islamic Africa will have a special role to play in the shaping of new macrohistories. Part of the challenge of writing deep time narratives is that in much of Africa, few written sources are capable of elucidating the inner workings of African systems of meaning prior to the colonial period. Evocative outlines of the intellectual worlds within which Africans constructed meaning in the deep past are now possible through historical linguistics, archaeology, spatial studies, oral traditions, and other means, but only in a few cases can these be set against a documentary record in the longue durée.[73] Arabic and *ʿajamī* writings—now extensively cataloged but rarely intensively examined—present a documentary record internal to African societies that can be productively placed in dialogue with these rich interdisciplinary sources of Africanist knowledge.

Historical linguistics can diagram a web of relationships between key concepts and practices over broad spaces and long periods of time, but it cannot offer concrete instantiations in the struggle to control meaning. Oral traditions (or for more recent periods, oral histories) can animate the past within African linguistic, historical, and ontological categories and provide powerful glimpses of meaning. But selected precolonial Arabic-script documentary sources can reveal the practical dynamics and specific discursive utterances that made meaning.[74] They can elucidate the quotidian knowledge practices and specific debates that shaped and reshaped worlds of meaning. The study of Islam in Africa offers an ideal laboratory for the writing of those provisional and flawed—but potentially transformative—macrohistories grounded in Africa.

This book does not and cannot fulfill all of these possibilities, but it can attempt to answer Feierman's call for new macrohistories rooted in Africa and capable of traversing long spans of time. By following this story of Islamic knowledge in West Africa from the deep precolonial past through to the contemporary era, I hope to shed light on processes of epistemological change in African societies where Islam was absent or did not provide the dominant framework for understanding. Through this study of Islamic knowledge transmission, we have a chance to elucidate what it meant "to know" in precolonial Africa in detailed terms and to reexamine with rare detail and precision nineteenth- and twentieth-century transformations in the mechanics and meanings of an African knowledge system. At the same time, this study also aims to furnish fresh insights on epistemic shifts in Muslim societies far from sub-Saharan Africa.

Structure of this Book

In addition to outlining the contents of this book and developing a preliminary sense of Qur'an schooling and its epistemology, this introduction has sought to move African Muslims in general from the margins of academic inquiry to its center. Both Islamic studies and African studies have been unwitting and unfortunate heirs to ancient and recent legacies of racial and colonial thought. A blind spot developed where Africanist inquiry and Orientalism met, and African Muslims disappeared. This deep time study of their approach to Islamic knowledge brings them back into the picture. I have also used portions of this introduction to discuss, in the context of the book's overall argument about embodied knowledge, the foundational period of Islam and the original *Walking Qur'an*, Muḥammad himself.

Chapter 1, "Education, Embodiment, and Epistemology," is an interdisciplinary exploration of the philosophy of knowledge behind Qur'an schooling. I craft a detailed historical ethnography of the institution in Senegambia in the recent past and use it to open an exploration of how knowledge was conceived and transmitted. The chapter moves on to trace the specific kind of Qur'an schooling found here—and its view of the elements of knowledge—back to the early days of Islam. From there I develop the claim that the literal *incorporation* of texts (including ingesting them) was central to learning and embodying knowledge. Carrying the Book inside and making it manifest through deeds were inexorably linked. Throughout this work, this sort of embodied and actualized Islamic knowledge is crystallized in the image of the Walking Qur'an. Subsequent chapters refract the last thousand years of Senegambian history through its prism.

Chapter 2, "Embodying Islam in West Africa: The Making of a Clerisy, ca. 1000–1770," examines the constitution and transformation of an indigenous West African clerisy over the longue durée. These African teachers and scholars of Islam were the main vectors of Islamization in a subcontinent that was untouched by the conquests of the early centuries of Islam. They developed a distinct model for relations between temporal and religious authorities that allowed them to keep their distance (and preserve their autonomy) from kings. I carry my examination of the moral and political economies of learning and teaching the Qur'an down through the eighteenth century, paying particular attention to how the rise of the Atlantic slave trade caused this model of pious distance from power to break down, as some clerics became increasingly radical militants. Some things are worth fighting for, and by the seventeenth century, previously quietist men of letters were willing to take up arms against worldly kings who had the temerity to enslave free Muslims and sell them to Christians.

Chapter 3, "The Book in Chains: Slavery and Revolution in Senegambia, 1770–1890," focuses on the problem of the enslavement of *huffāẓ* (keepers) of the Qur'an in Senegambia from the 1770s to the onset of French colonial rule in the 1880s. With clerics understood as embodied exemplars of the Book, such episodes of enslavement were not understood as merely violating Islamic law but rather more deeply felt as desecrations of the Book of God. This chapter documents a century of revolts, rebellions, and even revolutions in Senegambia that were sparked by the enslavement of "the walking Qur'an." The chapter's centerpiece is a dramatic revolutionary movement led by African Muslim clerics and their peasant disciples, who overthrew hereditary slaving kings in 1776, abolished the Atlantic slave trade in the Senegal River Valley, and may even have abolished the institution of slavery in the newly established clerical republic. This chapter is essential reading not just for anyone interested in the history of the Muslim world but also for anyone interested in slavery and abolition in modern history.

Chapter 4, "Bodies of Knowledge: Schooling, Sufism, and Social Change in Colonial Senegal, 1890–1945," expands on these themes of slavery, social justice, and Islamic knowledge as expressed in struggles over access to Qur'an schooling in Senegal from the 1890s to the 1940s, the heyday of French imperialism in West Africa. Former slaves and other marginalized groups used the formal abolition of slavery in the French colonial state to stake claims to dignity through Qur'an schooling. From within the epistemology of embodiment and against regional traditions of bodily stigmas attached to low-status persons, they struggled to remake the substance of their beings through Islamic education.

This effort to remake supposedly "impure" bodies as bodies of knowledge drove a diverse set of previously imperceptible political and educational transformations in colonial Senegal, including the rise of mass Sufi orders and newly emergent patterns of French and Muslim schooling. Even the French regime's basic administrative approach to African Muslims, Islam Noir, was informed by this intense period of changing societal claims on Islamic knowledge. This racialist policy of segregating supposedly syncretistic (and therefore nonthreatening) African Sufis from more "orthodox" (and therefore militant) Arabs produced unforeseeable effects in the knowledge practices of Senegalese Muslims. It is part of the reason the classical approach to Islamic knowledge not only survived colonial rule in Senegal but thrived within it.

Chapter 5, "Disembodied Knowledge?: 'Reform' and Epistemology in Senegal, 1945–Present," resumes the narrative in the period of decolonization after World War II and follows it through Senegalese independence in 1959 and down to the present. The quarantine of Islam Noir had helped safeguard classical approaches to Islamic knowledge in Senegal from the instrumentalization of Muslim schooling that touched other parts of the Muslim world. New "Arabic schools"—as they are usually called in Senegal—arrived late and have not displaced Qur'an schools. Instead of withering, the latter have thrived, assimilating elements of modern epistemology instead of being assimilated into it. Quotidian struggles over schooling in contemporary Senegal are producing hybrid approaches to knowing that stretch the interpretive capacities of standard oppositional models of Sufism and Salafism, tradition and reform.

In the conclusion, I wrap closing arguments about West African history and competing ways of knowing in Islam around my observation that Qur'an schooling has long been seen as an index of the social and spiritual health of West African Muslim communities. The stubborn relevance of classical ways of learning and teaching Islam in much of Africa and the relative neglect (or invisibility) of such schooling in much of the Arab world are revealing. Those interested in Islamic knowledge, I suggest, should be paying more attention to Africa than we usually do.

1 EDUCATION, EMBODIMENT, AND EPISTEMOLOGY

If the Qur'an were on an untanned hide and was thrown into a fire, it would not burn.
—Saying attributed to the Prophet Muḥammad

The *Taalibé*'s Plight

A recent Human Rights Watch (HRW) report, *Off the Backs of the Children: Forced Begging and Other Abuses against Talibés in Senegal*, opens with these lines:

> At least 50,000 children attending hundreds of residential Quranic schools, or daaras, in Senegal are subjected to conditions akin to slavery and forced to endure often extreme forms of abuse, neglect, and exploitation by the teachers, or marabouts. By no means do all Quranic schools run such regimes, but many marabouts force the children, known as talibés, to beg on the streets for long hours—a practice that meets the International Labour Organization's (ILO) definition of a worst form of child labor—and subject them to often brutal physical and psychological abuse. The marabouts are also grossly negligent in fulfilling the children's basic needs, including food, shelter, and healthcare, despite adequate resources in most urban daaras, brought in primarily by the children themselves.

This report is typical of how NGOs, human rights organizations, and casual observers have seen the *daara*. Its disclaimers not withstanding, HRW's depiction of Qur'an schooling, along with many others like it, conveys the notion that *daaras* offer no education worthy of the name and are sites only of child endangerment, abuse, and neglect. In such portrayals, Qur'an teachers are accused of the most cynical forms of exploitation. HRW tells us that marabouts ought to be humble ascetics but are instead leading lives of wealth, ease, and comfort "Off the Backs of Children." With no concrete fiscal data of any kind, the organization speculates freely about the sources and size of marabout revenues.[1] Its policy recommendations include a United Nations investigation of *daaras* as a form of *contemporary slavery* but not aid for marabouts. When the latter receive assistance, HRW claims (again without evidence), they "do not adjust the practice of begging at all, but merely use the assistance to obtain even greater net income."[2] These tropes of slavery and cynical exploitation are linked to corporal discipline. Such "beatings," as HRW calls them, are administered to force children to bring more money to their greedy, affluent marabouts:[3] "Beatings were most frequently reported within the context of failing to return the daily quota, although there were tens of talibés who were also beaten for failure to master the Quranic verses."[4] The testimony of HRW's child informants—that corporal discipline was meant to serve a pedagogic purpose—is dismissed.[5]

On alms seeking, child labor, and corporal punishment, as on many other topics, the report does not contextualize its data. Instead, HRW indulges in unsubstantiated claims about the quality of Qur'anic education, which it does not attempt to measure or document in any way: "Tens of thousands of talibés in Senegal are failing to receive either a religious education or an education in other basic skills."[6] More troubling is that nowhere does HRW seriously ask why parents send their boys away to learn the Qur'an in this way. The report's authors acknowledge that nearly all students in such *daaras* were taken there by their parents, most of whom are fully cognizant of the hardships their children will endure.[7] But this only leads them to condemn parents, too, making them coconspirators in child neglect and endangerment. Nowhere in "Off the Backs of the Children" does HRW come to terms with the fact that many parents are sending their sons to such schools because they *want* them to suffer significant hardship in their pursuit of Islamic knowledge. Nor do these outside observers grasp that marabouts are expected to discipline their charges, especially their live-in students (*njàngaan*).

The Untanned Hides of the Children of Adam

Such sensationalist depictions of the *daara* have drawn a fair amount of attention. In the process, they have helped raise advertising revenues for multimedia conglomerates and donations to human rights organizations, nongovernmental organizations (NGOs), and the numerous Christian mission groups that attempt to proselytize Muslim children in West Africa. The plight of the *taalibé* has become a cottage industry. In most cases, the outrage is certainly sincere and motivated by a desire to protect children, but it is based on a shallow understanding of what Qur'an schooling means to—and does for—African Muslims. When the *daara* is framed in this way, religious freedoms and parents' rights tend not to enter the equation. This kind of caricature of the *daara* did not originate with human rights groups. Sene-

Early twentieth-century postcard illustrated by cartoonist and colonist Édouard Herzig (1860–1926). Herzig, a white settler in Algeria, painted racial, cultural, and religious caricatures of North African Muslims. Colonial administrative reports on Qur'an schooling in North and West Africa tended to exaggerate the themes he distorted visually here. Much contemporary reporting on Qur'an schooling in West Africa does as well.

galese colonial and postcolonial archives are full of government reports—beginning in the 1850s—that resemble *Off the Backs of the Children.* Attacks on Qur'an schools were a major component of French assimilation policy and the colonial *mission civilisatrice* (civilizing mission) in Africa. My goal here is neither to rehash attacks on Qur'an schools nor to highlight their imperialist precedents.[8] Instead, I want to develop quite a different framework for understanding the disciplining of the body and the taming of the ego that take place in the *daara.*

■ This chapter offers an interdisciplinary exploration of the epistemology of Qur'an schooling. My analysis here is based largely on oral histories, autobiographical narratives, and archival accounts of dozens of students who grew up in Senegambian Qur'an schools during the twentieth century. It is also informed by roughly three years of living in Senegal and participant observation in Muslim intellectual and social life. Finally, these sources are augmented by Arabic texts about—and practices of—schooling that range in time from the early days of Islam down to the present. These include hadith reports, teacher training manuals, treatises on the pursuit of knowledge, and other texts. My goal is to construct a kind of historical ethnography of the *daara*, the Senegambian Qurʾan school, in the past century or so and to use this portrait as a window onto the role of embodiment in Islamic epistemology.

This means paying careful attention to controversial practices within the *daara*—among them mendicancy and corporal punishment—and attempting to understand the role they play in schooling as well as the epistemology underlying them. In short, it means beginning our inquiry with how bodily discipline shapes lowly clay into the Walking Qurʾan. This brings us to the saying that opens this chapter. Many students who grew up in Senegambian Qurʾan schools in the twentieth century cited an aphorism (often purported to be a hadith) that any part of the body struck—or more specifically, *scarred*—while learning the Qurʾan would never burn in the hellfire. I have not yet found such a hadith, but in all likelihood, this was an oblique reference to the Prophetic saying that is the epigraph of this chapter: "If the Qurʾan were on an untanned hide and was thrown into a fire, it would not burn."

Many classical theologians understood this saying to mean that the body of one who memorized the Qurʾan was exempt from the hellfire.[9] Indeed, my interlocutors often discussed it in this context: people who had memorized the Qurʾan spoke of being promised freedom from the fire.[10] This idea was sometimes discussed as a full-body absolution for the *ḥāfiẓ*, but more often it was represented as the liberation of the specific limbs that had been corporally chastised. It was as if the saving Word of God had been beaten into those pieces of flesh, thus sanctifying them. Some people showed me their scars, proudly or solemnly indicating where the short lashes often used in the *daara* had written the Qurʾan on their previously "untreated hides."

YAR: EDUCATION, DISCIPLINE, AND THE LASH

West African Muslims have attached a profoundly positive value to suffering and hardship in pursuit of knowledge.[11] In fact, in Wolof, the association of physical discipline with education is encoded even at the level of language. Contemporary Wolof speakers use the word *yar* primarily to mean "educate" or "raise." It is also the most common noun meaning "education." Yet the root meaning of the word *yar* is far more concrete—a "lash" or "switch." Only by extension did the word come to mean discipline, moral education, and education more broadly. In the first-person testimonies, *yar* was a defining symbol of life in the Qur'an school.[12] An indication of its symbolic importance can be found in the illustrations that decorate the pages of the Cahiers Ponty. Three images far surpassed the others in frequency of representation: the Word itself (either portrayed as book or tablet), the teacher, and the lash.[13] Many who had lived the Qur'an school experience remembered the discipline as formative, positive, and foundational. Many considered it central to a sense of self and wished to (and did) transmit it to their children. A small but not insignificant number of others had bitter memories of the discipline. For all, physical discipline—whether valued positively or negatively—was central to the meaning of the Qur'an school.[14]

In the Cahiers Ponty, descriptions were quite vivid. One student provided detailed accounts of the most extreme punishments, known as *ñadd* and *kata*, which were usually reserved for the most troublesome *taalibés*. The *ñadd* is a beating issued with the child held suspended in the air; the *kata* is the pinching of the earlobe with the fingernail or the squeezing of the foreskin or some other sensitive extremity with the hand and sand.[15] As violent as such scenes are, many people consider them an integral part of the educative process. In the words of a former student I interviewed, "One who studies in hardship knows best."[16] Because it entailed alms seeking, hunger, thirst, and generally greater hardship, consigning a child to the care of a Qur'an teacher—the kind of live-in study (*njàngaan*) that scandalized HRW—was almost universally understood to be the most rigorous form of Islamic education. Parting with sons for the sake of God and His Book was also considered an important component of moral education for boys and a powerful symbol of piety.

For Muslims, the Qur'an is the purest divine revelation, and it is taught to children at the very dawn of reason and moral responsibility. In Mālikī legal thought, a child is judged sufficiently mature to begin ritual prayer at the age of seven, precisely the same moment that children were usually sent to Qur'an school to be entrusted with the very essence of the Muslim faith.[17] Against the backdrop of such a paradox, the disciplining of the body finds its logic. The teacher has a sacred duty to protect the sanctity of the Word while producing an educated and disciplined child.

This profound responsibility is most artfully captured in Cheikh Hamidou Kane's brilliant novel, *Ambiguous Adventure*, which examines the epistemological (he calls it philosophical) clash between the schooling traditions of Muslim Africans and modern colonial ways of knowing and being. The Qur'an school is Kane's symbol of Islam, and his protagonist, Samba Diallo,

Yar. Advanced *taalibo*, with switch in hand, teaches young *gariibus* the Qur'an in Fuuta Tooro, 2005. Photograph by Rudolph Ware.

begins his ambiguous adventure in the Qur'an school of a pious and humble teacher whose devotion to the Word of God is expressed in an unrelenting brutality whenever his students corrupt that Word with faulty recitation. The novel opens with Samba being savagely corrected—some might say tortured—for making a mistake in his recitation. His ear is pinched until it bleeds and he is threatened with hot coals, yet Samba does not rebel against the discipline: "This sentence—which he did not understand, for which he was suffering martyrdom—he loved for its mystery and its somber beauty. This word was not like other words. It was a word which demanded suffering, it was a word come from God, it was a miracle, it was as God Himself had uttered it. The teacher was right. The Word which comes from God must be spoken exactly as it has pleased Him to fashion it. Whoever defaces it deserves to die."[18] My interviews with *taalibés* demonstrated that the pious submission (*islām*) exhibited by Samba Diallo was not inculcated only in fictional students. Yet one should be careful not to exaggerate the importance of physical discipline in Qur'an schools. Often enough, the lash or switch was there as a formality, a symbol of the school, and mostly as an idle threat.

Engendering Hardship

Whether corporal punishment was merely symbolic or all too real, some of the people I interviewed argued that learning the Qur'an was supposed to be hard. They reminded me that the revelation of the Qurʾan was physically painful to the Prophet. Traditions report that the first revelation was so alienating that the Prophet begged his wife to cover him, that his physical state changed during revelation of the Qurʾan, and that when he received revelation while riding on a domestic animal, the animal's back bowed under the weight.[19] From this perspective, hardships experienced while learning the Qurʾan made sense. According to Ponty student Demba Beye, the goal was "to form men used to suffering and struggling, capable of adapting themselves to any kind of life, capable, too, of living without bitterness, far from their parents."[20] Men I interviewed often used similar formulations, and discussing the hardships endured at times constituted a kind of mild masculine bragging as much as a rhetorical defense of the Qurʾan school.[21]

Hardship as a key element of the educative process was, of course, gendered. Girls were never *njàngaan*. Unless they received instruction from highly educated family members, they attended school only during the daylight hours. Consequently, their education was perceived as deficient. In reality, however, an education that was in some ways more practical resulted. Most sources agree that girls' literacy training often began immediately in the *daara* (because girls were not expected to stick with it for long), whereas boys were usually not taught to read or spell until much later. Girls often acquired vernacular literacy, whether in Fula *ʿajamī* or Wolofal, earlier than did boys, though children of both sexes usually left the Qurʾan school with literacy skills in their own African languages.

Girls were spared the humiliation of begging by societies that refused to expose them to its risks (and did not seek to cultivate autonomy and independence in the same way), but they, too, received an education designed to teach humility. Girls faced (usually light) corporal punishment and some forms of bodily discipline, but they were generally spared other kinds of hardships seen as central to the education of boys. Female students were usually required to labor in teachers' households, often under the supervision of a master's wives or daughters. Female students would be required to fetch water, go to the market, cook, and wash clothes—household tasks that were gendered female—to effect a change in their character.[22]

As with boys, this education was supposed to produce bodily dispositions or "postures of submissiveness."[23] Anta Njaay, who studied the Qurʾan in Tivaouane in the 1970s and 1980s, remembered these as important gendered components of instruction: "This is how a woman dresses, this is how a woman sits, this is how a woman speaks," her *sëriñ* would tell her. Girls who arrived to school in inappropriate attire would be dismissed and told to return wearing something "ladylike." Repeated violations of dress code could result in physical correction. Male live-in students were explicitly expected to wear tattered rags, loincloths, and other sparse clothing meant to promote humility and toughness. Girls' bodies, conversely, were to be concealed. Girls should also forgo profane, loud, unreserved, and excessive speech to carry themselves like ladies.[24]

Taxañi (going out to fetch wood) was gendered male and the structural equivalent to carrying water.[25] But male students could also be assigned tasks that were ordinarily gendered female as a means of instilling humility and because the work needed to be done. According to Sega Gueye's Cahier Ponty, in the morning, the *njàngaans* were required to sweep the house of the *sëriñ* with the palms of their hands. Then, under the watch of the advanced students, the *njàngaans* took care of his animals and got them grass for fodder. Fierce punishment awaited the shiftless or absent-minded: "If one forgets even one time to get grass, the school transforms itself into hell: the marabout, representing Satan, brutally strikes the damned, the *talibés*." They were also required to carry the *sëriñs'* children, fetch water, and complete countless other tasks.[26]

YALWAAN: THE QUEST FOR ALMS

Historically speaking, *yalwaan* (begging for food and alms) was an important part of the Qur'an school experience for most boys. This custom contributed to the maintenance of boys who lived at the school, who almost never paid tuition as such. Neither the student nor his parents paid for the child's instruction as a *njàngaan*; instead, they formally consigned rights to the child's labor to a *sëriñ*. Parents of *njàngaans* and ordinary *taalibés* alike offered gifts (*hadiyya*) to teachers, both voluntarily and after boys reached specific memorization milestones. Students who lived at home and came to the Qur'an school only to memorize the Book with teachers often made scheduled gifts to replace the labor owed to their teacher. On some occasions, however, they donned tattered rags like their live-in classmates and begged door-to-door, even in their hometowns, an experience some students described as particularly humiliating.

Perhaps influenced by growing negative perceptions of begging, many Qur'an school students and teachers with whom I lived and spoke decried the abuse of *yalwaan*, arguing that in the good old days, students did not beg much; instead, they farmed. HRW and especially journalistic treatments of the plight of the *taalibé* perpetuate this assumption. This is plainly false. Alms seeking seems always to have played some role in Islamic education in

Senegambia, and the alms bowl is a widely recognized symbol of the West African clerical class among other social strata. Many European sources, some from as early as the beginning of the seventeenth century, specifically attest to *yalwaan*. It appears prominently in the account of a Portuguese traveler in Saalum: "It is the ritual of the young people, as long as they study with the *bexerins* [teachers, clerics], to subsist on alms. There is no *bexerin* who does not have with him ten or twelve young people, to whom he teaches reading and writing, doing all of this on tablets and studying at night by firelight. During the day they seek alms in the name of God."[27]

Yalwaan has become more prominent as a consequence of urbanization and of the fact that fewer clerics now farm for a living, but *yalwaan* always existed alongside the students' farm labor.[28] Whether or not people nowadays want to admit it, many *taalibés* and almost all *njàngaans* were fed primarily from the food they could beg from society at large.[29] Giving students food and charity was understood as a community responsibility, and attention to it indexed the spiritual health of the Muslims.

Many twenty-first-century Senegalese, especially urbanites, oppose alms seeking, but people that I interviewed usually considered some measure of *yalwaan* essential to a proper education because of its capacity to humble the children of Adam. One *ḥāfiẓ* I interviewed in Tivaouane painted a verbal picture of a day in the *daara*:

> I have a filthy boubou [robe]. It's filthy, but I can't wash it. There is soap, but no one will wash it for me. Now it's raining. I don't go inside. I sleep outside. There's nowhere for me to go, no room for me to go into. And still it rains. I take a floor mat and wrap it around myself. . . . I'm wet, but I have no choice. . . . When I get up at four in the morning, I go out to *yalwaan* carrying a pot. What am I begging for? Sugar, rice, millet. . . . When I go, I go barefoot. I tremble because I am wearing only a light garment. . . . Afterward, you pour in your millet, and they give you a text. You recite it. Then you go *taxañi*, looking for dead wood in the bush, [still] without shoes. The sun is hot. . . . You beg. You're miserable [*yangi tumuranke*]. . . . You say, "For the love of God [*ngir Yàlla*], I have nothing to eat. God is the Lord of all mankind [*Allah rabb al-anām*]! Put a little aside for me.[30]

■ Because it was thought to produce humility and good character, *yalwaan* was esteemed by some teachers who did not require or even use the proceeds of the children's quest for alms. In his Cahier Ponty, Abdelkader Fall wrote in glowing terms of his Qur'an teacher, Amadu Jóob. Jóob had several hundred students, extensive fields, and a reputation for piety and scholarship throughout the Senegal River Valley. These fine traits made him *no* more forgiving in collecting alms from his *taalibés*: "Around eight o'clock they come back to the *serigne* [teacher], where they pile the proceeds of their collections into a large calabash. The poor fool whose bowl is not full had better watch out! He will be beaten in front of his comrades by Serigne Amadou, who thereby teaches him to 'be resourceful [*se debrouiller*]' like the others."[31]

By eliminating financial need from Sëriñ Amadu's motives for sending his *taalibés* out to seek alms, Fall is clearly making claims to his instructors at the French school. Ponty students were acutely aware that teachers in the French school generally thought of alms seeking as begging. Some students seemed to share this assessment, but many sought explicitly to defend the *daara* against its opponents. Modibo Bamany, a student from French Soudan (now Mali), directly defended alms seeking: "The white man must not think ill of the *garibou* [*gariibu*, a Fula term for a mendicant Qur'an student]. The Garibou is not a beggar; he does not ask for alms because he is a victim of the misery of his parents. No; it is custom and his religion that oblige him to do it. It is also not by necessity that the marabout has them ask for millet here and there; no, he wants to shape their education, make men of them."[32]

This training in humility—especially for boys who are generally thought of as more prideful and aggressive—was still deeply valued when I did interviews in the early years of the twenty-first century. Ibrahima Bàjjan, the shaykh of a prominent school in Tivaouane, summarized the point of *yalwaan*: "Pride does not enter the garden [*Réy du dem àjjana*]." It must first be removed from the children of Adam to make them useful servants of God. In his school, funded by a prominent branch of the Tijāniyya Sufi order, children do not seek alms for their maintenance, but they are required occasionally to seek alms so that they know what it is to *yalwaan*.[33] This is, in fact, the case in many contemporary *daaras* that are funded by pious gifts. Children are made to seek alms once or twice a year as part of their spiritual training.[34]

YOR: POSSESSING THE BOOK

Why did so many former *taalibés*—in my interviews and in the Cahiers Ponty—stress the importance of *yar* and *yalwaan* in colonial and postcolonial contexts where such discipline was visibly condemned by the state and others? Why would Qur'an school teachers who had no need for the proceeds of *yalwaan*—some claim to have redistributed them as alms to the poor—insist that their *taalibés* go out to seek alms? Why was *yar* (the lash) so important as a symbol of the schools? I heard many similar answers to this question in my conversations with former students, but the most colorful and illustrative came from Ibrahima Bàjjan. At his school, older students studying the religious sciences walk through the rows of beginning Qur'an students carrying short lashes, and I witnessed (light) physical correction firsthand. He explained that discursive teaching (*jàngale*) without moral education (*yar*) is useless. For him, it was akin to "taking a bowl and putting food in it without washing it first."[35] The implication was clear: one could not simply take the Word of God and dump it into the corrupted low flesh of the children of Adam. One needed to clean out the vessel first.

Over the years, I have heard numerous similar formulations. For Bàjjan, the image of a child's fragile young body as a vessel needing to be prepared to bear the Word of God was explicit. Hunger, thirst, fatigue, physical pain: all constituted bodily means for producing moral, emotional, and spiritual results, for reshaping sensibilities. One used the body to transcend the body. Countless former students recounted to me, either directly or across time in the pages of their Cahiers, that the physical hardships were intended to *toj xol bi* (literally "to break the heart" of the child) and then to *defarat jikko* (rebuild character).[36] All this *discipline* was meant to produce *disciples* (*taalibés*), *disciplined* Muslims worthy of keeping the Qur'an.

Embodiment and Epistemology

The approach to schooling that I encountered in the testimonies of former Qur'an school students was a bodily approach. Islamic knowledge was being transmitted as much through bodily practices as mere words. This focus on bodily transmission of religious ideas expresses an understanding of knowledge as a thing that inheres in the body. What it meant "to know" in the context of Senegambian Qur'an schooling differed dramatically from what it meant for many contemporary Westerners. Knowing was produced as much by the limbs as by the mind. Imitation of the teacher's gestures and comportment was as much a part of the educative process as the texts that one was required to read. Memorization of texts allowed for a personal possession of the Word in the body, without requiring recourse to a written source external to the self. The people were the books, just as the Prophet was the Walking Qur'an. Islamic knowledge was embodied knowledge.

Evidence of the salience of this approach appeared everywhere in the testimonies of students who grew up in Qur'an schools. One former student interviewed by a French sociologist two generations ago talked about how the embodied practical training began even before children were sent to the Qur'an school: "Religious consciousness is acquired on the basis of the religious practice of the family. . . . When one prays the father calls even the kids who are only four years old. They have no consciousness at that moment, but the fact that they get in the habit of putting their foreheads to the ground, of rising up at the same time as the adults, that is something. When the father prays everyone comes behind him, even the little ones. From that point one explains to them the entry into relationship with the Eternal, the hereafter, with God."[37]

Another former student wrote in similar terms about the respect in his home village of Dagatche, Senegal, for the Mālikī legal principle that children should be encouraged to pray at age seven and physically disciplined for neglecting prayers by age ten:[38] "For the prepubescent, and therefore [legally] incompetent child, prayer cannot have the character of an absolute obligation. Nonetheless in Dagatche, as in many Muslim societies, tradition has it that one enjoins him to pray at age seven and that one beats him so that he fulfills this obligation at age ten. This is so that as an adolescent, these things will be profoundly anchored in his heart, made familiar to his soul, and constitute habitual gestures for his limbs."[39]

These and countless other sources emphasize the extent to which the shaping of religious sensibilities was an embodied process. In some Qurʾan schools, beginning students were required to receive their lessons with their legs folded in the *jalsa* (seated position) used in ritual prayer and to remain in that position for hours while memorizing the lessons.[40] Whether moving the limbs or fixing them in place, disciplining them was a corporeal support for writing the Book in the memory, mind, and imagination.

Human beings learn with all of their senses and with the whole of themselves, not simply with the mind. One Qurʾan school teacher from Fuuta Tooro, Mokhtar Kebe, made this point abundantly clear in a presentation at the Islamic Institute of Dakar during a 2007 Institute for the Study of Islamic Thought in Africa conference. He talked at length about the first lesson for students in his school in Kaedi, Mauritania. He described dipping the child's finger in the homemade ink used at the school and using it like a pen to trace the first letter of the Qurʾan, *baa*, on a wooden tablet. He explained that he had the students look at the shape of the letter with the eye, feel the movement of shaping it with the hand, hear the sound pronounced with the ear, and then repeat the sound with the tongue. All the senses were explicitly engaged. After writing the whole of the *basmala*, he erased the letters with water and gave the children the liquid to drink, internalizing the word into their bodies in the most direct fashion.[41]

A typical coeducational Senegambian Qur'an school, 2005.
Photograph by Rudolph Ware.

The Sweetness of the Qur'an: Part I

Learning the Qur'an was not all bitter; it was also sweet. A number of the former students I interviewed in 2001–2 used the Wolof word *banneex* (pleasure, delight, satisfaction) to describe their experience of learning the Qur'an. Amadu Bassiru Jeng, a Murid *taalibé*, used the term repeatedly.[42] Qur'an schools were forbidding places, and the corporal punishment administered by teachers was legendary, but learning the Qur'an was also surrounded by an air of mystery, power, and excitement. A man from the Village of Ngabou, outside of Touba, known as Vieux (Old Man) Faal grew up in the 1930s and 1940s as the child of Fulɓe pastoralists who showed little interest in sending him to the *dudal*. At the age of twelve, he sneaked away to listen to the children reciting what he knew were holy words. He returned home and told his father that he wanted to study the Qur'an. His father, struck by the sudden show of piety, took him to the *ceerno* the next day. Faal remembered being enchanted by the *dudal*'s sense of holiness and feeling that he could no longer be excluded from the secret world of knowledge that the Qur'an school represented.[43]

Knowledge had a powerful allure for many students, often sparked by the sensory experience of hearing the Qur'an recited. A Ponty student, Sega Guèye, recalled this feeling from his first days in the *daara* and recorded his memories of hearing the recitation of the advanced students—those who wrote the verses on their tablets by themselves instead of having them written by the master: "More than once, an astonished passer-by stops suddenly, overtaken by this beautiful reading. Seduced ourselves, we stop and with a glance ask each other if we will ever reach their seemingly inaccessible level. . . . Their reading is absolutely singular: the voice remains low, the eyes fixed on the words, with a calm and withdrawn air."[44]

A number of accounts, both written and oral, depict the Qur'an as a kind of solemnly seductive song. Students learning the Qur'an often rock as they recite, using their bodies to keep the beat.[45] Ponty student Abdelkader Fall evokes this feeling in words that slip from prose into poetry: "Bodies sway; the *talibés* are possessed by the mysterious rhythm. Frantically reading, each one modifies according to his tastes the sacred text of which he understands nothing. Sacred music, the pious come to listen."[46] Much meaning could be made without understanding the words.[47]

Not all the pleasures of learning, of course, were, strictly speaking, sensory. A great many students relished the sense of accomplishment that came with memorizing new verses.[48] Others spoke of experiencing rushes of discursive or analytical understanding as they neared the end of the memorization and began to glimpse the meanings of verses and suras. One student recalled intense satisfaction when, after memorizing the Qur'an and beginning to study Arabic grammar, he realized that he could assimilate the grammar and vocabulary with incredible speed because he had thousands of sample sentences in his head.[49]

Qur'an schooling also offered simpler pleasures. Teachers often treated children to sweets, told jokes and funny stories, and otherwise made themselves beloved. Many Qur'an teachers were remembered as kind and gentle. The stereotype of the stern Qur'an teacher, while containing a kernel of truth, is nonetheless a stereotype. Some did not employ corporal punishment or did so only sparingly. Shaykh Lo Njaay, whom I interviewed in Touba, described his teacher as "a kind person; he did not have the habit of beating the children. . . . He would try to please you for you to learn. . . . He had compassion."[50] Lansiné Diané, a Ponty student from Guinea, saw his teacher as balancing the carrot and the stick: "Severe, but paternal, familiar with children, he knows their whims and tastes and knows just as well how to amuse them as to punish them."[51]

VENERATION OF MASTERS: *ḤUBB*, *KHIDMA*, AND *HADIYYA* (LOVE, SERVICE, AND GIFTS)

Whether stern, kind, or both, teachers were often beloved figures. Learning to respect, love, and serve the *sëriñ* has always been one of the most important aspects of religious socialization in the *daara*. Its corollary was that students' personal sense of piety often came to be conceived as the extension of a relationship with a human teacher and guide. When asked if she kept a favorable opinion of her teacher in spite of the fact that he was very severe, one student replied with an unequivocal affirmative: "Yes, a good memory, very good, because even now the verses that I recite, I say that I owe them to him. . . . He has been dead a long time . . . [but] even now, when I pray, I think of him."[52] She was expressing a sense of gratitude toward her deceased master because she owed her ability to fulfill the basic ritual obligations of her faith to his stern commitment to the Word. Shariif Sulaymaan Aydara, whom I interviewed in Touba, expressed a characteristic feeling of indebtedness to his *sëriñ* by alluding to a proverb: "I honor him and I thank him very much. Because *whosoever teaches you a letter of the Qur'an is your master.* I honor and thank him because he taught me to work, he taught me to persevere patiently [*muñ*] and to confront life!"[53] Receiving the Qur'an from a teacher produced a moral debt that could never be fully paid but that could be satisfied through service and pious gifts.[54]

Oral traditions of the Murīdiyya Sufi order about the Qur'anic education of Maaram Mbakke, great-grandfather of Amadu Bamba, illustrate the teacher's role as a vessel of *baraka* (blessing). Maaram studied with the Fulɓe scholar Samba Caam sometime during the first two decades of the eighteenth century. Cheikh Babou relates the story of Maaram's final day at the school: "Because of his respect and devotion to Samba Caam, for whom he worked tirelessly during his stay at the school, Maaram earned knowledge and *baraka*. . . . The day of Maaram's departure . . . Samba Caam gathered all the disciples in the yard of his school. . . . He declared to the assembly of disciples: 'Anybody who is in this school to seek knowledge, the sciences are still here, but to those looking for *baraka*, I say that Maaram has earned it all.'"[55] Love, service, and gifts were understood as the keys to unlocking the benefits of knowledge. Indeed it is still widely held that without receiving a teacher's gratitude (*ngërëm*) and blessing (*barke* in Wolof), one cannot profit from one's learning.

Some students sensed that simply by being in the physical presence of a teacher, one could be transformed by his *baraka* or perhaps by his inner state (*ḥāl*). Shaykh Lo Njaay, a Murid I interviewed in Touba, was among those who claimed that the most important part of an education was simply "being in front of the teacher [*nekk ci kanam sëriñ bi*]."[56] This concept, rendered in classical *adab* literature as *ṣuḥba* (companionship), was partly built on mimesis—that is to say, on the assimilation of gestures, mannerisms, and dispositions through extended physical proximity. This process was understood not only as a physical imprinting of the self but as a moral and spiritual one as well.

Companionship of this kind was strongly tied to *khidma* (service), which could mean everything from massaging a teacher's weary limbs to making his tea, burning incense in his room before he retired for the evening, and countless other tasks to lighten his burden.[57] Service of this kind played a central role in breaking the ego and instilling humility. Murid *taalibé* Amadu Basiru Jeng talked about this process of performing menial labor for a *sëriñ* as "lightening oneself [*woyofal sa bopp*]," declaring that this "lightness" allowed one to "rise," since "heavy things get left behind [*lu diis des ganaaw*]."[58] His expression echoed a major educative value common to the classical tradition as a whole but particularly emphasized in the Murīdiyya. As Amadu Bamba (the order's founder) wrote in his lengthy treatise on the etiquette of seeking knowledge (not only Sufi knowledge), "If you seek knowledge, strive to satisfy your master to please God. Be with your Shaykh like a slave [*mamlūk*]; you will attain, thanks to him, the rank of kings [*mulūk*]. Know that one obtains no favor without veneration according to what has been reported. In measure with your veneration of your Shaykh will you obtain what you desire, and thanks to him you will attain felicity."[59]

PERSONIFICATION, EMBODIED EXAMPLE, AND CHAINS OF AUTHORITY

Only after memorizing and internalizing the Qur'an and reshaping one's bodily deportment to resemble a living carrier of the Qur'an did one go on to study the religious sciences, geography, mathematics, or medicine. The vessel of the heart had been washed so that all knowledge poured in thereafter would be fruitful. And once one proceeded on to study the Islamic religious sciences, the emphasis on internalization and embodied example was not abandoned.

The standard model in West Africa was that an *ijāza* (permission to teach a specific text) was not issued until it was not only understood (and often memorized) but also actualized or embodied. When the master saw that the disciple's character and behavior had been shaped in light of the knowledge acquired, permission was granted. The possession of knowledge was inseparable from its actualization in character and deeds. *ʿIlm* was inseparable from *ʿamal*.[60] Understood in this way, knowledge could not be separated from the person of its possessor; it was personified—or embodied—knowledge.[61] The authority to transmit knowledge resides in this kind of human connection between the master and the disciple, a relationship that supersedes that of the student to the text. William Graham wrote thoughtfully on this point: "What is crucial here is the fundamental presupposition that truth does not reside in documents, however authentic, ancient, or well-preserved, but in authentic human beings and their personal connections with one another. Documents alone, without a line of *persons* possessed of *both* knowledge and righteousness to teach and convey them across the years, are useless as instruments of authoritative transmission. It is 'the golden chain of sincere Muslims' that guarantees the faithful copying, memorizing, reciting and understanding of texts—not only those of the *Ḥadīth*, but those of the Qurʾan and all subsequent works of Muslim piety and learning."[62]

Graham refers to this as the "isnad paradigm" and makes a compelling case for its general acceptance in the world of classical scholarship. While I agree that this ethic was central to Muslim scholarship everywhere before the nineteenth century, I want to suggest that embodied example has been particularly central to the transmission of knowledge in Mālikī chains of knowledge transmission—precisely the chains that have produced the scholars of the African West.

Recent work by Yasin Dutton, based in part on earlier work by ʿUmar Faruq ʿAbdallah, has offered precious insight on the role of practical example—what I would call embodied example—in the teachings of the Mālikī school. Both men have argued that the *ʿamal* (deeds) of the people of Medina constituted an independent source of legal rulings in the Mālikī school, a source that could—and often did—supersede authentic hadiths.[63] A classic example is the question of the position of the arms in prayer. Most followers of Mālikī rite hold their arms at their sides while standing in prayer, a position usually referred to as *sadl*. The followers of the other Sunni legal schools pray with their arms folded. A number of hadiths, identified as authentic by Mālikī authorities, confirm that witnesses saw the Prophet Muḥammad praying with his arms folded (*qabḍ*). These hadiths form the primary basis for the three other schools' definition of this position as the normative practice of the Prophet, and all of the other schools approach texts in related ways.[64] A smaller number of hadiths describe the Prophet praying with his arms at his sides, and scholars have challenged the authenticity of some of these.

Why, then, do most Mālikīs pray with their arms at their sides? Because according to Ibn al-Qāsim (d. 806), one of the earliest authorities in the chain of Mālik's teachings, Mālik himself had never seen a person in Medina, the Prophet's city, pray one of the five daily prayers with arms crossed.[65] In the reasoning of Mālik and those who followed his approach, the embodied example of the people of Medina was often the preferred source for defining the normative practice. Why? Because Mālik (711–95) served as the imam in the Prophet's city only a few generations after the Prophet himself, receiving the practice of Islam from his father and grandfather in the Prophet's city. He often preferred the example of the people of knowledge in Medina to hadith. A hadith could contain an isolated report or transmit a deed of the Prophet that was never intended to be normative.

Many early authorities distrusted the way isolated reports could gain the status to define norms simply by being transmitted and then written down. One of Mālik's teachers put the problem this way: "One thousand from one thousand is preferred by me to one from one. One from one would tear the sunna right out of your hands."[66] Hadiths are, structurally speaking, always one-to-one reports, even when they are corroborated by many other similar or identical reports. The example of the practice of a whole community transmitted a norm from one thousand to one thousand. Transmission from one whole generation to another in actual embodied practice was a check against idiosyncratic innovations and unprecedented interpretation.

Mālikī teaching came to stress practical, personified, human, *embodied* example in the transmission of knowledge.[67] While the construction of knowledge in the other Sunni and Shiite schools always focused on embodiment, followers of the school of Mālik may have emphasized this idea more than followers of other schools. Moreover, Mālikīs continued to use a definition of normative example (sunna) drawn not only from words and deeds of the Prophet himself but also from those of the early Muslims more broadly.[68] According to the closing lines of Qayrawānī's (922–96) *Risāla*, an early text still transmitted and studied widely in West Africa, "Following the path of the righteous forebears leads to success also. They are the models on whom we should base our lives. They are the leaders in interpreting that which they interpreted. They are also to be emulated in evolving rules and regulations to govern the lives of Muslims. Although they differ, their differences do not carry them away from coming to agreement."[69]

Early Islamic authorities—perhaps especially, though by no means exclusively, Mālikī authorities—called on *people* to light the road when texts might argue against one another. This focus on practical physicality was not restricted only to the study of the law; rather, the study of the law reflected and amplified a broader focus on practical transmission in the epistemology of Islam.[70]

Drinking the Qur'an

Memorization and recitation, mimesis and service, personification and practical example: these all exemplify corporeal knowledge practices. But the physical ingestion of "knowledge"—glimpsed briefly in the account of Mokhtar Kebe's school—is embodiment of a different order. The practice of "drinking the Qur'an"—actually imbibing the ink used to write verses from the Book—is closely associated with Qur'an schooling in West Africa. This practice particularly illustrates the role of embodiment in the epistemology of classical Qur'an schooling, but it is also a singularly revealing example of the ways in which a narrow focus on syncretism has worked to the disadvantage of both African and Islamic studies. If we begin to see embodiment as epistemology, this seemingly arcane practice from the African periphery of the Muslim world might produce revealing insights about the history of knowledge in Islam.

In Senegambia and indeed throughout West Africa, one of the most important physical objects differentiating a modern Arabic school from a Qur'an school is the former's use of mass-produced notebooks and ballpoint pens. In the Qur'an school, wooden tablets remain the primary medium for—and symbol of—instruction.[71] In Wolof, such a tablet is called an *àlluwa*, from the Arabic plural *alwāḥ*. Writing is done with reed pens (*xalima*) that dispense a homemade ink (*daa*), fabricated with water, gum arabic, and either charcoal or the soot from cooking pots.[72] When students memorize a verse of the Qur'an, they erase the lesson written on their boards with water and often drink the liquid, which is understood to be charged with the spiritual power of the Qur'an. Sometimes particular verses are written to help enhance a child's ability to learn the Book; at other times, verses understood to possess healing properties are given to children who fall ill in the *daara*.[73]

The use of the wash water from the *alwāḥ* in this way has long been noted as particularly prevalent in sub-Saharan Africa. Lamin Sanneh, now an academic scholar of Islam, attended a Gambian Qur'an school in the 1950s. He recalled that "a common practice at the school was to collect the water with which we had washed our slates if the relevant portions were from highly auspicious parts of the Qur'án. We collected this water in small bottles and took them home for use as medicine. We had to obtain Teacher's permission for that, but he was never known to object. In fact, it was he who told us which sections of the Qur'án were useful in that way. We could not recall a time, however, when he taught us that the holy water could help us acquire quick minds, and yet it was precisely this hope that sent many parents in search of the right Qur'án medicine, at great expense and trouble, which they made their children drink."[74]

This practice, along with the prevalence of Qur'anic talismans in sub-Saharan Africa, is usually explained as a kind of "Africanization" of Islam. Scholars suppose this to be a use of Qur'an as a sort of "African fetish," either decrying the practice as heterodox or implicitly celebrating an African cultural survival against the imperialist intrusion of Islam. In the best-known article devoted specifically to the topic of Qur'anic "erasures," Abdullahi Osman El-Tom, writing on the Berti of the Sudan, transmits a characteristic scholarly understanding of the practice: "The drinking of the Koran itself is confined to the peripheries of the Islamic world. Its origins might, therefore, relate to the religious system which existed prior to the intrusion of the Islamic culture, and which can still be seen in a number of existing practices."[75] This is a typical portrait of a seemingly "superstitious" or heterodox "African" practice of Islam. The use of the *miḥāya* (as the liquid is called in Sudanese Arabic) or *kiis* or *saafara* (Wolof) perfectly exemplifies how the significance of African practices of Islam have been misrepresented and misunderstood.

PEDIGREES AND PRECEDENTS

Drinking the Qur'an certainly represents no animist innovation. The practice is probably as old as Islam itself. In attempting to historicize the quotidian practices of Qur'an schooling, I stumbled across documentary evidence that traces the genealogies of drinking the Qur'an in West African schools all the way back to the end of the seventh century—to within a generation or two of the foundation of Islam. In Mālikī teaching texts written in North Africa in the ninth and tenth centuries, such practices and ideas are traced back to the earliest generations of Muslims.

In a book of guidelines for Qur'an school teachers and students, the *Risāla al-mufaṣṣila*, Abū al-Ḥasan al-Qābisī (936–1012), a respected jurist in the city of Qayrawān, establishes the pedigree for the reverential treatment of Qur'anic erasures and for the potency of ingesting the Revelation, tying it back to the early days of Islam.[76] He cites extensively a similar—though much shorter—work, *Kitāb Adab al-Muʿallimīn* (Book of Conduct of the Teachers), written roughly a century earlier by Muḥammad b. Saḥnūn (817–70), the son of one of the Mālikī school's major authorities. In fact, apart from Mālik b. Anas al-Aṣbaḥī (711–95), the eponym of the school, Saḥnūn b. Saʿīd (776–854) is perhaps the most important figure of early Malikism and is sometimes credited as the intellectual and jurist most responsible for the final victory of Mālikī Sunnism over Khārijī and Shiite competitors in North Africa during the ninth century.[77]

Saḥnūn is also conventionally credited as the final editor for Mālik's *Muwaṭṭaʾ*, an early collection of hadiths, legal precedents, and rulings that Mālik used for teaching and judging during his lifetime and that were compiled and published shortly after his death. It is widely studied and used by Sunni authorities in all four of the major schools. Saḥnūn was also the primary author of the *Mudawwana*, a compilation of Mālik's teachings collected by his students, the most prominent of whom was Saḥnūn himself.

Whatever his intellectual and legal achievements, Saḥnūn apparently still taught the Qurʾan to small children throughout most of his life, and his son transmitted his teachings about the proper conduct and methods of schoolmasters in the *Kitāb Adab al-Muʿallimīn*. Saḥnūn reported that Anas b. Mālik, manservant of the Prophet and one of the most widely cited sources of traditions in the first few decades of Islam, was asked about erasing the Qurʾan from the *alwāḥ*:[78] "How was it with the learned in the era of the imams Abū Bakr, ʿUmar, ʿUthmān and ʿAlī—may God be pleased with them?" Anas replied, "The learned had an *injāna* [a clay bowl] and the students took turns bringing water to pour into the bowl to wash the tablets. Then they dug a hole in the earth and poured this water in where it was absorbed into the ground."[79]

These same bowls can be seen in most Qurʾan schools from Senegal to Sudan, though they are often now made of plastic. Indeed, a number of interlocutors in Senegal reported to me the practice of pouring the filled bowls into holes or obscure wooded areas or into a pit underneath the Qurʾan school hearth so that no one would tread on the Word of God. This rationale was confirmed by the Cahier Ponty of a Mauritanian student: "As everyone knows, one must respect all of the Qurʾan, even the water that washes it. One must wash the tablets in a place off the beaten path [*dans un endroit à l'ecart du chemin*] so that the feet of men and the paws of animals do not mistreat it after having received the blessed water."[80]

■ It was precisely in this context that al-Qābisī and Ibn Saḥnūn introduced the hadith of the *injāna*, cited above. Muḥammad b. Saḥnūn asked his father whether it was acceptable to erase with the tongue. He said, "This is not a problem, but you must not do it with the foot; one can erase with a rag or something else like it." In short, one must not tread on God's Holy Word; moreover, one must not even wipe a slate board clean with something as low and dirty as the foot. Here we have simply a set of statements about the sanctity of the Word and an appropriate stance with respect to its sanctity. But there was more to the question of erasure.

In the *Kitāb Adab*, Muḥammad b. Saḥnūn cites hadith on the merits of erasing Qurʾan tablets with the tongue, thereby incorporating the Word of God physically. On the authority of the Qāḍī of Tripoli, Abū al-Aswad al-Qaṭṭān (830–918), Muḥammad b. Saḥnūn reports that Ibrāhīm al-Nakhaʿī (666–715), a prominent member of the generation following the Prophet's (*tābiʿūn*), said, "It is a sign of the qualities of a man deserving of the name that one see him with ink on his clothes and on his lips." Muḥammad b. Saḥnūn adds, "There is an argument in favor of the opinion that there is no trouble in *licking the Revelation*. . . . Often Saḥnūn [his father] would write something, then erase it with his tongue."[81]

In all likelihood, the practice of drinking from the Qurʾan school's *injana* was already current in North Africa in Qābisī's time and probably in Saḥnūn's as well, even if there is only explicit mention of licking the wooden boards and collecting the water in a pot. While the obvious next step of drinking the wash water may have been a recent innovation, it is much more likely that it was known but not explicitly mentioned in the texts, especially since drinking the Qurʾan in healing contexts was a widely accepted practice. In any case, if we take seriously the statement attributed to al-Nakhaʿī, the practice of ingesting the Qurʾanic Word while learning goes back at least to the late seventh century. Whatever the specific means of bringing the Qurʾan into the body of the seeker of knowledge, the understanding was that the Word itself had merits and the agency to produce fortuitous results.

In the early 1930s, more than one thousand years after Muḥammad b. Saḥnūn wrote of "licking the Revelation," Amadou Wane wrote an essay about his life at the Qurʾan school of Ceerno Hamadi: "[The teacher] takes my little right hand; he writes upon it, with great care and in large characters, the first letters of the first verse: ʻ = ba—signidié—mimarack—alif—lam-bam—ha—sagirou.' This done, he orders me to lick the holy writings. Then he copies them onto a small tablet that he nearly fills with his large writing. Squatting, legs folded [in the *jalsa* position], I receive the tablet on my thighs. Thierno Hamadi has me repeat the letters successively, one by one. He exaggerates the pronunciation to help me grasp it."

THE SWEETNESS OF THE QUR᾿AN: PART II

The bodily assimilation of the Word and its power was connected directly with its discursive transmission. The use of the *basmala* is both practical and symbolic. The Qur᾿an's first verse, the *fātiḥa* (opening), is a fitting tool to open the mind of a student as well as to open study. Of course, it is also literally the invocation of God, meaning "in God's name," and is thus uttered to invoke God's blessing for all sorts of undertakings.

This "opening" occurred prior to the discursive instruction, but it also followed and reinforced it. Wane continues, "The third phase is the inscription of these same characters on a very large cake. The belief is that these writings, when absorbed, render the whole body apt to receive divine instruction. Smaller cakes are distributed as alms for prompt success and brilliant study."[82] In this former student's formulation, it is not the mind that is prepared for study but rather "the whole body." It is also striking that this body is constructed as a passive recipient of "divine instruction," conditioned by God's speech itself. This practice was also mentioned by another Ponty student, Baba Ndiaye: "To acquire a prodigious memory, one makes [the new *taalibé*] eat a nice millet cake already 'blessed' by the master."[83]

In Wane's account, the physical incorporation of the Word is not limited to the student alone but involves a community, which is then bound corporally to the pious act through the sharing of food. A similar account is presented by another of the Ponty students, Abdelkader Fall, though in his *daara*, the cakes were presented only to the other students in the school rather than to the community at large.[84] However broadly that community might be defined, the sharing of food at this moment marks it as a sort of communal sacrifice.[85]

Such practices were—and are—widely reported in West African Qur᾿an schools. Among the Jakhanke clerical diaspora, children also lick part of the *basmala*—in this case, from both hands. The students then take an offering of pounded grain home for their parents.[86] Renaud Santerre reports that in Bandiagara (Mali), the *basmala* is imbibed rather than licked or eaten.[87] Based on anthropological fieldwork in Jenné, Mali, Geert Mommersteeg specifies that in addition to the *basmala*, marabouts habitually add verses from the Qur᾿an chosen to facilitate learning. He specifically mentions Q 20:25–28 and Q 87:6.[88] In the first of these, from Sura Ṭaha, the Qur᾿an recounts Moses' words of prayer when given the mission to preach to Pharaoh: "*O Lord! Swell my Heart. Ease my task for me. Untie my tongue. So that they understand my speech.*" These words offer a prayer befitting both student and teacher. The second example, from Sura al-ʿAlā, is perhaps a more direct invocation intended to produce an effect on the child: "*We will make you recite so you shall not forget.*" In all of these cases, the Qurʾan is being ingested for the purpose of increasing intelligence and ensuring fruitful study. God's speech possesses its own agency, a natural conclusion since in the Qurʾan, God has the power to say "be" and it is (*kūn fa yakūn*).

■ This understanding of the agency of God's word is not unique to West Africa, and although it has been discouraged or disparaged as "magic" by some reformist interpretations of Islam in the past two or three centuries, such an understanding is clearly operative in many healing practices throughout the Muslim world. For example, Jonathan Berkey's work on knowledge in medieval Egypt mentions the use of Qurʾan for healing, referring to it as a "popular practice" in spite of the fact that he was finding it used mostly by learned scholars. He saw this detail as an incongruity: "What is intriguing, however, is the close spatial proximity of cultural processes and artifacts which, at first glance, seem to be so different: on the one hand, the disciplined transmission of religious knowledge, of the legal and theological sciences which lie at the core of Islamic identity . . . on the other, a medicinal cure clearly drawn from folk memory, a cure with only the thinnest Islamic veneer, in the form of those inscribed Qurʾanic verses, which barely conceals its pre-Islamic origin."[89]

Much like El-Tom, Berkey finds the logic of Qurʾan erasure (*maḥw*) beyond the pale of Islam in spite of the fact that scholars-qua-healers were its expert practitioners. Indeed, healing was the subject of El-Tom's article "Drinking the Koran." Contrary to El-Tom's reading, however, the use of the Qurʾan for healing purposes spread directly from what he called "orthodox Islamic centres," where they have a long history. In fact, they are described in detail in a number of medieval medical treatises in the well-known Ṭibb al-Nabawī (Medicine of the Prophet) genre. Many medieval scholars recommended physical assimilation of the Word of God (through ingestion and/or bathing) as a central aspect of healing. Ibn al-Qāyyim al-Jawziyya (d. 1350), often claimed as a medieval forefather by contemporary Salafis who often reject such practices, endorsed this practice unequivocally, along with the writing of talismans from verses of the Qurʾan, both of which he traced to the era of the righteous forefathers (*salaf al-ṣāliḥ*). Al-Jawziyya, a student of Ibn Taymiyya, the medieval scholar of reference for Wahhabis, claimed that his teacher engaged in both practices. None of this should be altogether surprising, since there are very well-known hadiths wherein verses of the

Qur'an were used for healing purposes and the practice was endorsed by the Prophet.[90]

But what of the role of bathing and ingesting the Word of God in the actual embodied transmission of knowledge? The more than twenty-five thousand manuscripts cataloged over the past generation by scholars of Islamic West Africa do not include a single copy of any work known to be by al-Qābisī. While arguments from silence can be dangerous, I think it likely that al-Qābisī's text was not taught widely if at all.[91] Even if dozens of copies existed from Darfur to Dakar, I would not suppose that the practice was learned from reading al-Qābisī or from Saḥnūn. The practice was likely passed down over the past thousand years with little or no textual justification, from master to disciple, from one generation to the next via practical example. It is only fortuitous that the trace of the custom was preserved (though heretofore ignored) in the North African texts to show its antiquity and the likelihood that it is the source for later developments farther south rather than the simple invention of syncretistic West Africans, as El-Tom and others have assumed. For scholars, this should also serve as a reminder: most of what people do exists first and foremost (if not exclusively) as embodied practice.

■ The healing and schooling practices outlined here depend on a particular conception of the agency of the Word of God. This understanding is being erased in many parts of the Muslim world by modern interpretations of Islam that understand and teach Qur'an in narrowly literal and discursive ways. But in West Africa, Muslims continue to understand and transmit knowledge in ways that do not shy away from the esoteric implications of believing the Qur'an to be the verbatim speech of the Creator.

The success of the "reformists" in portraying their own interpretations as normative has cast such practices in the shadow of "superstition," where they are further obscured by the blackness of the Africans who maintain them. Africanists, for their part, have done little to remedy the situation with a narrow focus on the "Africanization" of Islam. African Islamic practice certainly has absorbed many cultural and even sometimes cultic elements from the societies wherein it has taken root. In this respect, it differs in no way from Muslim societies outside Africa, but the narrow-minded focus on syncretism has made it impossible to recognize what should be clear and plain: African Muslims sometimes conserve and elaborate modalities of Islamic understanding and practice after they have been largely abandoned elsewhere in the Muslim world. The equation of racial essences with religious purity and orthodoxy can admit no such possibility, and thus we have remained blinded to the simple facts of the pedigree and antiquity of such a deeply Islamic practice as drinking the Qur'an.

Blood and Ink

Attention to this seemingly arcane practice highlights another—still more unfathomable—practice that poses serious problems of orthodoxy for literalist and "reform-minded" Muslims: drinking the cupped blood of a holy person. Cupping is an old practice in a number of humoral systems of health maintenance, believed to restore balance to the body. It was—and still is—used in Arabia, often, though not exclusively as a treatment for specific illnesses. It involves making a small cut, often in the arm, and then draining off a small quantity of blood.

But what to do with the blood? Especially if it is the blood of the Prophet himself? A number of stories of people drinking the cupped blood of holy persons circulate in Muslim societies in Africa and beyond, and they seem to have as their archetype several hadiths about companions of the Prophet drinking his cupped blood after he suffered serious illness.[92] Of course, the Qur'an (2:173) explicitly forbids the consumption of blood of any kind, and the act appears so shocking that some Muslims have simply concluded that the hadiths are apocryphal. However, the hadiths and the continued circulation of analogous stories make perfect sense when seen in the light of the discussion of drinking the Qur'an.

The stories come originally from a number of hadiths, none of which appear in the collections of Bukhārī and Muslim but which are nonetheless attested in many early works of history and biography. A composite version of some relevant hadiths appears on the website of Saudi resident and well-known Salafi hadith specialist Muḥammad Ṣāliḥ al-Munājjid.

> ʿAbdallah b. al-Zubayr came to the Prophet whilst he was being cupped, and when he has finished he said: "O ʿAbdallah, take this blood and pour it away so no one will see it." When he had departed from the Prophet, he went and drank the blood.
>
> He said: "O ʿAbdallah, what have you done?"
>
> He said: "I put it in the most secret place where I thought it would be most hidden from the people."
>
> He said: "Perhaps you drank it."
>
> He said: "Yes."
>
> He said: "Why did you drink the blood? Woe to the people because of you and woe to you because of the people."

In another version of the story, the Prophet's response is rather different: he tells ʿAbdullah b. al-Zubayr, "The fire will never touch you." Another tradition transmits a similar story about one of the Prophet's companions, Safīna:

> The Prophet was treated with cupping, then he said to me: "Take this blood and bury it where animals and birds cannot reach it," or he said: "People and animals." So I took it away and drank it. Then he asked me and I told him that I had drunk it, and he smiled.

A similar story is told about an unnamed slave of the Quraysh, the Prophet's paternal clan:

> The Messenger of God was treated with cupping by a slave belonging to one of the Quraysh. When he had finished the cupping, he took the blood and took it behind a wall, then he looked to his right and his left, and when he did not see anyone, he drank the blood until it was all gone. Then he came back. The Prophet looked at his face and said: "Woe to you, what did you do with the blood?" I said: I hid it behind the wall. He said: "Where did you hide it?" I said: O Messenger of God, your blood is too precious to spill on the ground; it is in my stomach. He said: "Go, for you have saved yourself from the Fire."[93]

HOLY WATERS

In these narrations, the ambiguity in dealing with such a seemingly contradictory practice is obvious. In one version, the Prophet condemns the act. In another his approval is apparent, as he smiles. In the other two, the immediate lesson is uncertain, as the Prophet says, "You have saved yourself from the fire," though it is unclear in at least one narration whether this is because the speaker has rectified a lie. Al-Munājjid's conclusion that all the narrations that seem to approve of the practice are "weak" allows him to dismiss them.

Islamic studies scholar and hadith specialist Denis Gril, conversely, sees these hadiths, which are widely represented in compilations and biographies of the Prophet, as authentic. I am most interested in the narration in which the Prophet says, "The fire will never touch you," because it gives the sense that the sanctifying bodily substance of the Prophet conveys immunity from the fire. This interpretation is supported by another report highlighted by Gril: At the battle of Uḥud, Mālik b. Sinān is reported to have sucked the blood from the Prophet's wounds. He responded by saying, "My blood is mixed with his; the fire will never touch him."[94] This statement recalls the idea that fire could not burn a copy of the Qur'an, whether that copy were on an untreated hide, the bruised limbs of the corporally punished Qur'an student, or the servant who drank the blood of the Walking Qur'an.

A similar story is told in the circles of the Tijānīya about the Sufi order's founder, Aḥmad al-Tijānī (1737–1815). It is claimed that Sīdī ʿAlī al-Tamāsīnī (1766–1844), one of Tijānī's earliest and most illustrious disciples, cupped him and did not know what to do with the blood. As in the other stories, Sīdī ʿAlī refused to pour out the precious liquid where someone might trample on it. When he could not find a place to pour it, he drank it. In this context, the approval is unequivocal. Wolof poet Abbas Saal praises the love and devotion evident in Sīdī ʿAlī's treatment of Shaykh Tijānī's blood.[95]

■ *But what is most striking in all of these stories is that the context is identical to that of the Qur'an school at the moment when one must dispose of the wash water from the slate boards.* The disciple is looking for a place to dispose of a precious liquid brimming with the power of the Word of God. But this liquid cannot be left just anywhere. The solution is also identical: rather than pouring it where it may be trod on, the logical solution is to drink the blood, just as one would drink the Qur'an-infused water from the *alwāḥ*. The unspoken association is that the blood that coursed through the veins of the Prophet or a *walī* (friend of God) such as al-Tijānī was analogous to the dark liquid that carried the power of the Word. The saint literally was the text. While such a statement may chafe the sensibilities of reform-minded Muslims, it has been such a wholly unremarkable idea for many Muslims that it has rarely been consciously expressed as such. Nonetheless, people have long acted on it.

In twenty-first-century Senegal, adepts of the Ṭarīqa Murīdiyya (the Murid Sufi way) recount stories of the passing of Amadu Bamba Mbakke, the order's founder. It is said that there is a large hole in the ground on the very spot where he made his ablutions while under house arrest in Diourbel.[96] For generations, his followers and disciples have returned to this place to take away handfuls of sand in the hope that the dark liquid that rolled off his limbs as he washed might have penetrated the soil, sanctifying it. This is precisely the sort of practice that has earned the Murīdiyya its reputation as the archetypal "syncretistic" African Sufi order since the time of Paul Marty. Yet there is nothing particularly African or even Sufi about this example. An ironic illustration of this is the case of the allegedly anti-Sufi fourteenth-century scholar Ibn Taymiyya, whose lifeless body was subject to precisely the same treatment by the people of medieval Damascus. "Damascenes seeking 'benefit' and baraka drank the water in which Ibn Taymiyya did his ablutions; and after his death some vied to drink the water with which his corpse was washed."[97] More than simply blessing and benefit are being sought. Rather, if the true saint is, like the Prophet himself, the Walking Qur'an, then by ingesting wash water or even blood, disciples are absorbing the Word of God. The dark liquid that rolls off the living limbs, that courses through the pulsing veins, that washes over the lifeless corpse of the Walking Qur'an—all are subject to the same reverential treatment as the text of the Qur'an itself.

Epistemologies, Modern and Classical

The logic of this whole approach—of equating the body and the text, of teaching the text via the body—must seem quite perverse to many modern Muslims. The educational approach in most secular schools and many modern Islamic educational institutions posits a wholly different role for the body. The approach in most modern education rests on a Cartesian divide between the mind and the body. A teacher acts primarily on the intellect, and when religious ideas are understood, the mind of the believer will compel the body to apply them. The mind orders the body, and the body responds. The idea that one could "learn" through osmosis makes no sense in this understanding because it violates central conceptions of what knowing is. The key discipline in this approach is grammar, and the main skill to be acquired is linguistic facility in classical Arabic. Such linguistic facility is understood to produce superior understanding of the manifest meaning of verses of the Qur'an and hadith texts, which, in turn, allows students to absorb—or even synthesize—a system of religious rules based on simple deductive reasoning.

Grammar (*naḥaw*) has, of course, long been an important discipline for advanced students studying the religious sciences in traditional fashion (*majlis*). I encountered a number of students for whom grammar immediately followed Qur'an memorization. But in the new approach to schooling, mnemonic possession of the Qur'an is not a prerequisite for studying Arabic grammar. Instead, the usual technique in many such schools—in West Africa as well as in Arabic-speaking countries—is to teach classical Arabic using the techniques of modern foreign-language instruction before or concurrent with memorization. As many scholars have noted, memorization—taking possession of a text within oneself—usually plays a greatly diminished role in this new kind of schooling and is indeed considered anti-intellectual. Arabic language acquisition and communicating the meanings of verses take clear precedence over memorization, which often proceeds very slowly.

There are many stories of students who, once exposed to a modern educational ethic, no longer considered the mechanics of the classical model as "knowledge" at all. An excellent example is found in the work of Brinkley Messick on Islamic schooling in Yemen. Messick juxtaposes two distinct styles of reading in the person of Muhammad Aziz, whose education in the 1980s and 1990s is re-created in some detail. Muhammad is presented as a young scholar whose hybridized education—a mix of a small amount of Qur'an schooling, much modern state education, and personal isolated reading of Islamic texts—helps to illustrate a shift in recent approaches to reading in Yemen. Striking in Aziz's story was the moment when he decided to abandon the formal study of the Islamic religious sciences in the classical way. He was unable to continue when he was asked, as a prerequisite of study, to memorize a short (one-thousand-line) primer of Shāfiʿī *fiqh*, "a standard opening procedure in the old system. It was a step preparatory to regular lesson circle instruction in which the text would be recited or dictated by the teacher together with his commentaries, and, if necessary, further explanations. Although the text in question is very short, twenty pages in one lithograph edition, and is in the mnemonically accessible form of a poem, Muhammad 'did not see the point' of memorizing it and, although he tried, was unable to do so."[98] Though Aziz was deeply interested in learning from venerable shaykhs and strongly attracted to the classical style of education, he was nonetheless unable to engage in it. Knowledge as a discursive object rooted in understanding and analysis, not memorization, was hardwired into him. Despite his desire, he could not internalize a text in this way.

KNOWLEDGE, KEPT AND CARRIED

The epistemic chasm separating the classical from the modern system is illustrated by the story of how "Joorngal Calaaga" Kebbe, an eighteenth-century Senegambian scholar, came by his unique nickname: "Joorngal was very proud of himself because he had learned the Qur'an by heart; moreover, as soon as he heard of someone who had learned the Qur'an, he went to see him and wrote from memory a *hizb* of the Qur'an every day right in front of him until he finished the whole Qur'an, without the other ever having to correct him, so correct was his memorization. He named himself Joorngal Calaaga, which means 'the dry board of Calaaga,' for no one had ever dampened his tablet to correct it. He carried it dry to the corrector, who returned it to him the same way."[99]

For Joorngal Calaaga Kebbe, the highest honor possible was in "knowing" the Qur'an faultlessly. Even today in Senegambia, many classically trained scholars will commit to memory dozens of works of law, Sufism, and poetry, making the knowledge their own, a part of their being. A famous story is told of Abū Ḥāmid b. Muḥammad al-Ghazālī (1058–1111), the author of *Iḥyā' ʿulūm al-Dīn* (The Revitalization of the Religious Sciences), one of the most celebrated works of scholarship in the Islamic tradition and a widely esteemed work in Senegambia. Ghazālī, according to his biographers, was once robbed by highwaymen. He showed no interest in the loss of his worldly possessions except for his books and notes. He is supposed to have pleaded with the robbers: surely they would have no use for his manuscripts and notes; why not leave them? He would be lost without them. One of the thieves then reproached the master—What kind of *ʿālim* could be robbed of his knowledge if deprived of his books? From that point on, Ghazālī memorized all of his own writings—including his notes—just as he memorized the works of the scholars who came before him.[100]

Perhaps the most striking vindication of the wisdom of this method lies in the whole and partial copies of the Qur'an found throughout the historical record of slavery in the Americas. West African Muslims who underwent this process of embodied knowledge transmission became the books they studied. They were Walking Qur'an. The manuscript copies of the Qur'an and fragmentary legal texts they produced under the most difficult circumstances imaginable bear witness across the centuries. Knowledge possessed within the self in this way was tenacious. One could be stripped naked, beaten, and starved in the hold of a slave ship, shipped thousands of miles from home, and put to a lifetime of labor in unfamiliar surroundings without surrendering one's knowledge.[101]

God's Vice-Regents: The Dynamic Islam of the Children of Adam

Many Muslim modernists have shared the perception that "traditional" Islam, with its conception of knowledge and its transmission along with its modes of interpretation, were stagnant and unchanging. In other words, these Muslim intellectuals shared in the colonial discourse of modernity. Yet the "traditionalist" mode of knowledge production was never as stagnant and backward-looking as they imagined. The "traditional" understanding was built on perfecting the children of Adam, molding their characters into that of the Qur'an so that they might understand their proper relationship of service to God and fulfill their Qur'anically prescribed role as His vice-regent (*khalīfa*) on Earth (Q 2:30). Doing so entailed not only the preservation of texts but also, and more important, their internalization—first practically and spiritually, then discursively so that religion could be performed or enacted in any conceivable real-world context by expert practitioners. This is what many former students said in diverse ways when I routinely asked what the *daara* does for a person: "First of all, the *daara makes you into a person*, a true human being. What is a true human being? Wherever you may find yourself, you can handle it and carry yourself properly. You won't say things you shouldn't say; you won't do things you shouldn't do. It awakens you to the world. It lets you know who your Lord is. . . . What the *daara* does for the character of a human being is something only the *daara* can do."[102] The goal was not the unchanging transmission of an identical mode of comportment and practice. *The goal was—and in some cases remains—the creation of authentic human beings who carry with them the irreplaceable core of scriptural knowledge illuminated by human example in an unbroken chain returning to the Prophet, then via the bridge of revelation to Jibrīl, and finally to the Almighty Himself.*

That core of practical and discursive knowledge, which implies a disposition toward the world, allows for the creation of what linguists might call the articulate native speaker: the interlocutor who has mastered the rules of grammar and syntax and can produce new speech acts suited to any foreseen or unforeseen context without necessarily needing conscious reflection. Traditional Islam never made change impossible or even undesirable, but it did seek to keep it from the unqualified. This mode of knowledge transmission facilitated and nurtured change while assuring that its agents embodied core teachings in their persons. Michael Chamberlain's characterization of the medieval scholarly community in Damascus beautifully captures this idea: "What is striking about the greatest shaykhs is the frequency with which writers praised their inventiveness and individual virtuosity. . . . Shaykhs did not duplicate an unchanging body of cultural forms. Rather they struggled to acquire a sense of deportment that allowed them to manipulate these apparently fixed cultural forms gracefully and naturally, much as athletes or musicians repeat single movements in ever-changing situations. Also like athletes and musicians, they lauded unexpected virtuosity in the use of an apparently invariable 'tradition.'"[103] *Mastery has always been the precondition for improvisation.*

IT IS ONLY INK ON PAPER!

No textual source can detail correct practice—much less correct belief or correct intention—in all of the unforeseen circumstances a human being may encounter. This is one of the most pernicious fictions of the modernist Islamic ethic: that texts are transparent and that grasping their manifest meaning makes their prescriptions clear.[104] Reformers purport to make texts easily accessible to all Muslims, as though one can simply open the Qurʾan, hadith texts, or the constitution of Medina; make an effort of mind; and have immediate and unambiguous prescriptions for an Islamic life.

The Islamic scholarly tradition distrusted books and reason exercised in isolation. The Qurʾan itself is best understood as a transmitted line of recitation and interpretation rather than a book as such. ʿAlī b. Abū Ṭālib, the Prophet's young cousin and one of Islam's most important early intellectuals, is supposed to have made this point explicitly. In a heated argument with Islam's earliest literalist extremists, the Kharijites, he turns to a written copy of the Qurʾan (*muṣḥaf*) and says, "O *muṣḥaf* inform the people!" In the story, even the Khawārij can only reply with the truth: "It is only ink on paper, we argue on the basis of what we have transmitted from it!"[105]

Medieval seekers of knowledge were warned, "One of the greatest calamities is taking texts as shaykhs."[106] The classical model trusted authoritative individuals. *Samʿa*—hearing, whether hadith or an oral lesson from an authoritative teacher—was understood as infinitely superior to reading from books.[107] Reading texts in isolation encouraged idiosyncratic interpretations and omitted a great deal of contextual information. It transmitted an impoverished, decontextualized, "disembodied" knowledge. In the Internet age, when Islamic knowledge is increasingly words on a screen instead of ink on paper, textual sensibilities may favor isolated reading more than ever before. Many Muslims now acquire basic elements of religious knowledge without any direct human interaction at all. Embodied transmission of Islamic knowledge is being eclipsed by disembodied consumption.

With an epistemology of embodiment in sight, early teaching texts such as Mālik's *Muwaṭṭaʾ* and Saḥnūn's *Mudawwana* can be better understood. They are *not*, properly speaking, books. They are best understood as mnemonic devices meant to unlock a set of oral teachings. The authoritative transmission of this broader teaching was guaranteed by the chains of authority (*isnād*) mentioned earlier. Metaphorically, the text was only the seed of an oral teaching. Knowledge bloomed as a consequence of the gestures, facial expressions, and moral state of a teacher. The student was the fertile soil in which the seed would be planted, but the teacher and all of the subtleties of the personal transmission of the knowledge were the sun and the rain. A flower of knowledge simply could not bloom without a master. These flowers are what the classical tradition sought to cultivate. From within this older paradigm, the modern approach—with texts read in isolation and "disembodied" Internet fatwas—must seem to simply pass along lifeless seeds.

CHARACTER AND PRACTICAL MASTERY

Isolated reading was thought particularly dangerous when practiced by those who had not undergone thorough character training (*adab* and *tarbiya*) through study of the Qur'an and service to accomplished masters. Omitting character training risked inscribing whatever might be buried in particular individuals' hearts—spiritual illnesses, personal interests, or political projects—onto their understanding of Islam itself. One of the striking facts of the modern ethic of knowledge transmission in Islam is that it has frequently been dominated by intellectuals who underwent no training with shaykhs. Sayyid Qutb, one of the founding fathers of Islamism, is an excellent example. His masterwork, *In the Shade of the Qur'an*, is often sold alongside classical *tafsīr* (exegesis) in Islamic bookstores around the world, but Qutb was trained as an academic literary critic, not an exegete.[108] In the words of Arabic literary scholar Issa Boullata, "Sayyid Qutb's Qur'anic commentary is not similar to works of exegesis known as *tafsir*. . . . It is rather a free expression of his feelings and thoughts as he religiously reads the Holy Book he loves."[109] The work contains almost no reference to classical *tafsīr*. Qutb was part of the first generation of Egyptians to study in state schools and modernized Islamic educational institutions. He attended an Egyptian Qur'an school (*kuttāb*) for only a single day and was shocked by what he saw, especially the practice of licking the slate boards clean.[110]

If the classical tradition does not seek to produce carbon copies of previous scholars, it does still insist on a kind of practical mastery in scholarship. Broadly speaking, the rational, text-based transmission of Islam of the twentieth century has not been similarly insistent. If mastery is the prerequisite for improvisation, then practical application of learning is certainly the road to mastery. Piano virtuosos do not learn to play from manuals. They learn to play from master teachers and then from applied, embodied practice. No book could explain what their hands can do. Humans' subtle abilities to teach through gestures, facial expressions, emotional states, bodily movements, and inflections of voice are all lost to an epistemology that conceives of reason and texts as the ultimate guides.

REASON, DISCOURSE, AND DEBATE

The classical tradition seeks to produce human beings who embody within their persons certain core ideas and ideals and consequently are capable of improvisation. In spite of stereotypes, reason, discourse, and debate were always encouraged—after certain essentials were mastered. In fact, memorization and internalization of texts worked hand in hand with reason to stimulate scholarship and debate. In early-nineteenth-century Senegambia, Gaspard Mollien witnessed what he called a "literary conference" of marabouts held at the home of an *ʿālim* named ʿAbdullahi and attended by Diai Boukari (Bukaari Njaay), Mollien's own guide and interpreter:

> One of these marabouts was reading aloud; some young men attentively followed him in their books; and Abdoulai, who was blind, explained the difficult passages. The discussion afterwards turned to the obscure meanings of different passages of the book, which was the history of Mahomet. One of the young men took the book and read aloud; the others, under the direction of a Marabout, corrected the faults which had crept into the copies of the same work which they held in their hands. The most profound silence prevailed among these young men, who appeared to be really studious. Boukari, my Marabout, had an opportunity of displaying the depth of his knowledge of the Arabic language, for they addressed divers questions to him, which he answered in a manner that surprised all his hearers. The class was held in Abdoulai's cottage, which was completely that of a scholar; a bed made of a mat, a leather bag filled with books, a pitcher of water, and two or three vessels for ablution, composed the whole of the furniture.[111]

The passage captures the physical setting and tenor of a meeting of the minds in the 1810s in Senegambia. ʿAbdullahi, the sightless scholar, highlights the centrality of *hearing* in classical approaches to knowledge. Many traditionally trained scholars, it is worth noting, were blind. This story also highlights the important place that argumentation and discursive intellectual exchange held for scholars.

The notion that scholars trained in this tradition only repeat what came before them is simple caricature; the dynamism and ingenuity inherent in their approach was quite explicit. First, as some scholars have noted for medieval Europe, this kind of mnemonic possession of texts leads to a continuous engagement with their contents.[112] Writes Renaud Santerre of the Fulɓe scholars (*moodibaaɓe*) of northern Cameroon in the 1960s, "Unlike ours, the *moodibbes'* library, their memory, is always in use: No separation exists between the library and its user. Always open, always operating, it remains continuously at the latter's disposal."[113] This kind of engagement with texts leads to constant (even subconscious) juxtaposition and rearticulation of constituent pieces of mnemonically possessed knowledge. Instead of producing dull minds, this kind of possession of texts stimulates scholarship. Mokhtar Kebe made this point explicit at a conference on Islamic educa-

"Diai Boukari," or Bukaari Njaay, from a sketch by Mollien that was published in French and English editions of his traveler's account in the 1810s. Courtesy of Melville J. Herskovits Library of African Studies, Northwestern University.

tion in Senegambia in 2007. In response to the suggestion that the model of Qur'an schooling and classical study might be out of date, he replied that he chooses to use this model because it produced the prolific scholars of previous eras, among them Imam Ghazālī, Ibrāhīm Niass, and Amadu Bamba.[114]

The Tablet of History

Senegambian scholars, like Muslim intellectuals elsewhere, proclaimed—and produced—original insight, but it stood side-by-side in productive tension with reverence for early authorities and was validated by their chains of transmission. A quotation from the scholarly corpus of Amadu Bamba Mbakke captures this dynamic nicely. It is from *Masālik al-Jinān* (The Itineraries of Paradise), a poetic engagement with the legacy of Ghazālī and a number of other classical works. It includes many lengthy passages that subtly or overtly argue against the interpretations of previous authorities even as it valorizes those authorities:

> Do not turn away from [this book] due to my lack of renown in this era.
> Nor turn down its benefits merely because I am from among the blacks.
> The most honored servant with God is, without a doubt, the one most abundant in piety
> For blackness of body signals neither weakness of mind nor lack of understanding.
> O wise one, do not abandon my verses, thinking I do not practice what I preach.
> Do not give away God's favors by preferring only the ancients; this breeds ignorance.
> For it happens that a man of a recent era knows secrets unknown to the ancients.
> "A shower may precede a deluge, but the advantage is with the deluge, not the shower."
> You who doubt my verses, don't forget the hadith: "My community is like the rain."[115]

Bamba does not finish the line because doing so would break the poem's rhyme, but he also expects his readers to know that it ends with "Who is to say which part is better, the first or the last." Murid interlocutors often explain these verses by saying that Bamba meant that the drops of God's rain that fell in Arabia were only the drizzle (*wiis-wiis*) to announce the downpour of Islam that was coming to Africa. Among blacks has come a true flood of Islam.

Using a range of contemporary and ancient sources, this chapter has established an outline of classical Islamic education and its contemporary manifestations in West Africa. Education centered on the three Rs—reading, writing, and recitation. But it was also accomplished through the three Arabic Hs (*ḥubb*, *khidma*, and *hadiyya*—love, service, and gifts) and the three Wolof Ys (*yalwaan*, *yar*, and *yor*-alms seeking, bodily discipline, and internal possession). All of this attention to the body sought to produce not unthinking replication of texts or even practices but rather people who embodied core texts and practices and thus could perform Islam in novel contexts. Once this goal is acknowledged, the rationale for the historical exploration of an epistemology of Islam is apparent. The best place to study knowledge transmission in Islam is not in texts but rather in the place where knowledge had truly to be written—by the children of Adam on the tablet of history. The remainder of this book will thus proceed chronologically, moving from the deep past, ca. 1000, to the present. Against the backdrop of this epistemology of embodying the Qur'an and core Islamic texts and a tradition that requires *transmitting* them through direct contact, we will see that perhaps Islam is best characterized not only as "discursive tradition," as anthropologist Talal Asad has suggested, but also as a dense web of fully embodied encounters.[116]

2 EMBODYING ISLAM IN WEST AFRICA

THE MAKING OF A CLERISY, CA. 1000–1770

The ink of the scholar is more sacred than the blood of the martyr.
—Saying attributed to the Prophet Muḥammad

The Ink of Scholars

At the end of the eighteenth century, near the end of the period examined in this chapter, Mungo Park, a Scotsman, was traveling through Senegambia. Most Europeans who came to know West Africa well during this period were slavers, but Park was not. He was indeed there in service of commerce, however, working in conjunction with British groups interested in discovering the sources of the Niger River and the city of Timbuktu, famed in Europe as a city of learning—and especially wealth in gold—since the late fourteenth century. Traversing the predominantly Muslim regions of Senegambia and heading inland into parts of West Africa that were still religiously mixed, he spent two years (1795–97) in the region. In 1799, he published an account of his West African odyssey, *Travels in the Interior of Africa*, which commends its author as an astute observer, fine writer, and reflective thinker. In it, Park noted the preference for teaching over militancy in deepening and spreading the faith among West Africans:

> Religious persecution is not known among them, nor is it necessary; for the system of Mahomet is made to extend itself by means abundantly more efficacious. By establishing small schools in the different towns, where many of the Pagan as well as Mahomedan children are taught to read the Koran, and instructed in the tenets of the Prophet, the Mahomedan priests fix a bias on the minds, and form the character of their young disciples, which no accidents of life can ever afterwards remove or alter. Many of these little schools I visited in my progress through the country, and observed with pleasure the great docility and submissive deportment of the children, and heartily wished they had had better instructors, and

a purer religion. With the Mahomedan faith is also introduced the Arabic language.[1]

In spite of his evident biases of race and religion, Park was obviously a practiced observer whose account captures a number of key elements of Qurʾan schooling in a pithy way. He shows the centrality of instilling submissive postures of obedience and connects them to instruction in Arabic literacy and the formation of durable character traits and habits of mind.

Park's claim that religious persecution was unknown suggests that in the places he had traveled, Muslim scholars took seriously the Qurʾan's command to preserve freedom of conscience—*There is no compulsion in the religion* (Q 2:256). But a historical narrative is also embedded in Park's account. He clearly suspects that by visiting these humble schools, he is bearing witness to the process through which the religion had spread throughout West Africa.

CLERICS AND CLERISIES

Park's instincts were correct. Islam reached most West African communities not via jihad but via African Muslim intellectuals. The conquests of the first Islamic century did not reach sub-Saharan Africa, so whether or not the Prophet actually said that the "scholar's ink is more sacred than the martyr's blood" (some say those words instead came from early mystic and scholar Ḥasan al-Baṣrī, d. 728), ink was clearly far more important than blood to the spread of Islam in sub-Saharan Africa. Armed with reed pens, wooden slate boards, and the Book they carried within their bodies, *clerics* brought Islam to sub-Saharan West Africa.

It is often said that Islam has no clergy, and it is true that in Sunni Islam there is no officially sanctioned body of religious specialists. But Islam has had many clerics and many clerisies. The *Oxford English Dictionary* defines cleric as "a priest or religious leader . . . especially a Christian or Muslim one" and clerisy as "a distinct class of learned or literary people." Throughout this volume, I often use these terms to refer to Muslim religious specialists in West Africa. In most academic works on Islamic scholarship, *ʿālim* (scholar, person of knowledge) and *ʿulamāʾ*, its plural, are used in this way. Both terms now carry a strong connotation of textual scholarship that does not fully capture the social roles of learned people in earlier eras in West Africa or beyond.

Furthermore, in West Africa, *ʿulamāʾ* was not necessarily the preferred term for religious leaders in the centuries under study in this chapter. First, an Arabic term widely used in North Africa (and the Sahara) for a holy person, *mrābiṭ* and its Europeanized equivalent, "marabout," were prevalent. Second, local languages developed varied terminologies (*sëriñ*, *ceerno*, *moodibo*, *karamoko*, and others), all of which mean "teacher" but also connote spiritual power.[2] Finally, at least one of these terms, the Wolof term *sëriñ* (*bi-sëriñ* in its archaic form), is likely derived from an Arabic term, *bashirīn*, that seems to have been more commonly used than *ʿulamāʾ*. Park, like most European visitors to West Africa from the 1450s until the nineteenth century, referred to the clerics of the region—whatever their ethnic or national origins—as *bushreens* or, following Portuguese orthography, *bixirins*.

This term strongly links teachers with the spread of Islam; its primary meaning is "evangelist." In modern Arabic, this word refers mainly to Christian proselytizers, but historically (in West Africa at least), it was firmly tied to Muslim teaching and missionary activity. This seems entirely fitting, since its singular form, *al-bashīr*, is one of the praise names for the Prophet Muḥammad, the embodied archetype of all Islamic teaching and preaching.

The original Walking Qurʾan—the role model for the clerisy—was not only the exemplar of teaching and preaching but also the embodiment of spiritual leadership, supernatural power, and even healing ability. All of these facets of religious authority came to be embodied within the clerical lineages of West Africa, and all were tied to the Qurʾan. Nearly all clerics taught the Book for all or part of their lives. Some also taught *exoteric* worldly sciences such as mathematics, astronomy, or, more rarely, history or medicine. But nearly all also employed *esoteric* sciences, drawing on their literacy and their spiritual power as carriers of God's verbatim speech.

Whether through writing talismans (*ṭilāsim*) drawn from the Qurʾan, engaging in Islamic divination (*khaṭṭ al-raml*) or Qurʾanic numerology, or leading the prayer for rain (*ṣalāt al-istisqāʾ*), as the Prophet himself did, *they acted on the unseen world to produce results in the seen world.* They healed bodies with the wash water from the slate boards along with herbal and humoral remedies.[3] They healed the land by bringing rain.[4] And they healed communities by fighting sorcery.[5] This social sickness was approached both through social and spiritual interventions. The former included arbitration of disputes, counseling within and between families, and, when acting as judges, by making people swear oaths on the Qurʾan to abandon harmful magic.[6] Spiritual means included not only intercessory prayer but especially writing of protective, proactive, and therapeutic talismans as well as water-soluble Qurʾanic "solutions" for bathing or ingestion.[7]

Finally, a clerisy is a *distinct class* of learned people. While it incorporated people from many different social origins, the clerisy was seen as a class apart. Its members were known for a more rigorous practice of Islam and more advanced levels of literacy and scholarship than was possessed by their nonclerical neighbors, even those who were also believing Muslims. This clerisy was composed of clerical lineages, extended families that specialized in teaching the Qur'an. These West African clerical lineages have been astonishingly durable and distinctive social constructs, recognizable for a thousand years by their family names (Cissé, Turé, Dramé, Ba, Lo, Diakhité, and others) and professional activities.

■ In this chapter, I explore the construction of this indigenous clerisy from roughly 1000 to the last quarter of the eighteenth century. These clerics spread Islam using not swords but rather humble wooden boards. Through the power of the Qur'an inhering in prayers, talismans, and their own embodied persons, they made the faith a fundamental element of West African life. For the earliest period (from roughly 1000 to 1500), I use a wide angle of vision and consider material from a broader West Africa to develop a regional metanarrative on the social positioning of Islamic knowledge over the longue durée. Here I draw on a range of sources, including Arabic-language histories, geographies, and travel accounts. Some of these sources are available in excellent European-language translations, but whenever possible, I consulted Arabic originals and modified translations for clarity, so I take responsibility for the translations here unless otherwise noted.

As the chapter moves closer to the present in the sixteenth through eighteenth centuries, the focus narrows to Senegambia, and I treat the social history of clerical communities in greater detail. Here, I employ a number of European-language travelers' accounts where they shed light on dynamics of Islamic knowledge. I also employ archival documents (French and British) from seventeenth- and eighteenth-century Senegambian trading colonies—Saint-Louis and Gorée in Senegal and James Fort in Gambia. These colonial settlements sat at the mouths of rivers or on islands and were centers for shipping Africans (Muslim and otherwise) away to be slaves in the New World.

THE EMERGENT ATLANTIC CONTEXT

The Euro-American trade in African slaves, commonly (and euphemistically) called the Atlantic slave trade in spite of its Indian Ocean components, was the largest forced migration in human history. It carried roughly 15 million Africans away from the continent in European and American vessels from the 1440s to the 1880s and delivered those sturdy enough to survive the Middle Passage mainly to Atlantic ports of call. Senegambia was first visited by Portuguese slavers in the 1440s, and over four hundred years the trade produced profound social effects within the region's Muslim societies. Over time, it came to severely strain the pacifistic sensibilities of clerics and their general position of remaining aloof from politics. From the early seventeenth century forward, some became militant critics of the amoral comportment of kings who called themselves Muslims but sold other Muslims for European rum, guns, and consumer goods—all blatant violations of Islamic law.

Even the Euro-American slavers themselves contrasted the arbitrary violence and conspicuous consumption of slaving kings with the temperance and measured justice of clerics. According to a French slaver's account from the late seventeenth century, "If negro kings were as equitable in their wars as their *maraboux* are in Justice, one would not see their subjects not only groaning under the weight of their irons, but also sold and delivered to foreign merchants as slaves."[8] Ordinary Muslim peasants as well as many non-Muslims began to flock to the relative safety of clerical communities, where justice was less capricious and where kings were loath to meddle in the internal affairs of the clerisy.

Long before the rise of the Atlantic trade, clerical communities had been understood as inviolable spaces. The bodily sanctity of holy men (and sometimes women) and long-established regional traditions of clerical political neutrality made them off-limits to worldly authorities. Kings were not supposed to pursue even criminals onto the holy ground of a clerical compound, the asylum of which was theoretically absolute. As the Atlantic political economy expanded to enslave Muslims in great numbers, it produced a moral and political backlash. These clerical communities first became safe havens, then sites for exploring alternative models of polity, and finally staging grounds for revolution.

The dynamic explored here culminated near the end of the seventeenth century, when a multiethnic coalition of clerics abandoned regional traditions of pacifism and chose to fight against slaving kings. All of these stages of social engagement by the clerics illustrate the intellectual and social dynamism of the classical model of Islamic knowledge. These scholars did more than just reflexively copy or blindly imitate. They struggled to find in Islamic thought and practice appropriate models for engaging the world around them. For most of this period, that struggle meant developing a tolerant, peaceful approach to proselytizing, and for this they carefully drew on the most liberal of Mālikī legal and ethical models. But by the end of the seventeenth century, the Atlantic slave trade and burgeoning *bayḍān* racism were creating a world where Muslims could be indiscriminately enslaved if they happened to be black. Under these circumstances, some broke with the past and contemplated taking radical action.

Blood and Ink Revisited: Clerical Lineages

To understand why clerical communities in Senegambia became loci for early resistance to Atlantic slaving requires a basic understanding of the central role and particular forms of clerical authority in a broader West Africa. Clerical communities centered on the teaching of the Qur'an, agriculture, and sometimes trade are very old institutions in this part of the world, going back for at least a millennium. Here, the Islamic epistemology of embodiment outlined in chapter 1 intersected in uniquely powerful ways with regional traditions of endogamous occupational groups that predated Islam. Under these special circumstances, Islamic knowledge came to be seen as inhering in the very bodies of religious specialists.

Occupational specialization is one of the oldest forms of social organization in West Africa, predating the rise of the great medieval empires and forming a basic component of many of the societies of West Africa and the southern Sahara.[9] Endogamy, social segregation, and hierarchy were often so rigorously observed within these occupational groups that colonial ethnographers usually characterized this as a "caste" system. Birth into a particular category fixed one's formal social status regardless of one's actual professional activities. The difference between "casted" people (griots, blacksmiths, leatherworkers, and so on) and wellborn or noble groups was understood to be an embodied distinction.[10] By the medieval period, earlier less stratified, more egalitarian forms of occupational specialization had given way, and the "castes" were clearly hierarchically ranked. Islam seems to have played some significant role in this process of marginalizing endogamous occupational specialists, especially smiths and griots, the two original endogamous guilds. Hereafter, the bodily composition of "casted" people would be considered different from—and less pure than—the substance from which the free were cast. This taint of low birth was understood to be passed through the blood and other bodily fluids.

Specialists in Islamic knowledge both fit within this regional social logic and redefined it, infusing it with their own dynamics.[11] For our purposes here, it is useful to highlight the fact that birth into the clerical category functioned in ways similar to the "caste" system of the broader society. Within such families, an almost bodily discourse of predisposition to Islamic learning was not uncommon.[12] But the bonds of master-disciple relationships and the shared value of travel in pursuit of higher learning gave the clerical lineages an elasticity and regional scope that other categories generally lacked.[13]

These were extended family networks with unique spatial and social range. Clerical family histories and individual biographical and hagiographical accounts are replete with stories of travel in pursuit of knowledge, months or years spent studying with a specific teacher and building affective ties that outlasted the individuals concerned and evolved into familial connections. Often enough, the sojourn of a disciple would end with his master arranging to grant him a wife from among the community members.[14] If a master was particularly pleased with the piety, knowledge, and comportment of the disciple, he might give the hand of one of his own daughters. Such marriages could sometimes cross the lines of social origins. A slave who mastered the Qur'an and was then freed before pursuing the study of the religious sciences could marry into the clerisy. The clerical class was not immune to the hierarchies of the broader society and in many ways reproduced them, but the dynamics of educational distinction meant that even though it was relatively rare, casted people, slaves, and the descendants of slaves could become honored clerics through pursuit of knowledge.[15]

TIES THAT BIND—PART I

If status in West Africa was understood to be determined by birth and transmitted by blood, *then here again, the clerisy enacted an unspoken analogy between the blood of the cleric and the ink of the slate board.* In these lineages, the wash water from the slate board could be thicker than blood. More often, however, blood and ink ran together. Disciples became kin. Bonds of love, knowledge, and mutual obligation tied scholars together across space and time. One Wolof word for going away for study, *laxas*, literally means to be "tied" to the master scholar. In polygynous societies where pursuing higher learning meant traveling to study a specific text or discipline with a shaykh, no matter how distant, links of parentage and discipleship became *intertwined* across the entire region.

These ties frequently crossed the bounds of language, nation, and whatever incipient notions of "race" were developing in Senegambia and the southern Sahara from the fifteenth century through the nineteenth. Fula speakers studied with masters in Wolof country; Soninke and Mandingo clerics circulated widely and operated many of the oldest and most established schools. Even Arabo-Berber *bayḍān* crossed "racial" lines to honor ties of blood and ink. *Sūdānī* (black) teachers often formed important links in *bayḍān* chains of knowledge transmission, and the two groups frequently intermarried. Over time, however, *bayḍān* became increasingly unlikely to give their own women in marriage to the families of their black teachers or disciples.[16]

The interethnic, international, and interracial ties of blood and ink were a key element in the constitution of clerical communities. Living exemplars of the Qurʾan traversed West Africa, benefiting from the traditional inviolability and safe passage afforded scholars and crisscrossing the subcontinent to build webs of affection, kinship, and scholarship. Even at the height of the Atlantic slave trade, one late-eighteenth-century European observer noted, "in spite of war, marabouts often pass from one country to another without fear of being made slaves."[17]

The mobility of these Walking Qurʾan made Islam a familiar feature of West African life. Itinerant scholars, teachers, and preachers were known even in non-Muslim or religiously mixed areas. Clerical families tended to produce far more religious scholars than one particular area could possibly require, and the mark of the social maturity of a scholar was opening his own school. Large clerical families produced dozens of *huffāẓ*, many of whom would then go out to remote villages and open Qurʾan schools. The natural and social reproduction of these clerical lineages scattered scholars throughout the region, and by the eighteenth century, few villages lacked a Qurʾan school teacher.

These teachers not only taught Islam with words but used the Word to heal and to protect. They lived as bodily exemplars of Islam. They used wash water from *alwāḥ*, talismans, and prayers to heal and protect individuals and communities. Slowly but surely, they became key symbols of Islamic identity. Because the Qurʾan school, which often received both Muslim and non-Muslim children, was the key institution for spreading Islam, the dynamics of master-disciple relationships infused the societal understanding of Islam. The clerical class as a whole was generally accorded the veneration accorded to an individual's own Qurʾan teacher. The *ḥubb*, *khidma*, and *hadiyya* (love, service, and gifts) earned by one's own Qurʾan teacher were lavished on the clerical class as a whole. In societies where occupational specialization and complementarity were deeply rooted values, the notion that clerics were embodied physical examples of Islam was particularly powerful.

Making a Clerisy in the Age of Empire

The origins of a discernible West African clerisy go back to the heyday of the great West African empires of Ghana (ca. 600–1200), Mali (ca. 1220–1450), and Songhay (1464–1591). These were among the largest, wealthiest, and most powerful states anywhere in the world from the eighth through the sixteenth centuries. At their height, they spanned two thousand miles or more from east to west and five hundred miles or more from north to south. The emperor of Ghana, an eleventh-century source claimed, could put two hundred thousand men on the field of battle, forty thousand of them archers. While such a claim may not be literally accurate, the impression of overwhelming military strength certainly was.[18] Attempts to describe the wealth of such kingdoms were even more breathless. Contemporary Arabic sources from the fourteenth century claim that Mansa Mūsā of Mali brought so much gold on his pilgrimage in 1324–25 that when he passed through Cairo on his way to the Ḥijāz (the portion of Arabia containing the sacred cities of Mecca and Medina), he devalued the gold currency in the largest and wealthiest city in the so-called heartlands of Islam for more than a decade. A 1352–53 account from the premodern world's most famous traveler, Muḥammad Ibn Baṭṭūṭa, confirms that there is no overstating the security, wealth, and highly organized administration of Mali at its height. The key to all of this wealth and power was a monopoly on the lucrative West African gold trade, which supplied much of the Western Muslim world and Europe.

GHANA

The first empire, Ghana, predated the arrival of Islam in the region by several centuries. Indigenous West Africans (the ancestors of today's Soninke speakers) founded the centralized kingdom, which seems to have become an empire sometime before 600 by subsuming other peoples and states. Ghana was built on an already advanced trading civilization that moved goods over great distances within West Africa and had precocious urbanized mercantile centers such as Jenné, which appears to have had a population of at least forty thousand (and maybe significantly larger) as early as the eighth century.[19]

The gold trade became much more important in the eighth century, when camels had come into regular use for crossing the Sahara, and the Islamic conquests of North Africa were integrating the region into Muslim mercantile networks that stretched across the known world. Ghana's rulers accommodated foreign Muslim merchants from the ninth century forward, though the rulers themselves did not convert to Islam until the end of the eleventh. During the intervening centuries, Islam took on an increasing role in the empire.

Ghana was already a *very* old polity when it was first described in detail in Arabic sources in the eleventh century.[20] Cordoban geographer Abū ʿUbayd al-Bakrī (d. 1094) compiled information from merchants and travelers and wrote of the land of gold, describing a large, wealthy, and powerful empire. In 1068 he noted that "Emperor Manīn led a praiseworthy life on account of his love of justice and friendship for the Muslims." Al-Bakrī also described the role of Islam in the empire: "The city of Ghāna consists of two towns situated on a plain. One of these towns, which is inhabited by Muslims, is large and possesses twelve mosques, in one of which they assemble for the Friday prayer. There are salaried imams and muezzins, as well as jurists and scholars. . . . The king's town is six miles distant from this one. . . . Between these two towns there are continuous habitations. . . . In the king's town, and not far from his court of justice, is a mosque where the Muslims who arrive at his court pray. . . . The king's interpreters, the official in charge of his treasury and the majority of his ministers are Muslims."[21]

This pattern of spatial segregation was an expression of the oldest known sort of social organization of space in West Africa's complex societies, wherein lineages specializing in certain occupations were grouped into relatively autonomous—though interrelated—wards. This form of sociospatial organization had roots at least as far back as the beginning of the Common Era.[22] As the Sahelian imperial states converted to Islam over the course of centuries—a process led by scholars—the physical segregation of Muslims and non-Muslims often became the spatial segregation of religious specialists, a pattern that persists in many parts of West Africa.[23]

Though it is not explicit, al-Bakrī's account strongly suggests that many of the Muslims in Ghana in the eleventh century were indigenous West Africans. First, there are the large numbers of mosques, and the presence of a mosque even at the non-Muslim king's compound. Second, he does not specify whether the many literate Muslim scholars in Ghana were of local or foreign origin, calling them only "the Muslims," but in other parts of the text he readily identifies people as either Arab or *sūdān*. Moreover, al-Bakrī juxtaposes the Muslims not with the people of Ghana but rather with the followers of the king's religion, indicating that there were people of Ghana among the Muslims. Al-Idrīsī, writing before 1154, identifies the kings and people of Ghana as Muslim; al-Sharīshī, writing before 1222, is clearer, noting that the empire of Ghana contained numerous centers of religious scholarship and thus conveying the strong impression that a local tradition of scholarship was well established in Ghana by the late eleventh century if not earlier.[24]

MALI

Ibn Baṭṭūṭa (1304–77), the famous North African world traveler, paints a fuller picture of Islamic learning in West Africa. Baṭūṭa visited in 1352–53, more than one hundred years after a new imperial center, Mali, had ascended to rule over all the lands of old Ghana and to extend its dominions in every direction.

When Ibn Baṭūṭa arrived, Islam was at least three hundred years old in Mali. He was, nonetheless, sharply critical of gender relations among the Muslims in the empire. He criticized both Berbers in Walata and Mandingo Muslims in Jenné in particularly harsh terms, describing both groups as too liberal in their treatment of women and too unconcerned with covering the female body. While covering women was one of the principal public markers of Muslim identity in North Africa, Ibn Baṭṭūṭa's ethnocentrism did not blind him to the great importance West Africans placed on *their* most important public symbol of Muslim identity, Qur'an schooling. Even on holidays, some Malians made their children study or punished them for failing to do so: "I went in to visit the *qāḍī* on an *ʿīd* day and his children were tied up. I said to him, 'Why do you not release them?' He said, 'I shall not do so until they learn the Qur'an by heart.' One day I passed by a handsome youth from them dressed in fine clothes and on his feet was a heavy chain. I said to the man who was with me, 'What has this youth done—has he killed someone?' The youth understood my remark and laughed. It was told me, 'He has been chained so that he will learn the Qur'an by heart.'"[25]

Ibn Baṭṭūṭa's account definitely establishes the presence of a distinct black clerisy in the empire, with numerous *qāḍīs*, muftis, and imams of local origin. But in addition to providing insight on Qur'an schooling and the local clerisy in Mali in the fourteenth century, he also offers precious clues about earlier histories of Islamic scholarship. Among them is the first explicit textual reference to the Soninke tradition of Islamic scholarship emerging from old Ghana. He mentions the towns of Kābara and Zāgha, alluding to their reputation as centers of scholarship: "The people of Zāgha are old in Islam, they are religious and seekers after knowledge."[26]

THE JAKHANKE

Though transcribed as Zāgha by Ibn Baṭṭūṭa, the town to which he is referring is often rendered as Jāgha, Jākha, Jakhaba, Jā'ba, or simply as Jā'a or Jā, the point of origin for what may be the oldest collection of clerical lineages in West Africa, the Jakhanke.[27] This branch of the Soninke clerisy came

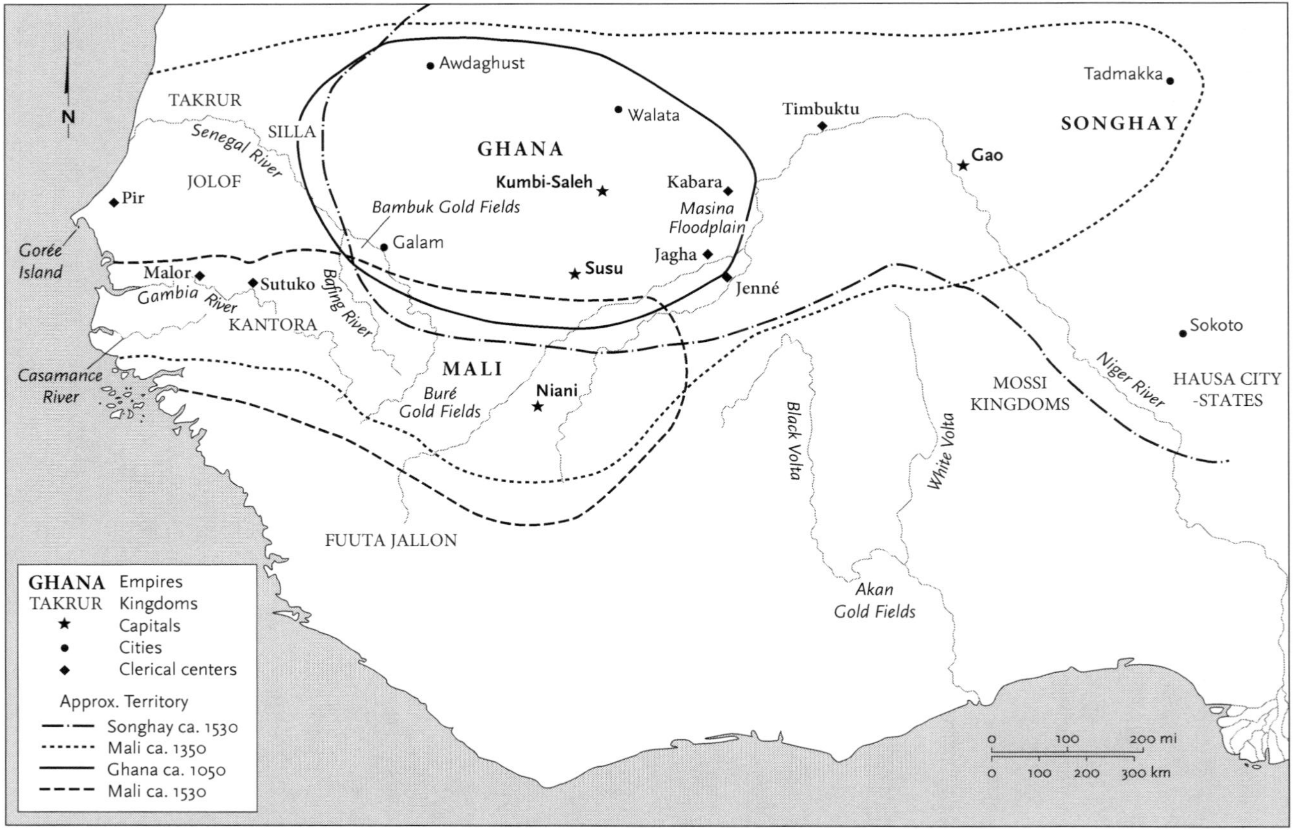

Map 2.1: Imperial West Africa, ca. 1000–1600

to be associated with its most famous luminary, al-Ḥājj Salīm Suwarī Siise (or Cissé), who probably lived in the second half of the fifteenth century and the first half of the sixteenth.[28] Al-Ḥājj Salīm is credited with institutionalizing the learning and teaching of three texts as the basic core of Jakhanke scholarly tradition: the *Muwaṭṭaʾ* of Mālik b. Anas, the *Tafsīr al-Jalālayn*; and the *Shifʿa* of al-Sabti (d. 1149). Accomplished scholars studied many other works as well, but memorizing the Qurʾan and studying these three writings marked one as a full member of the Jakhanke scholarly community. This community eventually formed a diaspora that spread throughout West Africa and developed a radical theological and legal approach to the separation of scholarship and politics. According to the framework of its greatest analyst, Ivor Wilks,

—Unbelief is a result of ignorance (*jahl*) rather than wickedness.
—It is God's will that some remain in *jāhiliyya* longer than others.
—There is no obligation in religion, and true conversion occurs in God's time.
—Jihad is not an acceptable means for converting non-Muslims.
—Jihad is legitimate only in self-defense to protect Muslims' survival.
—Muslims may support non-Muslim rule as long as they are allowed to practice Islam.
—Muslims must present an example to be emulated so non-Muslims will come to Islam.
—Scholarship must be the center of Muslim life to keep Islam from being corrupted.

Wilks notes that these "dicta do not at any point conflict with Maliki orthodoxy"; instead, they represent a radical adaptation of earlier Mālikī doctrines that allowed Muslims to live peacefully with non-Muslim neighbors.[29] "Armed" with this kind of tolerant approach, Juula and Jakhanke, Muslim merchants and clerics, respectively, enjoyed great freedom of movement to and through the non-Muslim lands to the south of the empire. Muslim intellectuals spread far and wide throughout West Africa, opening Qurʾan schools, teaching the sciences, and slowly drawing much of the western Sudan into the scholarly traditions of Islam.

Though it cannot be fully documented in the current state of research, elements of Jakhanke doctrines guiding relations with non-Muslims, though associated with al-Ḥājj Salīm in the fifteenth century, likely stretch back to the founding of the *sūdānī* clerisy.[30] Formal political neutrality was, along with the spatial segregation, an important condition imposed on merchants and Muslim religious specialists alike. In ancient Ghana, clerics lived and served at the mercy of temporal rulers and were forbidden to take up arms. The Jakhanke were both pursuing virtue and making a virtue of necessity when they elaborated their doctrines of maintaining pious distance from worldly power. In this, they may have drawn—as other West African scholars have—on a story told about Mālik b. Anas, eponym of the Mālikī school of Islamic law. It is said that when he was called to the court of the Abbasid caliph Hārūn al-Rashīd, he replied that he would be ashamed to have the angels see him knocking at the door of a king for a worldly matter.[31]

This pattern of clerical autonomy continued under the empire of Mali. In return for forsaking politics, *sūdānī* clerics enjoyed great freedom of movement among polities and a high degree of autonomy within their own communities.[32] Many sources confirm that spatially distinct clerical communities were considered inviolable spaces. Maḥmūd al-Kaʿti (d. 1599), author of the *Ta'rīkh al-Fattāsh*, suggests that Jāgha itself may be the archetype of a clerical sanctuary: Jāba "was governed by *fuqaha'*. The king of Mali never entered within, and no one had authority there except for the *qādī*. Whoever entered this city was protected from the king's violence and oppression. Even if he had killed the king's own children, the latter could not claim blood money. *They called it the city of God.*"[33]

MOODIBO MUḤAMMAD AL-KĀBARĪ AND TIMBUKTU

Al-Kaʿti's references to Jāba draw a direct parallel with the celebrated city of Timbuktu, where scholarship flourished under Mansa Mūsā (r. 1312–37) and his descendants, who gave gifts to clerics, built mosques and schools, but did not meddle in the city's internal affairs: "This city of Timbuktu in those days had no other magistrate other than the judge; it had no chief, or rather it was the *qāḍī* who was chief of the city and in his hands alone held the right to unbind and bind."[34] This more famous "city of God" is known in detail from two lengthy histories written near the end of the Songhay imperial period (1468–1591). Though the Timbuktu chronicles—the *Ta'rīkh al-Sūdān* and the *Ta'rīkh al-Fattāsh*—were written later, they yield precious insight on the evolution of the West African clerisy from 1300 to 1500. A close reading of them makes it clear that the scholarly efflorescence of Timbuktu grew from the same roots as the clerisy of ancient Ghana. Kābara, one of the towns mentioned by Ibn Baṭṭūṭa, was central in establishing the scholarly tradition of the most famous city of knowledge in sub-Saharan Africa.

The authors of both the *Ta'rīkh al-Sūdān* and the *Ta'rīkh al-Fattāsh* claimed Arab descent, and their writings helped constitute *bayḍān* identity and religious authority in the late sixteenth century. But whatever notions of "whiteness" they constructed for Arab and Berber peoples, they did not deny the foundational role of black scholars in establishing Timbuktu's renown. Al-Saʿadī, the author of the *Taʾrīkh al-Sūdān*, makes it clear that the earliest foundational tradition of scholarship in the town was a *sūdānī* tradition: "The Great Mosque and its tower minaret were built by the sultan al-Ḥājj Mūsā, ruler of Mali, after he returned from the pilgrimage and seized control of Timbuktu. . . . The first appointees to the imamate were *sūdānī* jurists, who held the office during Malian rule and part of Tuareg rule. . . . The first of the *bayḍān* to lead people in prayer in the Great Mosque [did so] during the latter days of Tuareg rule and the early days of the reign of Sunni ʿAlī (1464–92)."[35] Both chronicles make it clear that the town's best and brightest scholars during the fourteenth and fifteenth centuries were black.

The embodiment of this early black tradition of scholarship was Muḥammad al-Kābarī (d. 1450). Moodibo Muḥammad was likely of Fulɓe, Soninke, or perhaps even Mandingo background. Like many West Africans, he may well have been of mixed-ethnic parentage. Whatever the case, he was very clearly dark-skinned, according to al-Saʿadi, and just as clearly the most famous teacher of the early fifteenth century in Timbuktu.

> Among the revered men of Sankore was this shaykh, I mean the *faqīh* Moodibo Muḥammad al- Kābarī the pre-eminent shaykh. . . . He settled in Timbuktu in the middle of the ninth century [A.H.] . . . and was the contemporary of many shaykhs there. Among them [was] the jurist Sīdī ʿAbdul-Rahmān al-Tamīmī. . . . Moodibo Muḥammad al-Kābarī attained the very pinnacle of scholarship and righteousness and was the teacher of the jurist ʿUmar b. Muḥammad Aqīt and Sīdī Yaḥyā [al-Tadillisī]. . . . So numerous were his students, it is said, that he let no month go by without one of them finishing with him a reading of the *Tahdhīb* of al-Barādhʿī (d. 1039). At that time the town was full of *sūdānī* [black] students, people of the west who excelled in scholarship and righteousness. People even say that interred with him in his mausoleum (*rawḍa*), there are thirty men of Kābara, all scholars and saints.[36]

The text mentioned in this quotation indicates the seriousness of al-Kābarī's teaching, since complete extant manuscript copies of this text in Mauritanian private collections range from 450 to 790 pages in length.[37] But it also highlights that Kābara produced countless accomplished scholars.[38]

This rigorous tradition of scholarship attracted not only "black students from the west" but also those who considered themselves "white," whether from near or far. Sīdī, the honorific meaning "lord," is among the titles used to refer to people claiming direct descent from the Prophet. Even those who claimed such noble genealogies submitted themselves to the scholarly authority of Timbuktu's scholars. Sīdī ʿAbdul-Raḥmān al-Tamīmī left the Ḥijāz when, in the words of one scholar, "he realized that the scholars of Timbuktu surpassed him in knowledge of Islamic jurisprudence."[39] ʿUmar Aqīt, of Saharan *bayḍān* origin, did not consider that the blackness of Moodibo Muḥammad's skin made him unfit as a teacher. Nor did Sīdī Yaḥyā Tadillisi, who crossed the desert from North Africa to study with al-Kābarī. Sīdī Yaḥyā was an accomplished scholar and claimed descent from the Prophet. Though recognized as the saintly and scholarly paragon of the age by some, he reserved this kind of praise for his teacher, whom he eulogized in verse:

> It is the loss of a noble chief that rouses the heart's distress, a cultivated *faqīh* who passed along pearls of wisdom
> Through good teaching, ease of understanding, and sharp analysis of the *Tahdhīb* with fine delicacies of wisdom
> This master was Muḥammad Moodibo, possessing fine intelligence, long-suffering [for the sake of knowledge] but fortified with endless patience
> Will it be possible after him, for us to find another who can explain everything?
> O Arabs will there be another like him?[40]

Al-Saʿadi copied those verses from his father's hand. On the authority of his father and his father's teachers, he relays a story that suggests that al-Kābarī excelled in the *bāṭin* sciences of the religion as he did in the *ẓāhir.*

> One day in the first ten days of the Dhū-l-Ḥijja the shaykh went out to buy an animal for the Feast of the Sacrifice. The animals were on the other side of the river. The shaykh, accompanied by one of his disciples, began to walk upon the river. The disciple [*talamīdh*] followed him, since this seemed to him the thing to do at the time—God only knows why. The disciple sank right in the middle of the river just as the shaykh reached the other side. The latter called out to his disciple, stretched forth his hand and pulled him out of the water. Then he said "What compelled you to do that?"—"When I saw what you did, I did it," he replied. "How could you compare your foot to one that has never walked in the path of disobedience to God?"[41]

"People of the West"—The Senegambian Clerisy

The throngs of "people of the west who excelled in scholarship and righteousness" that came to Timbuktu in the imperial age certainly included many from Senegambia. Though at the fringes of the imperial authority of Ghana and Mali, Senegambia was devoid of neither states nor clerics, though neither is sufficiently documented before the arrival of the Portuguese at the coast in the middle of the fifteenth century. The earliest mention in Arabic sources of a state in the Senegal River Valley comes from al-Bakrī, who writes of the state of Takrūr converting to Islam under the rule of a king named Wār Jābī b. Rābīs (d. 1040–41).[42] There are, however, a number of tantalizing hints of substantial adherence to Islam in this part of Senegambia during the tenth century.

Oumar Kane, perhaps the most prominent expert on the early history of Takrūr and Fuuta Tooro, transmits oral traditions claiming that eleven clerical families of Soninke origin have been present in Fuuta Tooro since the tenth century. Kane also suggests that the first Qur'an schools in this predominantly Fulɓe region were founded by Soninke scholars in this period. Both assertions are probably correct, though they are difficult to substantiate.[43]

Some of the most compelling evidence adduced by Kane in favor of a foundational Soninke influence on Islamic religious culture in Takrūr (a region later known as Fuuta Tooro) comes from the Fula language itself. Kane notes that the root *jula* can be found in a variety of Fula terms associated with religion and trade: *julaade* (to engage in commerce), *juulde* (to pray), and *njuulu* (prayer).[44] Both Juula and Jakhanke are often called "Juula" by outgroups. "Juula" itself often means simply "merchant," "cleric," or even simply "Muslim" in some contexts. While linguistic speculation without careful long-term reconstructions can be risky, the etymology is quite plausible. In Wolof the words meaning "to pray [*julli*]," "to be pious [*jullite*]," and even "Muslim [*jullit*]" are all drawn from these same roots, whether directly from Soninke or through the intermediary of Fula. Fula and Wolof, languages that are spoken almost exclusively by Muslims and that draw much day-to-day vocabulary from Arabic, contain many words of non-Arabic origin for religious observance. This suggests that *Arabic*-speaking clerics played little role in proselytizing.

Ṣanhāja Berber clerics speaking Znaga, however, seem to have had a significant role, another phenomenon visible at the level of loan words. Along with the terms for prayer, the names of the daily prayers indicate early proselytizing with a limited role for speakers of Arabic. In Wolof and Fula, only the first prayer of the day retains even part of the form of Arabic (*fajr*), but the prayers *tisbaar*, *takkusaan*, and *timis* (*ẓuhr*, *aṣr*, and *maghrib*, respectively) appear to be derived from Znaga (Ṣanhāja) Berber. Senegambian languages also do not use Arabic names for the major religious holidays. The Feast of the Sacrifice (ʿĪd al-Aḍḥā in Arabic), and ʿĀshūrāʾ, the tenth day of the Muslim year, are called Tabaski and Tamkharit, respectively, suggesting Berber origins.[45]

TAKRŪR AND THE ALMORAVIDS

The *al-Murābitūn* (Almoravid) movement was a predominantly Berber puritanical movement that originated in the southwestern Sahara and ultimately established a ruling dynasty in North Africa and in Andalus (Muslim Spain) in the eleventh century. An earlier generation of scholars assumed that the Almoravids conquered Ghana and converted its rulers, but this theory has now been thoroughly debunked.[46] It is unknown whether the Almoravids even had significant *influence* in Ghana. But evidence shows that Almoravids specifically, and Berber clerics more generally, were important in the early history of Senegambia proper, to the west of the imperial heartlands. There appears to have been substantial religious exchange and cooperation, however, not unilateral influence or coercion from light-skinned Muslims. ʿAbdullah ibn Yasīn, the founder of the Almoravid movement in 1042 (or 1048, according to al-Bakrī) "when dismayed by Ṣanhājan resistance to his puritanical reforms, contemplated withdrawing among the Sudan, 'among whom Islam had already appeared.'"[47]

While these words may simply refer to Wār Jābī's conversion some years (or perhaps decades) earlier, it is also possible that early Soninke Qurʾan teachers—as Oumar Kane implies—had already made progress in Takrūr as early as the tenth century. If this is true, then the king's conversion might have marked the fruition of clerical efforts rather than a top-down Islamization. In any case, at least one documentary source suggests that an approximate date of 1000 for the spread of Islam in Takrūr may be a bit too late. By the last quarter of the tenth century, Cairo already had a neighborhood that housed "permanent pilgrims" from Takrūr: "A quarter of Bulaq, the suburb of Cairo, became known as Bulaq al-Takrūri, according to al-Maqrizi, because there lived al-Shaykh Abū Muhammad Yusuf ibn ʿAbdallah al-Takrūri: 'Many miracles, *karamat* were reported of him . . . and he is said to have lived during the reign of al-ʿAzīz ibn al-Muʿiz' (975–996)." An alliance between Takrūr and the Almoravids is the most likely explanation for medieval accounts stating that four thousand black soldiers fought alongside the Almoravid ruler Yūsuf b. Tāshfīn at Zalāqa in Spain in 1087.[48]

THE WALKING QUR'AN IN JOLOF

The Jolof Federation (ca. 1250–1550) emerged later in the area south of the Senegal River Valley and between the heartlands of Ghana and the Atlantic coast. It was a large, multiethnic polity with a core of Wolof speakers divided into four major states: Jolof, Kajoor, Bawol, and Waalo, but the capital in Jolof also ruled for extended periods of time over the Takrūr in the north and the Sereer states in the south.[49] The Wolof entered history at the edges of the large imperial states and in the aftermath of Takrūrī and the Almoravid movements of Islamization. From the beginning, the Wolof were fully integrated into the networks of schooling and Muslim identity emerging in the western Sudan. In addition to the Soninke, Mandingo, and Berber clerics, this phenomenon likely included Takrūrī clerics speaking Fula.[50] Njaajaan Njaay, legendary founder of the Jolof Federation, is reported to have lived in the thirteenth century, in which case he would be a rough contemporary of Mali's first emperor, Sunjaata Keita. Njaajaan is said to have been the son of Abū Dardai, one of the lieutenants of the Almoravid movement, and a Fulɓe woman, Fatimatu Saal.

This may be a typical case of claiming famed Arabic and Islamic origins, or it might perhaps mark a more formative Saharan influence on the Wolof than on the more centrally located *sūdānī* imperial polities. In any case, the founder of the Jolof Federation himself was portrayed literally as a *ḥāfiẓ*: "In some versions of the oral tradition he is said to have emerged from the river with a Qur'an in his hand in order to settle a dispute among some fishermen. Indeed it is reported that the first emperors of Jolof were required to recite the Qur'an in its entirety before being enthroned."[51] Either the first rulers of the Jolof Empire were required to be Walking Qur'an, or the griots—no friends of the clerisy in Jolof when the tales were collected in the 1960s—wanted us to believe that they were.

The earliest European source, Venetian merchant Alvise Cà da Mosto, visited "the King of Senega" (likely the Buurba Jolof) in 1455–57 as well as the Atlantic coastal province of Kajoor. In the latter, he found Ṣanhāja clerics at the dammel's court, confirming the impression that at least in this westernmost province of Jolof, Berbers were present and playing an important role, though it is unclear whether they were teaching the Qur'an in village communities, and they do not appear to have established independent clerical communities at this time.[52]

"Cities of God" in Senegambia

Cà da Mosto gives little insight into how clerics were perceived or the inner workings of their communities in Senegambia. But André Alvares d'Almada, a Portuguese slaver present in the region in the 1580s, captures the centrality of Muslim schooling here in a pithy though ethnocentric way: "There are a great many *bixirins* in these parts, and they put into the heads of the other people many [strange] notions, and they tell [them] many lies. . . . *The ordinary people are greatly devoted to them and pay much attention to what they tell them.* The *bixirins* make many charms which they give to the people, who have much confidence in these charms and expect much from them."[53]

While some clerics taught the Qur'an in villages throughout the region, there were also important centers of clerical authority. Almada's account highlights the antiquity of such settlements. He considered the Mandingo clerical settlements in the Cantor Kingdom on the Gambia River to be the region's oldest and best:[54] "In this district there are more devout *bixirins* than in all the rest of Guinea, because there are many establishments of this religion throughout the district, and many *pilgrims* who go from kingdom to kingdom. On the North side of the river, there are three large major establishments, corresponding to monasteries with us, which arouse great feeling and devotion in the blacks, and in which these 'monks' live and [also] those who are studying to become *bixirins*."[55] D'Almada identified Malor and Sutuco as major clerical establishments in this region, with another unnamed establishment at the river's mouth.[56]

His Jesuit countryman, Beltesar Barreira, gave a similar account of such independent clerical communities in 1608, specifying that they were autonomous settlements on lands granted by temporal rulers: "Kings . . . give them lands to inhabit and consequential privileges. In these settlements they have mosques, and the *bexerins* form schools in which they teach reading and writing in the Arabic script, which is what they use in their amulets. . . . When one of the *bexerins* visits either this kingdom or any other which accepts their religion, as happens annually, he is received and respected as if he came from heaven. Among those accompanying him are some youths who are under instruction and these daily write their lessons and read them out aloud."[57] Both accounts highlight the importance of schooling to such settlements and the sense of awe and respect that scholars—as living exemplars of God's Word—produced from the mouth of the Gambia River to the bend of the Niger and beyond.

Further, both accounts highlight the fact that it was not only the clerics that inspired reverence and pilgrimage but the spaces themselves. That is to say, a complex relationship has long obtained between clerical spaces and the bodies of clerics, mediated by the very earth that envelops their bodies. One of the factors that makes these settlements focal points of pilgrimage and reverence is that they are the burial places of scholars and saints. That the city of Timbuktu was understood to be hallowed ground for precisely this reason is apparent from the Timbuktu chronicles. Al-Kaʿti dedicates several pages to "tombs that procure the fulfillment of vows that are made near them," discussing the healing attributes and special powers associated with the tombs of particular clerics.[58]

In such places, more than just the bodies of the scholars (believed to be worth visiting whether alive or dead) are sanctifying the ground. This comes across clearly in the history of Pir, the first clearly documented clerical community in Wolof country, founded ca. 1600.[59] For centuries, people have come to the site of the original Qurʾan school at Pir to take home handfuls of dirt, which they then mix with water, using the solution for bathing.[60] Here, the earth itself is being treated the same way as the wash water from the *alwāḥ*. It is being mixed to make a dark liquid charged with the spiritual energy of the Qurʾan. Once again, we see that a parallel is being drawn between the bodily substance of holy individuals and the text of the Qurʾan.

SANCTITY AND SANCTUARY

Such spaces were sacrosanct. The blood of the children of Eve should never be shed on such ground, blessed as it was by the bodies of the walking Qurʾan and the wash water from the slate boards. Usually beginning as a Qurʾan school farm and often gradually developing into extensive clerical compounds, these spaces were a kind of *mahram* (forbidden space), off-limits to temporal authorities. As such, they were understood to be safe havens from political violence.[61] In exchange for this kind of autonomy, kings expected clerics to stay out of politics. We might see this neutrality as the minimum condition of patron-client or landlord-stranger relationships.[62] Kings held clerics to be incapable of wielding political power. In this view, birth and experience conferred war, statecraft, honor, and valor on the hereditary nobility. Clerics, who begged for alms, accepted gifts, and exercised a "craft," were dependent client groups.[63] They were weak, while kings were strong. Yet characteristic of the wider logic of specialization and interdependence, kings needed clerics. Kings often granted land in exchange for services provided at the court, usually prayers, writing of talismans for war or diplomacy, and secretarial services.[64] The land grants offered in return for such services were often in marginal areas at the edge of established political units. This arrangement suited clerics seeking distance from power as well as rulers seeking to buffer "secular" settlements from the influence of clerics.

As clerics slowly grew in influence, the two distinct sociospatial orders competed for clients. The villages and towns aligned with the clerisy were structured by master-disciple relationships and provided an alternative framework of allegiance and identity as well as moral and political order. In Wolof country, the villages and towns aligned with kings became known as *ceddo* communities, taking their name from the class of crown slaves who increasingly came to mark the power of the temporal order during the Atlantic era. The spatial marginality of clerical communities, conceived of as a kind of quarantine by ruling nobles meant to enforce such communities' weakness, sometimes backfired. Distant autonomous communities were not subject to close surveillance, and within them a communal ethos of independence and solidarity could be quite strong. Segregation always has the potential to become congregation.

In a context where power and authority meant primarily wealth in people—whether subjects, descendants, followers, disciples, or slaves—such clerical communities posed an obvious potential risk to political authorities.[65] Moreover, Islamic discourse and practice provided an epistemological, cultural, and moral register to orient communities. At the head of this moral universe was the master (*sëriñ* in Wolof, *ceerno* in Fula), who, when understood to possess the requisite knowledge, sanctity, and spiritual power, could lead a large following. The social weight and political potential of these communities did not pass unnoticed by temporal authorities.

In Fuuta Tooro, the Deeñanke ruling dynasty heaped scorn on the clerical class, known collectively as Tooroɓɓe, claiming that their lowly social origin—the word "Tooroɓɓe" alludes to seeking alms—made them incapable of rule.[66] Wolof rulers did likewise but obviously did not believe their own propaganda: they tacitly acknowledged the threat by formally requiring that anyone joining the clerical community must abandon all claims to political authority. Clerics were also generally forbidden to marry women from royal families out of fear that such unions, as well as the heirs they might produce, could pose political threats.[67]

The tension is captured in the story of the founding of the school of Pir. It was located in Kajoor, which was, after the Jolof Federation dissolved around 1550, the most powerful of the Wolof states. Pir was one of the most important places of study for both Wolof and Fulɓe clerics, drawing disciples from all around the subregion. Encompassing roughly seventy square kilometers and at least sixty distinct villages or wards, all of them founded by *qāḍī* (usually pronounced *xaali* in Wolof) Amar Jégi Faal or his descendants and disciples, Pir is exceptionally large and well known but is also typical in its composition and history.[68] The negotiations between Qāḍī Amar Faal and the dammel of Kajoor, Maaxuréja Kuuli, can be seen as archetypical of the kind of accord in which a worldly ruler made a concession of land to a well-born cleric. This account, transmitted in a cottage-press printed version by well-known griot and public historian El-Hadji Demba Lamine Diouf, is a composite version of the tale:

> Khali Amar Fall: I have not come here to dispute your power. I am a servant of God. After studying the Sacred Book in the Sahara I seek to devote myself to religion forever. I want nothing which might distance me from God. That's why I have come here, so that you might install me in a place of devotion where I will be able to teach the Holy Book to all who wish [to study it], a place where I could have the quietude necessary for worship of the Almighty.
>
> Dammel Maaxuréja Kuuli: I have perfectly understood what you have just said. I give you my accord for we are both heirs to the throne of Kajoor. As for power, we can get along if, as you say, you are not here to dispute with me [for it]. You have come in search of a land where you could establish yourself with your talibés and where you can be alone to devote yourself to God. As for me, I will see to your needs. I will assign you land that you will develop and where you will receive any man desiring to share your faith, if he respects the conditions that we have previously defined. All that I ask of you is that you not dream of abandoning your religious principles and covet the power I hold. Be sure, also, to bar the route to whoever may try to take this power away from me. We will join forces to deal with such an eventuality. Thus we will live together on the grounds that we have just defined.[69]

The history of the establishment of clerical communities throughout Senegambia and beyond is replete with similar stories.[70] The king conceives of the cleric as his man, bound to keep his peace and even to fight to help him preserve it. Here, Faal agrees but reminds the ruler that only struggle for the sake of God—jihad—will ever cause him to take up arms. As the worldly authorities in Senegambia became invested in the political economy of the Atlantic slave trade, perhaps it was only a matter of time before struggle for the sake of God became a fight against kings rather than for them.

The Rise of the Atlantic Economy

In the early of the sixteenth century, African coastlines were turning from backwaters to superhighways and investing previously obscure elites with unprecedented power, wealth, and importance. The dammel of Kajoor was one such elite magnified by the expansion of an Atlantic economy that needed slaves for New Spain and the sugar plantations of Brazil. In the 1520s, he asserted independence from the Jolof Federation, and by 1549, he had seceded.[71] In the century between first Portuguese contact with "Jalofos" in the 1440s and the secession of Kajoor, the slave populations of Mexico and Peru steadily gained more Senegambian Muslims, with Wolof and Fula speakers probably constituting a majority by the first half of the sixteenth century.[72]

Catholic priest Alonso de Sandoval, perhaps the most important church author on slavery in the early seventeenth century, explicitly instructed that slaves from Senegambia must be baptized on arrival in the colonies because they would not have received even a cursory baptism at their ports of embarkation. His account, published in the 1620s, almost two centuries after Cà da Mosto's account of Islam in Jolof, highlights the central role of schooling in spreading Islam in Senegambia, but it also perpetuates the fiction that Islam is a recently arrived Arab import: "What most shames me . . . is the care and work that the Moors give to perverting these black nations with their false Mahoma. In our days, and before our very eyes, they have introduced the Mohammedan sect in four of the most important and populous kingdoms of Guinea, those of the Berbesi [Sereer], the Mandingas, the Wolofs, and the Matomos, and others. To carry out their goals, they introduce schools where they teach reading and writing, telling them that this will help them in negotiations all over the world and in doing business with all the merchants."[73]

The growing number of Wolof and Fulɓe slaves in the New World was directly related to Kajoor's struggles to develop the military capacity to achieve independence from Jolof. Iron, horses, alcohol, tobacco, consumer goods, and possibly early firearms would have constituted the major imports. In these developments, one can see the beginnings of the new slaving regimes that would mark Senegambian history.

Slavery was not new here. Wolof rulers, like other kings of the imperial age in West Africa, used slave labor, but with the rise of new militarized regimes from the sixteenth century forward, slavery increased in scale and scope.[74] Furthermore, slave-exporting elites increasingly retained as well as sold slaves, eventually forming some into the personal military forces of rulers. In Wolof country, these military Crown slaves came to be called *ceddo*. As time passed, they became the main pillars of support for the royals, particularly in Kajoor but also (if to a lesser extent) in the other Wolof states. They began to bypass the institutions of local representation that ran through the Wolof states and had been part of the formal structure of the Jolof Federation. In Kajoor especially, large *ceddo* armies and tyrannical tendencies were quick to emerge. Slowly but surely, typically autocratic and predatory Atlantic elites were emerging in Senegambia.

By the end of the sixteenth century, some evidence indicates that this process was beginning to mark the divide between rulers and clerics in new ways. Some Europeans were seeing close association between clerics and kings as detrimental to transatlantic trade, particularly in slaves, and beginning to favor dealing with nonclerics. D'Almada related the story of a dammel who "drank no wine, [and] preferred the conversation and friendship of *bixirins* and Moors to that of our people, and in his day almost all of the trade and commerce with our people was lost."[75] The Atlantic economy depended on trading partners who bought alcohol, clothes, and weapons, which accounted for roughly three-quarters of the European value of the goods traded for slaves in Africa.[76] When trading partners favored a more austere clerical lifestyle, when they did not drink or indulge in lavish displays of conspicuous consumption, the slave trade suffered.

The rise of typically Atlantic elites—and increasingly brutal and arbitrary slave armies—in the Wolof countries produced significant critique. A well-known story attributed to Kocc Barma, a seventeenth-century member of the *laman* class, the traditional landholding patricians of the Jolof Federation, directly criticizes the rise of *ceddo* armies and the despotic centralization and autocracy that accompanied them. Numerous tales recount raids by a dammel's *ceddo* against one of his own villages. In such stories, the king typically reproaches a village for being slow to pay taxes or for an insult to the Crown or for killing a *ceddo* who stole food or people. In reality, these were often simple pretexts, designed to produce slaves for export. Kocc is supposed to have said to the corpse of a man murdered in one such raid, "Go tell our ancestors that today death is preferable to life. Go tell our forefathers that in their days, command was in the hands of free men who knew the meaning of honesty and duty; that they are fortunate to enjoy the respite of the grave; for today it is the slaves who command; these are slaves who execute the unjust wishes of their masters to gain their favor. Go tell them that there is no lack of men who want well-being, but those who attain it are no more."[77]

Kocc Barma's struggle against the unjust centralization of power was ap-

"Thiedo," or *ceddo*, drawn from life by Abbé Boilat, ca. 1850. Note the large bottle of eau-de-vie. Courtesy of Melville J. Herskovits Library of African Studies, Northwestern University.

parently more than rhetorical. In 1647, he engineered the last successful dethroning of a dammel by the traditional councils of electors.[78] Kocc Barma was a politician, not a cleric. After the mid-seventeenth century, the dammels silenced the traditional political representatives of the people all too easily. From that point forward, resistance to the arbitrary exactions of kings would have to come from the clerics and their *taalibés*. The clerisy's age-old doctrines of political neutrality and pious distance were beginning to break under the weight of the Atlantic slave trade.

TUUBANAAN

The most famous early instance of clerical resistance to temporal authorities' heavy engagement with slaving and the Atlantic economy was the Tuubanaan (from Arabic and Wolof *tawba* or *tuub*, meaning "repentance") movement in and around the Senegal River Valley in the 1670s. The basic elements of the received story—treated two generations ago by Curtin and Barry and not substantially revised since—is that sometime around 1670 a Saharan scholar of Berber descent, Naṣīr al-Dīn, undertook a revolt against the Ḥasānī Arabs in the Southwestern desert. The Banī Ḥasān were nomadic Arabs who had begun to enter the region in significant numbers in the fifteenth century, gradually establishing themselves as a warrior elite in the power void left by the decline of the great West African empires that had once ruled the desert. Naṣīr al-Dīn criticized the religious laxity, banditry, and amorality of the Ḥasān and claimed that the Zawāyā, the predominantly Berber clerical lineages of the desert who possessed Islamic knowledge, should rule.[79]

The sensibilities toward Islamic knowledge in Naṣīr al-Dīn's *zawāyā* community mirrored those farther south: this was a bodily possession of knowledge. Naṣīr al-Dīn is said to have commanded his disciples to carry their *alwāḥ* between their bodies and their bridles when they mounted their horses in case they should die in battle. These soldiers almost literally carried the Qur'an into battle as a shield. Naṣīr al-Dīn himself was the subject of the intense bodily reverence that was owed to a living exemplar of God's Holy Book. In the words of a *zawāyā* poet, his followers were deeply devoted, treating his saliva with the reverence of the wash water from a slate board: "They sought the influence of his virtues down to his saliva, which they collected to suck; in the water with which he rinsed his mouth and that they drank; in the leftovers from his meals, which they ate."[80]

The argument that such esteemed exemplars of piety and knowledge should rule resounded strongly with the clerical classes of Senegambia, who also suffered political marginalization at the hands of warrior elites frequently considered impious and unjust. The ties of blood and ink that connected Saharan and Senegambian scholars helped the movement spread rapidly south of the Senegal River. The Saharan movement was crushed in 1674, with Naṣīr al-Dīn killed in battle, but the movement spread effectively in the south, in large part because it carried an explicitly antislavery message. The substance of that message was recorded by Louis Mareau de Chambonneau, a French slave trader who fought to quell the uprising: "God in no way permits kings to pillage, kill, nor enslave their people, but to the contrary, [He enjoins kings] to maintain them and protect them from their enemies, the people not being made for the kings, but the kings for the people."[81]

According to Chambonneau, the movement installed rulers in Fuuta Tooro as well as the major Wolof states of Waalo, Kajoor, and Jolof. Chambonneau describes how once the Tuubanaan were in power, the flow of slaves immediately slowed to a trickle, highlighting the incongruity of clerical rule and Atlantic slaving.[82] In response, French slavers made common cause with the deposed rulers, supplying arms, men, and cannon support from gunboats in the Senegal River beginning in 1674 and leading to a definitive routing of the clerical party by the end of 1676.[83] Restored to power, the slaving kings dealt the clerics a painful retribution, capturing them en masse and thus violating age-old taboos against harming holy persons. Jean Barbot, a French slaver, recounted in his memoirs that the brak of Waalo resolved never again to suffer clerics in his land "but to sell all such as they should find in their country for slaves. I am apt to believe there was one of this sort among the slaves I purchas'd at Goeree in the year 1681. . . . This black priest was abroad for two months before he spoke a word, so deep was his sorrow. I sold him in the American Islands."[84]

Chambonneau, too, described the vengeance exacted by the brak of Waalo after he had regained his kingdom with help from the slavers: "For the whole year of 1676 he did nothing but kill, take captive, and burn the lands of the Toubenan, all the way to the site of the residence of Bourguli [Buur Jullit, Muslim king, the title of Tuubanaan rulers] destroying the millet and cutting it down while green so that the people of the country were forced to eat boiled grass, carrion, and bits of leather. [This] I saw on my trip in Foutes [Fuuta] in the month of July 1676, and whole families offered themselves to me as captives, provided that they be fed."[85] The Muslims of Senegambia were sold across the desert and sea, perhaps in unprecedented numbers. The devastation was complete and was followed by a generation of retribution against the clerics who had participated.

A number of elements of the story can be reexamined. As it has been told until now, this episode has been unduly colored by the pervasive assumption that Islamic ideas always moved from north to south and from white to black. In fact, a fair amount of evidence suggests that this movement began not in the desert with Naṣīr al-Dīn but rather in Kajoor, in the heart of Wolof country. As early as the 1650s, a prominent cleric, Njaay Saal, seems to have engineered a number of attempts to capture state power in Jolof. He has been portrayed by Curtin and others as a "lieutenant" of Naṣīr al-Dīn in Senegambia, yet to my knowledge no sources explicitly connect him with the *bayḍān* (white Arabo-Berber) leadership of the movement.

Saal then served as the *qāḍī* of Kajoor before claiming the throne for himself in the 1670s. A. B. Diop, historian of the royal family of Kajoor, describes Njaay Saal and the *lingeer* (head of the royal matrilineage) as the main protagonists in the events of the 1670s in Kajoor, the largest and most powerful Wolof state. *Lingeer* Yasin Buubu had offered herself in marriage to Njaay Saal, who was a cleric with a large following. She took with her a number of her Crown slaves and other royal followers, adding them to the already impressive entourage at the Saal compound (in Xellere). The dammel of Kajoor then sent his forces to punish the *lingeer* and the cleric who was so audacious as to marry a royal. The rebels defeated the dammel's soldiers and engineered his replacement by their own candidate, Fali Géy. Although brought to power by the clerical party, Fali Géy was surprised in his quarters drinking trade brandy (*sangara*), a symbol of the *ceddo* lifestyle, and was killed by Njaay Saal's disciples.[86] In one account, these events turned Yasin Buubu against her husband, and in all accounts the death of the dammel rallied the *ceddo* against the clerical party. Njaay Saal then attempted to claim the title of dammel for himself, only to be killed in open battle by a faction of the Kajoor royal family.[87]

Prior to Njaay Saal's rise, three successive dammels—Maaxuréja (who granted the land for the foundation of Pir), Bira Mbanga, and Dao Semba—were extremely unpopular rulers who imposed draconian sumptuary restrictions on their subjects and were famous drunks. In the 1960s, griots still sang, "*Mbanga, Mbanga, bu lekkul mungi naan* [Mbanga, Mbanga, if he's not eating, he's drinking]!" According to Diop, Mbanga was "a glutton who satisfied himself in orgy." Dammels of this era were said to have forbidden peasants to consume salt or even engage in sexual relations with their spouses. In this period, the peasantry fled increasingly to the communities of the Qur'an and away from the *ceddo* villages and especially from the pleasure tents of the kings.

With this background, it is clear why the clerical movement of the 1670s was wildly popular in the Wolof country, particularly Kajoor. But in spite of this popularity, the French slavers and deposed rulers joined forces and returned to power by the end of the 1670s in all the Senegambian and Sahara states. This was typical European policy in Africa. When one could not simply take slaves directly, one could nonetheless help arm people who had no qualms about slavery against those who might. Europeans were willing to ponder any course of action that might "stimulate" the slave supply. A particularly revealing late-eighteenth-century proposal suggested inciting the Moors to attack kingdoms deep in the interior. The more common strategy was to stimulate desire for consumer goods as a way of inciting kings to pillage. The same proposal recommended this method to turn the kingdom of Jolof into a slave supplier by making "annual presents to the king of the Yoloffes to get close to him and to bring into being new needs [*faire naitre des besoins*] and then commit him to making pillage on his neighbors; all these reflections are a bit barbaric, but they are the result of a Commerce that has become indispensable."[88]

More than ever before, African rulers came to depend on foreign imports and saddled themselves with debt. They soon turned to enslaving their own Muslim subjects. By the 1700s, Atlantic trade goods that had once been luxuries used to recruit a following were now necessities required to remain in power. Moreover, the thorough penetration of arms throughout the region made quick profitable expeditions against poorly armed inland peoples a thing of the distant past.[89] Kings whose power depended on large entourages and huge numbers of subjects and dependents were frequently required to give up the very human basis of their power, selling their own subjects to liquidate debts to European slave traders. French sources were explicit about this practice, making no pretense of having acquired their slaves in "just wars" on the African continent. Saint-Louis slave dealer André Brüe singled out the dammel of Kajoor, Latsukaabe Faal (r. ca. 1695–1719), for engaging in this practice, though he was only one of many:[90] "Negro princes always have a ready resource which allows them to procure more slaves: they sell their own subjects. They never lack pretexts to justify their violence and rapine. The dammel [Latsukaabe Faal] used this method because he was already deeply in debt to the Company, and he knew that his credit would not be extended."[91] Such debts had to be liquidated; otherwise, Europeans sometimes enslaved their erstwhile slaving partners to recover what was owed.

The situation was no different for the rulers of Fuuta Tooro, the Saltigis.[92] They, too, often promised slave deliveries beyond their means to receive the arms and goods with which to maintain their following, only to find themselves forced to sell their own subjects to make ends meet. A detailed 25 March 1731 letter from an anonymous French slaver illustrates a typical set of demands from an eighteenth-century Saltigi, along with French skepticism about the Saltigi's ability to deliver on his promises: "He demands 100 double-barrel shotguns and twenty common [rifles], pistols, swords, and powder, shot and flint [delivered] by the boat that will carry his customs. He assures that there will be captives enough to load 3 ships. Something which should absolutely not be counted on."[93]

Weakened by the clerical revolution more than the rulers of Kajoor, Waalo, or Jolof, Fuuta's leadership became hopelessly indebted not only to French slavers but also to military support from *bayḍān* groups in the desert in the century following the Tuubanaan movement. Moroccan warrior groups raided from the desert, as did Saharan *bayḍān*. Saltigis and other princes of the Deeñanke ruling dynasty turned a blind eye as Saharans captured the Muslim peasants of Fuuta and sold them across the desert or to French ships in the river. Indeed, the princes themselves engaged in the practice.[94] For a century, the Wolof and Fulɓe Muslims of Senegambia were victimized by increasingly predatory, despotic, and arbitrary rulers.

Kings and Clerics

In the eighteenth century, after the Tuubanaan movement and its repression, clerical communities were establishing quite a different political reputation. Francis Moore, an employee of the Royal African Company of England, was in the Gambia River region from 1730 until 1735. His published journal contains lengthy descriptions of clerical communities:

> In every Kingdom and Country on each Side of the River [Gambia] there are some People of a tawny Colour, call'd *Pholeys* [Fulas], much like the *Arabs*; which language they most often speak, being to them as *Latin* is in *Europe*; for it is taught in Schools, and their Law, the Alcoran, is in that Language. They are generally more learned in the *Arabick*, than the people of *Europe* are in *Latin*, for they can most of them speak it, tho' they have a vulgar Tongue besides, call'd *Pholey*. They . . . are not subject to any Kings of the Country, tho' they live in their territories. . . . They have Chiefs of their own, who rule with so much Moderation, that every Act of Government seems rather an Act of the People than of one Man. This form of

Government goes on easily, because the People are of a good and quiet Disposition, and so well instructed in what is just and right, that a man who does ill, is the Abomination of all, and none will support him against the chief. . . . It is universally look'd upon as infamous to violate the Laws of Hospitality towards them. As their Humanity extends to all, they are doubly kind to People of their own Race, insomuch that if they know one of them being made a Slave, all the *Pholeys* will redeem him. . . . They are strict *Mahometans*; none of them (unless here and there one) will drink Brandy, or any thing stronger than Water and Sugar.[95]

Moore's portrait of the Fulas attributes their form of government to Fulɓe ethnic characteristics. But similar accounts from other contemporary European sources make it clear that such clerical communities were found in predominantly Mandingo, Soninke, Wolof, and Berber zones as well. Moreover, these were usually multiethnic communities even if they had an ethnolinguistic core community.

■ *Ceddo* kings sold their own subjects to liquidate debts and to import liquor and guns. Clerics developed a reputation for never selling their own people. The differences between the two factions could hardly have been starker. With the benefit of hindsight, the appeal of the clerical movement is obvious, but at the time, the hereditary kings and warrior elites still held a decisive military advantage. Moreover, the weight of history and culture was on their side: the nobles were the socially acknowledged specialists in the arts of war and diplomacy. More important perhaps, they imported arms from the sea and horses from the desert. Many Africans no doubt decided to cast their lot with the strong even if the strong sometimes sold their own. Some rulers sought to use the carrot as well as the stick to control the swelling clerical party, giving concessions of land and titles to some Wolof and Fulɓe clerical groups in the aftermath of the Tuubanaan.[96] While such concessions may have softened some clerics' critiques and blurred the line between the clerisy and the nobility, these were the exceptions that proved the rule.

Slowly and steadily, the more powerful and autonomous clerical communities gathered people around them. As princes took away people and their possessions, the remaining men and women fled to the clerics. To make their allegiance meaningful and perhaps to help make sense of a world turned upside down by *ceddo*, these people took on a new engagement with Islam. Most Senegambian Muslims had previously left careful consideration of Islam to its "caste" of specialists, the clerics. Now, however, many began to adopt a lifestyle that had once been mainly the sign of belonging to the clerical community. Public articulation of Muslim identity became stronger, reinforcing the veneration of clerics that marked the region's religious culture.

The numbers and influence of Fulɓe, Wolof, and other clerics burgeoned. The bonds of marriage and discipleship (blood and ink) that tied them together were now sacralized by the spilled blood of brethren lost, those Walking Qur'an who had been killed or enslaved in the reprisals that followed the Tuubanaan revolution. Subsequent generations of scholars were held together by more powerful bonds and a common cause—the fight against the illegal enslavement of Muslims by kings who knew only the law of the strong. These scholars studied together at Pir and other schools; they built families and extended family networks. One hundred years after the Tuubanaan, the regeneration of the clerisy was complete, and they again became strong enough to stand against the kings. In so doing, they would be stirred to action by outrage at the enslavement of those who embodied the Word of God.

3 THE BOOK IN CHAINS

SLAVERY AND REVOLUTION IN SENEGAMBIA, 1770–1890

Whoever frees a believing slave, God will free his every limb from the Fire as he has freed those of the slave.
—Saying attributed to the Prophet Muḥammad

The Book in Chains

In 1770, Sulaymaan Baal, a Fulɓe teacher, was making his way back to Fuuta Tooro. Homeward bound after years of travel in pursuit of knowledge, he had visited the homes and schools of scholars all over West Africa, including the *bayḍān* clerics of the southwestern Sahara. Along with his disciples, he was now leaving the Saharan fringes and heading for the Senegal River Valley. The trip took them through dangerous country, controlled by Ḥasānī Arabs known to be highwaymen, bandits, and slave raiders. Armed only with the canes of shepherds, the wooden boards of *taalibés*, and the traditional immunity of the people of knowledge, they crossed hostile territory. When the slaves of a Ḥasānī chief found the party of scholars drinking from his well and tried to deny them hospitality, they claimed their rights with their staffs. When the chief himself arrived, he "found them beneath the trees next to the well and saw that they had hung their wooden boards in the trees."[1] Perhaps struck by the piety of these men who would not let the Word of God touch the ground, he gave them clemency.

Arriving safely at the Senegal River, Ceerno Sulaymaan Baal found a man held in bondage in a riverboat. The man was reciting the Qur'an aloud. Sulaymaan Baal rushed toward him and asked how he had come to this fate. He replied that he had been traveling to the town of Bakkel when the princes of the region captured him and sold him to the owners of the boat in which he was being held. The owners were now taking him to the white slavers at Saint-Louis. "Ceerno Sulaymaan told the occupants of the boat: 'Release him, he is a Muslim and thus free.' They responded, 'What you say means little to us. We bought him with our money.' Ceerno had with him a student who was called Aali Mayram and who was gifted at wrestling and very physically strong. He fought the occupants of the boat by himself, defeated them, and brought out of the boat the man who was reading the Qur'an. The Shaykh released him and ordered him to leave."[2]

Did seeing the Book in chains crystallize for Sulaymaan Baal the gravity of the problem facing the society he knew? Historians can only guess at the emotions this sight must have stirred. We do know that immediately after returning to Fuuta, Ceerno Sulaymaan Baal began preaching against the injustice of the Deeñanke, the hereditary nobility of the country, and especially their princes, the Saltigis. We also know that Fuutanke society had suffered massive enslavement of its free Muslim population for more than a century. But change was coming. Within a generation, the Senegambian clerisy would end the rule of kings in Fuuta Tooro, virtually halt the sale of Fuuta's Muslims into Atlantic slavery, and drive the Ḥasānī warriors from the banks of the Senegal River back to the desert fringes.

The story of the revolution that Sulaymaan Baal (d. 1776) started—and that ʿAbdul-Qādir Kan (d. 1806) finished—is a centerpiece of this chapter, and this chapter is a centerpiece of this book. One of its central premises is that much of the Senegambian past can be understood as the historical expression of an epistemology. In chapter 1, I painted a portrait of that Islamic epistemology of embodiment, arguing that the goal of Qur'an schooling was not simply to transmit discursive knowledge but rather to remold the body into a living vehicle of Islamic knowledge, a Walking Qur'an. A related idea, which I explored over eight centuries of West African history in chapter 2, was that certain people who fully internalized the Word of God—usually socially recognized scholars—were sanctified beings.

The main argument of this chapter is that the enslavement of the bearers of the Qur'an galvanized resistance to the enslavement of Muslims. If clerics were understood as embodiments of the Qur'an, then enslaving them was akin to desecrating the Book of God. *If attempts to burn ink-and-paper copies of the Qur'an sparked emotional reactions from Muslims worldwide at the beginning of the twenty-first century, how would Senegambians respond to seeing the Walking Qur'an carried away in chains?*

■ This had become a sadly familiar spectacle. The enslavement of Muslims by their rulers reached epidemic proportions during the eighteenth century, when roughly half of the total volume of the Atlantic slave trade was carried.[3] In this chapter, I examine oral traditions, Arabic manuscripts, archival documents, and European travelers' accounts from the long nineteenth century to retrieve narratives in which the enslavement of bearers of the Qur'an and their families served as proximate cause for revolt. Dozens of such stories have been hiding in plain sight. They occur so frequently that it is clear that they are a trope of the oral tradition and literature of Senegambia. But they are corroborated by so many other kinds of sources—from European slavers, abolitionists, colonial archives—that it is equally clear they are usually historical events. Seeing the Book in chains was both a real and metaphorical point of no return.

Men of letters took up arms. Muslim peasants, their disciples, and even slaves joined their rebellions. They went to war and conquered states, choosing to forgo long-established traditions of clerical pacifism, neutrality, and pious distance from power. They chose to incur the moral risks of exercising worldly authority rather than brook such an abomination.

THE PROBLEM OF SLAVERY IN ISLAM

In a recent overview of slavery and abolition in Islamic thought and Muslim societies, W. G. Clarence-Smith notes that Orientalists and historians have uncritically accepted the idea that slavery was an indelible institution within Islam.[4] There were a few dissenters, including Hans Müller, the world's foremost authority on slavery in Arabic, Persian, and Turkish sources, who argued that slavery was best understood as an economic rather than religious institution.[5] A century earlier, G. W. Leitner countered British claims—used to justify colonial conquests in Africa—that slavery was "the inevitable consequence of Mohammedan government." His rejoinder is as pertinent today as it was in 1884: "This is as great a libel on that religion as the assertion would be on Christianity, that it was in favour of slavery because Christ, although confronted by one of its cruellest forms in the Roman Empire, did not attempt to legislate, as Muḥammad did, for its eventual abolition in this world, but merely promised spiritual freedom to the repentant servants of sin, whether bond or free."[6] Leitner reminds us that scholarship that makes slavery appear an ineffaceable part of any world religion rather than part of worldly history is usually mere rhetoric.[7]

Clarence-Smith notes, however, that Orientalists were not alone in seeing slavery as a natural part of Islam. Many Muslim religious scholars saw it this way as well. But he shows that slavery's standing in Islamic law was contested. Some *ʿulamāʾ* challenged every aspect of the production and sale of human beings from the seventh century through the nineteenth. Some argued that no legal precedent existed for the forms of enslavement practiced during the expansion of the caliphate.[8] Others sought inspiration in the Prophet's example and noted that although the Qurʾan did not explicitly forbid slavery, its strong calls for pious manumission would have succeeded if not for the venality of the caliphate. Others noted that the Prophet himself freed anyone he had ever owned before he died.[9] If the sunna was so important, they suggest, Muslims should have done likewise. Still others challenged the weak legal basis for aggressive jihad, hoping to curb enslavement by curbing war.

But mainstream jurists usually disregarded such arguments, along with Prophetic sayings such as "The worst of men is he who sells men."[10] Muslim jurists codified slavery, a matter of pre-Islamic law in the lands that became the caliphate, as if it enjoyed the unambiguous approval of God and Prophet. These medieval jurists were functionaries in expansionist slaving states, so it is not surprising that they protected property rights and condoned slaving and slave trafficking. Nowhere in the history of Islamic legal thought is the worldly imprint of the caliphate as clear as in the sophistry used to make perpetual aggressive jihad (and its corollary, slavery) appear as divinely ordained.

As Clarence-Smith wrote, "Such exegetical exercises had the paradoxical outcome of seeming to mock the Qur'an."[11] The Qur'an discusses slavery as a fact of human society, neither condoning nor condemning it. Countless verses promote manumission. Countless sayings attributed to the Prophet echo the call. Nonetheless—and without support in any foundational text—many scholars came to see slavery as a legitimate punishment for unbelief.[12] Slowly, a "fragile Sunni consensus" on slavery's permissibility gathered the strength of precedent and became an unquestioned part of Islamic legal practice.[13] But even this consensus was disputed, especially in the African West, where successive generations of jurists in Timbuktu pulled at the loose threads of this consensus.[14]

"GOD WILL FREE HIS EVERY LIMB"

In a recent edited volume, two prominent scholars turn this chapter's epigraph on its head in an effort to portray slavery as a fundamental element of Islamic law and piety: "Since the freeing of a slave might be a way for an individual to be freed from the torments of hell," they reason, "to abolish slavery would be to eliminate a possible path to redemption." They conclude that for this reason and because the Qur'an and the Prophet acknowledged the existence of slavery, slavery was part of the religion of Islam, and Muslims would never have considered abolition without the impetus of the Society for the Abolition of Slavery in the nineteenth century. They conclude that "there was never any formal movement for the abolition of slavery, or even the suppression of the slave trade, in the Muslim world."[15]

This chapter, based on previously unused source materials, demonstrates the falsity of the claim that Islam did not—and could not—strive to abolish the slave trade without inspiration from the West. The story of ʿAbdul-Qādir Kan and the revolutionary clerics of Senegambia turns this facile imperialist narrative upside down. Rather than learning abolitionism from Christian Europeans, these African Muslims showed them how it was done. Evidence suggests that in 1787, when the Society for the Abolition of the Slave Trade held its first meeting in London to *discuss* how to gradually end the trade, the Almaami ʿAbdul-Qādir Kan had already abolished it in Senegambia. The British did not abolish the slave trade for another twenty years. Moreover, the leading member and founder of that society, the Reverend Thomas Clarkson, knew all about the African abolitionists as early as 1789, and he wrote publicly of the Almaami ʿAbdul-Qādir, proclaiming him as a role model for the Christian kings of Europe.

ʿAbdul-Qādir Kan was a Qurʾan teacher and a specialist in Mālikī law. None of his writings have yet been uncovered, so what he may have thought of earlier scholarly precedent and juristic reasoning remains unclear. What is clear, however, is that none of the Almaami's law books had a prescription for the ills his society was facing. The enslavement of free Muslims (categorically forbidden by all *ʿulamāʾ*) had long been a problem, but it usually occurred only in isolated instances. The numbers of Muslims being sent into Atlantic and Saharan slavery in the Senegal River Valley in the century after the Tuubanaan was unprecedented, and slaving kings had murdered and enslaved countless Walking Qurʾan in retribution. Interpreting and actualizing Islam—the goal of the classical learning that the Almaami embodied and taught—meant pondering radical action. It meant interpreting Islamic law and values in an utterly changed world and improvising an Islamic solution. *Sources suggest that for Almaami ʿAbdul-Qādir, this solution involved not only ending the Atlantic slave trade from his lands but freeing the slaves within them—abolishing the institution of slavery.*

Contemporary sources claim that he effected abolition by offering freedom to any slave who would recite a verse of the Qurʾan. Whatever earlier Mālikī scholars may have thought, Kan apparently did not think that even a single verse of the Book should be kept in chains. Muslim legal authorities had struggled with this idea for centuries. Many rejected the idea that enslaved converts should be immediately freed, but a fundamental incompatibility existed between the dignity associated with Islam and the indignities of slavery. Al-Wansharīsī, a fifteenth-century North African scholar, was asked, "How is it that the profession of the monotheistic creed, which saves from death and from punishment in the other world, does not save from the humiliation and suffering of slavery?"[16] His answer rings hollow: slavery was punishment for *past* unbelief. With his deeds, the Almaami answered differently. It appears that his position was that the "monotheistic creed," "There is no god but God," should free people in this world as it frees them in the next.

Skeptics had long responded that freeing slaves who converted would lead to dissimulation. Hadith reports, quoted by Muusa Kamara in his history of Fuuta Tooro, claim that Islam's second caliph, ʿUmar b. al-Khaṭṭāb (r. 634–44), used to manumit any slaves he found praying. "It was said to him, 'Verily they are deceiving you.' He said, 'By God let us be deceived in favor of him who deceives us for God.'" He did not want to be the owner of someone who made the *ṣalāt*.[17] The fear that some would pretend to accept Islam to escape slavery does not seem to have bothered the Almaami any more than it bothered ʿUmar. Fuuta oral tradition reports that for him, the Muslim was anyone who said, "*La ilaha illa Allah*," even if it was pronounced "*ra ira'a ira Arra*."[18] This saying was supposed to refer to the accent of non-Muslim peoples from southern Senegambia whose tongues and customs were alien to the people of Fuuta. The point of the story is that *anyone* willing to profess Islam should be freed.

"*God will free his every limb from the fire as he has freed those of the slave.*" Perhaps Kan was less concerned with the worldly risks of losing the labor of slaves and more concerned with the everlasting benefits that might come to someone who freed not one or two believing Muslims but every one that he could. Perhaps when he struggled to free the slaves who recited a single verse of the Qur'an or stammered through the profession of faith, Almaami ʿAbdul-Qādir sought eternal bodily redemption not for himself (he was already a *ḥāfiẓ*) but as expiation for all the "sellers of men" among the Africans and the Muslims.

The Wise and Virtuous *"Almammy"*

Clarkson's *Letters on the Slave Trade* (1791) is one of the main sources for reconstructing the Almaami's abolitionist stance. The book is both an impassioned argument for abolition and a detailed account of trading from Senegambia.[19] Clarkson interviewed slave-ship captains, slavers, and travelers to detail the means through which people were reduced to slavery in West Africa. He became connected with Réné Geoffroy de Villeneuve, a French botanist who spoke fluent Wolof and had spent most of three years living on the Senegalese mainland in the mid-1780s. Over several weeks of meetings, Villeneuve detailed the slave trade from large ledgers in which he had recorded notes from his travels; he also detailed the Almaami's resistance, which was quite well known to slavers. Clarkson devoted the final lines of the book to recapitulating the story of the Almaami's struggle to end the slave trade:

> To the sovereigns of Europe the wise and virtuous Almammy sets [an] illustrious example in extirpating the commerce in the human race; and when we consider this amiable man as having been trained up in a land of slavery, and as having had in the introduction of such a revolution all the prejudices of education and custom to oppose; when we consider him again as sacrificing a part of his own revenue; as refusing the presents of Europeans; and as exposing himself in consequence of it to the vindictive ravages of the agents of the latter, he is certainly more to be respected than any of the sovereigns of Europe, inasmuch as he has made a much nobler sacrifice than they, and has done more for the causes of humanity, justice, liberty, and religion.[20]

Clarkson specified not only that Kan had abolished the slave trade in his own country but that he had refused Europeans passage either overland or along the Senegal River in their efforts to acquire slaves further inland. "Not satisfied with these proceedings, he made a decree as a discouragement to the Slave Trade in the beginning of the year 1787, that whereas slaves made in other distant countries had been accustomed to be passed, in their way to Fort Saint-Louis, through his dominions, no such passage should be allowed them in the future, and accordingly, at the proper season of the year, he put his decree into execution by stopping the passage of slaves."[21]

As the British would later fight to stop the passage of slaving vessels on the sea, Kan stopped slave ships in the Senegal River. European merchants responded with bribes, assuming that his resistance was mere pillage: "They tried him next by many and rich presents. But he sent them all back, adding, that he would not only hinder the route of the slaves for that year, but as long as he should live; and that if the whites should attempt any depredations on his subjects in consequence of his determination, he would retaliate."[22]

Clarkson was unequivocal that the Almaami abolished not only the trade but slavery itself, sometime before 1787: "His next step was to prohibit the sale of the persons of men, and to abolish personal slavery in his own dominions, giving encouragement to agriculture and manufactures in their place."[23] *These assertions are among a number of sources (explored below) that suggest that this African Muslim state may have been the first in the modern world to abolish slavery and the slave trade.*

Clarkson was not Kan's sole contemporary to make this claim in print. Baron Roger's novel, *Kelédor* (1828), contains the claim as well, though he does not date this abolition to the 1780s, when Villeneuve learned of it, but rather to 1775 or 1776, when Kan was appointed Almaami: "He declared that no free man from Fouta could ever more be reduced to captivity, that trade would introduce no new slaves into the country, *and that every former slave who could read a passage from the Qur'an would immediately gain his freedom.*"[24]

Though *Kelédor* is a work of fiction, the claim deserves to be taken seriously. First, it is made as a statement of fact in the book's footnotes rather than as part of the narrative. Roger was governor of Senegal when he published the book, and he spoke with his own authoritative voice in these notes. He had also been involved in establishing agricultural installations around Dagana at the fringe of Fuuta in the 1820s and knew the country very well. Finally, the book is not speculative; it is a piece of historical fiction based on Roger's travels in Fuuta and his inquiries into its history.[25] Though many details are fictionalized, the work is also largely biographical. Recent research shows that *Kelédor* was based on a life history narrative of a real person, Clef d'Or, who fought alongside the Almaami in the 1790s before being enslaved and sent to the new world. As a free man of some standing, he returned to Senegal and told his remarkable story to Baron Roger in the 1820s.[26]

AFRICAN MORAL RESISTANCE AND THE ATLANTIC SLAVE TRADE

If this chapter poses a challenge to Islamicists who pretend that slavery is an indelible part of Islam, it likewise challenges Africanists who pretend that slave trading posed no moral problems for Africans. John Thornton's *Africans and the Making of the Atlantic World* is emblematic of this viewpoint. Thornton's basic argument was that Europeans were unable to dictate the terms of slave exports from Africa and that Africans were willing participants and beneficiaries who had little reason to question slavery or the trade.[27] While some Africans unquestionably participated, many others opposed participation. Recent work shows that Africans who opposed the slave trade did so on moral and political grounds rooted in local idioms and experiences.[28] In a recent work—perhaps crafted in response to this literature on moral *resistance*—Thornton asks about the ethical frameworks African used as *justifications* for participating in the European slave trade from Africa. "African leaders *clearly participated voluntarily* in the slave trade," he writes, "but that does not mean that they did so without recognizing the ethical problems the trade presented."[29]

Thornton and some other scholars refuse to see the *prisoner's dilemma* that Atlantic demand for slaves created in Africa.[30] Instead, he persists in arguing to accent "voluntary" participation and limit European agency: "African leaders were not necessarily forced into the slave trade through their own inabilities, or the inabilities of the their countries to prevent it."[31] This stance cannot be maintained. Africanist historian and activist Walter Rodney once reproached scholars for this kind of analysis, which, under the guise of claiming agency for Africans, holds them primarily responsible for the trade in African flesh. He noted that this approach conveniently downplays the role of Europeans and creates the impression that "without European demand there would have been captives sitting on the beach by the millions."[32]

Thomas Clarkson had heard such complacent arguments before; they were made all the time by slavers. Clarkson knew better than to be taken in by such apologetics. He blamed Europeans for cultivating partners in crime: "If the conduct of the Europeans and Africans were to be compared, I fear the former would have all the reason to blush. The Europeans are represented as flocking themselves, or as sending their agents, to the courts of the African kings; as seducing these by intoxication and bribery to subvert the just principles of government, and to become wolves instead of shepherds to their people; as suggesting schemes of treachery and violence, and as being receivers of the prey. The Africans, on the other hand, though they have some bad laws and customs among them, may attribute them in great measure to the Europeans."[33]

We saw at the end of chapter 2 that when slaving kings were defeated by clerics opposing the trade, French slavers made common cause with the deposed rulers, providing soldiers, gunboats, and ammunition. Throughout Atlantic Africa, Europeans helped to feed the "wolves" and starve the "shepherds." We also saw that Europeans consciously "stimulated" slave supply in any way they could: by raiding directly, by inciting Africans (and Arabs) to raid for slaves, and by providing arms and ammunition on credit. Other consumer goods—so crucial for maintaining a following—were advanced on credit as well, stoking a wildfire of debt and competitive consumption that swept inland, fueling the slave trade.[34] When we consider that an estimated 350,000–400,000 guns per year[35] were entering West Africa in the second half of the eighteenth century, it becomes obvious that the fundamental dynamic that shaped ethical action in Atlantic Africa was the fact that even if you were not willing to trade in slaves, someone else was—and soon he would be coming to make you a slave.

Ceerno Sulaymaan Baal and the Early Years of the Revolution

Two of the major sources for accounts of the revolution are Arabic-language manuscripts on the history of Fuuta Tooro written in the late nineteenth and early twentieth centuries by classically trained Fulɓe intellectuals, Siré Abbas Soh and Shaykh Muusa Kamara.[36] Both were completed with moral and financial support from key French colonial interlocutors, especially Henri Gaden. Both Soh and Kamara carried out oral historical research among the clerisy and consulted innumerable manuscript sources. Soh's account of the early years of the movement was based in large part on a no-longer-extant manuscript written by a participant in the 1770s revolution.[37]

Ceerno Sulaymaan Baal's struggles against the Deeñanke and the Ḥasānī Arabs began in 1770 and ended with his death in 1776 (1190 A.H.).[38] After pulling the Book in chains from the riverboat, he returned to Fuuta and became a popular preacher, delivering a biting critique of the Saltigi. He began by touring the country, "preaching and demanding the people to name their own imams among their *ʿulamāʾ* and to liberate themselves from the yoke of the Deeñanke and the *bayḍān*, who demanded tribute from them."[39] Oral histories collected in the 1960s by David Robinson and James Johnson indicate that Sulaymaan Baal took the war of words straight to the king, coming to the court of Saltigi Sulay Njaay and preaching to the people about the king's iniquity. Sulaymaan Baal reportedly reproached Sulay Njaay for having more than one hundred wives, to which the Saltigi is supposed to have responded that he had only three or four and that the rest were concubines from among the *ceddo* who were his slaves.[40] This affront to the honor of *ceddo* women—and labeling them slaves rather than clients—is presented as integral to their eventual allegiance to the clerisy. In one account, Sulay Njaay was assassinated by the same *ceddo* whose honor he had defamed.[41] In any case, Sulay Njaay died mysteriously in the early 1770s.[42]

In the struggle for succession, pretenders from different parties vied for position, and Ceerno Sulaymaan capitalized on the popularity of his preaching and support from the Saltigi's *ceddo*, whom he apparently treated as free, to gain power in central Fuuta. While swaying the *ceddo* was important, so, too, was persuading the clerical lineages to participate in armed struggle. The oral tradition highlights the participation of a council of scholars who tested Ceerno Sulaymaan's fitness to lead a movement that was larger than any one man.[43] Bonds of blood and ink stretching back to common study at Pir in the eighteenth century or the Tuubanaan in the seventeenth century held together this clerisy.[44]

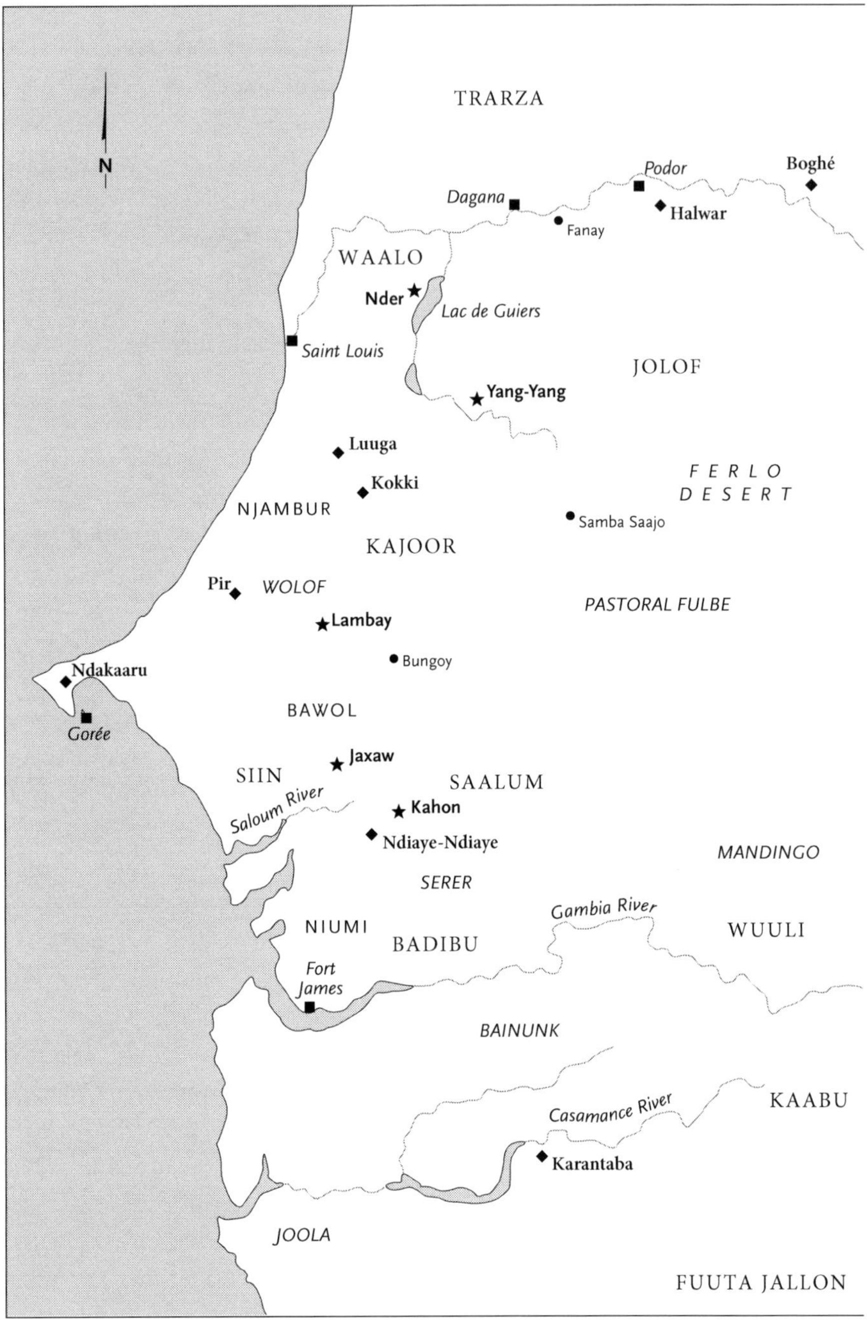

Map 3.1: Senegambia, ca. 1800

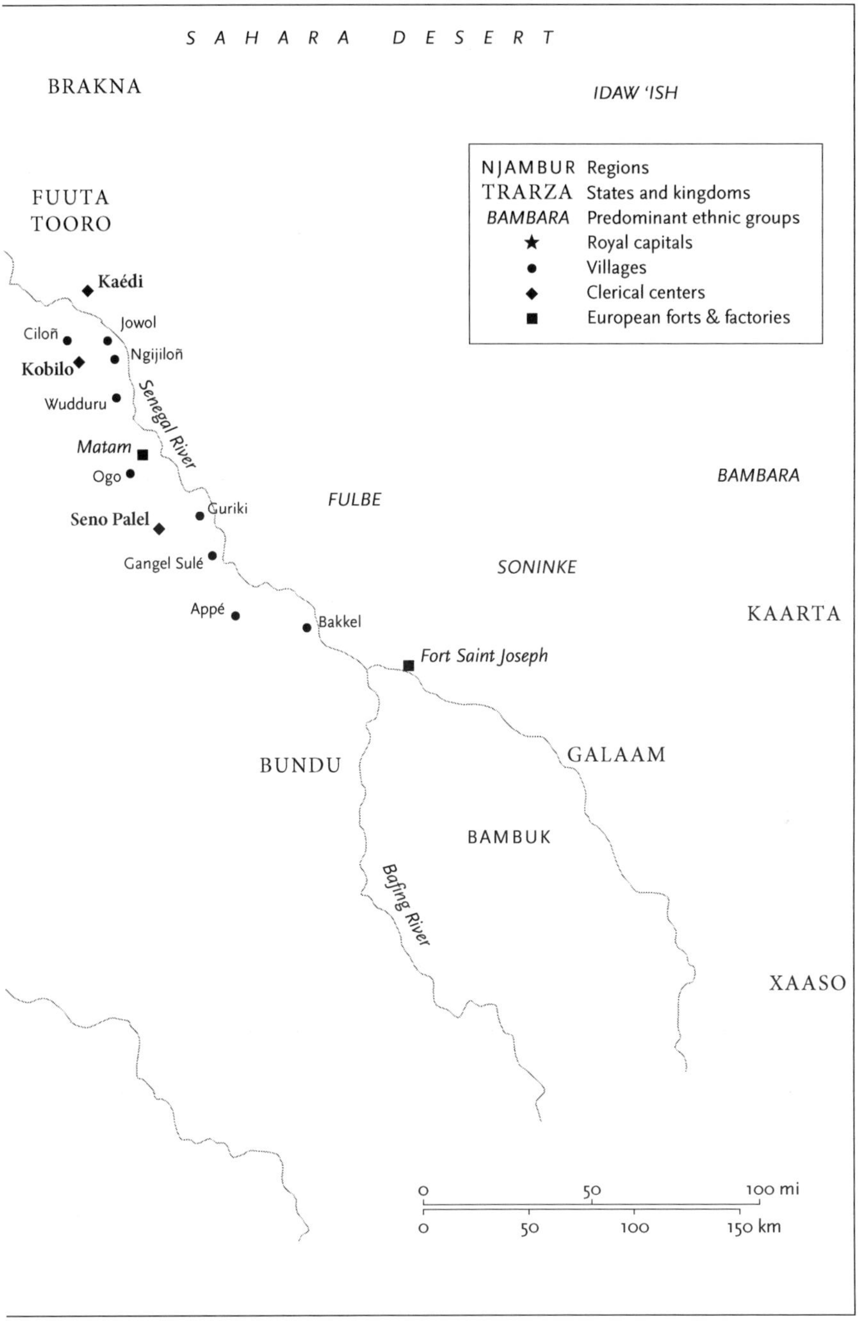
SAHARA DESERT
BRAKNA
IDAW 'ISH
NJAMBUR Regions
TRARZA States and kingdoms
BAMBARA Predominant ethnic groups
Royal capitals
Villages
Clerical centers
European forts & factories
FUUTA TOORO
Kaédi
Jowol
Ciloñ
Ngijiloñ
Kobilo
Wudduru
Senegal River
Matam
Ogo
Guriki
Seno Palel
Gangel Sulé
FULBE
SONINKE
BAMBARA
KAARTA
Appé
Bakkel
Fort Saint Joseph
GALAAM
BUNDU
BAMBUK
Bafing River
XAASO
0 50 100 mi
0 50 100 150 km

The struggle against the Saltigis and the Banī Ḥasān was rooted in knowledge. An example of the alliance of Sulaymaan Baal and the family of Ceerno Buubu Kaasum, the Jaawbe Jammbo branch of the Jah [Dia], illustrates how such allegiances at the outset of the movement were framed with reference to knowledge of the Qur'an: "Know that God put the Jaawbe Jammbo at the disposition of Ceerno Sulaymaan Baal, thanks to Ceerno Buubu Kaasum, who was from among them and who had twelve sons who were *huffāẓ*. When the latter and his son(s) came to obey Ceerno Sulaymaan, the Jaawbe Jammbo did the same and fought the [Saal of] Laam Tooro."[45] The bonds of affection and solidarity that made them one were bonds of embodied knowledge rooted in their status and self-perception as the living carriers of God's verbatim speech.

A number of other clerical families joined the Jah, leaving the clerics with a formidable coalition and significant military support from the former *ceddo*. Ceerno Sulaymaan presided over the rise of the movement and led the first years of battles. The Deeñanke had been unable to resolve their succession disputes, leaving the Tooroɓɓe party under Ceerno Sulaymaan the de facto masters of central Fuuta, while three pretenders to the Deeñanke throne controlled separate portions of Fuuta.

Word of the revolution seems to have reached Saint-Louis and Gorée—under British control at the time—as early as 1773, when a letter reported the rumor that "a Marabou (Mohammedan) king from the interior lands . . . is very powerful, and . . . will not look to end his conquests until the Kings follow his religion and renounce eau-de-vie [trade rum or brandy], after which he will leave them with a monitor [*surveillant*] and leave them alone. The brother of Çidy Mokhtar has joined his party thanks to the presents he received, and soon, I am assured, the Marabou will wage war on Çidy Mokhtar, on King Brac, and on the Damel."[46] This letter suggests that the characteristic diplomatic stance taken by Fuuta's new rulers was already established by 1773 and that control over central Fuuta was already well established. With his coalition of peasants, former *ceddo*, and clerical families, Ceerno Sulaymaan Baal was consolidating control in Fuuta and preparing to bring the revolution to the rest of Senegambia.

"His Name Is Still Used to Scare Children"

Baal's efforts were thwarted by Charles O'Hara, British governor at Saint-Louis. An abundance of British archival evidence suggests that he played a key role in the events of the mid-1770s. Forbidden to conduct trade of any kind on his own account, O'Hara nonetheless enriched himself illegally through massive slaving and misappropriation of funds. When word reached the colony of the rise of a clerical party that would be reluctant to trade in slaves, he appealed to the emir of Trārza to raid Fuuta Tooro.[47] As with the French response to the Tuubanaan, the British response here almost certainly included supplying arms and ammunition as well as financial incentives.[48] Trārza's chief, ʿAlī al-Kawrī, may also have seen the Saltigi's death as a prime opportunity to impose his will on Fuuta Tooro. With help from O'Hara, Trārza struck the Senegal River Valley and raided for slaves.[49]

The fighting was brutal and began to strongly favor Trārza by the middle of 1775, as is demonstrated by O'Hara's August letter to his superiors. It has been cited in a handful of sources, always as evidence of the depredations of the Moors in Senegambia or even as evidence of the brutal "Arab slave trade." Yet it was a Briton, Charles O'Hara, who was fueling the chaos while concealing his involvement: "Within these two months, the Moors have totally subdued all the different nations of negroes inhabiting the banks of this river in the neighborhood of Senegal. They have killed and sold many thousands, and obliged others to fly the country."[50]

In fact, O'Hara's profiteering was not limited to side deals with Trārza. The racially diverse French-speaking inhabitants of Saint-Louis accused him of stealing slaves, goods, and free persons alike, activities that led to punitive raids (probably from Fuuta) against European boats in the Senegal River. The French-speakers recounted several incidents in which O'Hara had partnered with Africans to produce slaves, only to turn on them and enslave his erstwhile partners. "And this is the way he uses all the Kings about the country, fraind [*sic*] to one today & turn enemy to him Next day. Therefore we are constantly in disturbance."[51] O'Hara's chief lieutenant, Matthias McNamara, suggests that O'Hara personally enslaved so many Fulɓe that he provoked war on the colony and a blockade against trade: "Governor O'Hara having sent to the West Indies many of the Pooles, or Fullars, on his destroying Fort George it made such a breach with that nation which I fear will never be settled, they having lately cut off a vessel of cargoe on a voyage to Gallam, this state being independant [*sic*] will entirely destroy our trade here."[52] This letter shows that the blockade against the French in 1787 was not a new policy. The Almaami or perhaps even Sulaymaan Baal had instituted an embargo against slave trading on the Senegal River as early as 1776.

McNamara wrote to the secretary of state in London as acting governor of British Senegambia on 1 July 1776, after a June coup had deposed O'Hara. At this point, he further explained the animosity O'Hara had sown: "The chief of the Pooles or Fulla country still resents the injuries done him by Governor O'Hara. *I have sent messengers to him, none of which have ever returned*, so that I never could get any satisfactory answer from that chief, but understand that he means to stop the Galam Fleet. However to guard against him, I have purchased the Dorset sloop of 90 tons as a convoy, which, well manned & armed, I hope will force her way through."[53]

The leaders of the revolution had obviously had enough of the Europeans. McNamara's effort to force through the Fuutankoobe barricade of the Senegal River did not produce the desired effect. O'Hara had brought chaos to the Senegal River Valley: "By the intestine wars and depredations of the Moors on all the adjacent kingdoms to this River, they are entirely depopulated & dispersed."[54] This was just part of O'Hara's legacy in Senegambia. His kidnappings and arbitrary violence were the stuff of legend. In 1811, thirty-five years after O'Hara was relieved of duty, the last British lieutenant governor of Senegambia mentioned in an official report that the name "O'Hara" was still used in the mainland kingdom of Waalo to frighten children.[55]

THE DEATH OF CEERNO SULAYMAAN

In 1773, the clerical movement was on the verge of victory. By 1777, O'Hara's support of an invasion from Trārza had created three years of "continual war."[56] Almost exactly one hundred years earlier, Chambonneau had intervened in a similar way to ensure that Muslim clerics would not withdraw Senegambia from the Euro-American slave trade. Perhaps some of the clerics thought that their movement was coming to a similar end and that they, too, would be sold as slaves in punishment when Ceerno Sulaymaan was killed sometime in 1776 in a fight against the Banī Ḥasān. A serious though perhaps not unanticipated problem of leadership resulted. Ceerno Sulaymaan often led his troops into battle, and Muusa Kamara claims that he routinely prepared them for the possibility of his death:

> I do not know if I will die in this battle, if I die name a knowledgeable imam, pious and ascetic, who does not interest himself in this world; and if you find that his possessions are growing, depose him and take his possessions from him; and if he refuses to abdicate, fight him and hunt him so that he will not establish a tyranny which his sons will inherit. Replace him with another, among the people of knowledge and action, from any of the clans. Never leave power inside one clan alone, so that it does not become hereditary. Put in power the one who merits it, one who forbids his soldiers to kill children and old men without strength, to undress the women, and most of all to kill them.[57]

This soliloquy is too poetic to have been said in such a neat form, but it is likely that a leader who fought at the head of his troops would discuss such matters.

In any case, the solution to Baal's succession had apparently already been partly faced. A number of sources agree that Ceerno Sulaymaan Baal never claimed for himself the title of Almaami, offering it instead offered to two humble teachers. The first was ʿAbdul-Karīm, who taught Qurʾan and the sciences at Seno Palel. When he refused, the clerics turned to ʿAbdul-Qādir Kan. Kan was a teacher of Qurʾan and Mālikī *fiqh* in Appé, a village on the eastern fringes of Fuuta, near Bundu, where he had long served as an independent *qāḍī*, arbitrating disputes between Muslims. Like much of the movement's leadership, he had studied at Pir. Heir to the traditions of the clerisy outlined in chapter 2, Kan's father, Hamadi, had studied the Islamic sciences in Jāgha, the archetypal West African city of God.[58] That he was a direct heir to this center of clerical autonomy and pious distance from power perhaps helps explain why Kan was not interested in becoming Fuuta Tooro's first imam. Like many clerics, he probably considered politics a shamefully worldly concern. Muusa Kamara's account also strongly suggests that he did not fully trust some of the clerics involved and that he was particularly concerned by the presence of some unlettered Deeñanke princes who had sworn their fealty to the clerics.[59] In the end, however, he reconsidered his position and accepted the imamate when Ceerno Sulaymaan Baal was shot dead in the ever worsening battles against the Ḥasān.[60]

Almaami ʿAbdul-Qādir Kan and the 1776 Revolution

In the ideal of the clerisy, the basis of political authority would be religious knowledge, not an inherited familial title. They chose to call their first ruler only *al-Imām* (Almaami in Fula). He would rule in the name of Islamic learning rather than in the name of narrow familial interests. Not surprisingly, knowledge sacralized his inauguration: "Almaami ʿAbdul-Qādir asked them to read the Qurʾan in its entirety, which they did, then he asked them to read the *ʿIshrīniyyāt* known among us by the name Ibn Mahīb, which they did. He then asked them to read *Dalāʾil al-khayrāt*, which they did. Afterward he said to them, 'May the learned commit themselves to setting me back on the right path if they see that I am in error.' And the learned did so swear."[61] In 1776, after reciting the Book of God and two famous devotional poems honoring the Prophet, no fewer than fifty chiefs of Fuuta swore never to betray the first Almaami of Fuuta Tooro, ʿAbdul-Qādir Kān. It would be thirty years before some of those present that day would break their promise and plot to assassinate him.

Very shortly after assuming power, Almaami ʿAbdul-Qādir turned the tide of the battle with the Ḥasān. How he did so is still unclear. His enemies remained in league with the British until the early 1780s.[62] Trārza was well-armed and ruthless and had been laying waste to the valley for three or four years. Johnson and Robinson offer little explanation for how Kan gained the upper hand in the war.[63] Internal sources such as Muusa Kamara's account stressed the role of esoteric practices to unlock the power of God's speech against their enemies: "They say that Ceerno Sulaymaan Baal or Almaami ʿAbdul-Qādir put the [Qurʾan] verse: 'Leave our country or enter our religion' in a pentagon, empty in the middle, and in this space they listed the chiefs of the Deeñanke, as do the people of this art; and God Most High is the most knowing."[64] Secret sciences were certainly widely employed by the clerics in this struggle. But clerics rarely depended *only* on work in the unseen world to produce results in the seen. A close reading of the sources suggests that one particularly earthly intervention by the Almaami may have been decisive.

A PRECOCIOUS ABOLITION?

Johnson and Robinson noted that the Almaami consolidated his rule through a series of successful military campaigns against Trārza from 1776–77 forward, culminating in a decisive victory in 1786. They also agree that the Almaami gave land grants to former *ceddo* of the Deeñanke on the north bank of the river for defensive purposes and to cut off the *bayḍān* groups' access to the river.[65] Because neither Robinson nor Johnson had access to Clarkson's manuscripts or the British archival material in their pioneering works they never asked what seems to me a pertinent question: *Did the Almaami free the slaves and commission them to fight?*[66]

Though it cannot be definitively demonstrated in the current state of research, I think it likely that this how the Almaami turned the tide against Trārza. The former *ceddo* who received grants of land in the river valley suggests this. The Sahara was home to many black slaves of diverse origins, and freeing the slaves of one's enemies had become a common tactic in military conflicts in both Africa and the Americas.[67] This strategy generally weakened political rivals since slavery was central to governance and often turned the tide of a war by swelling the ranks of one party as it emptied the other.[68] In some cases, domestic slaves were offered freedom in exchange for military service. Ceerno Sulaymaan won the allegiance of the *ceddo* by recognizing their claims to freedom and family honor. There is reason to believe that this was an important strategy used by both Ceerno Sulaymaan and the Almaami ʿAbdul-Qādir.

In spite of esoteric and political efforts to rid Fuuta of the Deeñanke, this goal was never fully accomplished. A French slave trader named Saugnier published a candid account of his activities in Senegambia from 1784 to 1786. It shows that Deeñanke princes in the far eastern regions of Fuuta continued to plague the Almaami nearly a decade after he assumed power: "They are commanded by a prince, who, by birthright, should have been king of the Poules; but the priests fleeced him, and chased him from his country. This prince is courageous, he makes frequent incursions into the land of the Poules, and sells all his captives to the neighboring Moors, who take them to Senegal. We always acquire some of them, *in spite of the treaty made with the Almamy to not buy anyone of his nation*, no doubt because one believes that this treaty only holds when one comes to his country in a convoy to go up to Galam."[69] His account confirms the existence of a treaty exempting the people of Fuuta from enslavement, but it also details French and Deeñanke efforts to circumvent the treaty.[70]

Saugnier also adds insight to Clarkson's suggestion that the slave trade had been effectively abolished within Fuuta in this period and that agriculture and industry were being pursued in its place. Of course, as a slaver, he lamented this development. "The trade we have with these people is nothing much. We pull from this country only the millet necessary for the colony, some tobacco and a little bit of morphil [unprocessed tusks]."[71] He also details the economic activity of the people of Fuuta in the colony: "The Poules come never or rarely to sell their captives; they bring their produce to the colony, but *they never drink*. Their palabres are not as long; and when they see some merchandise which they like, they give money which they have procured for themselves in the colony, by selling their millet, their furs, their morphil, etc. The merchandise which attracts them to the colony the most are iron and wool."[72]

In the current state of research, it is difficult to establish the precise nature of economic activity within Fuuta, but it appears that there was little if any slave trade and that merchants from Fuuta paid for goods in cash rather than in slaves. Saugnier's account also shows that Fuuta's agricultural productivity was, as Clarkson suggested, part of its ability to withdraw from the slave trade. Instead, the people of Fuuta traded food, especially to the French colony at Saint-Louis, which had a dense population and little cultivable land.

SANGARA

In the struggle against Trārza, the Almaami had the aid of Hammet Mukhtār, emir of Brākna, a smaller *bayḍān* polity that was frequently in competition with Trārza.[73] Observers in the 1780s had no doubts that Fuuta was the dominant partner in this arrangement.[74] Hammet Mukhtār owed his position of leadership in Brākna to Sulaymaan Baal's support in a coup against Hammet's brother, Sīdī Mukhtār, in the mid-1770s.[75] Hammet also appears to have been a sincere convert to the clerical cause; British customs lists include no shipments of alcohol to Brākna.[76]

Conversely, ʿAlī al-Kawrī of Trārza, the brak of Waalo, and the dammel of Kajoor continued to import liquor in exchange for Muslims. Would they abandon both of these traditional prerogatives of princes on the orders of a rabble of clerics, peasants, and former slaves?[77] French slaver Dominique Lamiral claims that he witnessed the reactions of the brak of Waalo and the dammel of Kajoor when they received the Almaami's ultimatum: "[Almaami vowed] to make the kings and the subjects a people of marabouts. He sent some ambassadors to order the king Damel and Brak to have their heads shaved and to wear a turban, and to impose on them the obligation of renouncing alcoholic drinks, and that in eight days he would come in person to receive their oath. Damel is a big drunkard and a coward: he had his head shaved and promised all that was desired. Brak, who is no more sober, but more resolute, was content to say in a very low voice, '*sa-sar-amday*,' which is the biggest insult one can utter in this country."[78]

Along with enslaving Muslims, drinking alcohol (*sangara*) was another way that kings flouted Islam, infuriating the clerics. Ḥasānī princes also drank, and many kings and *ceddo* from the sixteenth through the nineteenth centuries were obviously alcoholics.[79] Contemporary European accounts and oral traditions describe some rulers as drinking alcohol continuously every day without exception.[80] Clarkson's research with slave-ship captains led him to conclude that "seducing . . . by intoxication" was an explicit strategy of slavers.[81]

Archival sources confirm that these kings and *ceddo* drank a lot, even (or especially) on religious holidays. Customs lists from 1782 show that the brak received 150 French francs worth of "*eau-de-vie* that one gives to the king for each Mohammedan feasts." The dammel of Kajoor also received liquor "for the Mohammedan feasts of Corry, Tabarky, and Gamou valued at 150 FF."[82] That they imported *sangara* to celebrate the end of Ramadan (*korité*), the Feast of the Sacrifice (*tabaski*), and the Prophet's birthday (*gaamu* in Wolof, *mawlid* in Arabic) must have struck the clerics as perverse, especially since they traded the bodies of believing peasants for these intoxicants. Whether or not the dammel honored his oath to abandon *sangara*, he did swear fealty to the Almaami, enabling Kajoor to sit in peace while Waalo and Trārza faced an intimidating army.[83]

ARMAGEDDON

In Islamic eschatology, the Mahdī will be a victorious imam who comes at the end of the world to announce the return of Jesus and the beginning of the last days. He will be a soldier of good who will fight the *dajjāl*, the Antichrist. Many Muslims have expected his appearance to coincide with the end of a century in Islam's lunar calendar; the Almaami prepared for the biggest war anyone could remember in the millennial year 1200 A.H. (1786 C.E.) Some must have thought that the wholesale enslavement of the Muslims and the desecration of the Walking Qur'an were signs of Armageddon's approach. Rumors that the Almaami might be the Mahdi surely circulated as he prepared to face ʿAlī al-Kawrī, the chief of Trārza whose men had ravaged the Senegal River in the mid-1770s and killed Ceerno Sulaymaan Baal. Lamiral ignored Muslim eschatology, but his account captures the gravity of the moment:

> Finally the army started to march; it was composed of approximately thirty thousand men, most of whom were armed with lances; priests commanded it. It joined with that of Hamet Moctar, less numerous but better armed and more warlike. Everyone in these armies had a desire to conquer, but each one had a different goal. The Moors wanted to ravage everything and to take as many slaves as they could. The Peuls, on the contrary, commanded by priests, wanted to ravage everything not to take slaves, they said, but to submit them to the cult of Mahomet: *They cried liberty everywhere*: they said that they wanted nothing from the people, that on the contrary they came to set them free. They said to them, *so long as your king is not a marabou, you will not be free.*[84]

Lamiral was an avowed enemy of the London abolitionists, especially Clarkson, who was also instrumental in the creation of the first French abolitionist group, La Société des Amis des Noirs, in the late 1780s. His account comes from an explicitly antiabolitionist treatise, but even the committed slaver can only represent the battle of 1786 as the culmination of the clerical struggle for liberty.

The clerical coalition routed the slavers. The army of Fuuta killed ʿAlī al-Kawrī, the most feared *bayḍān* slaver, and "Almamy returned more powerful

The Army of Fuuta Tooro, from a sketch drawn by Mollien, ca. 1810.

and revered than ever."[85] He was extolled in poetry by the prominent *bayḍān* cleric Mukhtār b. Būnah al-Jakanī (d. 1805–6).

It has long been noted that Mukhtār wuld Būnah, as he is known locally, was a lifelong friend and confidant of the Almaami.[86] Robinson specified that the two men were classmates in the southwest Sahara, but academics have seldom noted that their teacher was a woman. Khadīja (or Ghadīja) bint Muḥammad al-ʿĀqil specialized in grammar, theology, and law and was considered by many of her peers to be the most accomplished *bayḍān* scholar of the eighteenth century. She taught the exoteric and esoteric sciences alike to a number of the most prominent figures of the late eighteenth century in the greater Senegambian Sahara.[87] Wuld Būnah's words capture the feeling of deliverance that swept over this clerisy, whose ties of blood and ink crossed national, linguistic, and racial boundaries:

> I pray that God forgive any sins of ʿAbdul-Qādir, the magnanimous ruler.
> May He guide him on the Right Path and aid him for the rest of his life.
> Servants of God, say Amen! When I pray to God for this imam.
> For a prayer for him is a prayer for all the Muslims.

Understand that I say God is satisfied with his actions, words, and intentions.
After the Holy Month, he led the campaigns to punish those who had attacked.
The progeny of Shem and Ham alike are grateful for his justice in all his deeds.[88]

FIGHTING FOR FREEDOM

This was a period of heady success for the Almaami. The French had to pay tribute to him, as did Trārza and Brākna, which were directly under his vassalage, as were Waalo, Kajoor, Bawol, and Jolof.[89] The Almaami had reassembled the pieces of the Jolof Federation and united Senegambia for the first time since the early 1500s. He sought to implement new political and economic policies that would end the enslavement of Muslims and indeed the entire Atlantic trade from Senegambia. When the French post on the island of Saint-Louis bristled at these terms, he cut off the supply of food that reached the coast, attempting to starve French merchants into compliance. Almaami ʿAbdul-Qādir attempted to normalize relations with the French, but on terms that were astonishingly favorable for an African sovereign in the Atlantic era. His 1785 agreement included prohibition of the enslavement of Muslims and heavy taxes on the French, explicitly referred to in later French documents as *jizya* (sharia-derived taxes for protected minorities in Muslim polities).[90]

The French were reestablishing control over what had been—for a generation—a British colony. The 1785 treaty was part of this, and thereafter observers began to pay closer attention to goings-on in Fuuta. Sometime between 1786 and 1789, Antoine Pruneau de Pommegorge, a former governor of the French fort at Saint-Louis, wrote an account that confirms not only that word about the Almaami was spreading but also the details and tenor of Clarkson's account of abolition:

> A marabout or priest of the law has managed through his intrigues, and under pretense of religion, to drive off Siratique-Conco, the legitimate sovereign and to make himself king of the country. He has forced all of the nobles of his kingdom to make themselves marabouts like himself. He has forbidden pillages and the taking of any captives at all throughout his country, and finally, by other political (and at heart very humane) means, he has been able to repopulate his vast kingdom, attracting many peoples there, where they find security. He is even becoming quite formidable to

all his neighbors, due to his good governance. Thus here is a man who gives a lesson in humanity to other civilized peoples [*peuples policés*] by forbidding in all of his states captivity and oppression.[91]

Pommegorge's account also highlights that migration into Fuuta from neighboring regions appears to have been significant, as the Almaami's stance about protecting anyone he could from enslavement was obviously widely known.

■ Saugnier and other French traders understood the treaty agreements with the Almaami to mean that they were forbidden to buy people from Fuuta. French merchants tried to circumvent the agreements and complained incessantly about the Almaami's "disruptions" of trade.[92] They tired of negotiations, punitive sackings of their vessels, and high customs, but they never seemed to grasp the basic problem: from the perspective of the clerics, no normal trade could be carried out between the parties as long as Muslims were being taken as slaves. A 1789 letter from Almaami ʿAbdul-Qādir Kan to Governor Blanchot of Saint-Louis highlights this. The missive was sent after three Tooroɓɓe children were purchased by two French agents under circumstances that are not fully clear. The Almaami's response, however, was unambiguous: "You can find another place to make your commerce, and we warn you that all who come to us for trade will be killed and massacred if you do not return to us our children. Would a hungry person nonetheless abstain if he were served a thing mixed with his own blood? We absolutely do not want you to buy Muslims, from near or far. . . . I repeat, this letter is to let you know that if your intentions are still to buy Muslims, you need only stay home and never return to our country, for all those who come can be assured of losing their lives."[93]

The Almaami continued to have his men harass French boats in the river when they would not abide by these terms.[94] Yet ʿAbdul-Qādir needed guns, which Deeñanke enemies with Bambara connections could acquire easily from the British on the Gambia.[95] And while he did not import *sangara* to distribute to his followers the way that *ceddo* kings did, trade goods were still extremely important for maintaining power and status. The centrifugal logic of the Atlantic era was that if a ruler did not trade slaves with the Europeans, someone else in his kingdom would. With enough guns for war and goods to secure the people's allegiance, those rivals would eventually take control of the country.

ʿAbdul-Qādir needed trade to stay in power, but he would not eat a thing mixed with the blood of slaves. Instead, he forbade the Europeans from using his river to reach sources of slaves in the interior, and his merchants sold millet, furs, and other primary products. In the end, the dispossessed Deeñanke, disgruntled clerics, and French and Bambara slavers thirsty for the trade came to take Fuuta away from the Almaami, but they did not succeed for another two decades. In the late 1780s, the Almaami was at the height of his power and popularity. He built mosques, appointed imams, and developed schools.[96] The second decade of the Almaami's rule, from 1786 to 1796, was a time of internal effort to try to remake Fuuta into the kind of just Islamic society that clerics had sought to build for centuries.

Kajoor Ablaze

In the mid-1790s, things began to come apart for the Almaami. When Amari Ngone Ndella Kumba Faal became the dammel of Kajoor in 1790, he was furious that his predecessor had sworn fealty to a lowly cleric. Like many worldly kings, he believed that nobility was found in the blood and at the point of a sword, not something one could earn through study and piety. He did not incite a conflict right away, but by the middle of the decade, the two nations were on the verge of war.

The precise sequence of events is difficult to untangle given the imprecisions in dating much of the oral material, but Amari Ndella seems to have refused to renew Kajoor's submission to formal overlordship by the Almaami of Fuuta Tooro. At this time, some clerics in Njambuur province in Kajoor began agitating against the new dammel. Though most spoke Wolof as their mother tongue, many were tied through marriage and scholarly connections to the Almaami and the clerics in Fuuta.[97] Malamin Saar was the *sëriñ* of Luuga, a major clerical center. In the oral traditions of the clerical families of Kajoor as related by Lucie Colvin, the dammel attacked them, capturing many of Saar's party and selling some of them—including one of Saar's sons—to the Ḥasān. This sale of *huffāẓ al-Qur'ān* prompted a fierce response from Saar and his followers, who gained retribution by capturing some of the dammel's men and selling them to French traders.[98] The dammel then had Malamin Saar assassinated.[99]

At this point, the *sëriñ* of Kokki, a school second only to Pir in reputation, called together the clerisy of Kajoor to determine how to "combat the villains who sowed tyranny and injustice on Earth and who shed blood without reason."[100] Again, the clerics were galvanized by the abuse and enslavement of the carriers of the Qur'an. These Wolof *sëriñs* then prepared themselves for open war against their dammel. But the dammel surprised them at Caxrew and exacted a brutal retribution for the challenge to his sovereignty. In the oral traditions of the clerics, he killed countless readers of the Qurʾan and reduced countless others to slavery.[101] The field at Caxrew was strewn with the broken bodies of Walking Qurʾan, and iron bonds were fastened to the rest as they were rushed away for sale to the French and the Ḥasān.

After hearing of the devastation of the clerics of Kajoor, the Senegambian clerisy as a whole was in an uproar. The *sëriñ* at Kokki, Balla Faxujja, wrote to Almaami ʿAbdul-Qādir to take action. The Almaami had studied grammar and rhetoric with the man's father in the first half of the eighteenth century.[102] He called on the loyalty of bonds of ink. Furthermore, the ruler of Jolof—once the imperial center of Senegambia but now a landlocked polity of minor importance—had lost a brother in the massacre of the clerics. He chose to ally himself with Almaami ʿAbdul-Qādir Kan to settle the matter. The latter sent emissaries to the court of the dammel to invite him to repentance, an Islamic lifestyle as defined by the clerics, and subordination to the Almaami, lest he face a jihad from Fuuta and Jolof. Their main religious dispute with the dammel was that it was against the sharia to enslave Muslims and especially odious to sell them to Christians.[103] Baron Roger's representation of the Almaami's message to the dammel captures this: "Reproach him for not sufficiently observing the religion and for not enforcing its respect in his states; tell him that it is against the law of God to arbitrarily reduce free men to slavery, *to not give freedom to slaves who read the Koran*, to sell Muḥammadans to Christians; tell him that he must from now on abstain from fermented drink, that he must repent."[104]

■ Mungo Park, the Scottish explorer who was in Senegambia in 1796–97 as these events unfolded, heard the story of what happened next from the griots countless times during his travels. According to Park, Almaami's emissaries came before the dammel bearing two large knives affixed to long poles: "The two knives were accordingly laid before Damel, and the ambassador explained himself as follows: 'With this knife (said he) Abdulkader will condescend to shave the head of Damel, if Damel will embrace the Mahomedan faith; and with this other knife, Abdulkader will cut the throat of Damel, if Damel refuses to embrace it:—take your choice."[105] The dammel's reply, that he wanted the Almaami neither as a barber nor as an executioner, suggested that he was ready for war.[106]

Almaami ʿAbdul-Qādir apparently sent another emissary, Tafsiir Hamadi Ibra Ba, a classmate from Pir, to extend another offer to the dammel. Conventional Mālikī stipulations regarding a jihad are that offers of peace in exchange for submission or accord should be made at least three times, and in fact as many as seven missions may have been sent to Kajoor to attempt a peaceful resolution. In any case, Tafsiir Hamadi was a sensible choice of emissary. Originally from Fuuta, he spent much of his time in Kajoor, where he had two wives and several sons. In a stunning move, Dammel Amari ambushed and murdered Tafsiir Hammadi and his party in the mosque as they prayed. He then deported the cleric's wives to Fuuta and imprisoned two of his sons.[107] *Tafsīr* (Qur'an exegesis in Arabic) is the usual title given in Fula to an exegete of the Qur'an. It is also used as an honorific, so whether Hamadi Ibra Ba was only a Walking Qur'an or also a walking exegesis is unclear. In either case, his murder constituted a brutal violation of stately protocol and clerical immunity. This was the last straw. There was nothing left but war.

■ At the end of 1796, Almaami ʿAbdul-Qādir Kan, who had vanquished the Deeñanke, brought Trārza to its knees, and abolished the slave trade from his dominions, departed for Kajoor at the head of a massive army estimated at roughly thirty thousand men. The oral traditions and contemporary accounts agree on most of what happened next. Crossing the semidesert region of Ferlo between Fuuta and Kajoor, the Almaami found that his enemy had pursued a scorched-earth tactic. According to Park,

> The inhabitants of the towns and villages filled up their wells, destroyed their provisions and abandoned their dwellings as he approached. By this means he was led on from place to place, until he had advanced three days' journey into the country of the Jaloffs [Wolofs—in this case, Kajoor]. He had, indeed, met with no opposition; but his army had suffered so much from scarcity of water, that several of his men had died by the way. This induced him to direct his march towards a watering place in the woods, where his men, having quenched their thirst, and being overcome with fatigue, lay down carelessly to sleep among the bushes. In this situation they were attacked by Damel before daybreak, and completely routed. Many of them were trampled to death as they lay asleep, by the Jaloff horses; others were killed in attempting to make their escape; and still a greater number were taken prisoners. Among the latter, was Abdulkader himself.[108]

Other accounts suggest that there were skirmishes between the dammel's forces and Kan's men as the latter crossed the Ferlo, and that there was a significant battle at Bunguye. In any case, the affair ended in a rout favoring the dammel. According to Shaykh Mussa Kamara, two internal narratives claim that Almaami ʿAbdul-Qādir Kan was brought to this end through treachery, betrayed either by one of his disciples or by the ruler of Jolof. But whatever the precise machinations of his enemies, several stories suggest that Almaami ʿAbdul-Qādir fought valiantly at the Battle of Bunguye, displaying a heroism well remembered by his enemies' griots. According to Ahmadou Bamba Diop, "In the words of the Cayorians, the hero of the day was the almamy, Abdou Khadre himself, who fought like a lion. Carried away by his own zeal, he got himself ahead, and his imprudence cost him his freedom."[109] The warrior-scholar was taken prisoner and put in chains.

THE ALMAAMI AND THE DAMMEL

The Almaami's life was now in the hands of the Dammel Amari. According to Park, the Almaami was brought before the dammel in irons and hurled to the ground. Amari Ngone is supposed to have asked him, "If the chance of war had placed me in your situation and you in mine, how would you have treated me?' 'I would have thrust my spear into your heart,' returned Abdulkader with great firmness; 'and I know that a similar fate awaits me.'"[110] But it did not. The dammel chose to spare his life. The Almaami was unimpressed by the reprieve. Kajoor traditions report that he replied to this clemency with defiance: "Truly a 'pagan'—even if a king—is nothing. If, favored by chance, I had taken you prisoner, your head would have long since left your shoulders and your soul rejoined the fire."[111]

The decision to spare the Almaami's life was stunning. Park, who heard the griots recount this part of the story with approval many times, seems to believe it only because he heard it corroborated "by Europeans on the Gambia, by some of the French at Goree; and confirmed by nine slaves, who were taken prisoners along with Abdulkader, by the watering place in the woods, and carried in the same ship with me to the West Indies."[112]

Some of the Kajoor clerics who had not participated in the uprising seem to have intervened and asked the dammel not to execute the Almaami.[113] The force of this clerical intervention may have been strengthened by a striking twist of fate. In the traditions of the school of Pir, the dammel had favored killing his enemy until he was dissuaded by one of his own court clerics: "This man that you wish to kill is Abdoul-Khadre Kane. He was a *taalibé* at the Islamic University of Pir. The day of your baptism [*ʿaqīqa* or *gente*—naming ceremony], Sëriñ Pir sent to Mbuul [capital of Kajoor] a delegation charged with celebrating the religious ceremony. The same Abdoul-Khadre took you in his arms to say the ritual prayers. If, by the grace of God, you have today become the dammel, you must honor his person and liberate him."[114]

Whether or not this specific interventions occurred, all sources agree that the dammel and his entourage shared a more general fear of killing the cleric lest they incur some sort of divine retribution.[115] In Roger's fictionalized account, even the Almaami's simple Qur'an students and ordinary soldiers inspired religious awe in their captors: the people of Kajoor requested that the prisoners write talismans for them.[116] According to Wolof traditions collected by A. B. Diop, the idea of violating the sanctity of ʿAbdul-Qādir's *body* particularly bothered the soldiers of Kajoor: "The dammel spared the life of the Almaami on the counsel of his leading warriors, who feared that the blood of such a man could only bring misfortune to the country."[117] Deeply rooted in the hearts of the people was the belief that the sanctified blood of an extraordinary *walī* (holy person, friend of God) touching the earth of Kajoor could have caused calamity, famine, or pestilence.

■ But if the dammel would not kill this particular cleric or sell him across the ocean as he had so many others, he nonetheless wanted to politically neutralize his foe and held him captive for three months.[118] If we believe the *bayḍān*, Fuuta, and Wolof written and oral traditions, then he performed a number of miracles during his internment, all of them fully consonant with his status as a powerful carrier of the Word. In some accounts, these miracles led directly to his release. In one tale, when challenged by one of the dammel's court clerics about the worldly intentions of his jihad, he is said to have reprimanded the cleric like a dog; the court cleric then "began barking exactly like a dog, the whole day he stayed in that state until the night, then he died."[119] This incident sparked the dammel to free the Almaami.[120]

Attacking the Almaami's Authority

Whatever the reasons for his release, the Almaami seems to have struggled to fully regain his power. In his absence, powerful Deeñanke families and disgruntled clerics made common cause. Returning from his imprisonment in 1797, the Almaami found that his home had been ransacked by enemies and that some of the Fuutankoobe elite (particularly in Ogo) refused to renew their allegiance to him. Kan contemplated swift action, but he took Mālikī understandings of the legal requirements for jihad very seriously. Though he was a specialist in law, he consulted another scholar, Hammadu Lamin Baal, on the legality of waging war on those who had sworn their allegiance (*bayʿa*) but now challenged his authority. Their deliberations centered on precedents in a Mālikī legal text, the Mukhtaṣar of Khalīl b. Ishāq al-Jundī (d. 1365), and the principle that those who willfully separate from the imam and refuse to follow his authority may be fought. Hammadu Lamin confirmed Kan's right to attack Ogo, but the latter demurred. Rather than burning the village of Ogo, he had a messenger symbolically light a handful of grass at the threshold of each home to indicate that they could have been burned but the Almaami wanted to keep the peace.[121]

Some Deeñanke had long sought to reassert their independence, and some clerics, especially in Ogo and Ciloñ, clearly resented his power and began directly to test the limits of the Almaami's authority. The first instance, which appears to have taken place in 1799–1800, involved the concealment of a murder case by a powerful family head, Eliman Coday Kan. One of his dependents had committed a murder, which he sought to conceal to save his kinsman from the Qur'anically mandated punishment (*ḥudūd*). Almaami ʿAbdul-Qādir insisted on its application in all relevant cases whether the offender was rich or poor. Kamara does not know whether capital punishment was in fact applied, but given the circumstance, it is likely that the offender was sent into hiding. For the crime of lying to the judge and concealing the matter from the Almaami, Eliman Coday was sentenced to lashes, but when the court's agent raised the lash to strike the man, he was shot dead by one of Coday's kinsmen.

Fuuta was reverting to what it had been under the Deeñanke—powerful clans made their own law. In roughly the same period, the Almaami alienated two powerful unlettered Deeñanke princes. ʿAlī Dunndu Kan and ʿAlī Sīdī Ba, for similar reasons. He attempted to enforce *ḥudūd* punishments in murder and rape cases involving their clan members. Scholars have represented this rigid interpretation of sharia as alienating, which it certainly must have been, and suggested that the Almaami may have been attempting to reassert his authority after a period of humiliating imprisonment.[122] This argument originally comes from *Kelédor*, where Roger opines that after his imprisonment, the Almaami "governed with such a restless, despotic spirit that he brought on a new revolution in which he was assassinated by the chiefs of the country."[123] This explanation comes directly from the clerics that undid Kan and his revolution.

I think it more helpful to see these rulings in the light of hadith, since the Almaami, a specialist in law, likely saw them this way. A very famous hadith concerns a wellborn woman from Quraysh (the Prophet's clan) who was convicted of theft. When it became clear that the *ḥudūd* punishment of cutting off her hand was to be imposed, members of her tribe hesitated and asked their clan chief to plead for clemency from the Prophet. He is said to have responded with a public address: "O people, those who have gone before you were destroyed, because if anyone of high rank committed theft among them, they spared him; and if anyone of low rank committed theft, they inflicted the prescribed punishment upon him. By God, if Fatima, daughter of Muḥammad, were to steal, I would have her hand cut off."[124]

If justice—especially capital punishment—is imposed only on the weak, it is not justice at all. For the Almaami, using the law against the weak or as a tool of enslavement was the definition of oppression. If the families of princes committed crimes, their "nobility" would not place them above the law. For many classically trained scholars, sharia is not only about *enforcing the law* but also about *dispensing justice*. The Almaami's application of *ḥudūd* and his fight against slavery are best seen in this light.

■ The rebellion of "princely" families became endemic during the last decade of the Almaami's reign. The final act was written when the Almaami waged war in Bundu against the dynasty founded a century earlier by cleric Mālik Sih.[125] The war against this Fulɓe clerical lineage was controversial for some in Fuuta, even though the incumbents were allied with the non-Muslim rulers of Karta who enslaved Muslims. By the last years of the eighteenth century, little in the lifestyle of the royal family of Bundu, whether founded by Tooroɓɓe or not, appeared to distinguish them from their non-Muslim Bambara allies. Park, who passed through Bundu in the late 1790s, remarked that all the "chief men (the king excepted) and a large majority of the inhabitants of Bondou, are Mussulmen."[126] This development was symptomatic of a broader trend. Each time clerics captured the reins of the state, they became indistinguishable from worldly kings. In Jolof, the first rulers in the thirteenth century had to recite the Qur'an from memory, but by the eighteenth century, the rulers neither prayed nor fasted.[127] Even the Deeñanke traced their ancestry to Koli Teŋella Ba, a Fulɓe cleric who lived in the 1500s and was described in the *Ta'rīkh al-Sūdān* as a paragon of justice.[128] Less than two centuries later, the Deeñanke were trading Muslims to Christians for rum. When clerics abandoned pious distance from power, they became the very thing they once detested.

Like other clerics turned kings, the Bundu royal family was no longer recognizably Muslim, but conflict with the Almaami was not caused by a general complaint of religious laxity. Once again the major issue was the enslavement of Muslims, particularly carriers of the Qur'an: "Imam Sega [ruler of Bundu] fell upon a village of the shaykhs of the country of Bundu and had taken prisoner many of their children; thus the shaykhs came to find Imam Abdulkader to complain of this and Imam Abdulkader sent to Imam Sega a letter in which he commanded him to return the children to their families; but Imam Sega refused to do so and it was then that Imam Abdulkader marched against him."[129] The version of the history told to Englishman William Gray roughly twenty years after the fact confirms the nature of the complaint. Gray specifies that an imam in one of the towns "preferred a complaint against Sega, the reigning chief of Boondoo, for having assisted the Kartans [Bambara] in the destruction of his town, and carried off his wife and daughter, both of whom he added to the list of his concubines, and for having destroyed his religious books, written by himself, and said to be so voluminous as to be a sufficient load for an ass."[130]

This story is striking because it includes the enslavement and abuse of a scholarly family as well as the destruction of "ink on paper." Sega is represented explicitly as the enemy of Muslims and the enemy of knowledge. ʿAbdul-Qādir rode out to battle against Imam Sega, defeated his troops quickly, and according to the best authorities, sentenced him to death without hearing his testimony.[131] This event seems to have sent shock waves through the broader clerical community. At this point, ʿAbdul-Qādir lost the support of his lifelong friend and classmate Mukhtār wuld Būnah, the prominent *bayḍān* scholar who had studied at his side in the *majlis* of Khadīja bint Muḥammad al-ʿĀqil several decades earlier.

Like earlier *bayḍān* scholars, Mukhtār wuld Būnah had not come south of the desert to teach Islam to blacks but rather to learn it from them. He was a friend and admirer of Kan, but such a summary execution could not be excused. Soh's history quotes Mukhtār wuld Būnah's words on this occasion: "I was disgusted with the religion of the whites [*bayḍān*] and I came to the blacks to learn their religion, and I left behind the doctrine of people who do not believe at all. But you, you have called this man in the name of Islam [and then summarily killed him]. Why have you acted in this way?"[132] In so many other instances, Kan, an expert in Qurʾan and *fiqh*, deliberated carefully before taking action. This time—as in the invasion of Kajoor—he acted rashly, a move that cost him dearly. Even the wise and virtuous Almaami could be touched by the arrogance of power.

FRENCH INVASION

During this period, trade in grain, furs, and tusks with the French broke down. The French had become aware of the Fuutankoobe disgust with the enslavement of *huffāẓ* and made kidnapping clerics a policy tool to leverage their negotiations, a strategy first recommended by Lamiral in 1791.[133] Gripped by the revolutions in France and Saint-Domingue (Haiti) and in the midst of a breakdown in their trading system on the Senegal River, the French were desperately trying to reopen the slave trade, if not in Fuuta, then at least through Fuuta to Bambara country. The island's French merchants were destitute. For most of the 1790s, they paid no tribute to the Almaami, who responded with a grain embargo. Commandant Blanchot at Saint-Louis then proposed a slave-raiding and pillaging expedition into Fuuta's western fringe to steal needed grain and make off with captives whose sale would solve the merchants' financial crises. The plan was framed not as a raid but as justice: "It is finally time to punish the ever growing and expanding insolence of the riverine peoples of Senegal [with] such a terror from the French government and the inhabitants of the Isle Saint-Louis that they will no longer be tempted to fall short in their commitments. In consequence, all the inhabitants of Senegal who had wanted to make the trip to Galam are invited to take every measure to arm themselves right away and join the two gunboats of the Republic . . . to punish Almamy for his ridiculous temerity and to make up for the trade at Galam that could not take place this year because of the Almamy's pillages."[134]

In the rainy season of 1804, the Saint-Louisiens took six hundred men in twelve boats to attack Podor and its hinterland. Governor Blanchot wrote proudly: "We devastated and burned ten villages in the country of Foute. . . . In one of these villages alone we counted 160 Poule negroes killed. Senegal [Saint-Louis] lost only two negroes, and there are a few others wounded, but a small number." Blanchot kidnapped sixteen people from Fuuta who were in the colony and sold them along with the 604 captives taken in the raid. He noted that at least three prominent clerics were among the enslaved.[135]

Furious, the Fuutankoobe pillaged French boats in 1805. Blanchot sent a punitive expedition to Fanaye on 18 August, firing cannons on the village and landing three hundred men, apparently with orders to burn and pillage but not to take slaves. The Fuutankoobe dealt a severe blow to the landing party, forcing them to retreat with thirty-two casualties, including a dead captain. The French sued for peace and normalization of trading relations, and Almaami ʿAbdul-Qādir Kan apparently authorized his allies among the Brākna to hammer out an agreement with Saint-Louis. Trade resumed in June 1806, by which time Almaami ʿAbdul-Qādir was dead.[136]

The Death of the Almaami

The combined forces of the Atlantic slave trade had been closing in on ʿAbdul-Qādir Kan for a decade, beginning with the dammel of Kajoor in the mid-1790s. The dammel, the French, the Deeñanke, the *bayḍān* slavers, the Bambara, even covetous political rivals within the clerisy were looking to overthrow him. Kan and his followers had overcome them with a decade of struggle from 1776 and then enjoyed a decade of liberty beginning in 1786. But between 1796 and 1806, Almaami ʿAbdul-Qādir's power declined. In April 1806, he was assassinated at the age of eighty-one.

According to Muusa Kamara, the murder occurred on 7 Safar 1221 A.H., or 26 April 1806. According to Siré Abbas Soh, the Almaami's rivals, including ʿAlī Dunndu Kan, Ceerno Molle Lih, and others, sent gifts of slaves to the Bambara king to purchase his aid in killing the Almaami.[137] In another account, it was not slaves but a *mudd* (a Qur'anic measure of weight) of gold.[138]

The Almaami's body lay in state for thirteen days (an unusually long time) before his first burial. He was later exhumed and moved to firmer soil, allowing his partisans, disciples, and loved ones to see him lain to rest. Many scholars from all over Senegambia and the southwest Sahara attended this second interment, thirty-seven days after the first. He was buried with honor this time, wearing a gift of a turban and fine burial shroud given by a prominent cleric.[139] Though neither cites it formally, both Soh and Kamara take their accounts of his burial from an anonymous manuscript, "The Chronicle of the Day the Emir al-Muminin ʿAbdul-Qādir Died": "People who attended the ceremony claimed that sweat rolled down his face, that his whole body was supple and damp and as they had found one of his arms and one of his legs bent, they stretched it without difficulty, and that his hair seemed to be oiled and combed. One of the attendees returned to the tomb some days later and reported, 'By God, the fragrance of musk wafted from his tomb and perfumed my nostrils!'"[140] This powerful image rhetorically establishes Almaami ʿAbdul-Qādir as a martyr: in Islamic discourse, martyrs are represented as being alive (there is no rigor mortis) rather than truly dead and as having wounds that exude a scent of musk. In fact, this description echoes closely a hadith about a martyr of the Battle of Uḥud who was exhumed after six months; his body had not decomposed except for a small change near his ear.[141]

More than simply affirming his status as a martyr, the stories of the Almaami's interment provide subtle but incontrovertible reminders that clerics were understood as Walking Qur'an. It is a curious coincidence that according to Muusa Kamara, "the first to visit (his tomb) was Ceerno Siise Salamata, who was called Ceerno Siise ʿDeereeji. ʿDeereeji means 'the Papers of the Book' [*waraqāt al-qirṭās*]."[142] And if an ordinary knowledgeable and pious scholar could be called the Papers of the Book, then it is fitting that a martyr and *walī* such as Almaami ʿAbdul-Qādir should be likened unto the Book itself, occupying another level in the very same register of embodied knowledge: "They say that among the miracles of Almaami Abdul, after his death, was the gushing of a pure white spring in the middle the valley [where he was buried] and which flowed toward the stream located east of his tomb. The people who lived in Fuuta all the way to the Ferlo came to this spring to implore his blessing and carried with them water from this spring."[143] Just as the water that erased the slate boards of *taalibés* could heal and perform miracles, so too could the erasure of Fuuta's greatest Walking Qurʾan send forth a precious liquid with the power to heal and bless.

POSTSCRIPT TO ABOLITION

The Almaami ʿAbdul-Qādir Kan's intrepid struggle against the slave trade has been mostly forgotten today, but it was so well known to the British governor of Senegal in 1811 that he mentioned it only in passing in a major report to his superiors in London: "It may be here necessary to remark that there has been greater facility in negociating with Almamy and less probability of again having disputes with him in consequence of the abolition of the Slave Trade, *a commerce which that Prince always opposed as being contrary to the Laws of his Religion*, and the means through which several of his subjects, followers of the Prophet, were led into Captivity."[144] The only new information passed along in this account concerns the result of British abolition of the slave trade in 1807, not the Almaami's abolition, which was common knowledge.

A little over a decade later, when Roger published *Kelédor*, the colony of Senegal was back in French hands, and he was its governor. In the novel, he reflected on France's formal abolition of the international trade in the 1810s, noting that the people of Fuuta considered themselves the first abolitionists: "Nothing could take away from these Foulhs the idea that in forbidding the trade in slaves the Europeans were emboldened [*determiné*] by their example. They are proud to have bypassed us in the progress of reason, justice, and humanity."[145]

Roger seems to dismiss the claim that European abolitionists could be inspired by Africans, but his novel is among many pieces of evidence that in fact confirm it. The Almaami inspired not only fictional work but real parliamentary interventions by Clarkson's Society for the Abolition of Slavery and

La Société des Amis des Noirs in Paris. At dawn of European abolitionism, before ideologies of racial and religious superiority could intervene to silence him, the Almaami's call to end slavery was heard all the way in Europe.

The people of Fuuta—including many from the clerisy—also helped erase the Almaami's legacy. Though they had once sworn never to betray him, they conspired in his murder and then moved on to the work of killing his revolution. Within a generation, the Tooroɓɓe, a multiethnic clerisy that had risen from low origins through knowledge, had become a slave-owning landed aristocracy. They closed ranks, nationalized and ethnicized their identity, and became worldly rulers. Once upon a time, anyone who had memorized the Qur'an and studied the sciences could become a *toorodo*, but now the Tooroɓɓe frequently denied Islamic education to nonclerics as a way to maintain their supremacy. While Almaami ʿAbdul-Qādir sought to free limbs of slaves from the yoke of slavery and the souls of slave owners from the fire, the clerisy retreated behind the complacency of the "fragile Sunni consensus" on the legality of enslaving non-Muslims and keeping in bondage even those who embodied the Qur'an as long as they had been bought or captured before converting.

In short, instead of using Islam as a shield against enslavement the way the Almaami did, most Tooroɓɓe used it as a sword, as have so many other Muslim elites. Sadly, this group included one of ʿAbdul-Qādir's sons, Hamadi, who asked for help from the state in undoing his father's abolitionist legacy:

> To help him regain possession of the slaves of his father . . . who did not use these slaves except in war and not for farming as is [now] the custom of the people of Fuuta. After the death of the Almaami, his son, Hamadi, wanted to put them back to work in the fields, but they refused. His brothers also disagreed and wanted the slaves to continue to live as they had during the time of the Almaami. Hamadi went to see [the new] Almaami Rāsīn in Ciloñ and [his] *qāḍī* . . . to ask their help by promising to give each one of them a share of these slaves if they were able to help him get his hands on them. When the slaves learned of this, they fled to [the villages of] Wudduru, Ngijiloñ, and Jowol, where the inhabitants offered their protection and forbade Hamadi al-Ḥājj to lay his hands on them. Some of these slaves had stayed in Kobilo [the Almaami's home village], and Ceerno Saydu Yero helped himself to some of them, and Hamadi al-Ḥājj did likewise with the rest. But [in the end] they managed to free themselves and join their brethren who had fled before them.[146]

■ So went Fuuta Tooro's Reconstruction. These "slaves" of the Almaami and their descendants had obviously lived free for decades, most likely since the Almaami freed the slaves and armed them. Now they had to flee from one of his sons and from opportunistic state-sponsored reenslavement. Some villagers and the rest of the Almaami's sons were ready to give them protection, but some clerics were ready to divvy up these Muslims as spoils.

Freedom for enslaved people, whether given in exchange for the promise to fight or for a single verse of the Qur'an, did not last long. By the 1810s and 1820s, many of the Tooroɓɓe clerics were enjoying the perquisites of power the way the Deeñanke had before them. This was a revolution betrayed. Like other revolutionaries, they discovered that it is easier to remain principled when outside of the corridors of power. This had been, of course, the basic rationale behind the West African clerisy's normative position of keeping distance from power. Though they still taught Islam, these were no longer clerics; they were now kings like any other—or worse, for Fuuta now had few independent clerics capable of autonomous critique of the state. In the nineteenth century, the clerics in Wolof country could no longer look north for aid in their struggles against the dammel of Kajoor.

The Nineteenth-Century Fight against the Dammel

On the Almaami's last day on earth, a small contingent of scholars, friends, and disciples refused to leave his side even as his enemies approached. They stayed with him and made the afternoon prayer together. After they had finished, the Almaami commanded them unequivocally to leave him rather than die in his cause. He made *duʿā* (supplication to God) for them to release them from his service and to say good-bye. They would have sat or kneeled before him, their hands open to catch the precious words of his prayers. He would have ended his prayer by blowing or spitting saliva onto those outstretched hands, whereupon the disciples would rub their hands across their faces, absorbing the saliva charged with the blessings of the Holy Word like water from the *alwāḥ*. One of only a handful of faithful sages to carry away the prayers of ʿAbdul-Qādir Kan from Guuriki was a young Wolof *sëriñ* from Kajoor, Njàga Isa Jóob.[147] Symbolic of the clerisy, whose ties of blood and ink so often transcended national and ethnic bounds, Njàga Isa serves as a critical link between the most prominent Senegambian clerical movement of the eighteenth century—which centered on Fuuta Tooro—and the Wolof countries, which would serve as the main theater for the nineteenth-century movements. Njàga Isa was from Njambuur, the province of Kajoor that was home to Pir and Kokki. It had been the center of clerical authority in the

Wolof lands' most powerful state for at least two centuries. In 1827, he led a revolt against the dammel of Kajoor, directed a disciple in the conquest of Waalo, and threatened Saint-Louis before reconciling with the dammel, only to have him kidnap Njàga Isa's daughter. His experiences highlight the dynamics of the clerisy in the first half of the nineteenth century.

■ Under Dammel Amari (r. 1790–1809), the illegal enslavement of clerics was a bigger problem than ever before in Kajoor. Beginning with his repression of Malamin Saar and the clerisy of Kajoor and culminating in the mass enslavement of the army of Almaami ʿAbdul-Qādir, Dammel Amari had probably killed and sold more Walking Qurʾan than any other ruler in Senegambian history. The only ones he spared, according to Kajoor traditions, "were those who were simple schoolmasters, incapable, he thought, of forming another coalition."[148] This was not entirely true; an important group of rebel clerics had escaped his grasp. As Dammel Amari sought to prepare a defense against the Almaami in 1796, a party of clerics from Njambuur, led by Jaal Jóob, fled to the village of Ndakaaru (Dakar), at the very edge of the dammel's territories. They built huge defensive walls at Bargny to thwart his pursuit and defended their independence there in a famous 1798 battle.[149] This city of God functioned as an autonomous village for nearly a century before the French colonized the mainland. When Njàga Isa Jóob took flight from the dammel of Kajoor in the 1820s, he was granted asylum here, in what is often called the Marabout Republic of Cape Verde.

Gaspard Mollien, traveling throughout Senegambia in 1818, made the "republican" nature of this state the subject of considerable reflection, since he saw it as unusual either for Muslims or Africans to have this form of political organization:

> This peninsula, which is not more than twenty square leagues, offers a remarkable fact, the founding of a republic favored, like that of Switzerland, by an isolated and difficult terrain. This is the place to make a curious observation about Muhammadanism, which, having founded only despotic empires in other places, or worse yet military republics, seems destined only to enlighten the negroes by inspiring in them a sense of independence. In effect, all the Muhammadan states I had the chance to visit on African shores are federated, while the pagan peoples groan under the most atrocious tyranny. Thus the Muhammadan Fulas and Mandingoes enjoy a very mild government; and the Wolofs are continuously exposed to the cruel whims of their masters.[150]

Mollien considered the Wolof rulers, especially the dammel of Kajoor, "pagans," a judgment that surely was transmitted to him by the clerics with whom he interacted. Like the rulers of Jolof, like the Deeñanke, and like countless others, the dammels of Kajoor had once been considered pious Muslims but after centuries in power were considered—at least by most clerics—as faithless worldly kings whose despotism and self-deification recalled the Qur'an's embodiment of human evil, the pharaoh.

In the decades between Njàga Isa's prayer behind the Almaami and his clash with the dammel, the enslavement of Muslims, particularly clerics and their families, was a major concern. Mollien mentions in passing that an important stop for traders in eastern Senegambia had been abandoned: "For two years past, these traders have not returned, because they have incurred the indignation of the inhabitants by carrying away the son of a marabout of this village for the purpose of selling him as a slave."[151]

Mollien is a very helpful source on the concerns of the clerics because he was not a slave trader and thus kept company mainly with clerics. Like Park, he was an explorer in search of the sources of the Senegal, Gambia, and Niger Rivers. Virtually all of the European sources for the region before Park and Mollien were slave traders, mostly frequenting *ceddo* courts. Some captured Muslims, all purchased Muslims, and a few, like Chambonneau, were directly involved in killing and enslaving members of the clerical class who rebelled against kings. Conversely, men such as Park and Mollien came to know the clerisy intimately and on friendly terms. Mollien was traveling the region in the aftermath of the dammel's assaults on the clerisy in the 1790s and was privy to the clerics' complaints: "The conversation generally turned on the cruelties which the dammel inflicted on his subjects. I often heard them swear never to receive any of the envoys of that prince. Some related that they had seen men lying in the grass near their village, and who were certainly only watching for the moment when they might carry off the women or children on their way to the spring."[152]

That the dammel should be uniquely detested comes as no surprise given the actions of Dammel Amari. Though the dammel during Mollien's time in Kajoor, Birama Fatma Cubb (1809–32), was not responsible for the wars, massacres, and enslavements of his predecessor, he nonetheless had to bear the hatred and enmity those depredations had wrought. As historian Lucie Colvin puts it, "A heritage of bitterness remained between the nobility and the marabouts. The marabouts regarded their rulers as enemies and continued to preach that it would only be a matter of time until they would be strong enough to overthrow the Damels."[153] Dammel Amari should be understood as a major breaking point in the history of the clerical movement. If specific incidents of illegal enslavement of Walking Qur'an often served as proximate cause in the seventeenth and eighteenth centuries, in the nineteenth century, such incidents were often unnecessary or unremarked. Dammel Amari's massacre and wholesale enslavement of clerics in 1796 and his open war against them at Bargny in 1798 were justification enough.

Certainly aware of this, Birima Fatma Cubb sought to enlist a *bayḍān* cleric from the Kunta family of Timbuktu, Abū Naʿam, known in Wolof as Shaykh Bunaama.[154] The Kunta were the most prominent "white" scholarly family east of Senegambia. Its members claimed descent from the Prophet Muḥammad, and Dammel Birima Fatma Cubb may have hoped to use claims to genetic nobility to trump the local Wolof, Fulɓe, Soninke, and Mandingo clerisies. Court oral traditions make of Dammel Birima a model pious king. He is best remembered for forbidding the *ceddo* to pillage goods and violate free women.[155] He comes across as trying to reform the *ceddo* and to get them to live by farming rather than raiding. But his efforts were too little, too late. A good dammel was still a dammel, and many clerics were no longer willing to suffer the tyranny of worldly kings who had for centuries sold Muslims for guns, horses, liquor, and fine garments.

Masters of the Sea

In the nineteenth century, the French became much more important than had ever before been the case. In contradictory ways, they helped create the conditions for the clerics' final victory over the *ceddo* kings. Finally expelling the English from the Senegal River area around 1810, France had a free hand in Senegal. The meaning of their occupation began to change dramatically. Senegambian populations had understood Europeans as merchants and "masters of the sea" since first contact in the fifteenth century; by the end of the nineteenth century, they were masters of the land.[156] The French presence affected clerical communities and movements in significant ways. As the French changed their emphasis from purchasing people to purchasing things, they became increasingly important in shaping debates over the enslavement of Muslims in Senegambia.

French economic interests tilted definitively in favor of clerical communities over the century. As the French first abolished the slave trade, then formal slavery itself in their small colony of Senegal, the clerisy was profoundly affected. *Ceddo* kings had once made themselves into ideal trading partners for Europeans by cultivating an appetite for eau-de-vie, firearms, and pillage. But by the mid-nineteenth century, they were becoming obstacles to the postabolition "legitimate commerce" Europeans were trying to build. The French began to seek clerical allies against pillaging slavers. But French anticlericalism and hatred of Islam were sometimes quite extreme, posing serious obstacles to such alliances. For example, Louis Faidherbe, the governor who initiated territorial conquest of Senegal in the 1850s, proposed in an April 1855 letter to his superiors that his efforts to conquer West African Muslims would be aided if the French could destroy the holy city of Mecca in Arabia to strike a symbolic and practical blow against Muslim unity![157]

While such a plan was known neither to his allies nor his adversaries, French attempts to dispossess Muslims of their lands became more and more transparent over the nineteenth century. From the 1830s forward, jihad movements based in communities of the Qur'an fought for their independence from increasing French encroachment. They sought to prevent a different kind of bondage from overtaking the Muslim communities they had struggled so hard to build. Again, Njàga Isa's story was predictive, as his men clashed with the French, leading to a dramatic and polarizing episode in Christian-Muslim relations in Senegambia.

THE MARABOUT, THE BLACKSMITH, AND THE FRENCHMEN

What prayer did Almaami ʿAbdul-Qādir spit into the hands of Njàga Isa Jóob on 26 April 1806? Historians can never know, but we do know that in the 1820s, Njàga Isa set himself on the same path to clerical independence that the Almaami had cleared; like his beloved mentor, this journey eventually led him to conflict with the dammel. His precise route would be different. By this time he was *sëriñ* of Kokki, the leader of one of the oldest and most powerful clerical communities in Wolof country, created in the first part of the eighteenth century. Like the Faal family at Pir, the Jóobeen of Kokki were of high birth but had abdicated their rights to political office upon joining the clerisy. Yet the Jóob family still used this high birth as a political weapon in Kajoor. Njàga Isa contracted a marriage with one of Dammel Birima's sisters, apparently attempting to develop influence over the dammel. At the same time, he was involved in preaching against the dammel. Using the kinds of prestige specific both to clerical and temporal registers, he built a significant following. Like Njaay Saal, who had married the *lingeer* Yasin Buubu 150 years earlier, Njàga Isa was a cleric poised to try to end the rule of the dammels with the help of a powerful royal woman.

Unlike Njaay Saal, however, Njàga Isa was unable to capture—even temporarily—the reins of Kajoor. According to Monserrat, a contemporary

French observer, Dammel Birima commanded Njàga Isa "to remain within the limits of his rights and his rank, or he would force him to put him in his place. Yagayssa [Njàga Isa] disregarded his orders and took up arms to defend himself against his king."[158] While the cleric had gathered many supporters around him, he was no match for Senegambia's most formidable army. Forced to flee into Waalo, he continued his movement there, drawing many of the local inhabitants into his camp. With Fuuta now strong enough to resist incursions from Ḥasānī raiders, Waalo had become the most severely raided region of Senegambia. Trārza raided with impunity, as did some pastoral stateless Fulɓe. In such circumstances, the preaching of an heir to the legacy of Almaami ʿAbdul-Qādir could be expected to gain converts to his cause, and he gathered swarms of followers. One was a man of the *tëgg*, blacksmith category, Jilé Kumba Jombos Caam.

According to a Njambuur oral source, Jilé Caam became "possessed by a spirit which would not let him stop reciting the name of Allah until he declared a jihad."[159] He did so, and with Njàga Isa rallying support from the broader Senegambian clerisy and many nonclerics, Jilé Caam directed a war against Waalo's beleaguered royalty. According to Monserrat, Njàga Isa established control over a portion of Waalo by 1829, though the royal family had not been fully vanquished. Divided and pillaged for decades, Waalo was the scene of civil war for as long as a year. When Jilé Caam took over military operations, probably in early 1830, the party vanquished the royal family. The royal army was routed in a matter of days in February or early March 1830. According to Monserrat, who obviously did not take a favorable view of Njàga Isa or Jilé Caam, the band went from village to village, forcing men (as the Almaami had) to shave their heads or lose them.[160]

The shaving of the head, now a universal bodily symbol of joining the clerical community (it mirrored the act of conversion and entering the ritual state required for pilgrimage), surely marked this initiation into the movement. But we should hesitate at the notion that this impromptu army was drawn up mainly by force. Again, Waalo had been utterly devastated, and many people were likely ready for revolution. According to Monserrat, Caam was referred to by at least one of his soldiers as "Madiou," which he glosses as "prophet" but which is clearly "Mahdiyyu" or "Mahdī." The movement likely had millennial aspects: in Waalo, as in Fuuta some years earlier, it appears some people believed that the world was coming to an end.

Perhaps a belief that the end was near helped with military recruitment, perhaps not. However Jilé Caam attracted recruits, his forces were large, motivated, and seemingly unstoppable in early March 1830. They sent the royal family into precipitous retreat to the French fort at Dagana. Caam's army pursued them, capturing a small French plantation along the way and threatening another that Governor Roger, author of *Kelédor*, had established at Richard-Toll. Feeling their interests threatened, the French decided to act. In official documents, the governor admitted that his motivation was not only the safety of French positions but also the desire to keep the dammel of Kajoor from defeating this movement and claiming possession of Waalo.[161] In other words, the fear of Kajoor and a covetous eye toward Waalo played a role in the French decision to intervene. This infamous intervention has echoed through the ages in the oral traditions of Senegambian Muslims.

■ French forces lynched Jilé Caam on 15 March 1830. The official story, related by Monserrat in his "précis" as well as the governor in his report to the ministry, is that the forces of Waalo carried out the death sentence, but the same governor admitted to a colleague two days later that French soldiers had hanged Jilé.[162] While the French maintained the cover-up with respect to Caam's execution, Monserrat proudly related the humiliation to which Jile Caam was subjected in his final moments on earth. The governor of Senegal personally interrogated Jilé regarding his motives:

> He responded that it was not him, that he was won over by the marabout Yagayssa [Njàga Isa], that he was in no way inspired by God, that he was not even a marabout, for before all this he was busy in his capacity as a blacksmith, that he had even worked for a long time on the island of Saint-Louis and that no one ever had any reason to reproach him. Someone from the governor's retinue wanting to have a little fun asked him—Do you drink eau-de-vie? "Oui Monsieur." Do you eat bacon ha! "Oui Monsieur. Give me, Monsieur, give me, I drink and eat anything I am not a marabout I tell you."
>
> He drank and ate everything he was presented with, he was little concerned with it, the mercy he implored concerning him much more, but an example was necessary, this affair not being able to end with a pardon, the whole country demanded his death and had their eyes fixed on the governor. . . . He turned him over to them, and he was immediately shot by the people of the country.[163]

The main reason for writing something down in colonial archives often was to make a lie hold as truth. But this lynching was not forgotten by oral historians, and in 1969, Colvin was shown the tree from which Jilé Caam's body had swung. When French colonial authorities complained of some clerics' hatred for whites or for Christians (*nasaraan*, or Nazarenes in local parlance), they forgot the long legacies of slaving and their complicity with the clerisy's bitter rivals. But they also underestimated how descriptions of white men hanging black bodies from trees could echo for centuries.

Njàga Isa Jóob escaped the battle and reconstituted some of the clerisy's forces. They headed south for the "Marabout Republic," founded thirty-five years earlier when another party of scholars fled after failing to topple the dammel of Kajoor. This party, too, ran afoul of the dammel, as Birima Fatima Cubb sent one of his generals to intercept them. Njàga Isa's forces defeated the *ceddo*, felled their general, and continued the march, reaching Ndakaaru (Dakar), the ancient fishing village that gave the small polity its name, sometime before 1 April 1830.[164] On that date, the French governor wrote to Eliman Dakar (*alimaan* is the Wolof pronunciation of "al-imam"), demanding that the Njàga Isa be relinquished, but the *sëriñs* would not compromise the traditional inviolability of a clerical compound. No ruler—white, black, or red—had the right to pursue people inside the cities of God.[165]

Doomi Soxna—The Children of Honorable Women

Njàga Isa remained in Dakar in peace until sometime after Birima Fatima Cubb's death in 1832. After Dammel Maissa Tenda Joor (1832–54) ascended to the throne, he made peace with Njàga Isa, and the latter returned to Kokki.[166] But the story did not end there. Some years later—probably in the 1840s—the dammel took an interest in one of Njàga Isa's daughters. He asked for her hand in marriage but was rebuffed. Maissa Tenda Joor took the girl by force, much as Imam Sega had taken the women he wanted from the clerics of Bundu almost a half century earlier. Njàga Isa had spent most of his life fighting to end just this sort of tyranny—the use and abuse of Muslims by worldly kings. He took up arms once again. Now an old man without much of an armed force, he resorted to pillaging the villages of the *ceddo* of Njambuur, futilely trying to exact some form of retribution. Eventually fleeing to Fuuta Tooro, he spent his remaining days in the village of Njuum, not far from Guuriki, where he had received the prayers of Almaami ʿAbdul-Qādir Kan in April 1806.

A few years later, in the 1860s, Maba Jaaxu Ba declared a jihad against the kings of Saalum and Badibu, in the border areas linking the Wolof, Sereer, and Mandingo kingdoms near the Gambia River.[167] His war was sparked by two separate incidences of the massacre and enslavement of clerics, which was a major concern of his movement. He declared jihad only after the king of Badibu stole a cleric's wife from his compound to take her as a concubine.

Maba Jaaxu Ba's war against the king of Saalum may also have been instigated by the murder and enslavement of *ḥuffāẓ*. Thierno Ka writes that in 1860, the king of Saalum "decided to attack the Qur'anic center of the village of Nandjigue [Nanjig]. Seventy among the readers of the Qur'an found their deaths there. Many others were captured. Maba Jaxu asked the Muslims of Saalum to buy back the prisoners. His request was granted by these Muslims."[168]

The account is apparently derived from oral histories gathered during Ka's extensive fieldwork in Rip. After the prisoners were ransomed, hostilities between the parties broke out afresh. Whatever caused Maba Jaaxu Ba's fight with the king of Saalum, the illegal enslavement of Muslims seems to have been his primary concern. His jihad soon encompassed nearby Jolof as well, bringing Ba into conflict with the French, whose territorial ambitions were now apparent. In an August 1865 letter to Governor Pinet-Laprade, Maba explained, "The motive for which I invaded Jolof is that the inhabitants of the country sold the free people who passed through there. . . . I warned them three times; in spite of my warnings, they did not want to abandon their bad habits. Peace to those who follow the path of justice! Sine, Baol, and Jolof are not yours. If now you wish to claim that they belong to you, protect the believers against the infidels."[169]

A MATTER OF HONOR

Many of the stories of the illegal enslavement of Muslims in the nineteenth century centered on the kidnapping of women and children. If the enslavement of clerics was a powerful symbol of violation, the true mark of the weakness of the clerics was the vulnerability of their dependents. Time and again, worldly authorities used and abused clerics' wives and daughters and took their children, prompting the clerics to rise against those authorities. The *ceddo* regimes were inimical to Islamic understandings of family, which centered on honor. Preserving the dignity of Muslim women was a constant struggle because pillaging Crown slaves and especially kings often simply took any women they wanted, as if the wives and children of others were theirs to use as they wished.

Accounts of ʿAbdul-Qādir's fateful march to Kajoor specify that many women and noncombatants marched behind the troops, preparing to celebrate the Almaami's next great triumph. According to Roger's fictionalized version of the story, when the defeat was apparent, a number of the women of Fuuta committed a kind of ritual suicide by holing themselves up in grass huts and setting them ablaze.[170] Whether this account reflects actual events is impossible to determine, but it highlights a very real problem. After a defeat, there was no respect for women, free or slave. They were almost certain to be raped by *ceddo* and then sold or distributed as booty, forced to live the rest of their lives as purchased women, concubines, with no standing, honor, or dignity.

Shaykh Muusa Kamara's account of the history of Fuuta includes a number of the stories of such women taken after the Almaami's fall from power, defining this practice as one of the primary evils of the age.[171] When the Bambara and Deeñanke murdered the Almaami, one of the Bambara captured his daughter and took her away to Bambara country, where she was either married or more likely taken as a concubine by a Bambara man, giving birth in her captivity to a son. After some time she was discovered and ransomed, along with her son, who was raised as a member of the community, bearing the patronym Kan.[172] Such stories span the period from the Almaami's fall through the 1910s, when Kamara set pen to paper. Such women's capture and sexual vulnerability posed a bodily threat to conceptions of family, community, and honor. This kind of gendered political violence produced the bitterest hatred of worldly authorities.

Breaking the Chains—Part I

In 1875, a young Amadu Bamba walked across his father's courtyard and heard the voices of two young men reciting the Qurʾan. This was no unusual sound; his father, Momar Anta Sali Mbakke, was a religious scholar and secretary for the ruler of Kajoor, Lat Joor Jóob (d. 1886). What was unusual was that the young men were captives, slaves distributed to the scholar by the dammel as payment for services at the court.[173] His reaction suggests that perhaps he experienced the same feelings that had spurred Ceerno Sulaymaan Baal to act when he heard a young man in bondage reciting the Qurʾan in the hold of the boat on the Senegal River a century before. Was it a sinking nausea? Was it a kind of heartbreak? Or was it blinding anger that overcame him as he saw and heard the Book in chains. A historian can only guess, but Bamba was obviously moved, for the young man (still in his early twenties) defied filial decorum and pressed his father for their immediate release.[174] This act would bring the young scholar into what seems to have been the first and nearly only polemical exchange of his career. It pitted him against Majaxate Kala, the dammel's chief *qāḍī* (*xaali* in Wolof), the man responsible for declaring these slaves licit.

Xaali Majaxate Kala was nearly twenty years Bamba's senior and a well-respected specialist in Islamic law. He was also probably Senegambia's foremost specialist in poetry. His masterwork on the subject, *Mubayyin al-Ishkāl*, was widely taught in Senegambian circles into the twentieth century. Indeed, Kala had taught this discipline to Bamba when he was a teenager in Saalum. According to Mamadou Lamine Diop, a close companion of Bamba and one of his biographers, "During this time he frequented Khaali Majaxate Kala, *qāḍī* of the damel, who was a scholar particularly renowned for the excellent quality of his poetry. Amadu Bamba frequented him to deepen his knowledge of the Arabic language. Sometimes he showed him poems that he had composed to verify their conformity to the rules of grammar, lexicography, and meter. Sometimes he detected mistakes, sometimes not. Their relationship continued in that way until the student surpassed the master in the art of poetry. So that the master, once focused on correcting the poems of the student, now aimed to learn them by heart."[175]

Though the account is designed to impress the reader with the intellectual superiority of the founder of the Murīdiyya, it also communicates the intimacy of the master-student relationship, which is sacrosanct and forms the core of the social logic of Islamic knowledge. This intimacy was torn apart by the enslavement of *huffāẓ al-Qurʾān*.

The confrontation between Majaxate Kala and Amadu Bamba is a famous moment narrated by historians of the Murīdiyya for generations. The story is still widely circulated in Murid circles as the first example of Bamba taking his characteristically aloof stance toward authority. Within the Murīdiyya, this is the story's most salient aspect. Yet this emphasis has obscured the fact that it was the visceral reaction to the desecration of a Walking Qurʾan that sparked Bamba's response.[176]

■ Here, I pull the narrative from its conventional context of explaining Amadu Bamba's stance toward the French or even his obviously deep commitment to Sufi principles, recontextualizing it in a longer-term historical narrative of the violation of the sanctity of the Qurʾan through the abuse, enslavement, and murder of those who embody it. This experience of seeing the Book in chains, I want to suggest, was primarily responsible for shaping Bamba's position with regard to political authorities. In this sense, he was heir to the history of the clerisy. In his father's courtyard that day, he came face-to-face with the same problem that had driven clerics to arms since the Tuubanaan movement in the 1670s. Bamba's reaction was different. Instead of attempting a jihad of the sword, he turned toward a new Sufi pedagogy to effect a jihad of the soul. While this story has usually been told as part of the history of Sufism, set against the longue durée, Bamba represents not a novelty but a return to what had long been the normative clerical posture of pious distance from power.

THE BATTLE OF SAMBA SAAJO

What, then, were the circumstances of the dispute between the dammel's *qāḍī* and his former student, and how was the dispute resolved? In January and February 1875, the dammel's warriors fought alongside the French against Amadu Shehu, a Fuutanke cleric who had declared a jihad against the colonial invaders. They handed his forces a stunning defeat at Samba Saajo, killing the cleric. A few years earlier, the dammel and Amadu Shehu had been partners fighting *against* the French, but in the middle years of the 1870s, the French saw an opportunity to end Amadu Shehu's movement by allying with Lat Joor and supporting his claims to rule Kajoor over those of his rivals. This shift unambiguously restored Lat Joor as part of the establishment, and he sought to quell the uprising of the clerical groups. Some of the *sëriñs* in his lands were in league with Amadu Shehu, and in 1874 they were threatening to overwhelm the dammel's forces.[177] In this context, Lat Joor joined forces with the French to defeat and kill Amadu Shehu. In the aftermath of the battle, Lat Joor claimed the captives as slaves and imprisoned and executed clerics suspected of complicity.

The sight of the broken and lifeless bodies of two Walking Qur'an from prominent clerical lineages in Kajoor who had allied with Amadu Shehu caused the young Amadu Bamba to renounce any political plans he might have been harboring. He was not yet twenty years old. Later in life, he wrote that at this very moment, he rid himself of any worldly ambitions.[178]

Xaali Majaxate Kala gave a ruling declaring the booty from the battle licit. He was no novice in matters of slavery law. Indeed, no less an authority than the *sëriñ* of one of Senegambia's oldest schools, Kokki, had requested that Kala issue a ruling on a complicated case a few years earlier. That such eminent scholarly authorities would appeal to his judgment affirmed both his scholarly record and his position of authority in the dammel's court. But sometimes the scholarship and temporal service could work at cross purposes. Close scrutiny of his record, made possible by the work of Claudine Gerresch, leads to the conclusion that Majaxate Kala was not above sophistry in his argumentation to produce fatwas favorable to the king.[179] In this instance, the argument that the sovereign should keep this substantial booty hinged on the claim that Amadu Shehu had "declared himself a prophet, a proclamation which justified spilling his blood and confiscating his goods."[180]

THE DAMMEL'S *QĀḌĪS*

Amadu Bamba's father, Momar Anta Sali Mbakke, who also served as a *qāḍī* for Lat Joor, was left in a very difficult position. He had previously given the opinion that Amadu Shehu's war against Kajoor could not be classified as a jihad since it pitted Muslim against Muslim and thus could only be understood as a worldly matter. This viewpoint justified Lat Joor's decision to resist Amadu Shehu's conquest of Kajoor, but it also thus forbade confiscation of goods or enslavement on either side. Majaxate Kala's new opinion gave the dammel a free hand in the situation: he could keep the slaves. In this context, Momar Anta Sali's freeing of the slaves must have appeared to be a direct contravention of Majaxate Kala's ruling.

This chain of events likely convinced Bamba of the fundamental injustice of both the dammel and the judges who served him. How could he risk being so closely tied to a worldly king who could fight on either side of a war and call it a jihad as long as it served his interests? Bamba had already apparently expressed concerns about the corrupting effects of political power on the scholar—first, according to Kajoor tradition, when Lat Joor personally ordered all of the villages in the area surrounding Mbakke-Kajoor to report at sunrise to Momar Anta Sali's fields and work, an unusual request that earned the cleric's gratitude. His son, however, was concerned with the obligation such a gift entailed and spoke of the cost of making rulings in the name of such a king.[181] In addition, oral sources speak of Bamba's concern about being closely associated with the court. M. L. Diop, one of Bamba's companions and biographers, says that he used to warn his father all the time about the risks, and his father would simply reply, "You are right, you have done well, God bless you" before reminding his son that their family's interests were at stake.[182]

Bamba is said to have once slipped a note into one of his father's books that said, "The most honest *qāḍī* will have to settle his accounts with God."[183] Sërin Bachir Mbacké (one of Bamba's sons and his chief biographer) also suggests that one of Bamba's earliest disciples, Masamba Jóob, reported that Bamba considered abandoning his father if he did not leave the service of the dammel.[184] While these intimate traces of family struggle are very difficult to date, there is no probable proximate cause for such extreme reproach other than the controversy of the illegal enslavement of the prisoners of the Battle of Samba Saajo. John Glover argues that Momar Anta Sali's decision to resign from service to the dammel at the urging of his son was made after this episode.

For his part, Amadu Bamba apparently did not see the matter as settled with his father's retirement from active service, but the younger man tempered his response in deference to his father and out of respect for his former teacher. Defiant but not disrespectful, he declined an invitation to come to the dammel's court to debate the matter with Majaxate Kala and the dammel's entourage. After Momar Anta Sali died in December 1881, Bamba's attitude changed. At his father's funeral, emissaries from the dammel came to make peace, offering him a courtesy position at the court. Bamba publicly and unceremoniously dismissed the offer, expressing what would become his characteristic stance toward worldly authorities: "I do not have the habit of visiting monarchs. I have no desires for their riches, and I seek honor only from the Supreme Lord."[185] He was rebuked for a lack of etiquette and for passing up a position of power, wealth, and authority, but Amadu Bamba had already seen where that road led.

THE COURT CLERIC

Perhaps concerned about the insolence of the young *ʿālim* or perhaps in a bid to keep a potential enemy close, the dammel continued to invite Bamba to visit the court. Bamba continued to decline the invitations, just as he had declined to debate the matter of the slaves from the Battle of Samba Saajo. But now, without having to defer to his father, he began to respond to these letters with clear signs of rebuke. In one, he paraphrased Imam Mālik b. Anas's refusal to visit the court of the Abbasid caliph Hārūn al-Rashīd, writing, "Tell the dammel that I would be ashamed that the angels see me going to see a king other than God."[186] The courier of his final letter to the dammel confirmed that the letter quoted an aphorism comparing court clerics to flies feeding on feces. The courier recorded the ensuing exchange between Majaxate Kala and the dammel:

> —What does he say? Asks the dammel.
> —It is not aimed at you, it is aimed at me.
> —In God's name, tell me what it says!
> —He says, "The Muslim scholar who curries the favor of a sultan is like a fly who feeds on filth."
> —I am the more despised, for if he compares you to a fly, he considers me as . . .[187]

According to M. L. Diop, they then resolved to treat Bamba like a barren patch in the midst of their field and simply work around him. A chance meeting brought the *qāḍī* to a village near Bamba's school sometime shortly thereafter. Determined to formally honor his former teacher and friend of the family in spite of the coolness between them, Amadu Bamba visited him. In the Murid sources, this meeting is portrayed as a matter of courtesy, though it certainly seems likely that Bamba grasped the opportunity to tell Majaxate Kala exactly what he thought of him. Bamba greeted the *qāḍī* formally and then prepared to leave, whereupon Majaxate Kala raised the question of the legality of the slaves, perhaps as an effort to finally settle the matter that had come between them. Bamba responded by giving his former master a concise lesson in Islamic law.[188] Diop's account of the exchange has Majaxate Kala saying,

> —In effect, my opinion is that Amadu Shehu having proclaimed himself a prophet and having imposed his domination by force, it was legitimate to kill him, confiscate his goods, and enslave his soldiers.
>
> A silence followed. Then Amadu addressed himself to the *qāḍī*. . . .
>
> —Who was it that bore witness that the man proclaimed himself a prophet?
>
> —All of Kajoor.
>
> —Can one accept in this regard, the testimony of the people of Kajoor, his enemies?
>
> —No, but that of the inhabitants of Samba Saajo who were present at the battle.
>
> —The inhabitants of Samba Saajo were surprised by soldiers coming from east and west, and the battle was a surprise attack. In this situation, what could they know of the true motivations of this war?[189]

The argument left Majaxate Kala speechless. While this version of the encounter is almost certainly too good to be true, it just as certainly captures the nature of Amadu Bamba's understanding of the illegality of the ruling. As far as can be determined from the sources, no witnesses had been produced to testify to Amadu Shehu's intentions. This ruling, like those that made up the original "fragile Sunni consensus" on slavery, was one of convenience.

■ If the meeting between Bamba and Kala did take place, it likely would have happened in 1882. We know from Cheikh Babou's oral sources that in 1882, Bamba was still preoccupied with the problematic ruling and was trying to undo the damage that Majaxate Kala had inflicted nearly a decade earlier. When Ibrahim Makodu Jóob, a cousin of Lat Joor, came to make his *njebalu* (the ritual of submission that binds disciple to master in the Murīdiyya), Bamba refused, insisting that the slaves from the Battle of Samba Saajo who remained in Ibrahim Makodu Jóob's possession be released first.[190]

Personal experience may have made Bamba particularly sensitive to the problem of illegal enslavement. In the mid-1860s, one of his younger sisters, nine- or ten-year-old Faati Mbakke, was kidnapped by slave raiders.[191] It could not have been difficult for him to imagine his sister held somewhere in bondage in spite of her piety and knowledge of the Qur'an. As with most clerical families, the Mbakke took pride in the fact that girls learned the Qur'an by heart and often studied the religious sciences. Later in his life, Amadu Bamba proudly displayed his daughters' knowledge of Qur'an to scholarly guests. Like the many women of Fuuta Tooro who had known slavery under the Bambara or the *bayḍān* in the nineteenth century, under Imam Sega, or under Dammel Maissa Tenda Joor, her honor and dignity might have been breached. Little wonder then, that he might hold in contempt people of learning who would allow pious girls and women to be so abused.

In May 1882, Majaxate Kala was also preoccupied with slavery. Using his position as the secretary of Lat Joor, he wrote to the governor of the French colony at Saint-Louis asking for the return of two of his own escaped slaves.[192] Though he was hardly a liberal, this was the second documented instance when he took advantage of his position as the dammel's chief scribe in this way. He had included in an 1876 letter to the governor a request that one of his fugitive slaves be returned.[193] For all we know, all three might even have been slaves taken in the Battle of Samba Saajo.

Some evidence indicates that a minor rapprochement occurred between the two men in the final years of Majaxate Kala's life. Sometime in the last years before his death in 1902, he wrote a poem in Arabic and Wolof lamenting his old age and Amadu Bamba's indifference to him.[194] Bamba responded to his now quite aged former teacher with kind words in a poem. But there is no indication that Bamba had softened his stance regarding the battle of Samba Saajo or the enslavement of Muslims. In light of the evidence, Bamba's characteristic stance toward political authority, which has so marked the Murīdiyya and Senegalese religious culture over the past century, may well have been framed in the moment when he saw and heard the Book in chains in his father's courtyard.

Slavery, the West African Jihads, and Clerical Rule

Majaxate Kala in some ways symbolizes the clerisy's compromise on slavery, whereas Bamba symbolizes an adaptation to the new circumstances. The affair laid bare the lessons of history. For more than two hundred years, since the time of Njaay Saal and the *tubanaan* movement, many clerics had sought to overthrow the kings to end their tyranny as well as their illegal enslavement and murder of free Muslims. Yet time and again, reformers had claimed power only to become precisely what they detested. However sincere their outrage at the problem of illegal enslavement, the political economy of West Africa in the period did not admit the possibility of political success without deep complicity in slave trading. The era was the height of the Atlantic slave trade and a period of unprecedented Saharan slave trade. In an area with such old Muslim identities, the weapon of *takfīr* (excommunication) had to be wielded to justify struggles over control of land and people—precious people who could be traded for guns, horses, and the machinery of war and statecraft.

The story of the Almaami is a reminder to Africanists interested in the slave trade in a number of ways. First, Africans abolished the European slave trade *dozens* if not *hundreds* of times, but that trade would continue until Europeans stopped the demand for slaves, because economic and military incentives were always strong enough to undo abolition in any given kingdom or region. Second, the nearly complete erasure of the memory of the Almaami's abolition offers a reminder that the rulers who squashed African resistance to slavery (with European help) normalized the institution of slavery and erased earlier legacies of struggles. Like the Almaami's son, rulers reenslaved people and reestablished slave trades and pretended that they had inalienable customary or Islamic legal rights to do so.

When Europeans arrived in Africa and the Middle East as rulers in the late nineteenth century, they took the claims of such aristocrats as gospel and invested reactionary, masculine claims about sharia and customary law with the power of colonial governments and academic scholarship. They were only too happy to do so, since this viewpoint confirmed their sense of Eastern or African backwardness and gave them courts and chiefs who could institute repressive mechanisms of social control at little cost to the state. This was known in Africa as "indirect rule."

■ The activities of the two most famous jihad state builders in nineteenth-century West Africa are not considered because of lack of space and because they would have carried us too far beyond the bounds of Senegambia. Nonetheless, the jihads of Usman dan Fodio and al-Ḥājj ʿUmar al-Fūtī Taal fit the "Book in chains" pattern quite well. Dan Fodio's major critique of the Hausa kings of Gobir was not their tolerance for the syncretistic spirit possession cults known collectively as *bori* that have so captured the imagination of scholars interested in a kind of Nigerian Islam Noir but rather the illegal enslavement of Hausa Muslims and their increasing sale into Yoruba Atlantic slaving networks. Moreover, the actual fighting in Gobir began when the sultan captured a large number of the Shehu's Qur'an reciters and sold them as slaves rather than ransoming them. One of al-Ḥājj ʿUmar's most important pre-jihad texts was an 1844 document in which "he sharply criticized the laxity of ostensibly Muslim rulers who allowed Muslims to be enslaved and sold to Europeans."[195] This was a major feature of the slave trade from what is now Guinea. The sad paradox, however, is that while these two men fought wars in part to end the illegal enslavement of Muslims, the "jihads" of Dan Fodio and Tall might have produced more Muslim slaves than any other conflicts. Hausa-speaking Muslims were enslaved on an unprecedented scale by the Sokoto jihad, and al-Ḥājj ʿUmar's bloodiest fights were with the Muslims of Masina.

The lesson from Senegambia, Masina, and Sokoto may well have been the failure of the efforts to wrest power from corrupt kings and to place in power men of principle who understood the sharia. If one of the great lessons of this period in history in the West was that politics had to be separated from religion for the protection of the former, the history of the clerisy in West Africa demonstrated one final time that such a separation was necessary to protect the latter.

Bamba seems to have been particularly inspired by this kind of thinking. He had seen the shortcomings of Maba's movement firsthand as Bamba, his family, and many of the clerics of Kajoor were forced to march to Saalum in the wake of the *mujahid*'s retreat. He saw talented scholars like his own father and his once-beloved teacher Majaxate Kala try to control kings, only to become tools of their injustice. In 1882, rather than moving to the court or raising an army, he turned his attention to his school and a new pedagogy capable of transforming society from the bottom up rather than from the top down. The flexibility with which he and some of his contemporaries reached out beyond the usual clientele of wellborn families and clerical lineages made their movements dramatically successful. Majaxate Kala's letters to Saint-Louis, which had abolished slavery in 1848, were cracks in a crumbling edifice. The bonds of slavery soon would effectively be broken, and those who had once been held at arm's length from Islam because of the taint of capture or low birth would now clamor for full participation in Muslim society and for the honor of Qur'an schooling. The Sufi success in Senegambia was in large part predicated on the ability and desire to offer a fuller Muslim identity to those set free by the crumbling late-nineteenth-century sociopolitical order.

4

BODIES OF KNOWLEDGE

SCHOOLING, SUFISM, AND SOCIAL CHANGE IN COLONIAL SENEGAL, 1890–1945

The nobility of my community are the bearers of the Qur'an.
—Saying attributed to the Prophet Muḥammad

Bodies of Knowledge

Even as some fought a desperate battle to prevent the enslavement of Muslims by Muslims, precolonial Senegambia had been transforming itself into a slave society. Part of what made the rhetoric and reality of the revolutionary movements so powerful was that they had called on Muslim identity to cut across what everyone knew to be deeply rooted hierarchical distinctions of social status. These distinctions were powerfully embodied. Enslaved and "casted" people were not made from the same stuff as the free and noble. Slaves and other lowborn people had bodies and beings that were impure. Even in twenty-first-century Senegal, the corporeal taint of low birth remains a salient factor in social life, particularly affecting marriage patterns. At the end of the nineteenth century, such distinctions were even more firmly rooted, but the political order that upheld them was already crumbling. The French had begun to extend their military dominance from isolated coastal trading entrepôts to the mainland by annexing the Wolof state of Waalo in 1855. In 1895, after forty years of conquests, French authority encompassed much of the African West in a vast new imperial state, Afrique Occidentale Française (AOF).[1] This expansion fatally undermined the Senegambian martial monarchies that composed the old political order. The power relations that upheld systems of slavery and caste were irrevocably altered.

Just as important perhaps, the rhetoric of a French *mission civilisatrice* was accompanied by a commitment to end slavery in French West Africa.[2] This commitment was always incomplete, frequently half-hearted, and sometimes quite cynical. Yet even this effort was enough to create a space within which the enslaved could stake claims. They sought not only an abstract colonial legal status as "free" but also honor and dignity in the societies that had held them in bondage. Learning the Qur'an came to play a special role in this process. The esteem enjoyed by Qur'an reciters made schools ideal places for people of low status to earn respect. But from within an epistemology of embodiment, this went beyond mere social climbing. Shared belief in the transformative capacities of the Word made this something more. Embodying the Qur'an might allow slaves to redefine their beings. Some, it seems, dared to believe that the stain of slavery could be washed away with the water from the slate board. For if the bodies of the lowborn were not made from the same stuff as those of the free, could they not be made noble with knowledge? Would it not be possible—through internalization of the Qur'an—to remake the bodies of the enslaved and casted as free bodies? As Muslim bodies? As *bodies of knowledge*?

A PATH TO HONOR

The model had precedent. It was something of an open historical secret that much of the Tooroɓɓe clerisy in Fuuta Tooro came from humble origins.[3] The clerisy as a whole was not immune to embodied distinctions of caste; like other occupational groups, it tended to reproduce itself through endogamy. Moreover, its hereditary claims to Islamic knowledge could be decidedly proprietary and bodily, with embodied grace (*baraka*) seen as passed from one generation of scholars to the next.[4] Nonetheless, stories of individuals of low or slave birth who earned freedom and dignity through Islamic learning were not uncommon. Though only rarely, some from humble backgrounds did go on to become honored clerics.

Certain clerics perpetuated hereditary claims to an embodied grace but were nonetheless prepared—even eager—to accommodate the yearnings of the multitudes newly freed in law by the French. Indeed, many Muslim intellectuals had long felt ambivalent about the role of slavery in Senegambian society. This group included Amadu Bamba Mbakke. Murid oral tradition reports that an enthusiastic disciple once came to him offering the gift of a slave. He responded, "If you own him, then you own me, because he and I have the same Master."[5]

The story may or may not be apocryphal, but the Murīdiyya's role in offering dignity and Muslim identity to people of all sorts of backgrounds is not.[6] Nor were the Murids alone in developing a more inclusive vision of Muslim identity. Sufi leaders transformed and channeled a process of social change that was fundamentally driven by the claims for personal dignity of those previously held at arms length from Islamic knowledge. In so doing, these leaders focused on reformulating Islamic education and on making it accessible to previously underserved populations. Though frequently ignored, broad-based societal demand for Qur'an schooling was one of the major causes of the Sufi revolution of the nineteenth century. Skillful leaders such as Bamba, al-Ḥājj Mālik Sy, and 'Abdullahi Niass tapped into this demand, channeled it into Sufi structures, and thus developed organizations capable of transcending the limitations of clerical lineages.[7]

SUFISM AND SOCIAL STRUGGLE

If the *sëriñ* as a teacher and Walking Qur'an had dominated previous epochs, this was to become the era of the Sufi shaykh. Responding to newly liberated demand, clerics reshaped Sufism, once merely a body of knowledge within the curricula of advanced Islamic studies, making it into the most significant form of social organization in colonial Senegambia. *Taṣawwuf*, a private initiatory discipline, gave way to the *ṭarīqa* (pl. *ṭuruq*), a kind of spiritual and social organization that allowed Senegambian Muslims to act as a body. Grafting older notions of clerical lineage onto a Sufi framework, Sufi leaders guided a process that subtly altered the embodied ethic of knowledge transmission while, paradoxically perhaps, preserving it in one of the few forms durable enough to withstand a century of epistemological assault.

In ways both obvious and subtle, the French school was the leading edge in that colonial assault on African Muslim ways of knowing. Until the 1920s, a direct competition for students existed, and the French were losing. An early report on Qur'an schooling by the head of the Muslim Affairs Office, Paul Marty, acknowledged, "It is painful to watch certain of the rural [French] schools stagnating with only a dozen students, while taken together the little marabout schools flourishing nearby reach a hundred."[8] For decades, the colonial state crafted legislation designed to move African children out of Qur'an schools and into French schools. But as was so often the case, the results of colonial interventions were contradictory and unpredictable.

At the same time that the French colonial state fought Islamic education with one hand, it was also—and not wholly unwittingly—reifying the power of marabouts, who defined their social and personal identities through teaching the Word. The destruction of military aristocracies had settled a centuries-long struggle between chiefs and clerics on terms that decidedly favored the latter. As chiefs quickly became petty bureaucrats within the colonial state, responsible for collecting money for taxes and men for labor and military conscription, they lost much popular legitimacy. Qur'an teachers and Sufi shaykhs became the most important African arbiters of moral, social, and political authority in the colonial state. This fact was not lost on the French officers at the middle and upper levels of the colonial administration. Some sought to curtail the growing influence of clerics; others sought to capitalize on it.[9] But most oscillated pragmatically between these positions in ways that ultimately helped reinforce already deep societal commitments to clerics. Wittingly and unwittingly, the French state preserved, extended, and deepened Senegambian engagements with Islamic knowledge even as it sought to weaken them.

French colonial authorities largely misunderstood and sometimes intentionally caricatured the nature and extent of those Senegambian engagements with Islamic knowledge. This corpus of colonial thought on West African Islam is the final body of knowledge to be examined in this chapter. Islam Noir was both an intellectual construct and an administrative principle that deeply shaped the ways in which state authorities in French West Africa perceived and governed their African subjects. A visible component of the colonial archive and of subsequent secondary literature, it has been the subject of a number of useful analyses, and I do not treat it exhaustively here. But at the end of this chapter, I do focus specifically on how Islam Noir—which read West African Muslims not as bodies of knowledge but as bodies of ignorance—paradoxically helped preserve the epistemological foundations of Senegambian Islam during a century of dramatic social change.

Impure Bodies

Yoro Jaw, a noble from Waalo and nineteenth- and twentieth-century French colonial chief whose reflections on Senegambian history and society form much of the basis for historical ethnography in the region, defined a *géer* as "any person of either sex untouched by captive [slave] or gnégno [*ñeeño*] blood, from the royal princes down to the last badolo [free peasant]."[10] Among the hierarchical Senegambian societies, including almost all Fula, Wolof, Mandingo, and Soninke speakers, "freeborn" or "wellborn" identity (to which I will refer using the Wolof term *géer*) has been defined negatively in reference to two supposedly inferior categories of birth, *ñeeño* and *jaam*.[11] *Ñeeño* are best defined as endogamous lineages of occupational specialists, though francophone convention has long labeled them *castés* or *gens de caste*.[12] "Casted" status encompasses many groups and subgroups, including smiths (*tëgg*), leatherworkers (*wuude*), weavers (*ràbb*), and griots (*géwël*), among others. Occupational specialization is one of the oldest ways of organizing social life in the region, and discourses on the essential differences regarding the members of the groups are quite old.[13] In all hierarchical Senegambian societies, *ñeeño* are considered "free" in that they are not the slave property of any other individual or lineage, but they are also denied status and honor by freeborn society, which considers them generally uncouth. Though often attached to specific lineages in dependent and subordinate roles, *ñeeño* were categorically distinguished from slaves and generally considered unsuitable for enslavement.

The distinction between *géer* and *ñeeño* is primarily understood in terms of the "pure blood" (*dërët ju set*) of the former and the tainted blood (*dërët ju gàkk*) of the latter.[14] However, the taint in the bodily substance of *ñeeño* that is supposed to mark their inferiority is not limited to the blood. David Gamble's description (based on fieldwork conducted shortly after World War II) of stereotyped historical memory of the precolonial griots captures the way in which the bodily taint of *ñeeño* was seen as causing a thoroughgoing ritual contamination: "In the past they had a reputation for drunkenness and licentiousness and were long resistant to Islam. At death their bodies were not buried in the ground or thrown into the sea, for it was believed that in such cases the crops would fail or the fish die. Instead their bodies were deposited in hollow baobab trees. Now [in the 1950s] they are buried in a section of the cemetery apart from the rest of the community."[15]

This taint was understood to be both material and spiritual. *Ñeeño* also had spirit-propitiation rituals associated with their artisanal production that made them spiritually dangerous. A mid-nineteenth-century account from Anne Raffenel makes this explicit while highlighting the antiquity of Senegambian tropes of bodily taint: "Their bodies would poison seeds and fruit, claim the other negroes, and they would poison the water and the fish as well; therefore they are neither buried nor thrown into the sea or rivers. [They are believed] to live in close contact [*dans un commerce familier*] with the devil, and this belief contributes in no small measure to forbidding them access to the ordinary burial site."[16]

The typical representation of "casted" people as either non-Muslim or inadequately Muslim is closely tied to their supposed interactions—or transactions—with unseen spirits. In certain Islamic discourses, interaction with jinn can produce ritual impurity. A connection between particular occupations—especially smiths and tanners—and impurity has been known in Muslim societies outside of West Africa as well.[17]

In Senegambia, interaction with spirits and spirit possession has also played an important though ambiguous role in linking *ñeeño* with witchcraft. In short, "casted" people have been thought to be significantly more likely than the freeborn to be "witches" or "eaters of people" (*dëmm*). Witchcraft was (and is) thought to be an inherited characteristic, a transmissible essence or subtle substance within the body. Although appearing among all categories, it is thought to be concentrated most heavily among *ñeeño*.[18] Notions of sexual impurity have played a major role in the imaginings of *ñeeño* bodies as well. "Casted" women, especially griot women, are thought to be more sexually promiscuous. Indeed, intemperate and unreserved comportment of all kinds is considered typical of *ñeeño*.[19] Connected with this kind of sexual impurity, sexual relations with casted persons were thought capable of exposing transgressors to bodily, social, or financial misfortune (*um*).[20]

Differences between "casted" and "free" were thus understood to inhere in the very matter of the body itself. Nowhere is this more apparent than in the legendary description of the origins of the *ñoole* "caste." This group was said to have emerged as offspring of a woman who conceived a child with the corpse of her already deceased husband. In this trope, sexual and bodily impurity are explicitly tied together. And, indeed, the material of the *ñoole* body is thought to differ from that of the free insofar as they are believed to decompose more rapidly.[21]

ENSLAVED BODIES

Tropes of bodily taint also were used to characterize slaves. Strictly speaking, enslaved people did not form a "caste" in Senegambian society. Slave status was political and legal.[22] Conditions of life for enslaved people could vary dramatically, from recently purchased trade slaves who were treated like chattel to *ceddo* families of slave origin, which formed a kind of military aristocracy. But if complex political and social hierarchies defined conditions of life in different ways, there is no doubt that *jaam*, *maccudo*, *rimayɓe*, and other local nomenclatures are best translated as "slave." In the hierarchical Senegambian societies, people of such status were assigned to the category of slave under extant understandings of Islamic law. They observed half of the mourning period observed by the free and had to compensate their masters for their absence should they be fortunate enough to make the hajj to Mecca.[23]

While slave status was formally quite different from that of *ñeeño*, enslaved people were nonetheless assimilated to the ideological framework explaining *ñeeño* inferiority.[24] In short, slaves too were thought of as impure, and as powerful carriers of a bodily taint. This is most clearly seen in the study of marriage patterns of *jaam* and their descendants, which were usually though not always endogamous. Abdoulaye Bara Diop clearly portrays this similar but not identical stain of low, tainted birth: "We know that *biological ideology* contributed to the segregation and reproduction of slaves; but it was attenuated, even contradicted, by the commonly advanced argument that slaves were reduced to a servile state by ill fortune (arms) and not by biological defect—contrary to the members of the inferior castes."[25]

It is important to signal that this was not, strictly speaking, a "biological ideology." No biomedical notions of the body or the abstract universality of its systems were intrinsic to it. "Commonly advanced" counterarguments notwithstanding, bodily explanations for the inferiority of *jaam* remain current today and affect the status of their descendants in many respects.[26] The taint of capture has clung not only to the persons of the enslaved but also to their descendants as a kind of corporeal pollution. The fact that slave women were often abused sexually certainly contributed to the notion that impurity inhered in—or adhered to—the bodies of enslaved persons and their descendants. In this conception, the offspring of a slave woman's body was by definition impure.

PROXIMITY TO AND DISTANCE FROM FAITH

Islam was supposed to be the affair of the freeborn. *Géer* defined the social inferiority of *jaam* and *ñeeño* through religious as well as bodily and political reference. This viewpoint was reflected in access to knowledge of the Qur'an. Several authors have suggested that in the precolonial period, enslaved and casted people rarely submitted their children to live-in instruction, which was understood to be the most pious, rigorous, and thoroughgoing kind of Islamic education. Ravane Mbaye voices this view—with pristine freeborn bias—in this excerpt from his *Thèse de troisième cycle*: "This principle of live-in instruction [*internat*] was scrupulously respected by almost all the families of noble caste. . . . As for the families of servile castes, their children were obliged to learn the trade of their parents, or they could be left to vagabond about without anything to learn at that age. Moreover, in their difficult situation, they could not pass up the help, minimal though it was, that their children could offer them."[27] For Mbaye, only those of noble blood and patrician means would be willing to part with their children for the sake of abstract religious principle. To give a son as a *njàngaan* (live-in student), was the mark of a family's piety, honor, and wealth.

As in many societies, inattention to the education of low-status people was justified with the allegation that such groups inherently lacked intelligence. The Cahier Ponty of one Fulɓe Qur'an student says that members of the Subalbe fishing caste were thought to have the intelligence of fish and that all the best wrestlers came either from this class or from among the slaves.[28] People from the lower status groups were understood to have strong bodies and weak minds. Clearly, the notion that the "servile castes" were impure by birth, dull-witted, and incompletely Muslim was a much more serious obstacle to instruction than the logistical difficulties posed by craft apprenticeship.[29]

Though both enslaved and casted people were held at arm's length from Islamic knowledge, the former probably faced much more significant obstacles to instruction before colonial rule than the latter. For *jaam*, access to rigorous Qur'an instruction as a *njàngaan* was extremely difficult for two basic reasons: they had little control of the time and labor of their offspring, and the act of consigning a child to a *sëriñ* was based on the transfer of rights in persons, which *jaam* did not possess. The child of a female *jaam* belonged to her master, whatever the status or condition of the father. Even when a suitor redeemed a female *jaam* through payment of a bride price, the labor of her children remained under the control of her original owner until those children married.[30] The exception to this rule was the offspring of a union between a slaveholder and his female *jaam*: she became a concubine (*taara*), gaining her freedom and that of her child. The status of the Wolof *taara* and their children as attested in nineteenth- and twentieth-century ethnographic sources mirrors precisely the formal legal status of *umm walad* (the mother of child) in Mālikī law.[31] However, the mandatory manumission of mother and child associated with this status were not always respected. More important, even when free, such women and children remained socially stigmatized as *jaam* because the taint clung to their bodies and persons whatever their precise juridical status.[32]

For the most part, the enslaved stood on the outside of the Qur'an school looking in. Enslaved men were almost never allowed to marry freeborn women, meaning that only a tiny number of enslaved men and women controlled their children's labor. Slaves could not give children to a *sëriñ* for education because those children were not their parents' to give. Slaveholders were much more inclined to use enslaved children in domestic and field labor to allow the owners' children to study the Qur'an. With access to live-in instruction barred, enslaved children might be able to obtain access to drop-in instruction, but doing so would have required both the consent of the master and perhaps gifts to reimburse the *sëriñ*. *Jaam* might obtain such consent but were unlikely to do so because their social inferiority was justified by the stereotype of the enslaved as bad Muslims, descended from impure and unbelieving origins. Moreover, the poverty of most *jaam* made it difficult for them to pay for instruction. Theoretically, whatever wealth an enslaved male could accumulate could not be passed on to his descendants but instead reverted back to the master.[33] In the face of such obstacles, few *jaam* could acquire serious Qur'an instruction, though some clerical families offered instruction to their slaves.[34] Freeborn ideologies projected the notion that slaves were ignorant and irreligious, but it was the power of the freeborn that shaped reality to meet the stereotype. Little wonder then that so many would struggle to draw out the egalitarian themes in Islamic thought and reclaim their worth by pursuing sacred knowledge, for was it not the Prophet himself who said, "The nobility of my community are the bearers of the Qur'an"?

Breaking the Chains—Part II

In 1848, France abolished legal slavery in its colonies, leading to a century of smuggling, pawning, "apprenticeship," indenture—the myriad practices used to hide slavery in plain sight. The tangled history of efforts to end slavery in France's African colonies cannot be told here, but understanding some of its dynamics is critical to the story that unfolded at the end of the nineteenth century and into the twentieth. In spite of the potential complications, the weight of this emancipatory moment was not lost on the enslaved, and in Saint-Louis on 23 August 1848, upon hearing of the forthcoming decree, "many of the freed slaves went down to the sea for what seems to have been a spontaneous ritual cleansing."[35] This moment is poignant evidence that the taint of slavery was indeed perceived as clinging to the body. Seeking to wash away impurity in the waters of the Atlantic, perhaps these people sought *liberation*. Unfortunately, they found only a fraught *abolition*, and even this was tasted only by a few in the middle decades of the nineteenth century, as it affected the enslaved population only in the coastal colonies under French control. The result was a series of bilateral exoduses wherein people in bondage in neighboring African kingdoms fled to the coast in hopes of living in freedom, while coastal slave owners sold people to the mainland to keep them in bondage. Pieces of this process were visible in the last chapter in Majaxate Kala's efforts to retrieve *jaam* who had escaped to Saint-Louis.

This dance continued until the 1880s, when French military expansion onto the mainland intensified and began to erase the line between lands with slavery and lands without it. Beginning with tentative steps in the 1880s, the colonial regime progressively enforced legislation emancipating slaves within the newly minted AOF. Martin Klein suggests that over a half century, the formal labor bonds of slavery were effectively broken in most of the AOF and that by 1930, they had all but disappeared in Senegal. This was a profound change, but it neither removed the blight of slave birth nor conferred respect on *jaam*. Those who chose to claim their social dignity in the societies that had held them in bondage had to shatter the stereotype that they were godless. Klein describes the role that Islamic education played in reshaping the damaged social dignity of slaves of the Fulɓe in twentieth-century Mali: "For many *rimaibe*, becoming free meant becoming Fulbe. They often reproach their masters for not giving them the Muslim education that would have facilitated assimilation. It is not enough to become Fulbe by decision of the state. Those who can, often seek to do so either through Islam or, for the richer, by paying for their manumission. . . . The former slave who becomes a practising Muslim is also staking out a claim to honor."[36]

In Wolof country, also overwhelmingly Muslim, the dynamics were similar: to be Wolof was to be Muslim. For many people, the only option for obtaining dignity through Qur'an schooling was to consign a child to the care of a *sëriñ*, because few slave families emerged from emancipation with the ability to pay for instruction in cash or in kind. Moreover, live-in instruction was the standard for rigorous assimilation of the Qur'an. Drop-in instruction could familiarize a child with the Book, but consigning a child to a master would allow him to become it.

FEMALE BODIES OF KNOWLEDGE

Live-in instruction was barred to most girls, as it was extremely rare to have girls consigned to the care of strangers outside of the lineage. Unless a girl belonged to a prominent clerical lineage, therefore, she would receive an inferior drop-in education. Wellborn girls suffered many of the same disadvantages as boys of *jaam* or *ñeeño* lineage with regard to getting access to a thorough Islamic education. For many people, girls' education was not a priority. While tropes of female bodily impurity certainly played a role in casting girls as second-class subjects in Islam, producing a hierarchically gendered social order seems like the most pressing reason. In the words of anonymous male elders interviewed by David Ames in 1950, "Why does a woman need an education to bear children, pound grain, and draw water?"[37]

In light of such prejudices, it is not surprising that fewer girls than boys attended Qur'an schools. Such attitudes notwithstanding, many girls did study the Qur'an. Incomplete but suggestive colonial census data from the second decade of the twentieth century indicates that in the cities of Dakar and Saint-Louis, boys outnumbered girls by five-to-one and four-to-one ratios, respectively.[38] It is unclear whether ratios were more or less favorable further inland. Abdou Rahmane Diop's Cahier Ponty suggests that such ratios may have been fairly representative. "The girls constitute a significant part of the personnel," he wrote, "thirty [of 150] between the ages of seven and fourteen; they are charged with taking care of small domestic chores [*petits soins du ménage*]. They are all externals."[39]

Such ratios seem to reflect fairly high attendance rates by wellborn girls and almost no attendance by girls from *jaam* and *ñeeño* origins. Modibo Bamany, a Ponty student from Bandiagara in Mali, noted that all of the girls in his Qur'an school were "daughters of bureaucrats, marabouts, or rich families."[40] Nonetheless, as Ousseina Alidou reminds us in her careful study of gender and Islamic knowledge in Niger, Qur'an schools still educated a much higher percentage of girls than did French colonial schools.[41] Hadiza Djibo notes that in 1918 in all of French West Africa, only 503 girls were enrolled in French schools.[42]

Qur'an schools thus had much better gender ratios than French schools in the colonial period, but they were still generally poor. The fact that all girls were by definition external students may mean that overall ratios would have been somewhat lower than the 16 to 20 percent indicated above since all of the Qur'an schools in Saint-Louis and Dakar were in fixed locations, like the *daara* attended by Diop. Itinerant schools enrolled few, if any, female students. Abdou Rahmane Diop notes that girls "participate in neither the night classes nor in 'diangue dieul' [*jàng njël*—dawn study]. As for the day sessions, they arrive later and leave earlier."[43] The data, however, is inconclusive; it is possible that some of the schools surveyed in Dakar and Saint-Louis were itinerant schools from further inland and thus the girls enrolled remained in their home villages. Also, since they were only drop-in students and never *njàngaans*, girls were probably undercounted in all censuses. Whatever the gender ratios for all of Senegal in the early twentieth century, by the end of the colonial period, state census materials gave the ratio at 22 percent.[44]

Local conceptions of what constituted properly feminine spheres of activity shaped these ratios and led to qualitative as well as quantitative differences in the sorts of instruction given to girls. Observing the instruction of the girls in his *daara*, Abdelkader Fall wrote, "It is not necessary that young girls be very well versed in the study of the Qur'an. They learn the last twenty surats which are relatively short."[45] Abdou Rahmane Diop noted that in addition to being limited in its religious ambition, the instruction of girls also focused more on the practical benefits of literacy: "The study of writing begins earlier with the girls, their instruction not needing to be advanced very far."[46] Under normal circumstances, girls were not expected to be long-term students in the Qur'an school.[47] They were expected only to learn enough of the Qur'an to pray and to learn the letters of the alphabet so that they could write their mother tongues in Arabic script for domestic purposes. The reason for the disparity in the education of girls was clear enough to Abdelkader Fall: "This negligence in a woman's studies is easily explained. One asks of her only one thing: to obey and to remain faithful to her husband. A native precept says, 'A woman is led to heaven by her husband.' This means that whatever wisdom or sanctity a woman possesses, she will never go to heaven if her spouse is not happy with her. This illustrates well how highly one holds a woman's obligations to her husband."[48]

Qur'an schooling was seen as a way to shape girls into proper Muslim wives according to local conventions. It is thus not surprising that other sorts of "domestic" education—both practical and moral—comprised a girl's lot and were transmitted by the *sëriñ*'s wives. In the words of Abdelkader Fall, "The marabout's wife teaches them to sew, to dye fabric, and inculcates in them notions of propriety [*bienséance*] and native politesse."[49] These gendered aspects of moral education (*yar*) require more attention. Girls were not spared the lash (*yar*) in the *daara*, and at a basic level, moral education for girls and boys was rooted in the same logic: the school should reshape character (*defarat jikko*). Girls would be required to perform menial tasks that might normally be performed by servants in the homes of free and wealthy families—washing clothes, fetching water, making trips to the market, running other domestic errands.[50] This process resembled the humiliation experienced by male *njàngaan* as they worked in the fields and sought alms.

Most *daaras* that had female students were coeducational, though in some instances, the boys and girls were taught in separate physical places of instruction especially as they neared adolescence. While they shared the school with boys, they rarely shared the same education. Most girls were asked only to learn to practice their religion and to write grocery lists and to leave "scholarship" to men. Even so, there were exceptions to the rule. According to Abdelkader Fall, "Some of the particularly intelligent ones are able to go much further. They often become devout women, entirely occupied by religion. It is among these that the marabouts choose their wives. If they do not become the wives of holy men, they prefer to remain old maids or to give their bodies and goods over to a renowned marabout without asking for a dowry. Such is the provision of custom."[51]

Girls from clerical lineages often did memorize the entire Qur'an, and some became erudite and productive literary scholars in their own right.[52] In the colonial period, two of Amadu Bamba's daughters, Maymunatu and Muslimatu Mbakke, became esteemed authors of poetry and prose in Wolofal and Arabic. Ruqayya Niass, the daughter of Tijānī shaykh Ibrāhīm Niass

Girls at a Qur'an school in Dakar, Senegal, from a mid-twentieth-century postcard.

of Kaolack, completed her studies and began composing Arabic-language poetry on moral and religious themes shortly after independence. Some of her writings specifically targeted women because she felt that there was a dearth of works that spoke directly to them.[53] Her writings help us to envision the cultural expectations incumbent on Muslim girls: "O Muslim daughter, when you awake in the morning at six o'clock . . . praise God that his name be blessed and exalted! Then go to the bathroom to wash. Then do the cleaning quickly and without laziness, lay out the blankets on the bed or change the sheets, arrange the pillows, sweep the house and its outbuildings. It is then that you prepare to pray: make your ablutions for prayer with water *as you learned at school.* Do not rub your body with sand without a valid excuse like the negligent young girls. Then offer your morning prayer, observing all the rules."[54]

The school appears in her exhortation as the site where girls learned how to fulfill basic religious obligations, reaffirming the *daara*'s central role in practical instruction. But this passage also draws attention to the heavy household burdens that curtailed the scholarly aspirations of many female Qur'an students. Niass and others took their schooling much further, but for most girls, the *daara*'s mission ended with the rudiments of faith and preparation for domestic life.

Thus Senegalese sociologist Yaya Wane could still generalize in the ethnographic present of the 1960s: "The prolonged study of the Qur'an is only incumbent on the boys of the free castes. . . . Whereas for the boys of the professional or servile castes and the girls of all castes, generally the social collective esteems that their stay at the koranic school can be of short duration, because the former have a métier to learn, and the latter must be prepared for their conjugal destination."[55] Whatever the decree of the "social collective" (freeborn males), twentieth-century students of all backgrounds had more opportunities than had been available in the past to pursue serious instruction. While there are few reliable sources for statistical analyses in recent periods, statistics from neighboring countries and direct observations suggest that by the first decade of the twenty-first-century, between a third and half of all Qur'an students were girls. If this is true, then much of the increase in feminine attendance likely has come from girls from the low-status groups attending Qur'an schools in unprecedented numbers.

CHANNELING THE DEMAND

Changing gender ratios are part of an overall increase in accessibility of Qur'an schooling for people who were generally considered second-class Muslims in earlier eras. The descendants of slaves in particular have received greatly improved access to religious education over the past century. The multitude of slaves who fled to Murid settlements in central Senegal seeking instruction and Islamic legitimacy in the order's *daaras* has been well documented elsewhere.[56] The slaves and subalterns who fled to the relative anonymity of cities and towns and sought Islamic legitimacy in Tijānī structures have been less well documented, but a number of scholars have made arguments that echo Lucie Colvin: "During the colonial period, when the towns became a refuge for low status persons escaping rural masters, the Tijāniyya recruited freely."[57] The Sufi orders sought to deemphasize social

Map 4.1: Senegal since 1900

origins, laying new stress on equality before God. They also provided an entirely new framework of social hierarchy. Moreover, they did so in delocalized spaces. Structures of caste and slavery were particularly well suited to the old agrarian village order. Murids established new villages, towns, and even cities in agricultural areas of the Senegambian interior. Tijānīs made formidable inroads in colonial cities and towns such as Dakar, Kaolack, Kebemer, Tivaouane, and Saint-Louis. The Sufi orders did not eradicate older orders of "caste" and hierarchy but made them less salient.

This decision was neither unconscious nor automatic; indeed, it required a careful and innovative effort to redirect the flow of history. Sufi legacies contained no automatic prescriptions for the development of an Islamic social order. As Louis Brenner has argued, "The emergence of *ṭuruq* [corporate Sufi orders] in West Africa . . . was not an accident but the result of conscious decisions by Sufi leaders who saw in them a potential not only for religious change, but also for social and political transformation."[58]

To further emphasize the point, it is useful to suspend the teleological term "Sufi leaders." As Brenner notes, these were first and foremost men issued from traditional clerical lineages. They were students and teachers of all the traditional disciplines of the Islamic sciences, including law, theology, and grammar. But they saw in Sufism the potential for new kinds of polity, society, and piety. To bring this about, they had to extend the reach of what had essentially been a private initiatory discipline. Sufism was a fixed body of knowledge, which had to be creatively mined and deployed to become an effective instrument of change. One of the key institutions in the articulation of new social meanings rooted in Islam was the school. Clerics' primary function as teachers and embodiments of the Qur'an guaranteed them a certain social importance and a base from which to broaden their influence. The marabout-*taalibé* pedagogical relationship became the foundation of—and model for—the Sufi *shaykh-murīd* relationship.

From *Taṣawwuf* to *Ṭarīqa*

The Sufi social revolution of the late nineteenth century was inextricably tied to teaching. By this time, centuries of effort by prestigious clerical families and village Qur'an school teachers had made preaching and teaching clerics the focal point of religious life for most Senegambian Muslims. To understand how Sufi structures elaborated on and modified structures of Islamic education, some background on the history of Sufism and its development in Senegal is necessary here. Sufism, often glossed as Islamic mysticism, began to appear as a formally distinct discipline probably in the second century after the *hijra*. It was thus roughly coeval with the emergence of *fiqh* and the other classical Islamic religious sciences of which it became an integral part. By the twelfth century of the Common Era, several hundred years later, it is possible to document the existence of large organized Sufi groups with distinctive ritual and organizational practices.[59] The Sufis called such organizations *ṭarīqas*. The word *ṭarīqa* in Arabic functions very much like the English word "way" in that it signifies both a manner of doing something and a path leading to a destination. The distinctiveness of each "way" was determined by the teachings of its founder, whose name was usually given to the *ṭarīqa* itself. Thus, the world's largest and most widespread Sufi *ṭarīqa*, the Qādiriyya, is named for ʿAbdul-Qādir Jilānī of Baghdad, who died in the twelfth century.

The Qādiriyya was probably the first *ṭarīqa* to appear in West Africa and was certainly the first to be carefully documented. Erudite members of southern Saharan clerical lineages probably followed the Qādirī way as early as the sixteenth or seventeenth century. The Qādiriyya was present in Senegambia and other parts of sub-Saharan West Africa by the eighteenth century.[60] By the early nineteenth century, the Qādiriyya had been joined by the Tijāniyya.[61] Until the nineteenth century, membership in the Qādiriyya and the Tijāniyya was limited almost exclusively to the spiritual elite of the clerical lineages. Distinguished clerics collected and exchanged Sufi initiations and supererogatory prayers (*wird*) to gain intimate experiential knowledge of God and spiritual authority. They were following the "way" of a *ṭarīqa* in the sense that they employed its means and followed its path; however, the *ṭarīqa* as a semicorporate entity and popular organization did not yet exist in Senegambia. In a manner of speaking, Sufism was represented by *taṣawwuf* more than *ṭarīqa*.

The beginnings of a change from elite to popular Sufism began late in the eighteenth century in the southern Sahara. Sīdī al-Mukhtār al-Kuntī began to reshape the practices of the order to move beyond the traditional confines of the Muslim lineage and out of the private realm of elitist, introspective *taṣawwuf*.[62] In the middle of the nineteenth century, al-Ḥājj ʿUmar Taal, a cleric from Halwar in Fuuta Tooro, launched a major Islamic reform movement and military jihad. Tijāniyya affiliation and identity were important components of this effort.[63] Al-Ḥājj ʿUmar had been named a *muqaddam* and *khalīfa* of the order, meaning that he was both authorized to distribute the order's *wird* and enfranchise others to do so. The success of ʿUmar Taal's political and social efforts among Fulɓe Muslims implanted the Tijāniyya-ʿUmariyya among the Tooroɓɓe clerical lineages of the Senegal River Valley, where it surpassed the influence of the older Qādiriyya.[64]

Both the Qādiriyya and the Tijāniyya spread to Wolof country through the bonds of blood and ink linking clerics throughout Senegambia and the southwestern Sahara. Clerics sought to augment their learning, prestige, and *baraka* through the study of *taṣawwuf*. They vied to accumulate short chains of initiation (*silsila*) relating them to great Sufi masters. Throughout most of the nineteenth century, the Qādiriyya and the Tijāniyya remained restricted to the clerisy. In the last two decades of the nineteenth century, a number of clerics developed visions that transformed Sufi orders into popular organizations. Bu Kunta, a Qādirī shaykh of Saharan origin, and al-Ḥājj ʿAbdullahi

Niass, a Tijānī shaykh in Saalum, played major roles, but the most significant transformations in the first two decades of the twentieth century were authored by al-Ḥājj Mālik Sy and Amadu Bamba Mbakke.

The lives and works of Sy and Bamba cannot be explored in detail here.[65] Yet some background is necessary, and a summary of the educational strategies they employed is central to my argument. Both men were born around 1855 to families of Fuutanke origin that had lived in Wolof territories for more than a century and had become linguistically and culturally Wolofized. Both pursued Qurʾan study in their youth, memorized the Qurʾan, and went through a prolonged phase of itinerant study in the Islamic sciences with respected teachers in Senegal and southern Mauritania. Both men became teachers early in life, beginning to offer Qurʾan instruction on their own around 1880 after first instructing in their fathers' schools. Bamba and Sy obtained advanced instruction in Arabic and the Islamic sciences, ultimately demonstrating their piety and erudition through the composition of religious poetry and prose. Both men were also committed Sufis, and it was in the realm of *taṣawwuf* that their intellectual biographies diverged and formed the basis for distinct approaches to educational reform.

Mālik Sy was born in Gaya in Fuuta Tooro, and his family had relationships with the Umarian branch of the Tijāniyya, though it did not apparently participate in ʿUmar's jihad of the sword. Amadu Bamba Mbakke was born in Bawol to a family affiliated with the Qādiriyya movement founded by Siddiya al-Kabīr. Both Mālik Sy and Amadu Bamba had watched Umarians and the other jihad movements of the mid-nineteenth century crumble under the weight of their own inconsistencies and French cannons.[66] Later, the French fictions of Islam Noir would hold that black marabouts were inherently quietist and disinclined to jihad as a consequence of their incomplete understandings of and commitment to Muslim doctrines. However, Muslim clerical groups led the most sustained and effective military resistance that the French encountered in the conquest of West Africa. Unlike the most famous clerics of the generation that preceded them, Sy and Mbakke entertained no notions of waging the jihad of the sword. By the time they had come of age, French colonial rule was a fait accompli. Early in their careers, they began to experiment with the use of Sufi structures and educational reform to promote Islamic practice and piety through peaceful means.[67]

By the early 1890s, both men were successful teachers, clerics, and scholars with flourishing *daaras* and the loyalty of many disciples. But like Sīdī al-Mukhtār and ʿUmar Taal before them, they hoped to transcend the limitations of the traditional clerical lineage through *ṭarīqa*. By 1903, Amadu

Bamba had announced publicly that the Prophet Muḥammad had granted him a *wird*.[68] He broke free from the Qādiriyya and created a new order, which he called the Murīdiyya, derived from the Arabic term *murīd*, which denotes the spiritual aspirant and disciple in classical Sufi instruction. *Murīd* is derived from the noun *arāda* and communicates longing, desire, and seeking. The Murīdiyya is the order of the seeker of God. A year earlier, Mālik Sy had founded a Tijānī *zāwiya* (Sufi lodge) in Tivaouane, and it became the center for a distinct subset of the order held together by his influence and instruction, the Tijāniyya-Mālikiyya.

AL-ḤĀJJ MĀLIK SY

Mālik Sy had diversified and strengthened his Tijāniyya affiliations during itinerant study as a young man. As a learned and committed Sufi, he sought the shortest chain of transmission (*silsila*) for his Tijānī affiliation, ultimately making connections with the *zāwiya* of the order's founder, Aḥmad al-Tijānī in Fez. He was made a *muqqadam* in the order, licensed to distribute the *wird* and to appoint his own lieutenants. His exceptional scholarship and propitious initiation into the Tijāniyya drew the attention of the wealthy and learned Muslims of Saint-Louis, who provided him with patronage in the early stages of his career.[69] After a phase of consolidation in the late 1890s in central Kajoor, where he ran an important school and developed extensive fields with the labor of his disciples, he moved to Tivaouane. His pedagogical approach, which was probably developed before the move, was a rigorous incarnation of the classical model: he taught the Qur'an to young students in the standard way. His instruction in the Islamic sciences was reputed to be of excellent quality, and it was infused with an important element of Tijānī *taṣawwuf*, including his own writings, especially his defenses of Tijānī doctrine. Armed with a solid education and the authority to initiate new members into the Tijāniyya, his students spread throughout Senegal, reproducing the model of instruction and Tijānī proselytism taught in Tivaouane.

Al-Ḥājj Mālik seems to have employed a conscious strategy of using the colonial infrastructure to proselytize and educate, sending teachers to the cities and the newly burgeoning railroad towns.[70] Al-Ḥājj Mālik enjoyed esteem among the French administration and was one of only a handful of Senegambians permitted to make the pilgrimage during the 1890s. Perhaps as a result, the French did not notice that his quietist educational approach had the subtle effect of subverting the French *mission civilisatrice* from its very centers. His model was to open Qur'an schools and *zāwiyas* in the same colonial towns that spread French schooling and material culture. Muslim affairs officer Paul Marty, the chief architect of Islam Noir, was largely ignorant of the form, content, and meaning of Qur'an schooling. He did, however, perceive the centrality of education in Mālik Sy's mission and described it in his 1917 volume, *Études sur l'Islam au Sénégal*: "The characteristic of the Zaouïa of Tivaouane is that it constitutes a veritable popular university. It has formed a considerable quantity of Qur'anic school masters who have spread out across Lower Senegal, forming in turn a new pleiad of masters thus contributing to greatly expand the rudiments of Muslim instruction. . . . The clientele of the Shaykh of Tivaouane is above all a clientele of lesser marabouts, propagators of instruction on the wooden tablet." Marty went on to name a number of Qur'an school teachers who offered classical instruction—and dispensed the Tijānī litanies (*awrād*) in Mālik's name—throughout Senegal.[71]

AMADU BAMBA

Like Mālik Sy, Amadu Bamba was a committed Sufi and teacher of the Qur'an. In his days as a student of the Islamic sciences, he experimented with multiple religious initiations in addition to his familial Qādirī affiliation.[72] He was searching for the shaykh who could guide him to the closeness with God for which he longed. He sought a shorter *silsila* and was reinitiated and consecrated as a *muqaddam* in the Qādiriyya by Siddia Baba, a descendant of Siddia al-Kabir, in Mauritania in the early 1880s.[73] But unlike Mālik Sy, Bamba never found a shaykh who could fully satisfy his longing as a *murīd*, a seeker after God. If Mālik Sy found what he was looking for in Aḥmad Tijānī's *zāwiya* in Fez, Bamba ultimately discovered that the shaykh he sought was within.

He reported a vision of the Prophet while in a waking state in the early 1890s and thereafter consistently referred to himself as the "servant of the Prophet" (*khādim al-Rasūl*). The full social articulation of this new ontological status was forestalled by his deportation to Gabon by French authorities in 1895.[74] When he returned to Senegal in 1902, his freedom was short-lived. Concerned by the size of his following, the French deported him to Mauritania a short time thereafter in the hopes that the Qādirī shaykh who had initiated him, Siddia Baba, could exercise some influence on him. But twenty years had passed since Amadu Bamba had been initiated by Siddia Baba, a man several years his junior. In the intervening years, Bamba had undertaken much study and many Sufi retreats, he had written countless pages of religious poetry and prose, and he had endured a seven-year exile in a non-Muslim land. Most important, he had seen the Prophet and had been personally guided by him.[75]

Amadu Bamba Mbakke no longer considered the *bayḍān* cleric his superior; in a written response to the suggestion that he was not sufficiently deferential to his host and spiritual guide, he made this fact abundantly clear: "I am not your disciple—as you know well—because I am forbidden from attaching myself to anyone on this earth. This is not because I disrespect or underestimate Shaykhs, but because the Messenger of God turned to me to educate me and promote me and there is no way that I can turn away from him."[76] Bamba garnered many disciples from among the *bayḍān* while in Mauritania, and the French ultimately realized that their efforts had failed and brought Bamba back to Bawol. Bamba then began fully actualizing a new concept of pedagogy for his new *ṭarīqa*.

Bamba had begun experimenting with a new Sufi pedagogy two decades earlier, even before his vision of the Prophet in the early 1890s. His path to Sufi-inspired educational reform began in earnest when his father, Momar Anta Sali, died in the early 1880s. Momar Anta Sali had at one time been the primary Muslim judge of the dammel of Kajoor, Lat Joor Jóob. At his father's funeral, it was suggested that Bamba, already an accomplished scholar, should likewise pursue a career at the dammel's court. Bamba rejected the notion publicly, expressing what would become his characteristic stance vis-à-vis worldly authorities: "I do not have the habit of mingling with rulers, and I do not expect any help from them. I seek honor only from the Supreme Lord (God)."[77]

Such statements had been the credos of most West African clerics for a thousand years. Bamba chose instead to occupy himself with the family school in Mbakke-Kajoor, immediately introducing radical changes.[78] He was rebuked for his refusal to associate with the dammel, just as he was later punished for his refusal to associate with the French. But his defiance of rulers was tied to a new Sufi vision for actualizing the timeless goal of the clerisy: a Muslim social order independent of temporal powers. His vision of this new order took shape through his pedagogical experimentation in the *daara* of Mbakke-Kajoor and later in Mbakke-Bawol. According to Cheikh Anta Babou, "The system that Amadu Bamba designed was a lifelong education geared towards the transformation of the character and behaviour of the disciples. It comprised three main steps: exoteric education or *taalim*, which aimed at feeding the brain by the study of the Qur'an and the Islamic sciences, and esoteric education or *tarbiyya* which aimed at educating the soul. The third step, *tarqiyya*, which was reached by only a small number of especially gifted disciples, allowed the elevation of their souls beyond the futility of material life and put them in a position of leadership in the community."[79]

This tripartite hierarchy of *taʿalīm*, *tarbiya*, and *tarqiyya* (instruction, education, ascension) is a classic pedagogical trope in many classical texts, and Bamba, like other traditionally trained pedagogues (not only Sufis), thought with it and through it. His writings and his educational practice show this concern, for he was as much interested in shaping the inner lives of his disciples as he was with shaping their external comportment.[80] The most dramatic innovation he introduced in this vein was the *daara tarbiya*.

DAARA TARBIYA

The *daara tarbiya* retains most of the basic forms and elements of the classical *daara*; however, the ostensible goal is not the memorization of the entire Qur'an but a taming of the soul. Bamba well knew that the Qur'an was usually only memorized by the sons of clerical lineages who pursued it as a matter of family obligation and the basis for a clerical career. Those individuals not descended from clerical lineages usually left the *daara* after a few years, having learned basic observance of Islam, literacy skills, and enough of the Qur'an to be able to pray and develop respect for the Word. Bamba must have seen this degree of attainment as insufficient for inculcating in them the level of piety that he sought. The flood of disciples that filled Bawol in the 1890s and 1900s was largely composed of people from slave and casted origins. Large numbers of unlettered adults and adolescents submitted themselves to Bamba's instruction. Most were well past the normal age for beginning Qur'an study. For them, the traditional *daara* was probably inappropriate and just as probably incapable of reshaping their inner and outer selves.

The *daara tarbiya* emphasized service to a Sufi shaykh as a guide and spiritual mentor. This was, in a sense, an extension of the traditional principle of *khidma* (service) as it was known in many Qur'an school communities, but it was imbued with new Sufi significance. For Bamba, the *daara tarbiya* was modeled on the relationship between the Sufi guide (*murshid*) and his *murīd*. The disciple would serve his shaykh to receive his *baraka* and emulate the shaykh's comportment. This vision of education, though new to Senegambia, drew its inspiration from classical Sufi educational principles.

In addition to reshaping education with the introduction of the Sufi-modeled *daara tarbiya*, Amadu Bamba pursued a missionary educational approach that paralleled the one employed by al-Ḥājj Mālik.[81] Bamba did not, however, conceive of his missionary approach in exactly the same way that Mālik Sy did, though Bamba apparently sent some teachers along the rail line and into colonial towns and cities. Consistent with a posture of distance from temporal authority, the cornerstone of the Murid approach was to colonize "new lands," establishing a *daara tarbiya* or a new village in the interior away from state authority, especially in Bawol and Saalum.[82]

Bamba's missionary approach to teaching differed from that of Mālik Sy in another respect. Bamba did not so much train cadres of teachers as he invested existing teaching lineages with his personal authority and delegated particular responsibilities to them. According to Shaykhuna Lo, a descendant of one of Amadu Bamba's first disciples, ʿAbdul-Raḥmān Lo, "In the time of Sëriñ Touba, he said, 'Find me one hundred people with the same family name who have all memorized the Qur'an and are capable of its exegesis.' Only among those named Lo could they be found. Within the children of this same family, there was also one who was called ʿAbdul-Raḥmān Lo—Sëriñ Ndam, Abdul-Raḥmān Lo. It was he who taught the children of Sëriñ Touba and other important *taalibés*."[83]

The Lo family had maintained Qur'an schools for centuries in the village of Ndame in the region of Njambuur. Bamba likely designated them to teach the Qur'an and the Islamic sciences to Murids because of their reputation for particularly rigorous scholarship and his close relationship with Sëriñ Ndam. The Buso family, Bamba's matrilineage, also had a strong teaching reputation and earned a special designation as a family of instruction within the Murīdiyya.[84] These families were entrusted to teach the Qur'an, and their most prominent scholars instructed the elite of the order and supervised the quality of instruction of the Islamic sciences.

■ Though Sufi organizations of some scale were established by the Kunta family and by ʿUmar Taal before the 1880s, these groups largely remained restricted to the clerisy. Before Amadu Bamba and Mālik Sy, Sufism had no real history as a mass movement in Senegambia. These two visionary Sufis and scholars implemented strategies to spread the influence of their orders and the reach of Islam. But why were their efforts so singularly effective? In 1880, Amadu Bamba and Mālik Sy were successful teachers; by 1910, they were the heads of the largest Sufi organizations in Senegalese history. How did they attract so many followers and disciples? How did Sufi initiation, a practice previously confined to the clerisy, become a primary principle of social organization for Senegalese Muslims from all backgrounds and walks of life?

Scholars have proposed many different responses to this question, and the answers are too complex to fully untangle here. However, no explanation of the popular success of Sufi orders in the late nineteenth and early twentieth centuries is complete without an understanding of the historical legacies of Qur'an schooling in Senegambia. The Sufi shaykh was a new sort of *sëriñ*: in fact, the word for Sufi shaykh in Wolof is *sëriñ*.[85] He remained the focal point of *baraka*, but Sufism now vested him with an institutionalized ability to make an impact in the unseen world. The older vision of the *sëriñ* as an embodiment of knowledge made Senegambian Muslims receptive to Sufi teaching. The Qur'an schools' esoteric approach to the Word was fully compatible with Sufism; thus, the Qur'an school made the ethos of Sufism legible to ordinary Muslims. Indeed in Wolof, the term *sëriñ* is used interchangeably to refer either to a teacher or a Sufi shaykh. The Sufi orders also benefited from the broad prestige and social influence of the clerisy. The strong social ties that linked *sëriñs* and *taalibés* made it possible to elaborate in novel ways on structures of personal allegiance and spiritual submission, turning them into widely accepted principles of social organization.[86]

Of course, the time could not have been riper for an infusion of new Sufi structures of education and society. The French had destroyed the hereditary Wolof kingdoms and the jihad states but had not filled the void with new social institutions. The end of slavery and the old social order may have made the need for new social structures particularly acute, but the importance of Muslim identity and the desire for Islamic legitimacy made clerics particularly attractive patrons. The clerical community provided a potential model for social reorganization in this time of change. Early efforts by al-Ḥājj Mālik Sy, Amadu Bamba, and al-Ḥājj ʿAbdullahi Niass to develop agricultural communities around Qur'an school farms are best understood as applications of this model. As the structures of their respective *ṭarīqas* developed, it seems to have become clear that a Sufi model of discipleship need not require the same sort of spatial localization. Disciples were connected to a new delocalized sort of clerical community through chains of initiation and ritual submission. The shaykh's blessing held together this new form of identity, allowing the Sufi community to become a Qur'an school writ large.

THE *SËRIÑ* AND THE SHAYKH

A specific example of the ways in which *ṭarīqa* structures represented a kind of delocalization of the social relationships of the Qur'anic community is the *toolu àllarba* (Wednesday field). In the Sufi context, the Wednesday field is cultivated on this day of the week by a shaykh's disciples.[87] It was among the most essential economic structures of the *ṭarīqas* in the past century because it allowed shaykhs to accrue annual revenue from the agricultural labor of disciples they almost never saw. Many rural Senegalese communities have Wednesday fields devoted to specific Sufi shaykhs, but the Wednesday field was originally devoted to the Qur'an teacher, a fact that has not disappeared from the historical memory of Senegalese Muslims. In a 1967 interview about the origins of the institution, a Tijānī farmer reported, "The Wednesday field dates back to the foundation of Islam. It was for he who taught the Qur'an. If one did not set aside a special field, one came to work on Wednesday in the fields of he who taught the Qur'an."[88] Drop-in and adult students as well as those who simply wished to accomplish a pious act cultivated a teacher's Wednesday field. Its extension to the adult disciples of a Sufi shaykh was based on the analogy between the student and the disciple. Senegalese Muslims accepted the practice because it constituted a precedent for expressing piety, fidelity, and obligation to a *sëriñ*.[89]

The Sufi orders not only built on the historical ties that bound *sëriñ* and *taalibé* but also modified and, at least initially, threatened them. Oral sources well remember the conflict between established Wolof clerical families, the *doomi soxna*, and Amadu Bamba in the early stages of his mission. The famous story of the submission of one previously antagonistic *doomu soxna*, Mañaaw Sylla, illustrates the economic dependence of the clerical families on their *taalibés* as well as their fear of the change the Murid movement wrought. When Amadu Bamba returned from exile in 1902, he is supposed to have asked Mañaaw Sylla,

> "Mañaaw, what was your occupations [*sic*] during my exile in Gabon?" Mañaaw responded; "every Friday we would cook a lot of food to give away in the form of alms, recite the Koran many times and pray God so that you never return to this land"; Amadu Bamba pursued, "Why were you doing that?" Mañaaw said, "Mbakke, we are *doomi soxna*, we live by our schools and the labor of our disciples and you were about to take all that from us." Amadu Bamba said, "Mañaaw, you [alone] are telling me this only because you are an honest man, but you were not alone in doing this"; he added, "but the man I am going to make of you will never again need the labor of pupils for his [livelihood].[90]

This ex post facto prophecy attributed to Bamba regarding the career of Mañaaw Sylla can stand in for the changes awaiting the clerical class as a whole. The Sufi revolution transformed the teacher-student relationship. By the end of the first decade of the twentieth century, the clerical families that taught the Qur'an and depended on the labor of their pupils and disciples had made their own submissions to the representatives of the major orders. They had become a part of the structure of popular Sufism. Clerics, who had earlier sought private initiations into *taṣawwuf* as elite badges of honor, were now part of semicorporate *tarixas*. Sufism had gone from a discrete and discreet body of knowledge to a public institution that allowed Muslims to act as a body.

Moving the Bar—Cash, Schooling, and Social Change

Demand from low-status people for an embodied dignity as Qur'an reciters was a driving force for social change from the 1890s forward, but by the first decades of the twentieth century, wellborn lineages seem to have begun using cash accumulated in the colonial economy to transform the relationship between status and schooling. Careful reading of first-person accounts from the 1920s and 1930s, particularly the Cahiers Ponty, suggests that as low-status people began to avail themselves of Qur'an schooling and offer their children to the care of *sëriñs*, the freeborn changed the manner of keeping score in the status game. They demonstrated wealth through payment and sought to guarantee privilege through the more expensive and less available French school. The *njàngaan*, once the son of the noble, was becoming the son of the subaltern. The social significance of mendicancy and servile labor in the *daara*, which had always mimed low status to teach resourcefulness to the wellborn, began to shift as these activities came to be associated with true poverty and low birth rather than their simulacra.

Wealth had always, of course, played a role in structuring access to Islamic knowledge. In the precolonial period, a family's wherewithal determined whether it would be able to send many children to be *njàngaans* or none at all. Wealth structured paid instruction as well. Payment in cash or kind appears to have long been an option for students of the Qur'an in Senegambia. Wolof kings and wealthy nobility are known to have hired *sëriñs* as personal tutors for their children.[91] In ordinary *daaras*, instruction was dispensed to external students who lived in close proximity in exchange for a day of labor in the teacher's fields or a "gift" delivered to the *sëriñ* on Wednesday (*àllarba*) that ultimately came to be called by that name.[92]

Payments were almost never structured or discussed as such; they were framed as *hadiyya* (gift). One did not pay to learn the Qur'an, nor did teachers demand payment. For this reason, remuneration varied greatly according to time, place, and circumstance. Nonetheless, some of these conventions became quite routinized forms of payment, though even such regular payments were structured and discussed as *substituting* for the labor of the *taalibés* rather than as tuition.

Payment was rarely formally binding because teachers of the Qur'an were usually reticent to demand payment. But in practice, students who did not provide at least token gifts could be excluded from real instruction and made to *taxawaalu* (stand by or audit).[93] Such deadbeat *taalibés* were unlikely to be blessed with the *baraka* of the *sëriñ*. A number of Cahiers Ponty also suggest that certain teachers freely let people choose what to give.[94] A colonial official who wrote a short ethnographic piece on family relations in Kajoor in 1939 mentioned the custom for payment at the end of study: "Parents of children who have come out of a Koranic school at the end of their religious instruction are expected to pay compensation to the marabout according to their means."[95] In Senegambia at least, this was the ordinary approach, though it was expected that these would be gifts of significant value, including large domestic animals and especially heads of cattle.

WEALTH AND STATUS

By the 1920s and 1930s, when the first detailed descriptions of financial arrangements for drop-in students appear in the Cahiers Ponty, payments were clearly routinized and based on colonial currency. Baba Ndiaye noted that external students paid "50 centimes" every Wednesday.[96] Médoune Fall affirms this view, reporting that *externes* paid 50 centimes every Wednesday for the right to have a weekend.[97] This token sum retained the form of the *àl-larba* payment, but it was hardly enough to reimburse the *sëriñ* for his time; hence, other payments were required. Abdou Rahmane Diop describes a sophisticated system wherein external students were required to pay for each of the chores from which they were exempted. Each live-in student owed his morning alms to the *sëriñ*, but since external students did not beg (*ne vont point mendier*), the *yalwaan* was replaced by a sum of between ten and twenty francs per month. Diop continues, "The *taxañ* is another charge due for those who do not gather dead wood for the night classes—it is fixed at ten to twenty francs. In order to be granted holidays one must, every week, on Wednesday morning, give twenty-five centimes. Likewise, to be able to enjoy the '*beurre*' [*bër*—annual vacation] a sum of five francs is claimed from the students. The internal students pay none of these charges."[98]

Another Ponty student, Baba Ndiaye, does not describe such a comprehensive tuition system in his *daara*, but he reports that external students paid a sum fixed at roughly ten to fifteen francs per month.[99] It is unclear how wealth articulated with birth to shape the *interne/externe* divide in the early twentieth century since none of the Ponty students commented openly on ascribed status, presenting Islamic education as freely available to all Muslims. But access to instruction as an external student obviously depended on a family's ability to produce a surplus. Although the costs were not necessarily exorbitant or even rigorously enforced, they could be obstacles to obtaining a Qur'anic education. Testimonials from life in the schools make it clear that by the 1920s, many previously marginalized people were flooding into the *daaras*. By that time, most live-in students were probably the children of poor peasant farmers (*baadolo*) and *jaam*.

For Médoune Fall, such a conclusion was so self-evident that it led him to secondary speculation about the nature of the historical connection between live-in instruction and poverty: "In the beginning . . . the country was led by a rather fetishist aristocracy that monopolized all the wealth. The first Muslims were all 'badolos' and slaves. Not being very rich, they had no means at all of paying for the instruction of their children; they confided them [to the marabout] and made them work."[100]

Other students corroborate the view that in the interwar period, most *njàngaans* were sons of the poor and powerless. Wealthy families, it seems, were becoming less likely to suffer their children being clothed in rags and begging from door to door than families of more humble origins. In his Cahier Ponty, Baba Ndiaye commented on the connection between one's family status and the *interne/externe* divide. "If the child belongs to a high family," he wrote, "whose reputation will not allow him to go asking charity from hut to hut, as compensation the marabout has recourse to wages."[101]

Abdelkader Fall identified himself proudly as an external student as he described the privileged nature of this category: "These are the sons of the well-to-do inhabitants of the village; I was one of these external pupils. In the morning after breakfast they go to the Qur'anic school and return home around noon. They go back out in the afternoon at the hour of first [afternoon] prayer (one pm) and return home after four pm. It is in this category that one finds the best students. They only study with the marabout without complicating their studies with chores."[102] Fall's testimony contradicts the idea that *njàngaans* were the most capable category of students with the plausible reasoning that the difficult life of a *taalibé* complicated scholarly achievement. But this description ignored the fact that *njàngaans* also engaged in *njang njël* (dawn study) from about 4:30 to 6:30, before the morning prayer, and studied again after sunset. The firelit studies (*dudal* or "hearth" is the name for a Qur'an school in Fula) more than doubled the hours of instruction that most live-in students received.

When they had the means, many families chose gentler fee-based instruction for their children, but certainly not all did so, in part because it meant far fewer hours spent in study. Moreover, normative discourses still upheld the redemptive qualities of suffering as a *njàngaan*. Médoune Fall wrote, "Even in well-off families, the father finds no fault in sending his son to lead this indigent's life. 'God blesses the father who has his son learn the Qur'an.'"[103] When a family sought to shelter its children from the hardships of the *daara*, "the father of a family is even criticized for having wished to free himself from the prescriptions of custom. He who places the happiness of his son above the obligations of religion is called a bad Muslim."[104] Modibo Bamany, another Ponty student, reinforces the classical sense that the best way to learn was as a student consigned to the care of a teacher. External students, "enjoying their freedom about town, do not give sustained attention to their studies, that's why with us, parents try to send their children as far away as they can when they take them to the school. The external student rarely finishes [memorizing] the Qur'an."[105]

Payment in cash for educational services did more than mark the affluence of wellborn and well-to-do families; it may also have opened up the possibility of pursuing education in French schools. Abdelkader Fall noted that attendance at the *école française* was an impossibility for the *njàngaan*, whereas the drop-in student was able to attend fairly easily: "The French school has come to compete with that of the marabout. It is above all the external boys who go to this [French] school because for the *talibés-ndianganes* it is out of the question."[106] If more *njàngaans* were drawn from the ranks of the poor and former slaves, then these groups would have had less access than wealthy *géer* to the French school. Some wealthy freeborn families paid for Qur'an instruction to maintain social superiority in Islamic terms while simultaneously benefiting economically from French education. In other words, some *géer* families, particularly in towns, used the French school as an avenue to wealth while still frequenting the Qur'an school to reinforce status.

L'École Française

French schooling thus shaped dynamics of Islamic knowledge transmission in important ways as perceptions toward live-in Qur'anic instruction—particularly in cities and towns—shifted dramatically. But the *école française* posed a more fundamental problem to the basis of Qur'an schooling. From the outset of colonial expansion, the colonial state promoted French schools in direct opposition to Qur'an schools. Louis Léon César Faidherbe, the chief architect of French military expansion, saw the colonial school as a crucial tool for naturalizing and legitimating French rule. In a March 1857 letter to the minister of the marine, he wrote, "The affair of the schools . . . I regard as the most important of all those with which I am charged."[107] The statement was only a minor hyperbole. This was the heyday of assimilation discourse in the French Empire, and Faidherbe took the idea more seriously than most. Michael Crowder has defined the notion of assimilation in French imperial discourse as the belief that "there were no racial and cultural differences that *education* could not eliminate. Thus the French, when confronted with people whom they believed to be barbarians, believed it their mission to convert them to Frenchmen."[108] Perhaps Faidherbe did not wish to convert Africans into Frenchmen, but he certainly hoped to use French schools to assimilate them to the colonial enterprise.[109]

In 1857, Faidherbe personally authored the first decree to that end. Throughout the latter half of the nineteenth century, French officials sought to restrict the free practice of Islamic education through legal measures. Their efforts were aimed first at the colonial outposts in Saint-Louis, Gorée, Dakar, and Rufisque and later at the whole mainland colony. Subsequent decrees in 1870, 1896, and 1903 were proffered in the name of the public good and the social welfare of children.[110] But they were primarily efforts to circumscribe the Arabic language and Islamic culture to the benefit of French language and social norms.

Such attacks were perceived not as assaults on a particular kind of schooling but rather as attacks on Muslim identity—yet another reminder that Qur'an schooling was seen as the central public symbol of commitment to Islam. In response to the 1896 decree, which sought to close the town's *daaras* whenever French schools were in session, the Muslims of Saint-Louis wrote, "The entire population of the city of Saint-Louis has the honor to address to you with a violent grief and unspeakable sadness in the heart and hopes from you the remedy to its affliction. We are damaged to our vital vein [*corde vive*], which is the teaching of our religion to our children, by a recent measure which, in bringing such a change in the Arabic schools of our city, gravely endangers the observation and preservation of our religion. The pain that we feel to see such a measure applied can neither be translated with the pen nor expressed with the tongue."[111]

This kind of French repression of Qur'an schools was intended to force children out of the *daara* and into the *école française*, but it provoked Muslim resistance that rendered ineffectual the first half century of colonial laws regarding Qur'an schooling.

Qur'an schools had been the primary public symbol of Muslim identity for nine hundred years in parts of Senegambia, so Muslim populations could only see these closures as direct attacks on Islam. Indeed, bitter memories of this period have not fully disappeared, particularly in clerical milieus.[112] But the French school did make significant headway among significant sectors of the population, particularly in urban areas. Qur'an schools were not, however, abandoned. At least one early colonial analyst of the Qur'an schools, Destaing, cautioned against any expectations of the demise of Qur'an schools in Senegal, whatever gains French schools might make. After noting that the families of Kajoor demonstrated a greater demand for Qur'an schooling than did North African families, he concluded that if the former "clamor for French schools, they will not easily forget the Koranic school."[113]

"DETESTABLE YOUNG ATHEISTS"

Many Senegalese Muslims deeply distrusted French education. In the Murid heartland of Touba, construction of a French public school did not occur until after independence. Children could sense the tension. Several Ponty students openly discussed hating the students from the French school. Modibo Bamany wrote, "They hate the students from the French school and pity them because they are in league with the whites."[114] While Bamany highlighted political and racial reasons for this hatred, Sega Gueye spoke of the religious dimension and how it led to a bodily revulsion: "The little *talibés* take the *écoliers* for young atheists. They hate them, despise them and distance themselves from their presence."[115] This visceral hatred of the French school and its agents contributed to an emergent moral dilemma about whether Senegalese Muslims should send their children to the French schools.

As much as the French school was despised and distrusted, it was just as clearly perceived as a route of access to wealth and power in the colonial order. The tension over how to properly educate Muslim children in these changed circumstances played itself out countless times. In the end, Senegalese Muslims made room in their lives for both sorts of schools. As early as the 1920s, official (and probably inflated) estimates concluded that the French schools had equaled the number of pupils educated by the *daaras*.[116] The pragmatic acceptance of the French schools was coupled with a widely respected compromise that children should study the Qur'an before enrolling in the French school or concurrently with it.[117]

This approach came to be thought of as producing pedagogical advantages, as Demba Beye recalled: "The Qur'anic school opens the intelligence of the little ones who, once at the French school, will make rapid progress."[118] The visible success of French schools in enrolling Senegalese Muslim students helped justify the administration's retreat from aggressive repression of the *daaras* to "malign neglect" in the early 1920s.[119] It is likely also that French retreat from the schools was conditioned by a changing relationship with Senegalese marabouts. After an initial phase of mutual distrust, both parties found that Sufi organization and colonial rule could coexist and provide economic and political benefits for both parties. The détente between marabouts and the state constrained the latter's desire to attack the schools.[120]

"THE GRAND TRIBUNAL OF REASON"

On balance, it is fair to say that repression of Qur'an schools failed to have a significant impact. In the long run, the ways of thinking and the models of schooling introduced in French schools were far more influential in reshaping Senegambian approaches to knowledge. Even this process should not be overestimated. After all, French schools were severely limited in their demographic reach, even in an educationally favored colony such as Senegal.[121] But documents like the Cahiers Ponty reveal the inner workings of a process of epistemological change. These documents required both implicit and explicit comparison of the modes of knowing experienced by young men who had studied in both French schools and Qur'an schools. When asked to give their recommendations about "how Qur'an schooling could contribute to the evolution of the country," many reflected on the proper relations among students, teachers, and texts: "The Qur'an school master will no longer be a preacher, but a simple teacher, specially prepared for this profession. The texts, which the student will understand, will then be able to guide him in his religious life. . . . The school master will do no more than assure the comprehension of texts."[122] Lack of comprehension was the main criticism. Most students thought that comprehension was important on intellectual grounds, but some understood its absence as a religious problem. Médoune Fall, for example, argued that a lack of comprehension went "against the spirit of the religion, for the Qur'an is a book of law and religious precepts; it is not enough to recite it; one must understand it."[123]

Instilling understanding, they believed, required a teacher, not a marabout. Indeed, many students clearly saw teaching as occupying a central role. The Ponty school was the most prestigious secondary school, so many of its graduates pursued careers in teaching. Their dreams of educating their compatriots highlighted the distinction between what they had come to see as thoughtless mimicry and enlightened use of intelligence. Wrote one Fuutanke student, "I will receive in my little school my young fellow citizens, I will be able, I dare to hope, to channel and orient this thirst for knowledge that they have in their blood. To their credulous minds full of mysticism, I will oppose rational critical thought."

Yet this very same student came dangerously close to acknowledging that Qur'an schooling was a precursor to an instruction more rooted in comprehension and discursive debate. He noted that after having finished the Qur'an school, the Toorodo child went on to higher study, where he translated the advanced books: "He comments [on them] and discusses with his colleagues principles and problems of sociology and philosophy." Yet even here, the weight of colonial indoctrination intervened, and before the sentence could even be finished, the lofty title of philosophy was briskly withdrawn since it was, he reminded, "a philosophy . . . based on beliefs and devoid of all rationalism."[124]

From this perspective, rationalism was the supreme orienting principle of all education and precisely what was lacking in the kinds of schooling that already existed among Senegambian Muslims. Another Ponty student, Médoune Fall, showed a similar reticence to equate the ways of knowing and learning even when he clearly saw a close relationship. He noted that the method of teaching the alphabet in his Qur'an school was "noticeably the same as that used in the French school: one begins with simple letters, then proceeds progressively to more and more complicated combinations. Nonetheless, let us hasten to say that intelligent and rational teaching goes no further than this stage."[125]

The pressure of indoctrination constantly weighed on students in these kinds of schooling environments. A small example from the Cahier Ponty of Youssouf Sakho helps to make the point. He describes the practice of the prayer for rain (*ṣalāt al-istisqā'*) in Fuuta, only to have his credulity and lack of rationalism promptly corrected when he concludes by saying, "and the strange thing is, the rain never hesitates to fall."[126] The teacher marks this line with a large red question mark, as if to say, "You can't really believe this." Further along, Sakho refers to blacks as superstitious and fanatical, disfavored by nature, and narrow-minded and still primitive. He concludes with a glimmering testimony to faith in reason and enlightenment: "As instruction penetrates the masses and the centuries roll on, day will break, shining and pure. If religion remains—which is desirable—all the fanaticism, all the erroneous beliefs will disappear and make room for firm knowledge, for ideas in accord with the Grand Tribunal of Reason."[127]

Such glimpses into the indoctrination of a young African Muslim student offer a reminder that epistemological change was not only a subtle change in understandings of knowledge. Sometimes it was a more direct reeducation.

This idea, in turn, highlights the extent to which *epistemological* change was driven by *ideological* attacks in the context of dramatic imbalances of power. All of these developments had irrevocably changed what knowing was for the few African students who studied at length in French schools. In the words of an ambivalent lament at the end of one Cahier, "I admire and at the same time pity this machine that is the Qur'anic school student. . . . I now feel incapable of schooling [*faire l'école*] that way."[128]

Colonial Bodies of Knowledge—Islam Noir

French schools laid claim to reason and taught their charges to see African Muslim ways of knowing as largely—if not wholly—irrational. Yet much of their administrative policy regarding Islamic knowledge was riddled with inconsistencies and depended on fully irrational forms of racialist thought. Born as a body of colonial knowledge, early narration of Muslim history in West Africa predictably depended on the logic of race. Many administrators downplayed the age and importance of Islam in "black" colonies.[129] Dark-skinned African Muslims were considered as neophytes, recently emerged from primitive tribalism. The French saw the profound success of Sufi proselytizers in the late nineteenth and twentieth centuries as a "conversion" from paganism instead of what it patently was—a kind of democratization of religious knowledge. They thought of Africans as "traditional" creatures moving slowly through history before colonial conquest. Some Europeans thought that blacks were biologically and culturally incapable of absorbing the Arabic language and Islamic doctrine and that this new "conversion" to Islam represented a political reaction to French conquest. The emerging racialized picture of African Muslims—Islam Noir—infantilized Senegalese Muslims, portraying them as ignorant, credulous, and blindly obedient to marabouts, who were transformed by French rhetoric into a kind of god-king, at once replacing both the cult of fetishes and the native chief.

Here, French scholars perceived the outlines of the epistemological orientation that embodied knowledge in Senegambia. In characteristic fashion, however, the dual lenses of race and Orientalism distorted the picture. Early-twentieth-century colonial thought equated Islam with texts and Africans with idolatry and ancestor worship. Thus, colonial observers could see only syncretism and heterodoxy in the Senegalese devotion to clerics. As Paul Marty wrote of the Murīdiyya,

> One can see in it all the native tendencies toward anthropomorphism and its practical consequence: anthropolatry. These blacks, tinted with Moha-

medanism, return to their antiquated beliefs, to the worship of a man, man as fetish, to the cult of Saints. The religious wave of Islam has passed, and behind it, once more one sees all the individuals of the same race gathering around a local religious hearth; all their moral, social, and juridical forces moving instinctively in the direction of the ancestral beliefs and practices; all their economic faculties concentrating around personages who, by mysterious divination or remarkable practical sense, have been able to pose as the representatives of these confused aspirations.[130]

■ The most blatant racism and the most explicitly racialized policies were not instituted immediately. Marty did not arrive in the colony until 1912 after being appointed by the new governor-general, William Ponty, who came to the AOF in 1909. These two men were particularly influential in shaping colonial racial politics. Ponty initiated a policy of divide and rule along ethnic lines.[131] *La politique des races* involved a kind of reification of ethnicity that was typical in colonial Africa. Ponty saw the "tribes [*peuplades*]" of West Africa as clearly distinct entities and discrete administrative units. Marty's job was to implement Ponty's racial policy in Muslim administration.

These efforts had important implications for Islamic education in Senegal. First, to promote ethnic identities over broader Muslim identities, Ponty outlawed the use of Arabic in correspondence between chiefs and the regime. This restriction also sought to reduce the influence of literate Muslim scholars, who controlled the correspondence between the chiefs and the central government. Second, Ponty discouraged the use of Arabic in any of the colonies' public schools. He saw Arabic education as an unnecessary and superfluous concession to African Muslims.[132] Thus, the state schools, which had periodically undertaken sporadic and limited experiments with Arabic in their curriculum, dropped these efforts.[133]

The elimination of Arabic represented a stark reversal of course. From the middle of the nineteenth century until Ponty's arrival, the colony of Senegal (and later the AOF) tended to administer sub-Saharan African Muslims much like North African Muslims. The French had been a colonizing presence in Algeria since the early nineteenth century, and that area served as the administrative crucible for later colonial ventures in sub-Saharan Africa. Algeria was to French colonialism what India was to British colonialism. Most administrators were trained and had their first experiences here before they were sent to other places.

Not surprisingly then, state-initiated educational reform and modernization—"functionalization," in Starrett's turn of phrase—were attempted in the AOF shortly after this process began in North Africa. But such efforts did not get off the ground. Ponty's *politique des races* actively discouraged importing models from North Africa on the grounds that doing so would spread Islam among half-animist populations. The role that racial logic played in aborting the functionalization of Islamic schooling in the AOF is most clearly perceived in the brief and inauspicious history of the colonial school that was once intended to modernize (and functionalize) Islamic education in Senegal.

THE MÉDERSA OF SAINT-LOUIS

The Médersa (from the Arabic *madrasa*) of Saint-Louis was founded in 1908. According to the law announcing the establishment of the new school, "The Médérsa created in Saint Louis has at its goal to form the instructional personnel of the Qur'an schools, to assure the recruitment of Muslim magistrates or interpreters and to incline to our ideas of tolerance and progress a young native elite capable of understanding and making [the natives] appreciate the civilizing role of France in Africa."[134] It was, in fact, the second such school in French West Africa, and it was conceived as part of a broader political strategy.[135] The purpose, in short, was to form cadres of teachers and clerics who would incorporate some elements from the French schools into their instruction and who would be, above all, loyal to France. In 1910, the first inspector of Muslim instruction for the AOF, Jules Mariani, elaborated on this mission. In addition to being trained as interpreters and judges for the Muslim tribunals, the students of the Médersa of Saint-Louis were destined to be "used as schoolmasters and compelled to give, under the authority of the administration, Qur'an and French instruction which will allow them to supplant, little by little, the marabouts formed outside of us."[136] In short, the process of modernization, standardization, and functionalization of Islamic schooling taking place across the Muslim world had reached French West Africa. Islam Noir as an administrative construct had not yet taken root.

The initial curriculum drew heavily on the standard corpus of works taught in the local circles of advanced study.[137] Mariani and the early staff and faculty appear to have been genuinely committed to providing substantive theological and literary training to the Médersa's students. Mariani believed that Médersa graduates had to have strong credentials in the Islamic sciences to be respected in the local scholarly community and thus useful to the regime. In a short article published in 1909 in the *Revue du Monde*

Musulman, he outlined in relatively positive terms the community of Muslim scholars in Saint-Louis. He also observed firsthand well-attended lectures on *fiqh* and other topics: "The professor," wrote Mariani, "explains in Wolof, and the students return to their homes and review the passages which were the object of the lesson. Hence they become capable of translating by themselves, without the help of a teacher, by making use of a commentary."[138]

Having interacted with teachers and students, Mariani "acquired the conviction that there are, among the blacks of Saint-Louis, people who really merit the name *lettrés* and who have assimilated the works they have studied." The culture of Islamic scholarship was so extensive that a learned butcher, Mourfay (Móor Fay), gave lectures at his home "surrounded by around twenty auditors, between twenty-five and forty years of age, who listened in the greatest silence to his explanations."[139]

Destaing, the Médersa's first director, took a similar view of the importance of a substantive Islamic curriculum for the school. Consequently, during the first years of the Médersa's operations, its biweekly program devoted forty-five hours to its Arabo-Islamic curriculum and twenty hours for French.[140] In 1911, after only three years of functional existence, the Médersa underwent major changes. Mariani left the AOF, and the position he had occupied was obviated by an administrative reorganization. Destaing accepted a position directing an Algerian Médersa, and his replacement died shortly thereafter. Finally, Souleymane Seck, a Senegalese who had been the original professor of Arabic at the Medérsa, was promoted to head of the Muslim tribunal of Saint-Louis.[141]

■ The logic of race intervened. The new director of the Médersa, Jules Salenc, lacked the commitment to Arabic instruction that his predecessors had possessed. In fact, he held the stereotypical belief that Africans could not assimilate the Arabic language and that Islamic high culture was of little consequence in Senegal. Years later, after he left the Médersa, Salenc wrote an angry letter in which he ridiculed the overly Islamic curriculum instituted by his successor, which he saw as futile among dull-witted blacks who were ignorant of Arabic and Islam.[142] Salenc's revised schedule more than doubled the hours dedicated to French instruction (forty-four) while reducing the hours for Arabo-Islamic instruction to twenty-eight hours, of which only three were dedicated to the Islamic sciences. The remaining twenty-five were devoted to the study of the Arabic language and pre-Islamic literature. Previously, theology and Qur'an exegesis had occupied nineteen of the forty-five hours devoted to Arabic-language instruction.[143] Like most "religious" schooling in the Arab world, Salenc's curriculum amounted to little more than secular education in the Arabic language.

The results for the Médersa of Saint-Louis were profound. Ponty had appointed Salenc, and his ideas and training as a schoolteacher in France were much more in line with the new governor-general's way of thinking. Marty was also clearly involved in the reorganization, which fell under his purview as the new director of Muslim affairs. He explained the reorganization of the Médersa as an introduction to Salenc's report in the *Revue du Monde Musulman*: "This year . . . the spirit of the school, the method of the teachers, and the pedagogy of the new instruction became clearer. In a country that is Islamized in its own way . . . we imperceptibly brushed aside, to the great satisfaction of all, an overly dogmatic Muslim instruction; one which was too religiously technical, one might say; and the Médersa has become a little native university where, alongside the cycle of French studies, one gives higher education in Arabic language, literature, and Muslim civilization."[144]

Beginning in 1912, the Médersa of Saint-Louis became nothing more than a school of colonial administration. It was closed in 1922, having trained a few hundred young men to be loyalist marabouts. The Médersa at Timbuktu, where *bayḍān* groups were now socially dominant, survived somewhat longer, largely because in the new *politique des races* and from within the framework of Islam Noir, an Arabic-language Islamic school could be justified as long as the students were "white."[145] However, the skin color of many people who claimed *bayḍān* status could hardly be distinguished from that of people considered black.

Race Thinking and Its Ironies

Thereafter, Ponty commissioned Marty to study various aspects of Islam, including Senegalese Qur'an schools. Relying heavily (if not exclusively) on *bayḍān* informants, Marty began to paint a racialized picture of Senegalese Islam in four studies completed within a year of his arrival.[146] In his study of Qur'an schools, finished shortly after he arrived in Dakar, Marty recommended that the state cease trying to impose impossible regulations on schools because they were useless, not dangerous. He argued that the problems that the French perceived in the *daaras*, such as rote instruction, a poor level of scholarship, and too much child labor and mendicancy, did not threaten colonial rule. He made his case, which contradicted received wisdom, by appealing to widely held stereotypes about blacks.

P. J. André, a captain in the Colonial Infantry who also wrote under the pen name Pierre Redan, published a lengthy treatise, *Islam et les races*, in which he endorses the suggestion of prior authors that the adoption of Islam by members of the Negro race—whom he equates with overgrown children—proves that their lasciviousness is stronger than their drunkenness. This is proved, he reasons, since when faced with conversion to Christianity or Islam, they have tended toward the latter, which permits them the harem but forbids them strong drink. "To these sensual pleasures," he writes, "we must add the simplicity of the monotheist doctrine of Islam, easy to understand for the primitive brains of the black continent."[147]

Marty employed similar caricatures to help make a case for ending legislation repressing the Qur'an schools. He agreed with his predecessors that rote pedagogy and excessive time in work and begging resulted in poor levels of scholarship, but he concluded that ultimately the "ignorance" of Senegalese Muslims was a boon for French colonialism, because it drained Islam's political potential. Marty downplayed the charges of fanaticism and child endangerment that had dominated early colonial thinking about Qur'an schools. He transformed them from dangerous sites for the socialization of potentially radical Muslims into harmless enterprises operated by ignorant charlatans.

For Marty, Islam Noir could run only so deep since blacks lacked the intelligence to properly understand the faith. In his report on Qur'an schools, he makes this view explicit when he discusses what he perceives to be poor training in the religious sciences in the Senegalese Muslim schools: "As for theological studies they are completely neglected. The Moors, who were and still are the agents of islamisation and the spiritual directors of the blacks, declare without hesitation that the brain of a black is absolutely impervious to Muslim dogma. It is the same with the grammatical studies that are so advanced among the Moors. The extreme subtleness of its morphological or syntactic gymnastics is beyond the intellectual reach of the black."[148]

■ Within this racist logic, all that was required to ensure colonial order was to isolate Islam Noir from more "orthodox" Arab or Moorish Islam and let it "evolve toward its own inferior and harmless destiny."[149] The intellectual construction of Islam Noir entailed a profound act of historical amnesia, because only a generation earlier, the French colonial state had fought many of its fiercest battles against West African Muslim clerics such as al-Ḥājj ʿUmar Taal, who called their wars against the French military "jihads" and justified them with scriptural references.[150] As Haitian scholar Michel Rolph Trouillot has written about the supposed impossibility of slave revolt in Saint-

Domingue: "when reality does not coincide with deeply-held beliefs, human beings tend to phrase interpretations that force reality within the scope of these beliefs."[151] That Islam was essentially Semitic and anathema to the animist essence of blacks was just one example of such a deeply held belief.

Segregating the bodies of West African Muslims from their supposedly more orthodox Arab counterparts became the principal concern of the Service of Muslim Affairs in the post-Marty period. Surveillance and censorship of all Arabic-language press that entered the colony and tight control over the pilgrimage were the main instruments with which this segregation was exercised.[152] Ironically, this policy did much to preserve the foundations of Senegambian Islamic practice and epistemology.

State surveillance of Qur'an schooling more or less disappeared overnight, as did efforts to produce competing state-sponsored Islamic schools. These two factors, as much as any others, were responsible for introducing dramatic changes in the ordering of knowledge in Arabic-speaking lands. In Morocco, for example, Dale Eickelman describes a complex of knowledge transmission very similar to what occurred in Senegambia but adds that it had already begun to disappear in the 1920s and 1930s in the face of a series of efforts to modernize and rationalize Islamic schooling.[153] The roots of such efforts might reasonably be sought in the *tanẓimāt* reforms of the nineteenth century in the Ottoman Empire. They were already quite advanced in Egypt by the 1920s after a long period under the direction of Muḥammad ʿAbduh (d. 1905) near the turn of the century. ʿAbduh's students and others who have been associated with the rise of early Salafi thought were closely linked to al-Azhar, and as early as the 1920s, the French colonial state began to seek specific information about individuals from West Africa who moved in such circles.[154] Islamic newspapers, among them Rashīd Riḍā's *Al-Manār,* that were very influential in the Middle East and in East Africa were banned in French West Africa.[155] Competing modernist conceptions of Islamic knowledge and especially of the schools that gave them life did not begin to penetrate Senegambia in meaningful ways until the last days of the colonial era, and their impact was not fully felt until alien rule had ended.

5 DISEMBODIED KNOWLEDGE? "REFORM" AND EPISTEMOLOGY IN SENEGAL, 1945–PRESENT

A man without any bit of the Qur'an in his belly is like a broken-down house.
—Saying attributed to the Prophet Muḥammad

Walking to Saudi Arabia

In 1940, a Fulɓe man, Maḥmūd Ba, began teaching the Qur'an in an unusual way in his hometown of Jowol, along the Senegal River, where the freedmen of the Almaami (see chapter 3) had once taken refuge from a cynical attempt to rob them of their liberty. Ba was descended from humble origins as well; he was not from the Tooroɓɓe clerical elite but rather was from a family of pastoralists. He began Qur'an study at the late age of sixteen but memorized the Book quickly and began study of the Islamic sciences before setting out on an overland pilgrimage to Mecca.[1] To this point, his story is unusual but hardly unprecedented. Some people from outside the clerisy became religiously inspired and memorized the Book. These Walking Qur'an—whether from the clerisy or not—occasionally literally *walked* all the way to the Ḥijāz in pursuit of Islamic knowledge.

Ba personified many of the contradictions of French colonial rule in Islamic West Africa. He was typical of the phenomenon driving chapter 4—people without conventional ties to the clerisy who made new claims on Islamic knowledge under French colonial rule. But he was also an outlier: the French tightly controlled the pilgrimage, making it a rarely observed pillar of Islam from the 1880s until the 1940s.[2] Inspired Muslims from the Senegal River Valley had been making overland pilgrimages since the tenth century, but these journeys were rare under colonial rule. Much had changed.

THE NEW NORMAL

What had changed the most from earlier centuries was not the West Africa that Ba left but the Ḥijāz that he found. The ideological content and epistemic mooring of Islamic knowledge had been transformed, perhaps irrevocably, by the establishment of the Saudi state. Ba completed his study of the

Islamic sciences in the 1930s as the modern kingdom of Saudi Arabia was taking shape. The Saudis had reconquered the holy cities of Mecca and Medina in the mid-1920s, and petroleum, which was quickly becoming the most important industrial lubricant and fuel in the world, was discovered in the kingdom early in the following decade.

The court clerics of the Saudi regime, all of them followers or descendants of Muḥammad b. ʿAbdul-Wahhāb, were building and generously financing educational institutions to shatter the prevailing impression that they were unlettered tomb-smashing heretics.[3] French colonial surveillance of the Arab and Muslim press in the 1920s (an important part of the quarantine policies of Islam Noir) provides massive evidence of Wahhabi disrepute. The French translated, summarized, and reproduced fatwas from all over the Muslim world that declared that the fifth pillar of Islam was not *obligatory* until the infidels could be driven from the Holy Cities. Some of the fatwas went so far as to suggest that the pilgrimage was explicitly *forbidden* until the Wahhabis were ousted![4] Al-Ḥājj Maḥmūd Ba was exposed to the novel pedagogies employed in the Wahhabi educational institutions that were beginning to flourish at that time.

When Ba returned, he opened his school in Fuuta Tooro. On a hand-carved wooden blackboard, he dispensed lessons to beginning students in Arabic language and grammar, devoting a relatively small portion of the time to memorization of the Qur'an. He dressed his students in white uniforms instead of tattered rags, and he forbade them from seeking alms. He put the burden of maintaining them on their families instead of the community as a whole. Parents were to pay regular tuition. In 1944, he moved a portion of his school to the new capital of Dakar before leaving Senegal for the town of Kayes in neighboring French Soudan (Mali) in 1945. In less than a decade, graduates of his al-Falāḥ school were operating similar establishments throughout northeastern Senegal, southern Mauritania, and western (French) Soudan.[5] This was the beginning of the Ḥarakat al-Falāḥ Li-l-Thaqāfa al-Islāmīyya al-Salafīya bi Sinighāl (Success Movement for Salafi Islamic Culture in Senegal).

Ẓāhir and Bāṭin

In a recent seminal work on Islamic schooling in West Africa, Louis Brenner argues quite persuasively that "a fundamental epistemic shift has been taking place in Mali [and in francophone West Africa more broadly], driven by social and political change, which has profoundly affected the ways in which Muslims see themselves and their religion."[6] He goes on to argue that a sea change is under way and that the esoteric episteme that characterized precolonial Islamic knowledge has, since the colonial period, been progressively if unevenly replaced by a rationalistic episteme associated with Salafism and reformist schooling. While I certainly agree that esotericism played a fundamental role in what I have called a classical approach to knowledge in West Africa, I see the defining characteristic of this paradigm as embodiment, not esotericism. A focus on memorization, personification of knowledge, corporeal practice, mimesis, and service were fundamental to the transmission of the *ẓāhir* (manifest) sciences as much as to the hidden (*bāṭin*).

Similarly, rationalism, supposedly the defining characteristic of the new modern ethic of knowledge, was never absent from the classical model. To the contrary—rhetoric, logic, and argument were central to its methods. As long as one had valid chains for the acquisition of basic knowledge, such exercises of reason were highly valorized. No less a philosopher, physicist, astronomer, and scholar of medicine than Averroes (d. 1198) was formed by the same Mālikī scholarly traditions that have animated West African intellectual life in recent centuries. While celebrated in the West for bequeathing a tradition of reason, he was also a Mālikī jurist, as were his father and grandfather before him.

As we saw in chapter 4, exclusivist colonial claims to reason were part of the propaganda imposed on African Muslims through French schooling. We should not be carried away by such characterizations. What distinguished the new way of knowing from the old was not that it *reasoned* but rather that it *rationalized*. The new way of knowing sought to make knowledge abstract, to divorce it from its particular embodied bearers, and to see it as a universally accessible and uniform good. Knowledge unbound from its embodied human bearers thus became quantifiable, alienable, and observable.

To my mind, one of the most significant and unheralded dates in the epistemological history of Islam is 1872. In this year, according to Anne Bang, standardized entrance exams were first used at Cairo's al-Azhar University. According to Bang, "Although these initial reforms were partly obstructed by the *shaykhs* at al-Azhar, they were nevertheless significant in the sense that Islamic education came to be seen as a predictable and structured process, where the competency of the student could be measured according to a fixed standard."[7] This is a weighty moment symbolically, because it signals a move to *reduce* or *rationalize* systems of Islamic knowledge to render them transparent and legible to state bureaucrats. New kinds of government sought unprecedented ways of controlling religious discourses and, most important, the *ʿulamāʾ* themselves.

POWER AND KNOWLEDGE

In the Qur'an as in the Old Testament, Pharaoh does not count heads except to better control bodies. Colonial states or states that sought to modernize in the face of colonialism initiated new forms of surveillance to better *instrumentalize* Muslim scholars, control Islamic knowledge, and ultimately manipulate populations. West African clerics had long distrusted such efforts. Some scholars curried the favor of kings by endorsing their every injustice and intrusion, but such scholars were usually not well respected. One such case was al-Maghīlī (d. 1505), a North African long miscast as an exemplar of "Islam in Africa" for his efforts to "purify" Islamic practice in the Songhay Empire five hundred years ago.

Al-Maghīlī's attempt at "purification" involved writing a legal opinion that gave Askiya Muḥammad Turé unlimited license for jihad, enslavement, political arrests, confiscation of goods, morality police, strict dress codes for women, and the expulsion of Jews.[8] Some scholars' presumption of superior "Arab orthodoxy" has led to his portrayal as a "reformer" of Africanized Islam. The accomplished scholars of Songhay's famous free city of God, as Humphrey Fisher and Charlotte Blum have noted, probably saw his pandering to the kings' political goals differently: "The clerics of Timbuktu must have despised al-Maghīlī as no better than a sycophantic court cleric himself, going at once to the ruler, instead of waiting with dignified patience for the ruler to come to him."[9]

But these new nineteenth- and twentieth-century states were more intrusive than any that had come before. They did not want merely "sycophantic court clerics"; they wanted to put each scholar and student on a grid to be named, placed, measured, disciplined, and rewarded through formal bureaucratic procedures. Prior (and now coeval) systems of embodied knowledge transmission had their own ways of accomplishing all this, but the means, mechanisms, and aims were diffuse. Recognizing, placing, evaluating, controlling, and rewarding scholars took place over great lengths of space and time and along embodied chains of knowledge. These processes were malleable and thoroughly personalized. Most of all, they were illegible to those who sought to fix knowledge and assign its metrics in space and time.

The fundamental definition of what knowledge *is* was changed by this new approach to governance and surveillance. Thus, before *ideological* indoctrination began in modern state schools, the *epistemological* assault was under way. This new way of knowing was not without its own appeal, and it was often quite seductive. But European colonial states in Africa were seldom (if ever) genuinely interested in educating large numbers of people, so the impact of European schooling was limited. Moreover, some Senegalese were always prepared to dismiss French learning as alien, infidel knowledge.

In the postcolonial period, the quarantine of Islam Noir was lifted and West African Muslims revitalized their connections with other centers of Islamic knowledge. Immediately after World War II, new Muslim schools were created with new kinds of Muslim teachers such as al-Ḥājj Maḥmūd Ba. This process began to pose a much more serious and persistent problem to traditional Qur'an schooling because the practitioners of the new approach were Muslims teaching the language of the Holy Qur'an and some religious knowledge, and they often held diplomas from prestigious institutions in the most famous cities in Islamic history—al-Azhar in Cairo, al-Qarawiyyin in Fez, or the Islamic University of Medina in what had become Saudi Arabia.

■ In this chapter, I develop two main interrelated narratives. The first is essentially an analysis of the political economy of Islamic schooling in postcolonial Senegal. This narrative centers on the development of a small group of Islamic reformers promoting a new type of school, usually known locally as the *école arabe* (or *école franco-arabe*) and an educational and social platform paradoxically inimical to Qur'an schools. I highlight the changing nature of state policies regarding "traditional" and "reformed" Islamic education.

After tracing the landscape in this way, I use a series of concrete recent examples to challenge Brenner's argument that an ineluctable epistemic shift is driving people away from Qur'an schools and toward modernized religious education. Instead, I see a remarkable dynamism among the proponents of the classical embodied paradigm, a dynamism often imagined to be beyond their capacities. Most important, however, these case studies shed light on the process of epistemological change in postcolonial Senegal. In short, I suspect that a hybrid epistemology is emerging before our eyes. Shifts in its modes of functioning and apprehension are driven much more by a series of quotidian—sometimes seemingly trivial—choices made by parents, teachers, clerics, and even children about the practical mechanics of transmitting Islamic knowledge than by any grand articulated ideological visions that either hypothetical Sufis or stereotypical Salafis might pronounce.

Reform and Epistemology

Salafism starts with schooling. Contemporary Islamic reform movements are almost always studied as political movements, but most of their activities are educative. Seeing the rise of Islamic reform through the lens of epistemology rather than politics or ideology, one's attention is drawn immediately to the centrality of education in the mission of most recent reformist movements.[10] Instantly salient, too, is the sense that their sensibilities regarding texts, reading, schooling, and intellectual authority seem much closer to our own than to those of Senegambian Qur'an teachers, for example. This should not be wholly surprising. While Islamic reform movements often claim a return to a pristine Islamic past, until recently, many of their earliest practitioners openly acknowledged that their approaches to education and schooling were deeply informed by engagements with Western education. In North Africa, a large number of the first generations of Salafi reformers were colonial schoolteachers.[11] Muḥammad ʿAbduh, who shepherded educational reform at al-Azhar, was unabashed in his desire to modernize Islamic schooling.[12] The Tablīghī Jamāʿa in South Asia grew largely out of a concern that traditional Qur'an schools there were no longer capable of providing what Muslim society needed.[13]

Ḥasan al-Bannā (d. 1949), the founder of Egypt's Muslim Brotherhood and thus the forefather of contemporary Islamism, rejected the traditional schooling that was still available in Egypt in his youth, choosing instead to pursue his education in modern state schools.[14] Much of the Brotherhood's early activity focused on education, and al-Bannā earned his living as a primary school teacher in the state system. In the first issue of the Brotherhood's journal, he noted that classical learning and scholarship did not fit with his habits of mind or those of his comrades: "We have had minimal benefit of the religious sciences because these books are written in a way that does not correspond to *modern methods of studying*. If a young man *with a modern education* asks you for a book that briefly and convincingly summarizes the Islamic creeds or the rituals of worship *in a way that fits his mind*, there is not a single book to recommend!"[15]

Al-Bannā's most famous disciple, Sayyid Qutb (d. 1966), was among the first generation in his village to attend modern schools, and himself organized concourses with the local Qur'an school to demonstrate the superior nature of the new teaching. As an adult, he did not formally study the Islamic religious sciences; he was trained as a literary critic in the Western academic tradition. Qutb is arguably the Islamist theorist most singularly responsible for framing aggressive exhortations to jihad among modern Muslim extremists.[16] Qutb was one of the first in his village to attend the new government school, and he attended the *kuttāb*, as the Qur'an school is known in Egypt, for only a single day. Strikingly, he was most disturbed by one practice in particular: the licking of the *alwāḥ*.

QURʾAN IN THE BELLY

This chapter's epigraph is not a euphemism meant to refer to simply memorizing the Qurʾan. The wording could have been, "in his heart," or even "on his tongue," if that were all that was meant. The former would have spoken of understanding it in a way that is both spiritual and discursive; the latter would have left ambiguity about whether this was simply meant to refer to the act of reciting the Qurʾan or perhaps "licking the Revelation." This saying is about believing in its power so much that one brings it into oneself to let it act on its own agency. By speaking of the belly, it is clear that ingestion of God's word is the intended meaning. This Prophetic dictum is about the transformative capacities of bringing the Word into the body. Neglecting the practice leaves the human body a broken-down shell, a ruin. No one knew better than the Prophet the power of the Qurʾan, when poured into the body, to repair, heal, and enlighten. The Qurʾan was inside him all the time, and people who sought to emulate his example should also be filled with the Qurʾan. The saying is also about bodily intimacy with the Word, about loving the Qurʾan so much that one licks one's tablet clean or that one drinks it rather than pouring it out where it might be tread upon.

In Rashīd Riḍā's preface to the *Tafsīr al-Manār*, he specifically derides putting the Qurʾan in the belly and argues that it is a book to be understood, not washed and ingested:

> The small boy will be taught by his people that the Qurʾan is the word of God Most High, without, however, comprehending what it means and without appreciating anything of the sanctity of the Qurʾan except the way it is sanctified by the Muslims among whom he is educated. And this way is twofold: on the one hand lies the idea that a specific verse, if written, then washed away, and finally drunk by somebody who is affected by a particular ailment will cause him to be healed. On the other hand [is the idea] that whoever carries with himself a copy of the Qurʾan is secure from jinns and demons and that in this way, God blesses such and such person, as it is a notoriously common habit among the populace much more than it is among the elite. Apart from the fact that these practices may or may not have a foundation whatsoever, we are of the advice that they involve an excessive devotional attitude [*taʿẓīm*].[17]

It is striking that Riḍā (d. 1935) is unconcerned about whether such practices have any foundation in the practice of the earliest Muslims, as they clearly do. He finds them to represent an excessive devotional attitude and therefore it does not matter whether this was the way of the people of knowledge from the beginning of Islam. Because it is of the body and appears superstitious, he associates the practice with the common people. In Africa, these practices are usually thought of as an "Africanization" of Islam. In all cases, it is associated with low, base bodies rather than the higher faculties of intellect.

Riḍā himself was a critical bridge between the Salafi movement, which was a loose intellectual tendency more than a real social movement, and the Saudi state's court clerics, the Wahhabis.[18] The latter were described in the early nineteenth century by Aḥmad b. Idrīs, a prominent North African religious scholar, as "miserable wretches who are bound inflexibly to the externalities of the law . . . and accuse of heresy those who oppose them."[19] After initial clashes, men such as Riḍā became staunch supporters of the Saudi state and Wahhabism, largely because the Saudi regime offered state jobs funded by oil money to scholars from all over the world willing to be associated with their peculiar vision of Islam.

Over the course of the twentieth century, this new hybrid modern Islamic reformism congealed. Massive state patronage of conservative scripturalists gave the Wahhabi state intellectual legitimacy. Slowly but surely, an obscure sect known mainly for *takfīr* (calling other Muslims unbelievers), destroying the tombs of scholars, and even trying to disinter the Prophet came to enjoy an image of strict orthodoxy. A group that was thought so heretical that its possession of Mecca put the fifth pillar of Islam into abeyance for some scholars used oil money and book donations to spread a version of Muḥammad b. ʿAbdul-Wahhāb's doctrines throughout the world. Driven by modernist sensibilities toward texts and Wahhabi fascinations with naming every novelty a *bidʿa* (blameworthy innovation), a new approach to Islam was born in the twentieth century. It was little interested in the long, embodied process of formation of scholars and time-honored traditions of subtle debate. It wanted things simple and clear and exoteric—the externalities of the law were conflated with Islam itself. This approach has been marked by (among other things) a tendency to disregard personified chains of authority and a thorough distrust of the body. I return to this particular point in the conclusion.

The social and political transformations that drove a move away from classical Qur'an schooling to new forms of modern religious education and discourse in the Middle East cannot be examined in detail here. What is important here is the idea that these shifts were not experienced contemporaneously with developments in Egypt, Syria, Arabia, and India. Nor were they cultivated by state co-optation of Islamic knowledge. Rather, they were transported—by men like Maḥmūd Ba—to West Africa almost fully formed after a half century or more of gestation elsewhere as the curtain of Islam Noir was slowly lifted in the years around World War II.

The Francophone Islamic Critique

In 1953, a reform-minded Senegalese from a Tijānī background who had long-standing ties to the clerical traditions of West Africa, Cheikh Touré, founded an organization that would combine features of French statutory associations and Islamic educational reform. The founders called the group the Union Culturelle Musulmane (UCM—Muslim Cultural Union). The UCM owed much to the distinct character of Cheikh Touré, who was closely associated with the reform movement until the 1990s. Like Maḥmūd Ba, Touré gained new perspectives on pedagogy outside of Senegal while studying in an Arabic-speaking country. He did not brave an overland pilgrimage to Mecca, but Cheikh Touré was one of a handful of students who overcame many obstacles to study in North Africa and Egypt during the 1940s and early 1950s as colonial restrictions on movement eased.[20] Upon his return, he was deeply committed to using education as a way to bring about social and religious change. Three months after its founding, the UCM began publishing a French-language newspaper, *Reveil Islamique* (Islamic Awakening), and opened its first school. Cheikh Touré managed the school while teaching Arabic, the Qur'an, and Islamic sciences.[21]

In 1957, he authored a book, *Afin que tu deviennes croyant* (For You to Become a Believer), in which he directed fiery prose at the marabouts, accusing them of complicity with colonial rule and misleading the faithful. For Cheikh Touré, the entire complex of esteem and affection for masters as embodiments of Islam was nothing more than a form of *shirk* (associating a created being with God). He also decried as "unorthodox" the fabrication of talismans, the other main esoteric application of the Qur'an's power employed by clerics.[22]

■ In the aftermath of World War II, independence movements throughout sub-Saharan Africa began to rapidly gain momentum. Students played an important role in these movements. In French West Africa as well as among African students in the metropole, a new discursive space was opening up that allowed for the articulation of aggressive critiques of colonial rule. The most prominent African Muslim student group of the time, the Association des Étudiants Musulmane d'Afrique Noire (Association of Muslim Students of Black Africa), published a newspaper, *Vers l'Islam* (Toward Islam), that was "international" in its orientation. One of its most prominent authors, Ciré Ly, was at one point studying in Paris, and the group drew much of its constituency from Muslim students from around West Africa who were congregated in the institutions of higher education in Dakar.

From the beginning, a unique component of this movement for Islamic reform was the preferred place of the French language as a medium. The movement was very young, and few participants had a "modern" Arabic-language education. Publications such as the *Reveil Islamique* and *Vers Islam* were targeted at a francophone audience.[23] As reformist intellectuals opened schools and began to publicly critique local Islamic thought and practice, they found that their French-educated counterparts often shared the same point of view. While this confluence was certainly driven by a shared political commitment to anticolonial struggle, the epistemological kinship—the shared sense of common sense—was as significant a factor as well.

Islamic reformers articulated a vision of self-determination with Muslim identity at its core.[24] The young journalists also highlighted the regime's preferential treatment of Christians, which Ly referred to as "eucharistic imperialism."[25] But they were quick to create common ground with African Christians as fellow People of the Book when doing so helped to promote anticolonial activism. The colonial state was not the only target of the reformers' displeasure. They also charged Sufi leaders with complicity with the colonial state. Two distinct yet intertwined threads of critique seemed to come together. First, the French-educated elite, raised on the notion of post-Enlightenment progress, saw these marabouts as "feudal" figures and obstacles to material progress and development. Second, Muslim reformers, exposed to Wahhabi and Salafi conceptions of Islam, saw the orders as a corruption of the sunna and as marring the purity of the religion.

THE REFORMIST CRITIQUE OF THE *DAARA*

It is strikingly paradoxical how much "reformists" who claimed to promote a return to the fundamentals of the religion have attacked Qur'an schools. The critique was informed by two important elements of the composition of the reform movement itself: the "modern" pedagogical strategies learned in French schools at home and Arabic institutions of higher education abroad, and the conviction that Qur'an schools were important in reproducing social and spiritual dependency on marabouts. Discourses on the inadequacies of the schools were part of French-educated Muslims' instructional legacy. The perception of the *école coranique* as a backward institution with obsolete pedagogical methods and negative social consequences permeated colonial educational culture.

The pedagogical superiority of modern techniques also seemed self-evident for many of those who had obtained an Arabic-language education abroad, particularly when, like al-Ḥājj Maḥmūd Ba, they had no family ties to the educational traditions of the clerisy. Maḥmūd Ba apparently never attended a French school, and he developed his ideas on the basis of experience abroad, but some of the many Senegalese Muslims who frequented both the *daara* and the *école française* perceived a need to change the *daara* based on purely local experiences. They simply felt that the modern methods of the French schools produced results more quickly. After learning to speak French in a short period in the *école française* and having spent much more time in the *daara* without acquiring any ability to speak Arabic, some simply concluded that the French school had better methods.[26]

Of course, value judgments about the efficacy of the schools were tied to changing perceptions about what the schools were supposed to teach. Learning spoken Arabic was simply not a significant goal of the Qur'an school. Even in Arabic-speaking milieus, traditional Qur'an teachers made little or no effort to explain verses to the children, thus allowing them to connect their own colloquial dialects to the text learned in school. Students were there to memorize, internalize, and learn to embody the Book. Purely literary and linguistic concerns entered the picture only after students advanced to higher studies.

The fact that the acquisition of the Arabic language came to be a more prominent goal of the reformers is related to their conception of the social mission of educational reform. They hoped to use Arabic as a vehicle for the transmission of technical as well as religious knowledge as a means of modernizing society. More important, they hoped to produce new religious sensibilities by making the Qur'anic Word more mundane and accessible to Senegalese Muslims. In the words of Muriel Gomez-Perez, who interviewed some of the founding members of the UCM, "The point was no longer only to memorize the Qur'an without comprehension or explanation of the text. Arithmetic, vocabulary, dictation, conjugation, geography, sciences and composition were introduced simultaneously. . . . These new methods of instruction also introduce, in the eyes of the militants, new decision-making processes. The elite is no longer the sole guardian of knowledge. Religious texts should be understood by all categories of society."[27] The *école arabe* would make religious knowledge more available and comprehensible to ordinary Senegalese Muslims. Unbound from the spiritual and social power of the marabouts, this disembodied knowledge would engender new political and social relationships.

At the core, however, the new role envisioned for the Arabic language in schooling was rooted in a new epistemology. As Robert Launay has cogently argued, reformists and modernists have tended to believe in the "transparency of signs," while classically trained intellectuals have tended to be persuaded of their opacity.[28] Reading in new ways, reformists confronted the Qur'an as full of self-evident rather than contemplative signs. From this standpoint, the key to unlocking the Qur'an's power seemed to be understanding its words. Closely related was the ability to easily speak classical Arabic, the language of the Qur'an, and to demonstrate verbal and rhetorical skill in it. Grammar as a discipline had always played an important role in the formation of Senegambian Muslim intellectuals, but in the classical system, it was pursued only at advanced levels of study, after memorization of the Qur'an was complete. For the reformists, grammar was often the first subject taught, even before Qur'an memorization, for what good was it to memorize the Qur'an, they thought, without understanding it?

THE REFORMERS, SCHOOLING, AND THE STATE

The colonial state imposed tight surveillance on reform-minded Muslims; the reformist critique of colonial power played a role in provoking this observation, but more threatening was the reformist social agenda. A model of education aimed at transforming social relationships and conceptions of religious leadership among West African Muslims threatened the colonial state. French governors and administrators had carefully cultivated what were always tenuous relationships with influential clerics. They were not eager to see the results of their efforts undone. The reformers, many of whom studied in Arabic-speaking countries and were labeled "Wahhabis," were seen as embodying a pan-Islamic threat or even as agents of foreign regimes.[29]

Thus, as the colonial period was drawing to a close and liberalization of political structures was becoming the order of the day, the Office of Muslim Affairs fought a rearguard effort and renewed religious repression. According to Jean-Louis Triaud, the office's main political goals in the early 1950s were "to combat the Wahhabis, bar the road to the development of Arabic instruction, [and] establish a barrier against Islamic expansion."[30] Al-Ḥājj Maḥmūd Ba, now in Mali, along with a handful of graduates from al-Azhar University in Cairo, were denied the right to open schools.[31] In Senegal, the government tried to close down UCM schools in 1954, but the group defied the state by mobilizing the support of key political figures Lamine Gueye and Leopold Senghor.[32]

Senegal's transition to independence from France in 1959–60 significantly changed the dynamic obtaining between the state and the reform movement, particularly regarding Islamic education. Independent politicians did not inherit the fear of Islam that had imbued the French Office of Muslim Affairs. Many of them sympathized with the movement. As priests of progress and modernization, they, too, hoped eventually to bypass the "retrograde" influence of marabouts over their *taalibés* and gain direct access to the people. More important perhaps, the vast majority of postcolonial bureaucrats were Muslims; modernized forms of Arabic and Islamic education appealed to their religious convictions as well as their modernist leanings. Senegal's first prime minister, Mamadou Dia, personally reached out to the reformers and promoted Arabic in the public schools. His reasons for doing so capture the mélange of Islamic and nationalist modernisms that made the movement appealing to the bureaucratic cadres of the government:

> For Islam to remain a factor of national liberation and development, it would have to purify itself of the slag which falsifies it and empties it of its humanism and its message. This was an exigency of the moment . . . to struggle . . . in favor of instruction in Arabic, considered by the colonial administration and the secular school as a language of subversion and a dangerous rival. If one wished to advance . . . , if one wanted Islam to become a factor of progress and development, it was necessary to courageously favor a return to a pure Islam. . . . The best way to restore Islam was to restore religious instruction, Islamic instruction. I thought that the Qur'anic schools functioning such as they were, were not sufficient. . . . It was necessary instead to reexamine the question through instruction of the language of the Holy Qur'an, by introducing it in the schools.[33]

Rid of colonial racism and the isolationist policies of Islam Noir, state functionalization got a fresh start in the early 1960s. The prime minister also made the examinations dispensed in the private *écoles arabes* formal equivalents of the primary school certification offered in the French schools.[34] Dia, who spent time in a Qur'anic school before studying in the French system, was a singularly effective champion for reformed Arabic-language education, but he also represented the perspectives of other French-educated urban Muslims.

The state did conceive another stimulus for the development of the reform movement. Beginning at independence, the Senegalese government began to fund scholarships for students to study abroad in Arabic-speaking countries.[35] Officials were responding to a demand that had been growing since the 1940s, but they were also cultivating new forms of Islamic leadership and new forms of Islamic education. Rather than repressing the emerging reformist movement, the state sought to co-opt and control it. In 1960, the government began using public examinations as a means of general recruitment of Arabic teachers for the public schools. Only 9 were accepted in 1960, a number that more than tripled to 30 in 1963; by 1970, state public schools had at least 243 Arabic instructors.[36] The increased use of the Arabic language in the state schools and the recognition of private examinations in the *écoles arabes* created a state-sponsored outlet for the talents and training of the students who had returned from abroad. This strategy created an avenue of employment for members of a social category that otherwise would have had few career options. Thus, rather than constituting a disgruntled mass of overeducated and underemployed Islamic militants, the reformers were now tied to state structures, weakening the danger of an independent and thus radicalized critique of power.[37] The importance of education to the reformers and the patronage of the state thus helped create a new category of Muslim teacher, the *ustādh* (Arabic professor).

The independent state retained much of the colonial government's disdain for the Qur'an school, which was perceived as backward both pedagogically and socially. For most politicians these schools were sites of indoctrination into the social structures of clerical—and now Sufi—authority. Within a decade of independence, the schools had become targets of renewed assaults from the state as well as reform-minded Muslims. A modern francophone education was still the most desirable option from the state's perspective; moreover, the fact that the modern Arabic schools often dispensed instruction in mathematics and natural sciences—unlike the more or less purely religious curricula in the *daaras*—made them attractive to modernizing elites as well.

The Postcolonial State and the *Daara*, 1960–1980

Beginning in the latter half of the 1960s, the state began to fix its gaze on the Qur'an school in an effort to press for reform and rationalization of the institution. In 1966, the Direction de l'Animation Urbaine undertook a census in the city and immediate suburbs of Dakar. The study sought to establish the nature and extent of the Qur'an schooling in the capital and establish a baseline to guide policies regarding the schools.[38] By 1969, a division of the Comité National Pour l'Action Sociale (CNAS) was prepared to act on the basis of the study.[39] CNAS officials saw the key problems as mendicancy, the lack of modern health care, and issues of social insertion—all but the last were complaints leveled by French observers throughout the colonial period. More than ever before however, *yalwaan* (alms seeking by *taalibés*) came to be perceived as a public nuisance. On the basis of the 1966 study in Dakar, CNAS concluded that Qur'an school teachers native to the city were not the cause of the problem; rather, the city had experienced a flood of teachers from inland and a swarm of impoverished rural children.[40] Many policymakers perceived that begging constituted a public nuisance and that the dire economic straits experienced by the teachers and students put the children at grave risk of health problems. CNAS's final concern was that by failing to provide a francophone education, the Qur'an schools left the students without real career outlets and no prospects for adaptation to modern life. The result, according to these officials, could only be a life of delinquency.

CNAS's analysis of the problems with Qur'an schooling was based solely on their perceptions of the mendicants of Dakar. Indeed, in this urban milieu, the public perception of *taalibés* and Qur'an schools appears to have begun to suffer. By 1978, when the Institut Islamique de Dakar (IID) conducted a public opinion poll concerning the Qur'an schools in the capital, respondents took an overwhelmingly negative view of the *daara*.[41] Nearly two-thirds of those polled (65 percent) found *taalibés* to be "annoying [*gênant*]" for reasons of vagabondage, delinquency, and poor hygiene, among others. More than half (52 percent) did not want their own children to receive such an education, while only 9 percent had no qualms about sending their children to a *daara*. Nearly half of the respondents (44 percent) found that Qur'an schools, such as they were, had no utility.[42] Such negative assessments of live-in *taalibés* may have reflected a disdain for the presumably humble origins of most such students.

The Dakarois consulted by the IID obviously had no great fund of public sympathy for the Qur'an schools or their students in the late 1970s. One can only speculate on the results of a similar poll conducted in rural areas or smaller towns, where the penetration of French and Arabic schools was less advanced, but it is hard to imagine that residents of those areas would have been nearly as disapproving. In fact, this seemingly general disdain for the *daara* and the *taalibés* was also closely tied to a rural/urban divide. Following a series of prolonged droughts beginning in the late 1960s, the pace of urbanization accelerated in Senegal, a phenomenon subsequently referred to as the *exode rurale* (rural exodus). State bureaucrats—and urbanites more generally—believed that throngs of rural poor were overburdening the social and material infrastructures of the cities.

HUMAN CLUTTER

This was, in fact, the case, however the terms of discussion regarding this issue in state circles and in the francophone, urban press were shockingly uncharitable, perhaps betraying a widely held assumption that many of new urbanites were ethnic others or the descendants of slaves. This suspicion is strengthened by the fact that by the 1970s, government officials, including President Leopold Senghor, began to speak publicly about the problem of *encombrement humains* (human encumbrance or clutter) and its negative effect on urban morale and the tourist industry.[43] The *taalibés* and their itinerant teachers were not spared the city dwellers' collective frustration. By 1977, Senghor's government responded to the problem by issuing strict laws against vagabondage and public mendicancy. However, some Muslim groups, including the Fédération Nationale des Associations Culturelles Musulmanes du Sénégal, an association with ties to the Sufi orders, lobbied for *taalibés* to be exempted on the grounds that alms giving played an important role in Senegalese Islamic culture.[44] To avoid offending religious sensibilities, particularly those of the Sufi elites, the vagrancy laws explicitly approved the *taalibés*' quest for charity: "Seeking alms during the days and in the places provided for by religious tradition does not constitute an act of mendicancy."[45]

The issue, however, was not resolved. The state's concern with the question of "human encumbrance" and its desire to promote modernized education led to a continued interest in Qur'an schooling. The government changed its tactics, attempting to mobilize the religious authority of Islamic reformers to bolster the case against the *daara*. In May 1978, the IID and at least two state ministries organized a major conference on Qur'anic instruction. It is unclear whether reformers or the state bore primary responsibility for the conference. The IID had been created with state approval and state funds and is best understood as one of the major state-sponsored outlets for reformers' talents. It was also the youngest and most visible Islamic institution in the capital city. The state could use the IID's Islamic prestige to raise the issue of Qur'an schooling without risking a direct backlash from the Sufi orders.

The government participants were the minister of national education, Abd El Kader Fall, and a representative from the Ministère d'État Chargé de la Culture (Ministry of State Responsible for Culture). The minister of education focused on the creation of a more well-adapted Qur'an school, "capable both of conserving its traditional values of religious grounding [*enracinement*] and of linking them with a general, even professional, formation. Thus the *talibé* turned adult citizen could remain an authentic Muslim and a competent worker, conscientious of his responsibilities as a man and a citizen."[46] The representative from the Ministry of State was not as generous, placing emphasis less on the "traditional" religious values and more on the application of a single rationalized program common to all Qur'an schools, the introduction of non-Islamic sciences in the curricula, parental accountability, and "curbing the scourges of vagabondage and mendicancy of the *talibés*."[47] Presentations by IID researchers mined similar themes, drawing conclusions from the institute's polls on the problem of the *daaras*.

LE PROBLÈME DU DAARA

For their part, the representatives of the *daaras* were put somewhat on the defensive by the modernist critiques from both the state and the reformers. Some made a point to mention that a number of their *taalibés* also attended French schools, while others simply said that students who wished to learn French would not be discouraged from doing so as long as this extracurricular study did not interfere with their study or manual labor. All offered detailed outlines of their pedagogical methods, which closely followed traditional methods. The representatives of the *daaras* all tactfully deflected criticisms of their schools, informing the state representatives that state aid to marabouts/teachers would remedy many of the alleged problems. Some placed the blame on parents who were, in the words of one representative, "struck as if with a kind of religious madness which makes them believe that learning is synonymous with mortification, humiliation, famine, vagabondage, malnutrition, and every kind of misfortune [and thus] have neglected their responsibilities to the children and to the latter's teachers."[48] Others targeted the ignorance of certain unqualified teachers. But overall, schoolmasters reminded the conference attendees that the Qur'an school was the single most important institution for the spread of Islamic culture in Senegal, that the call to teach the Qur'an to children was a noble one, and that if the state agents wished to see the schools operate in better conditions, subsidies should be provided.

In spite of the reformers' best intentions, the state took little action to reform Qur'an schooling. The government thought it unwise to attack the schools because doing so would have been perceived as an attack on Islam. Abdou Diouf assumed power from Senghor in 1981 and perhaps thought it better to consolidate rather than undermine his power base among the Sufi shaykhs. Nonetheless, under Diouf, the Senegalese state continued to develop its patronage of the reformist educational movement, creating in 1983 and 1984 new Arabic-language sections for state secondary degrees.[49] Instead of a policy of open hostility, the state quietly continued its patronage of the Islamic reform movement, perhaps hoping to stay above the fray while the reformers slowly undermined Qur'an schooling via their own educational agenda.

But again, the state's patronage policy was intended not only to slowly undermine the Qur'an schools but also to tie the reformers to the state and reduce the radical potential of "political Islam." In this way, state patronage also controlled and constrained the development of educational reform. Though some state agents certainly hoped to see the development of modern Islamic education, others just as certainly thought that the increased use of Arabic in the school system was a way of taming the development of Islamic education and guiding it in the directions preferred by the state. This policy had quietly succeeded throughout the 1960s and 1970s; by 1975, one Islamic reform organization estimated that between six hundred and seven hundred Senegalese students were studying abroad in Arabic-speaking countries, many with grants from the Ministre de l'Enseignement Supérieur (Ministry of Higher Education) as well as funding from the host countries and international Islamic organizations.[50] Most of the students returned to work as Arabic instructors in the state public schools or in private *écoles arabes*. The Islamic reform movement appeared to be under state control.[51]

REFORM, REFORMULATED

By the early 1980s, however, the movement was changing directions. Two main factors were at work. First, the new generation of students trained overseas came to maturity and began to achieve a sort of critical mass, allowing them to assert a certain autonomy vis-à-vis the state. Second, the reformers had come to understand that Sufi leaders enjoyed such deeply rooted popular support that overt anti-Sufi attacks would provide little benefit; the reformers had no similar constituencies or independent resource base. As a whole, the reform movement began to take steps to bridge the epistemic divide and move closer to clerics with whom they shared ideological and political concerns. In 1978, dissident members of the UCM, including its founder, Cheikh Touré, broke from the organization, which they felt had been compromised by state patronage. They founded the Jamāʿat ʿIbādu Raḥmān (Association of the Servants of the Beneficent). The Ibaadu, as they are commonly called in Senegal, appealed to the growing number of students returned from abroad, the graduates of Senegal's domestic Arabic schools, and many urban youths. Instead of railing against the Sufis, the organization refocused its efforts on education.[52]

The Jamāʿat ʿIbādu Raḥmān rapidly expanded the scope of the *école arabe* movement. According to one source, by the end of the 1980s, the organization had opened as many as three hundred schools in Dakar's surburbs.[53] Near the end of the preceding decade, the al-Falāḥ Salafi educational reform movement, founded by al-Ḥājj Maḥmūd Ba in the 1940s, became the Ḥarakat al-Falāḥ Li-l-Thaqāfa al-Islāmīyya al-Salafīya Bi Sinighāl and began to rapidly expand both in terms of educational activity and public prominence. Ḥarakat al-Falāḥ schools, which are quite numerous if still uncounted, are often reputed to be the best funded and best staffed reformist schools. The organization reportedly has received substantial financial support from private Egyptian donors, international Islamic organizations, and the Saudi government, although the Ḥarakat al-Falāḥ's directors maintain that their funding comes almost exclusively from school fees and private donations by pious Senegalese entrepreneurs.[54] In fact, both Ḥarakat al-Falāḥ and Jamāʿat ʿIbādu Raḥmān, along with a number of other Islamic education organizations, allegedly receive significant amounts of funding from Islamic NGO's such as the Zakat House in Kuwait, the World Association of Muslim Youth, and the International Islamic League.[55] The extent—and, in some cases, the existence—of such funding is the subject of some debate, but revenue sources from abroad appear to have helped the reform movement wean itself from state patronage in the 1970s and 1980s.

My experience cataloging clerical libraries in Fuuta Tooro between 2005 and 2007 confirms that Saudi patrons and Salafi groups from abroad made significant donations of books from at least the 1980s, especially Wahhabi and Salafi texts, as well as supposedly "proto-Salafi" classical authors such as Ibn Taymiyya and Ibn al-Qayyim al-Jawziyya who were otherwise not read much if at all in Senegambia.[56] Whatever their sources of revenue, Jamāʿat ʿIbādu Raḥmān and Ḥarakat al-Falāḥ, along with a constellation of smaller associations, focused on education rather than overt social critique throughout the 1980s. They enjoyed considerable success in promoting a new vision of Islamic schooling, though their success was largely limited to urban areas.[57] They gained ground because of urbanites' negative perceptions of Qurʾan schooling and because even in the cities, the state failed to meet citizens' demands for formal education. State schools did not accept all students who wished to attend, and those who gained admission often found school fees and equipment prohibitively expensive. The costs in most *écoles arabes* were significantly lower and often highly negotiable. Furthermore, the religious motives and entrepreneurial spirit of school directors meant that few were inclined categorically to reject students. The reformers focused on filling an educational gap that the state could not fill, and the *école arabe* movement flourished throughout the 1980s without directing a concerted discursive attack on the *daara*.

The Internationalization of the *Taalibés'* Plight

By the end of the 1980s, the state was prepared to launch another attack on Senegal's Qur'an schools. In 1989, the United Nations held a worldwide conference on the rights of children, leading ultimately to the creation of the International Convention for the Preservation of Children's Rights. Senegal signed the convention and in 1992 undertook a joint program with UNICEF on the "rehabilitation of the rights of *talibés*."[58] The campaign proceeded on many fronts. It was supposed to provide some financial support to marabouts/teachers who indicated a willingness to put an end to alms seeking and corporal punishment. It was also accompanied by a television, radio, and print media blitz designed to sensitize the Senegalese public to the plight of *taalibés*. The state newspaper, *Le Soleil*, highlighted the poor living conditions of *taalibés* and "uncovered" particularly shocking stories of neglect, such as the case of a blind *sëriñ* in Kaolack who was purported to be incapable of caring for his 157 *taalibés*, with tragic results.[59]

The plan to "sensitize" the public may be better characterized as a program to "sensationalize" the plight of the *taalibé*. Only the worst face of the *daara* was shown to the public, and no effort whatever was made to contextualize or historicize the harsh living conditions, corporal punishment, or mendicancy reported by the journalists. Furthermore, the financial support to marabouts that was supposed to accompany the plan was largely illusory. It was channeled only to a very small number of schools, all of which already met UNICEF and state expectations about what a modern education should look like. Some of these schools could not be characterized as *daaras* at all.[60] One was the Daara Association de Malika, which was founded (perhaps as an NGO) in 1980 by European expatriates living in the town of Malika, outside Dakar.[61]

In the judgment of many observers, this program to "support" the *daaras* was highly disingenuous, a simple pretext for an attack. Senegalese reformist intellectual Khadim Mbacké has suggested that the program was only an attempt to revive colonial assaults on the schools.[62] The newspaper published by the Jamāʿat ʿIbādu Raḥmān, *Le Musulman* (The Muslim) also "vigorously attacked the signing of the Convention on Children's Rights and accused humanitarian organizations of trying to take over the Qur'anic schools with the intention of damaging Islam."[63] Certainly, the prominence of western funding and imported ideals made it easy to perceive this new campaign as a new incarnation of the *mission civilisatrice*. But just as the colonial state did not hope to transform Qur'an schooling for purely humanitarian reasons, the postcolonial state also had its ulterior motives. The Diouf government may well have acceded to UNICEF's program out of a concern for maintaining a good international profile in the era of "structural adjustment," but the state's long-term desire to undercut independent Islamic social institutions certainly played its part as well. The state now had an external source of funding and moral credibility for an offensive against the *daara*.

MARABOUTS AND MODERNISTS

At first glance, the fact that the Ibaadu and other reform-minded Muslims chose not to endorse the state's attack on Qur'an schools in the early 1990s seems incongruous. Directors of *écoles arabes* could only profit from the weakening of one of their main competitors. Furthermore, many of the reformers, like UCM founder and leading Salafi figure Cheikh Touré, hoped to create an Islamic social order less dependent on the leadership of marabouts. The UCM's early leaders also believed that a "modern" Arabic instruction was an important means of eroding the spiritual authority of *sëriñs*. How, then, do we explain the fact that Jamāʿat ʿIbādu Raḥmān, the radical offshoot of the UCM, chose to forgo this opportunity to undermine the *daara*? The Jamāʿa's decision to back the Qur'an schools in print certainly was driven at least in part by a desire to separate its aims from those of the state and present a unified pro-Islamic stance. But its choice also provides a reminder that the reformers and the Sufis have not always been at odds.

Cheikh Touré, the author of the polemical anti-Sufi book, *Afin que tu deviennes croyant*, was the son of an important Tijāniyya lineage.[64] And if some prominent Tijānīs pressed for his imprisonment after the book's publication, others supported his right to free speech.[65] In fact, although reformists and marabouts can be separated for analytical purposes, they have been closely tied historically, and those close ties have always mitigated the antagonistic potential inherent in their relations. Several scholars have highlighted the competition between the reformers and the marabouts, but few have noted the underlying historical processes that have brought together Sufis and reformers, marabouts and Muslim modernists.

Indeed, from the very beginning of the movement for reform, clerical lineages have played a leading role. Many of the earliest Islamic statutory associations, founded in the 1930s, were created by religious scholars from well-known clerical centers.[66] By the late 1950s, many of the most prominent figures in the Islamic educational reform movement were important Sufi shaykhs. Some academic observers have perceived the involvement of the Murid and Tijānī elites in Islamic education as a belated—and perhaps even cynical—effort to fight the influence of new ideas that potentially threatened their social and spiritual hegemony. Roman Loimeier, for example, has argued that the dynamics of the Islamic reform movement have "forced the marabuts to generate ideas of their own in order not to lose their clientele to the reformers."[67] This contention is a bit misleading. Clerical lineages did not infiltrate or co-opt Islamic educational reform simply to compete; rather, they sought to participate in the elaboration of the clerisy's principal vocation: teaching. Many members of the clerisy must have sought to steer the educational reform movement away from what they would have seen as Wahhabi or Salafi excesses, but they did not wish to inhibit Islamic education. The judgment of noted reformist Khadim Mbacké textures our understanding of this dynamic. He reminds us that many of the famed study abroad returnees who did so much to cultivate the movement were the children or disciples of important Sufi shaykhs. They embraced the opportunity to study in Arabic-speaking countries "to benefit from a modern system of instruction allowing them to safeguard the cultural heritage of their ancestors while also developing it."[68]

For clerical families, the insulating tendencies of colonial rule and racialist policies designed to isolate Islam Noir were not without effect. In the middle of the nineteenth century, the sort of Islamic education dispensed in Senegal had much in common with education in most of the Muslim world. By the time of independence in 1960, however, the situation was quite different. The development of modern systems of Islamic and Arabic-language instruction elsewhere was almost exactly contemporaneous with colonial conquests that inhibited the circulation of people and ideas. In the 1880s and 1890s, Egypt's famous al-Azhar University, which had been founded in the ninth century, restructured its curricula with an eye toward modernization. In the Maghrib, a system of Qur'an schooling nearly identical to that in effect in Senegambia began to give way to modernist pedagogical practices only in the 1920s and 1930s.[69]

Tight control over the pilgrimage to Mecca and the close surveillance of Muslim clerics in Afrique Occidentale Française made travel difficult and impaired the communication of new pedagogies. Some clerical families attempted to surmount these obstacles by founding statutory associations—with educational priorities—as early as the 1930s, but colonial suspicion of Islamic reform limited the scope of their activities. Under the independent government, however, clerical lineages strengthened and renewed their connections to the rest of the Islamic world. The most successful, perhaps, was the extended family of Shaykh Ibrāhīm Niass, who developed relationships with Arab and Nigerian dignitaries and scholars while expanding educational networks all across Africa, from Senegal to Sudan.[70]

The desire to send students abroad should be seen in this light rather than as an attempt to co-opt Islamic reform. While a certain number of the returnees from abroad (perhaps those with weak ties to the Sufi orders) came armed with anti-Sufi conceptions of the proper Islamic social order, most sought not to destroy Sufi structures but rather to invigorate them with new pedagogical approaches used elsewhere.

Shaykh Tijaan Sy, the son of former Tijānī caliph Ababakar Sy and thus the grandson of al-Ḥājj Mālik, founded a francophone journal, *L'Islam Eternel*, in the late 1950s to contest the influence of the anti-Sufi reformers. Shaykh Tijaan had not studied abroad in North Africa or the Ḥijāz but had obtained an advanced Arabic-language education in the *zāwiya* at Tivaouane and in the Senegalese and Mauritanian networks. He was, however, in regular dialogue with the first generation of returnees, some of whom contributed to his newspaper. Shaykh Tijaan favored the modernization of educational practices in Senegal but obviously did not wish to demolish the legacy of his auspicious grandfather, al-Ḥājj Mālik. In a 1993 speech, Shaykh Tijaan Sy's son, Mustaafa, intimated his father's reasons for founding the journal: "When [the reformers] started to transgress the limits, Cheikh Tidiane Sy called them [together] and told them, 'Your way of proceeding is not judicious. . . . The preoccupation of each of us is religion. We must unify our efforts.' . . . When they created newspapers to harm Islam, [Cheikh Tidiane Sy] founded the review *Al-Islām al-khālid* [Eternal Islam]."[71]

In *L'Islam Eternel*, which Shaykh Tijaan Sy edited, he called for the modernization of educational structures and Islamic reform while affirming the mission of the Sufi orders and the *daaras*. In an editorial on "The Problem of the Religious Education of the Muslim Masses," one of the paper's contributors outlined its position on Qur'an schooling: "Muslim children must necessarily and obligatorily receive Qur'anic instruction. . . . Religious education is all the more necessary since the Muslim should not risk accomplishing an action except if he understands the divine prescriptions associated with it."[72]

The notion in force for the younger, reform-minded wing of the Tijāniyya was not a battle against Qur'an schooling and certainly not a war with the *ṭuruq* but rather a concerted effort by all parties to improve Islamic instruction and practice.

ʿAbdul-ʿAzīz Sy later founded another Tijāni-based reform movement, the Fédération Nationales des Associations Culturelles Musulmanes du Sénégal, which grouped together other Islamic associations.[73] In 1965, the Fédération began publishing a journal, *L'Afrique Musulmane*, with ʿAbdul-ʿAzīz Sy serving as the director of publication. It featured contributions from ʿAbdul-ʿAzīz as well as Shaykh Ibrāhīm Niass and was intended to highlight the Fédération's accomplishments, provide information on religious doctrine and practice, and offer commentary on popular culture from an Islamic perspective. It also aimed to rein in the perceived excesses of reformist associations:

> Islamic cultural associations have made an effort for many long years to take care of the instruction and education of the children on whom the future of the nation is built. But to circumvent difficulties, they have understood the necessity of coming together to harmonize their efforts and render more efficacious their means of action. This does not mean a formal condemnation of the methods adopted to this point by our predecessors. Much to the contrary, we admire their merit. In spite of the difficulty of contact with the outside world and the few means at their disposal, we owe the maintenance and even the expansion of Islam in the country to them. The young people who today have been able to pursue their studies abroad to return with experience gained in other Muslim countries were able to do so thanks to the initial formation received among our marabouts.[74]

Beginning, then, in the late 1950s, the Tijāniyya spearheaded an effort to guide the reform movement away from anti-Sufi critiques. The Dā'irat al-Mustarshidīn Wa al-Mustarshidāt (Circle of the Rightly Guided Men and Women), known generally as the Moustarchidine and founded in 1980 by Mustaafa Sy, has become the most significant of these Tijānī-based reform movements.[75]

The Sy family, however, was not alone in altering the trajectory of the reform movement and reconciling it with the structures of the Sufi orders. In 1968, the Niasse family branch of the Tijāniyya founded the Institut Islamique El Hadj Abdoulaye Niasse in Kaolack. The Murīdiyya also became involved in reformed Islamic education early on. In 1958, Shaykh Aḥmad Mbakke, the eldest son of the Murīdiyya's first caliph, founded the Institut d'Études Islamiques de Diourbel, and in 1974, Shaykh Muḥammad Murtada Mbakke, a younger brother of Amadu Bamba, founded a larger school, the Institut al-Azhar, in Ndàm-Bawol, a few kilometers from Touba.[76] These are only a few examples of modernized Arabic schools founded by members of Senegal's most prominent clerical lineages. The participation of key Sufi figures in the reform movement has blurred the line between the *reformers* and the marabouts. Indeed, as Leonardo Villalon has noted, "By the late 1980's . . . there were no clearly distinguishable boundaries between maraboutic and reformist Islamic organizations in Senegal. Rather there existed a proliferation of groups with varying degrees of ties to the state on the one hand and to the Sufi orders on the other."[77]

The political and social implications of the hybridized relations among the clerics, the state, and reformers are intriguing. They cannot, however, be fully untangled here. For the purposes of this study, what is most important is the way in which this dialogue between reformers and marabouts has brought the *daara* into a close dialogue with the *école arabe*. The children of clerical lineages often began their studies in traditional *daaras* before going on to study at one of the regional, Sufi-affiliated Arabic institutes and then to higher study abroad in Arabic-speaking countries.[78] After completing their studies, they then choose to operate family *daaras* or open their own institutions, much in the same way that their ancestors did. But many of these young men had acquired a different sort of training and new sensibilities. They began subtly inscribing new sorts of ideas and approaches into Qur'an schooling.

Pedagogies and Epistemology

To illustrate, I want to briefly examine two of the *daaras* I came to know during my field research in 2001–2. One is in Ngabou, a few kilometers outside of Touba, and is operated by two brothers, Shaykhuna and Xaliil Lo. The other is in Tivaouane and is operated by Ibrahima Bàjjan. The directors of both of these schools come from clerical lineages that have maintained *daaras* for centuries and that are intimately tied to the Sufi orders—the Lo to the Murīdiyya and the Bàjjan to the Tijāniyya. Any local or outside observer would unhesitatingly classify these institutions as Qur'an schools.[79] The children study their lessons on *àlluwas* rather than on a blackboard or paper, although in the *daara* in Ngabou, some older students carry notebooks as well as *àlluwas*. In each school, the Qur'an is the sole formal subject taught to children, with each child reciting his or her own specific lesson each day. All of the students sit on mats on the ground rather than at chairs in front of desks. In Ibrahima Bàjjan's *daara*, which is much larger than the Lo family *daara* at Ngabou, advanced students in their late teens and early twenties direct and police the younger students. They hold short lashes to correct the inattentive. The *daara* at Ngabou places less emphasis on corporal punishment, perhaps as a consequence of the school's smaller size, but it does take place. At first glance, there seems to be nothing modern about either of the schools. But initial appearances are misleading, because the social dialogue on the proper education of Muslims and the personal experiences of the teachers themselves have led to subtle changes in the ways in which education is dispensed.

Shaykhuna Lo studied the Qur'an and Islamic sciences within his family in childhood and early adulthood, using the time-tested techniques that clerical lineages have employed for centuries. In adolescence, he enrolled in the Institut al-Azhar near Touba. With the exception of a few hours of French and English per week, the entire curriculum is taught in Arabic. During his time there, he strengthened his grasp on the Arabic language and the Islamic sciences while learning mathematics, geography, and natural sciences, which quickly became his favorite subject. He returned to Ngabou and built a Qur'an school not far from his home. His father, a Murid shaykh, has many disciples in the village, so Shaykhuna had no shortage of students. He certainly did not need to change his methods to fill his *daara*. Nonetheless, Shaykhuna thought that certain kinds of changes were necessary. When I asked him why, he replied that the schools today must differ from those of yesterday because children are different. To give them the same things that he received, he had to proceed differently. Children in Ngabou are now as aware of developments in Italy and the United States as they are of events in their immediate surroundings. They know from radio and television what life is like in other places and about religious difference. Maintaining an education *solely* based on rote memorization could not, Lo argued, reach these children in the same way it reached his father and grandfathers.[80]

When Shaykhuna's younger brother, Xaliil, finished his cycle of studies, he took over most of the school's day-to-day operations, but the brothers shared a vision of making Qur'anic instruction succeed at its task of making children into Muslims in a changing time. They offer early instruction in literacy skills informed by their study in the Murid institutes for advanced study while laying more stress than was once common on the *explanation* of the Qur'an to students who have not yet memorized it in its entirety but are nonetheless mature and advanced enough to listen. The Los put what is perhaps a greater emphasis than their forbears on informal lessons in religious observance, such as prayer, fasting, and alms giving, though such instruction has always played an important role in many Qur'an schools. They also teach older *taalibés* the principles associated with those obligations, drawing on advanced study of *fiqh*.[81] At the same time, they do not reject and in fact have made a conscious effort to make *yar* (moral education and discipline) a central component of their education. They intentionally reproduce some of the hardships from their own educational experiences, not for the sake of suffering alone but rather to inculcate in their students a respect for work and the Word.[82]

■ Ibrahima Bàjjan's *daara* in Tivaouane is supported, financially and morally, by the Sy family branch of the Tijāniyya.[83] It was a flourishing school when he studied the Islamic sciences there in the 1970s, as it had been for generations stretching back to the era of al-Ḥājj Mālik Sy. Bàjjan did not go to a "reformed" Arabic school, nor did he study abroad, yet the changes he has implemented in the school's educational approach since he took over in the 1990s resemble those undertaken in Ngabou. There is a heavy emphasis on literacy skills and the translation of Qur'anic passages. According to Bàjjan, in the old days, "you went to study the Qur'an until completing it, [but] you didn't know what it meant or anything." He saw this as a problem: the students memorized the Book without understanding it; it was the focus of the *taalibés*' lives, but they did not know what it was. Now, in his *daara*, teachers explain the passages, telling students, "'This is what it means,' from the top to the bottom."

Bàjjan also instituted informal changes designed to make religious practice more comprehensible to students. Even the smallest *taalibés* in his *daara*, children of only four or five years of age, knew the legal prescriptions regarding correct accomplishment of ritual ablution. There is no *yalwaan* or onerous labor in his *daara* because, in his words, "We refuse to commit a wrong [*àq*] against the children." In the old days, he explained, a student was treated "like a sort of slave." At the same time, however, Bàjjan also respects and perpetuates a strict disciplinary regime, and I witnessed light physical correction of students firsthand. He argued that discursive teaching (*jàngal*) without moral education (*yar*) is useless.[84]

These schools are only two examples of a continuing process of social dialogue surrounding Qur'an schooling. The Lo brothers studied at modernized institutions that were nonetheless firmly located within the religious sphere of the Murīdiyya. They brought insights and pedagogies from their experiences home to their small village Qur'an school. Ibrahima Bàjjan did not study at a reformed school, yet his experiences and understanding drove him to change. At the same time, his changes were likely informed at a distance by the methods of the French and Arabic schools. The stereotype that Qurʾan schools have remained stationary or stagnant cannot be applied to these schools or to many other schools like them.

These institutions have not simply become modernized Arabic schools, and their directors do not wish them to become such. When I asked Xaliil Lo about the difference between the *daara* and the *école arabe*, he chose precisely the same language that Ibrahima Bàjjan had used months earlier and hundreds of kilometers away—the difference between *jàngal* and *yar*, which might be translated as the difference between *teaching* and *educating*.[85] In the *daara*, said Xaliil Lo, "we teach *and* educate: that's the difference. [In the *école arabe*,] Arabic comes first. But the moral education has a way to go."[86] Mansuur Caam, who does not teach the Qurʾan but studied in the *daara* and in Tijānī networks of "traditional" higher education, made a similar critique of the knowledge dispensed in the *écoles arabes*: although students learn good spoken Arabic and even much about religion, books are read without a component of spiritual education and thus too easily become *xam-xamu saay-saay* (cynical knowledge)—knowledge without faith or religious practice.[87] Similarly, Anta Njaay stressed that teachers in the modern-style schools are not held to any sort of moral standard but are responsible only for making sure that students understand their lessons. Qurʾan teachers, in contrast, are held accountable for children's behavior as well.[88] Put slightly differently: Arabic schools might train minds to know religion, but they do not train the children of Adam to embody it.

HYBRID EPISTEMOLOGIES

The borrowing of ideas and practices of schooling flows in both directions. If Qurʾan teachers increasingly borrow bits and pieces from French and Arabic schools, so too are reformist schools shaped by the *daaras*. Clear evidence of this comes from the village of Bokidiawé. One of the largest schools in this small village is run by Imam Aḥmad Sow. The school was founded in the 1980s as part of the Ḥarakat al-Falāḥ Salafi educational movement founded by al-Ḥājj Maḥmūd Ba. That the school and its director are Salafi or Ibaadu, as they are usually called in Senegal (referring to the Jamaʿat ʿIbādu Raḥmān), is evident from the imam's long beard and Arabic dress. He folds his arms across his chest when he prays, whereas most Mālikīs hold their arms at their sides. When he leads the morning prayer at his school, he does not pause long enough to say the Qunut supplication in the second genuflection of the prayer, as almost all Senegalese Mālikīs do. His library contains multiple works by Ibn al-Qayyim al-Jawziyya, a favorite "proto-Salafi" author, as well as a collection of Saudi fatwas and numerous other explicitly reformist works.[89]

Yet a major part of his school's educational success and longevity is in the compromises that it has made with the local scholarly tradition. While many reformist schools have focused on the Arabic language and explaining the meaning of the Qur'an, Imam Sow focuses exclusively on memorization and recitation, with the goal being the rapid and correct memorization of as many suras as possible. This approach was important to him personally but was dictated primarily by the desires of local parents. In this respect, the major tangible difference between his school and most Qur'an schools in the area is that his teaches the Hafs reading while all the other schools—like most Mālikīs—teach the Warsh reading. Similarly, Egyptian conventions of *tajwīd* (proper Qur'anic pronunciation) distinguish the recitations of his students. When I asked students at the school what attracted them to it, some said that the sensory experience of hearing this distinctive recitation drew them.

Furthermore, Imam Sow, though following no *madhhab* (school of Islamic rite), nonetheless teaches several core texts of Mālikī *fiqh*, including the *Risāla* of Qayrawānī, to advanced students in his school. When I expressed a certain surprise, given that many Salafis take explicit positions against *taqlīd* (blind imitation of legal authorities and particularly of the four major schools), Imam Sow explained that Islam was about being a good neighbor, so it was perfectly natural for him to respond to what his neighbors and coreligionists wanted from his school.

■ In this same small village of Bokidiawé is profound evidence that the classical tradition is not only informing more recent educational approaches but also thriving in its own right. Bokidiawé is home to what must certainly be the largest school for the traditional study of the Islamic sciences in all of Fuuta Tooro. The school of Ceerno Moodi Bokar Jaalo appeared to have an overall attendance of more than 1,000 students, each of whom learns one or more texts from specific masters. I observed a *fiqh* course on a commentary on the *Mukhtaṣar* of Khalīl b. Isḥāq al-Jundī (d. 1365) that was attended by between 100 and 150 students. In the classical fashion, the master reads from the Arabic text and then explains the passages in the vernacular—in this case, Fula. Some students were as young as fifteen or so, while others were middle-aged. All sat on the ground, with the teacher alone seated in a

Ceerno Moodi Bokar Jaalo in his *majlis al-ʿilm*, Bokidiawé, Senegal, 2005. Photograph by Rudolph Ware.

chair in their midst. This type of advanced study circle (the *majlis al-ʿilm* in Arabic) was long the primary means of transmitting advanced knowledge of the religious sciences, and in spite of recent challenges, some such advanced academies still thrive.

Moving back from the specific examples to the broader picture, we can see the outline of a discursive and practical dialogue on the proper way to educate Muslim children. The language of the discussion has been informed by Wahhabi ideas, developmentalist modernism, international children's rights discourses, Sufi thinkers, and Senegalese conceptions of *yar.* Like any living institution, the *daara* has had to be conversant with historical and social change to remain relevant. In practice, the often close relations between "traditional" clerics and "modernist" reformers in Senegal blur the line between the "traditional" *daara* and the "modern" *école arabe.*[90] Similarly, the modern Arabic schools have had to draw heavily on the religious curricula of the *daara* to satisfy the desire for religious and moral education expressed by many Senegalese Muslim parents.

The colonial state attempted to transform Qur'an schooling mainly through repression and through the promotion of modern francophone schools. Their efforts drew children to the *école française* but did not eliminate the *daara*. Personal experiences with the benefits of French education helped to give birth to the *école arabe* movement, but the full elaboration of an alternative educational model disassociated from the French school led to more important changes. Unlike the *école française*, the *école arabe* could not be dismissed as an infidels' school. Before the advent of the *écoles arabes*, there was no effective way of critiquing the pedagogical or social logic of Qur'an schooling without appearing un-Islamic. Moreover, the reach of the French school was always limited. The emergence of an alternative educational model has led to new dynamics but not to the death of the *daara*. Instead, some Qur'an teachers have begun to experiment with methods drawn from other educational traditions while retaining the core mission of teaching Qur'an recital, dispensing moral education, inculcating religious practice, and teaching basic literacy. The *daaras* continue to draw a numerically important clientele because their attributes still appeal to many Senegalese Muslims.

Yet much has changed. A critical advantage enjoyed by modernized Arabic schools is that they are increasingly recognized by government agencies as educational institutions. Diplomas from such schools allow students access to employment and opportunities for advanced study either domestically or abroad. It is not that the older more diffuse networks for rewarding classically formed scholars no longer function; rather, it is that state power does little to directly infuse them with incentives. Sufi orders, of course, play important roles in managing relations with the state, but they do so acting primarily as shaykhs with disciples, not as scholars with students.

Materiality and Epistemology

I end this chapter by revisiting its epigraph and the practice of ingesting the Qur'an. Drinking the water from the slate board, I have argued, represents an ancient practice associated with knowledge transmission in Muslim societies. Throughout this book, I have presented it as a powerful symbol of an embodied approach to knowledge and its transmission. I return to it here to highlight the role of materiality and small quotidian choices in shaping something as deep and broad as epistemological change.

When a child arrives at the *daara*, he or she either carries under the arm or is given by the master a hand-carved wooden tablet on which the first lesson is written. The tablet carries important social and religious meanings. It is the first implement of impending literacy and a universal symbol of the new position the student occupies.[91] According to Abdelkader Fall, "Tradition reports that the prophet Moussa [Moses] received the commandments on a tablet لوح. It is in memory of this tradition that one uses 'alouwas' to transcribe the Qur'an, sacred text emanating directly from Allah."[92]

Paper is the preferred writing surface in both the French and the Arabic schools, but very few *daaras* use paper for elementary study. Of course, for most of Senegambian history, paper was many times more expensive than wooden tablets, but this is less of a factor than it once was. The religious significance of the *àlluwa* remains central to its continued use. Before our first formal interview, Ibrahima Bàjjan and my host in Tivaouane, Amadu Faal, discussed at length the symbolism and spiritual power of the *àlluwa*. They concluded that "paper has no *baraka*"—one of the most basic reasons why the wooden tablet remains the preferred medium.[93]

The pens used to write on those tablets are not without meaning. In Wolof, they are called *xalima* (from the Arabic *qalam*). They are usually made from reed stalks or leaves from various sorts of palms rolled into tubes and dipped in a homemade ink (*daa*). Ibrahima Bàjjan and Amadu Faal agreed that mass-produced pens also had no *barke*.[94] They are almost never referred to as *xalimas* but instead are called by their French name, *stylo*, or more commonly by the brand name *bic*. Such commercial pens are generally considered inappropriate for inscribing the Qur'an on wooden tablets. When many Qur'an teachers, including Shaykhuna Mbakke, begin Qur'an study with children, they demonstrate how to carefully craft a pen from a hollow reed tube and how to dip it into homemade black ink so that it will write neatly on the wooden tablets.[95]

Like the tablet, the *qalam* is closely tied to revelation itself and was central in the first words of revelation granted Muḥammad:

> *Recite! In the name Of your Lord Who created,*
> *Created humanity from a clot*
> *Recite! And your Lord is Munificent*
> *He Who taught By the Pen.*
> *Taught humanity that which it knew not.* (Q 96: 1–5)

Teaching the children of Adam that which they knew not by means of the pen on the tablets of Moses reenacts the revelation of God's knowledge to the World.

A Mauritanian Ponty student, Sidi Mohamed, noted that the air of reverence surrounding these material objects instilled particular postures and dispositions toward the Word. This reverential air was particularly important, he maintained, since even in Arabic-speaking Mauritania, the children understood nothing of the meaning of the verses: "A moral education is slowly, imperceptibly prepared: the child, quickly accustomed to respect the Qur'an—the slate board, the ink, the reed, etc. are surrounded with a particular respect—'the Word of Allah' and convinced of the accuracy of this origin finds it quite natural to follow these 'holy recommendations' and, later on, as soon as he comes to grasp the full meaning of a verse, he applies it at first opportunity."[96]

Since the colonial period, more and more Senegambian Muslims have seen things differently. In his *cahier*, Médoune Fall argued that writing on wood and erasing it was a waste of time and that using paper would help children revise their lessons: "I believe that Muḥammad never forbade transcribing the word of Allah on something other than wood."[97] He was certainly not alone in this evaluation, as even some Qur'an schools now have their students write their lessons in notebooks after they have familiarized themselves with the *àlluwa*.[98]

But if many Qur'an teachers—like Ibrahima Bàjjan, the Lo brothers, and countless others—have continued to inscribe their lessons with reed pens on wooden tablets, they have had reasons for doing so. Perhaps they have thoughtlessly and doggedly clung to tradition for its own sake. Or perhaps they have understood that a simple material change, like writing with a mass-produced pen in a mass-produced notebook, could produce unanticipated changes in the way in which their students experienced learning and knowing. Making the thoroughly practical and seemingly self-evident transition to paper and pen obviates the problem of how to manage the erasure of the tablets. When class is over, one simply closes the notebook. The question of where and how to dispose of God's verbatim speech is no longer posed as a quotidian problem. Drinking the water thus charged no longer presents itself as a daily reality.

Whether or not one believes that the Qur'an is God's verbatim speech is irrelevant. Whether or not one believes that God's verbatim speech is capable of acting through its own agency is similarly irrelevant. The fact that this ritual left countless generations of *taalibés* feeling like they bore in themselves a heavy charge is beyond dispute. The notion that this embodied experience would produce particular sensibilities toward Islamic knowledge seems equally obvious. In this respect, what I have heard many times over the years in Senegambia is patent: studying seated at a desk is not the same as sitting on the floor with the legs folded in the position of prayer. Laying an *àlluwa* across one's knees is not the same as writing in a notebook. And chanting the Qur'an by firelight in tattered rags in the hours before the break of dawn is not the same as getting dressed up to go to school.[99] Thus even as knowledge practices on both sides of an epistemological divide seem to flow into and out of one another, bringing into being what may prove to be a nascent episteme, there are now and seemingly will always be in West Africa some who hold fast to the small material details of the Qur'an school.

CONCLUSION

THE QUR'AN SCHOOL, THE BODY, AND THE HEALTH OF THE *UMMA*

The people of the West will keep triumphantly following Truth until the Hour arrives.
—Saying attributed to the Prophet Muḥammad

The Plight of the *Taalibés* Revisited

I have spent nearly three years living in Senegal's urbane and cosmopolitan capital city of Dakar. As I write, it is a sprawling modern metropolis with a population of at least three million souls. I have lived for extended periods in four different neighborhoods, and in each there was a traditional Qur'an school within roughly two hundred meters of my home. Everywhere you go in Senegambia, you find a *daara*. *Taalibés* have rung my doorbell and stopped me on the street thousands of times. They do not ask for much, and whenever I have coins in my pocket I try to give them alms. Fifty FCFA (roughly ten U.S. cents) is often enough to send ten *taalibés* away happy, each one a penny closer to earning his keep for that day.

When I began researching Qur'an schools a dozen years ago, I shared Human Rights Watch's view that the *daara* was an exploitative and backward institution. I pitied the *taalibés* because I assumed that they were suffering awful exploitation, and I too wondered whether they were actually learning anything. Years ago, I began routinely asking *taalibés* to recite verses in exchange for alms. Sometimes I ask them to recite freely; other times I start a particular verse for them to finish. Some have an astonishingly beautiful delivery, others mumble, and most recite in a hurried monotone. But I can count on one hand the number of times they could not recite at all. Many of the dusty children dressed in rags that people see at traffic lights have hundreds of verses of the Book inscribed in their minds. One should not judge a book by its cover; these are fragile partial copies of the Qur'an that are walking between the cars.

Nowadays, many people never get beyond superficial encounters with *taalibés*. Some do not roll down the windows of their air-conditioned vehicles to respond to their call, *sarax ngir Yàlla* (alms, for the sake of God).

Sarax is the Wolofized version of an Arabic word, *ṣadaqa* (charity or alms). This is not the *zakāt* or fixed rate of alms intended for the poor. *Ṣadaqa* is not mandatory. It is given voluntarily, for the sake of God. Along with poor relatives and neighbors, those who are learning the Qur'an are ideal recipients of pious alms. In expatriate quarters as well as in some other affluent neighborhoods, doormen keep *taalibés* from ringing the bell and asking for *ṣadaqa*. But living in ordinary residential neighborhoods, even in a bustling city like Dakar, one gets to know the *taalibés*. One often sees the same groups of children every day or every few days. Shopkeepers and housekeepers, old women and young watchmen keep an eye on them. Many offer unsolicited gifts to neighborhood Qur'an teachers or buy medicine when they hear of a sick child. People rarely throw away food. Leftovers, sweets, soft drinks, and candy are saved for *taalibés*. With their deeds, the community is saying that these are our children; we must take care of them.

■ Taking care of *taalibés* is rooted more in commiseration than in compassion, more in empathy than in sympathy. One Ponty student highlighted this in the 1940s: "In Fouta, we generally tolerate these poor boys. We pity them and try to ease their pains with a maximum of generosity. The men, in seeing them, think of what they went through, the women of what their children are going through."[1] Traditionally, society saw itself in its *taalibés*, but this sensibility is now in danger, for many reasons: campaigns against urban mendicancy have unfairly focused on *taalibés* rather than on the scourge of urban poverty. Newspapers often sensationalize the plight of the *taalibés*. But the deeper problem is that new efforts to fix "the problem"—by NGOs, human rights groups, and the state—are driven by compassion but not commiseration. Colonial and postcolonial propaganda against Qur'an schools has not been framed by people who "think of what they went through" when they see *taalibés*.

Most Western critics and increasing numbers of urban Senegalese have never spent a single day learning the Qur'an in the *daara*. French schools and modern Arabic schools are concentrated in urban areas, especially Dakar. In some cases, two or three generations of wealthy urban Senegalese families have sent their children exclusively to French schools. People educated in these schools may *lament* the plight of the *taalibés* but do not *identify* with it. It holds little personal significance for them. It does not stir bittersweet nostalgia for the way their own bodies, character traits, and habits of mind were formed. It recalls neither their own childhood nor that of their fathers, brothers, and sons. Consequently, not only do they not identify with the *taalibés*, but they have missed important lessons—of the Qur'an as well as of life.

Rituals of Incorporation I

In the Qur'an school, people learn to make and live in a community. This sense of communal responsibility is under assault from individualistic materialism. While the consumer culture of late capitalism has certainly amplified this selfishness, from an Islamic perspective, this kind of proud, egocentric ambition is a sickness of the heart as old as the children of Adam. Exegetes of the Qur'an often say that when God formed Adam, the first human body lay in state for a time before being brought to life. During this time, Iblīs (Satan) would fly in through his mouth and out through his anus and say things like "This thing is hollow," and "It will spend its days trying to fill its emptiness." Satan planned to attack the children of Adam through this weakness of ours—we are always trying to fill our bellies. The point is that our need to consume can easily be thrown out of proportion and can distract us from more important things.

Modern society liberates and valorizes, stimulates and celebrates this endless pursuit of individualistic consumption. The Qur'an spoke directly to such excess in the Arabian society of the seventh century. Today it is often *read* as a legal *text*, but it was likely first *heard* by Quraysh as a piercing social critique. The Book reproached the people for making a society where the strong ate the weak, where the rich consumed the poor instead of feeding them. Qur'an schools have long been places where Muslims willing to accept the Book's challenge could struggle to make a different kind of society.

Incorporation can mean coming together to form a body, but it can also mean to take something into the body. Here I use it in both senses to show how the sharing of food and drink with *taalibés*—as alms as well as in other rituals—has constituted community. Filling the void inside us is necessary for our bodies to survive. But how to fill them? The Qur'an exhorts human beings to keep consumption in proportion and to make sure that everyone gets to eat. It says a society should be more than a collection of self-centered individuals who—as in West African characterizations of witches—prefer to eat alone or even to eat the flesh of others. In West Africa, Qur'an schools have played an important role in building unity and community through the *sharing* of food and drink.

This sharing begins on the first day at the Qur'an school, described here by Ponty student Modibo Bamany. In his account, the focus moves from the text of the Qur'an to the social bonds created through the Qur'an school:

> One gives the child the water washed from a tablet. He swallows a mouthful, and washes his face and hands with it. The marabout writes in his right palm بسم الله that the child must lick. Then one gives him a little tablet upon which is written بسم الله. He must spell out these words for the rest of the day: bi, as, mi, hi, la hi—The child's parents then bring a large calabash of porridge (it is claimed that the sweeter the porridge the smarter the child) for the little ones and a large dish of rice for the teachers. . . . The rice is shared among the wives of the marabout, the old women of the neighborhood, and the muezzins.

The community shares in the act, especially the women who do much of the work of taking care of the child, and the men who make the call to prayer that, like the school itself, serves as a visible and audible symbol of the community's commitment to Islam.

But this ritual of incorporation cannot end, Bamany informs us, without returning to the bowl of porridge. After all of the *taalibés* have eaten of the sweet pudding, "each one, taking a spoon in hand, must dump a bit of the cream on the new student: it is claimed, again, that the dirtier he gets, the smarter he will be; but still others claim that this is to teach him to tolerate having classmates, *to live in society.*"[2]

In the Qur'an school, people learn to tolerate the impositions of others and live as a community. They beg their daily bread—to calm the hunger in their bellies—from society at large. They learn that ultimately, no matter how wealthy or strong, each human being is contingent on the goodwill of others to survive. And when they leave the school, they are expected to be charitable to others; one who has subsisted only on alms is more likely to give them.

Some people, especially "the old women of the neighborhood," take it upon themselves to cook food or do laundry for the *taalibés*. They are sometimes paid small change for such services, but much of the time it is done as charity. My interviews and the Cahiers Ponty are filled with statements of love and gratitude to these "mothers of the *daara* [*yaayu daara*]." Some of these "mothers" were surely women who did not have biological children of their own but helped nurture the community's children. But the care and feeding of the *taalibés* has never been a burden that a handful of pious women were meant to carry alone. The people as a whole must fulfill this obligation, and in so doing, they built community in the most typically African way—through *sharing the same bowl.*[3]

No witchcraft, poison, or enmity can be present in food that is shared with the disciples of the Qur'an. This is the deeper significance of the *taalibés* begging for their food. *Taalibés* come by nearly every house, nearly every day. We must be at peace with one another to take care of them. As the children go door-to-door, they are sustained and nourished by the community's sacrifice, just as the community is spiritually sustained and nourished by theirs. In a typical gesture of reciprocity, from time to time the neighbors of a Qur'an school will come by to ask for a small quantity of the wash water from the slate boards for healing purposes or for general maintenance of total well-being.[4] The sharing of food and drink between the community and the Qur'an school marks them as a single household.

TIES THAT BIND—PART II

"Human clutter" as a way of thinking about alms shows how far community values have deteriorated in some cases. Many people now seem to see their own schools through the same "veil" (to use W. E. B. Du Bois's term) as the colonial state or NGOs. Du Bois also described this as "double-consciousness, this sense of always looking at one's self through the eyes of others."[5] Colonial racism and francophone education have certainly produced plenty of cultural estrangement, but more is at work here than just alienation. The harsh tone sometimes used to describe *taalibés* suggest that class, caste, ethnic, and national biases are interfering with the sense of community belonging. These are not *our* children. They are not Senegalese; they are from Guinea. They are not Wolof; they speak Fula. They are probably the poor children of slave parents who have abandoned them. They are not *my* children; why should I be bothered? I have my own family to feed. There is a danger that the community is no longer seeing itself as responsible for its *taalibés*. Many people, especially in the city, expect parents, teachers, the government, NGOs—*somebody*—to do something to stop these wretches from harassing people and cutting into disposable income that could be used for more consumption.

All of this misses the point. In African society, Islamic society, and in the many societies that are both African and Islamic, educating children was not left to the nuclear family. Schooling is a *community* responsibility. This idea is explicit among Mālikī scholars in West Africa, who usually characterize learning and teaching the Qur'an as a *fard kifāya* (collective obligation) of the community.[6] If some people are diligently attending to it, it is not incumbent upon each and every individual who knows something of the Qur'an to teach it. But if it is neglected or endangered, it becomes an individual obligation, a *fard ʿayn*, mandatory for every capable person, male or female.

The Prophet is reported to have said, "The best among you are those who learn the Qur'an and [those who] teach it."[7] Caring for these pillars of society—the Qur'an, its disciples, and its teachers—is a social obligation. Doing so constitutes fulfilling a responsibility on behalf of the community; if the community does not reciprocate, then it has left unfulfilled duties both to God and to his servants. Muslims (especially but not exclusively in West Africa) have long measured their social and spiritual fitness by the way they treat their *taalibés* and by the state of their Qur'an schools. When asked how many *daaras* were located in his small village near Touba, Omar Ngom, a Qur'an teacher interviewed in the late 1960s, captured this nicely: "Those who teach the Qur'an are fairly numerous here. In a village populated by Muslims, they can't be lacking. . . . In almost all the houses, one finds *daaras*. It is a good village of Muslims."[8]

■ Qur'an schooling is a mirror of the state of Muslim society. This is the basic argument that I wish to develop in these final pages. West African Muslims have long seen a direct relationship between Qur'an schooling and social well-being. In the remainder of this conclusion, I explore this idea, employing an explicitly anthropological mode of analysis. I also return to some of the analytical and theoretical arguments about embodiment and epistemology discussed earlier in the book.

■ In this conclusion I want to develop five basic points, the first of which I have already made:

1. Historically, Qur'an schooling is the primary index of—and avenue toward—social health in West African Muslim society.

2. The durability of Qur'an schooling over the past millennium is evidence of its flexibility and dynamism, not, as some would suggest, a sign of stagnation.

3. From this standpoint, the neglect of the classical style of Qur'an schooling outside of West Africa indicates a crisis in the Muslim community.

4. This crisis is tied to a changing approach to knowledge that is extrinsic in origin, individualistic, and materialistic and that denies the role of the body in Islamic knowledge.

5. In spite of new Islamic "orthodoxies" and other challenges of modernity, both Qur'an schooling and its epistemology of embodiment are thriving in West Africa and are likely to continue to do so for a very long time.

"The People of the West—A Mythic Tale"

"The Hour" in the epigraph to this chapter refers to the end of all things, which I suppose, befits a conclusion. The Prophet usually spoke only in cryptic fashion about the end of days. Or rather, the Prophet spoke clearly about *what* was coming but mysteriously about *when*. The only thing certain about the Hour is that it has never been closer. Many Muslims have long enjoyed speculating about such sayings, since they are impossible to either confirm or deny: Could the "west" refer to Jerusalem, whence the Prophet ascended through the heavens on his night journey? Does it refer to the Maghrib (North Africa), which draws its name from *gharb*, the word used for "west," in the saying. Might it refer to al-Andalūs, Muslim Spain? Or could it reference a broader Europe, "the West" in modern parlance? Allow me to note, if only in passing, that the westernmost point in the Old World is the city of Dakar. Wherever the original Walking Qurʾan was standing if and when he said "people of the west," the farthest west he himself could have walked before reaching an endless sea was the Cape Verde Peninsula, the site on which Dakar was built.

The people of Takrūr, living on the banks of the Senegal (the westernmost river flowing into the westernmost sea) were brought into the fold of Islam no later than the tenth century. Along with other Senegambians, the *Taʾrīkh al-Sūdān* referred to them as "people of the west who excelled in scholarship and righteousness."[9] The site of Dakar itself was once the far western edge of the Federation of Jolof, founded by Njaajaan Njaay in the thirteenth century. According to legend, he emerged from the Senegal River with a Qurʾan in his hand and made peace between fishermen in a fractured community. And for generations, before the seductions of the world turned them into kings like any others, all of the rulers of Jolof were expected to recite the Qurʾan in its entirety from memory.

In the sixteenth century, a worldly king, the dammel of Kajoor, seceded from Jolof. For a little while, the town at the cape, Ndakaaru, as it is still called in Wolof, was nothing more than a fishing village in his dominions. But the European slavers soon made it a port of call, though they usually stayed on the neighboring island that the Dutch named Goeree (Gorée). When the trade in human flesh made the dammel of Kajoor one of the most powerful men in West Africa, many of the people of knowledge rose against him to prevent him from selling Muslims for guns and clothes, tobacco and rum. From the seventeenth through the nineteenth centuries, a western province of Kajoor, Njambuur, was the epicenter of clerical resistance to the iniquities of kings. In the 1790s, a party of clerics fled from the dammel's retribution there and established a clerical republic on the site where Dakar now stands.

Time and again, such Muslim freedom struggles were thwarted by Europeans who did not want the trade in Africans to end. These Europeans offered arms, goods, and gunboats to help men like the dammel of Kajoor who were willing to sell black bodies to be consumed on plantations. Suddenly, at the beginning of the nineteenth century, Britain and France had a change of heart. Christian abolitionists, led by Thomas Clarkson—a great admirer of Senegambia's Muslim abolitionists—prevailed on European governments to end this shameful trade.

More cynical souls sought to profit from this, using abolition as a pretense for colonization. Europeans conveniently forgot that for centuries they had pruned some vines and nurtured others to make the African West a garden for slaves. Now they claimed that Africans—especially Muslims—were born slavers whose religion and morals knew nothing of freedom. They must be civilized—which meant conquered. Europeans became worldly rulers on the African mainland rather than mere flesh merchants at the mouths of rivers.[10] The French moved their base from Saint-Louis—an island where the Senegal meets the western sea—to the mainland. Ndakaaru became the capital of French West Africa. The new rulers opened new schools and began telling the Muslims that their ways of learning and teaching were no good. New Muslims soon came and did likewise. Through a millennium of drastic change, one thing has been constant: the "people of the west" have been learning the Qur'an on wooden tablets, with reed pens, and having the word of God inscribed on their bodies and souls. Perhaps this is what was meant by "following the Truth until the Hour arrives."

RESILIENCY AND EFFICACY

This kind of schooling is continuing to grow today, in spite of challenges, *because it works*. Senegalese sociologist Sokhna Diouf Faye has studied young men from the region around Touba who grew up in Murid Qur'an schools and were engaged in merchant activity in Dakar. She found that "the ideological foundations of the educational programs produce tangible effects; the statements of the [research] subjects distinguish between teaching, instruction, and education. This suggests a program not only to memorize the Qur'an, but also to develop intellectual dispositions and values. Modesty and solidarity are among these learned vales. The struggle for survival engenders development of entrepreneurial ability; but the active solidarity is a form of social security that the ideology integrates and transmits. *The meaning of work takes on a symbolic dimension*."[11]

Faye's research showed that recent state and NGO arguments that Qur'an students posed problems of "social insertion" were inaccurate. There is little indication at all that Qur'an schooling is unadapted to contemporary realities. In fact, French colonialists made this point all the time. They had no concerns that Qur'an students would not fit into society; rather, they were concerned that students in French schools were prepared only for salaried office jobs and tended to not be contributing members of society when they did not get such jobs.

Critics might respond that the success of the *taalibés* studied by Faye resulted from Murid patronage more than values. But all schooling produces networks of social patronage. In any case, we do not need to choose between these materialist and ideational interpretations of what many now agree are objective facts: Qur'an school students tend to do well in competitive market environments. The epistemology of the Qur'an school creates dynamic yet disciplined bodies capable of actualizing Islam under difficult circumstances. This is precisely what is being seen in the success of Murids in these domains, and it helps contextualize the statement that "the meaning of work takes on a symbolic dimension." Work takes on a symbolic meaning in the Murīdiyya because it allows one to actualize Islam. Murid interlocutors tried to explain this phenomenon to me in dozens of ways, but they kept coming back to one of Amadu Bamba's sayings: "Work is part of serving God [*Ligéey ci jammu Yàlla la bokk*]."

A different kind of research, also in the heartland of the Murīdiyya, has shown that Qur'an schools produce more than just industrious traders and thrifty, hardworking farmers. As always, Qur'an schools are producing *scholars*. The supposed ineffectiveness of the *daara* as a site for discursive and literary instruction has been vastly overstated. Doctoral research on literacy by Ulrike Wiegelmann in this region in the 1990s showed that Qur'an school students develop very good reading skills after two to four years of study, and 60 percent acquire writing ability. In rural areas, the rate of literacy among men over forty years of age was higher in Arabic than in French well into the 1990s.[12] This widespread literacy has subsequently expanded. After more than a decade of work in this area, I have reached the inescapable conclusion that the *daaras*—and the Arabic and *ʿajamī* literacy they impart—are flourishing.

None of these social, economic, or intellectual achievements are in any

A *sëriñ* instructs a *taalibé* in Medina Baye, Kaolack, in 2010.
Photograph by Rudolph Ware.

way limited to the Murid areas. My research trips to Fuuta Tooro and Kaolack in 2005, 2007, 2010, and 2013 confirmed that in such centers of traditional schooling and Sufi dynamism, Qur'an schooling is thriving. The African-American Islamic Institute, founded in 1988 by Shaykh Hassan Cissé (d. 2008), a grandson of Shaykh Ibrāhīm Niass and longtime *khalīfa* in his branch of the Tijāniyya, is another example of creative elaboration of traditional Qur'an schooling. This Qur'an and *majlis* school attracts students from America and all over West Africa, especially Ghana and Nigeria.

CREATIVE INTELLECTUALS

The persistence in maintaining and developing Qur'an schools in these areas and in West Africa more broadly is not the result of any unthinking commitment to tradition; it is proof of continuous adaptation to changing circumstances. African Muslims have tailored timeless understandings of Islamic knowledge to meet the needs of changing times. In *Peasant Intellectuals*, Steven Feierman has shown that long-term continuities in East African discourse and practice across different configurations of state and society are not signs of backwardness or stagnation.[13] They are the artifact of many thousands of conscious acts of creating and re-creating a discursive and practical tradition; they are the product of dynamic *intellectuals.*

Since Timbuktu became an international center for scholarship 700 years ago, people the world over who were able to look beyond race have seen that West Africa produces extraordinary intellectuals. This was true in the time of Moodibo Muḥammad al-Kābarī, "the very pinnacle of scholarship and righteousness," who taught Islam to *shurafā* from Fez, Mecca, and Baghdad in the fifteenth century. It was still true 350 years later, when a more virulent *bayḍān* racism had arisen, but a "white" scholar such as Mukhtār wuld Būnah could still proclaim that he was "disgusted with the religion of the *bayḍān* and came to the blacks to learn their religion."[14] He sang the praises of the Almaami, ʿAbdul-Qādir Kan, who fused knowledge of law with love of liberty and revolutionary resolve. In the nineteenth and twentieth centuries, men such as Amadu Bamba Mbakke and Shaykh Ibrāhīm Niass each wrote at least one hundred distinct works of poetry and prose that are widely read, sung, chanted, and embodied by their millions of disciples of all colors worldwide.[15]

Not all of the exceptional West African intellectuals were men. Clerical lineages in particular often produced accomplished female scholars. Khadīja bint Muḥammad al-ʿĀqil taught the manifest and hidden sciences to her brothers, to Mukhtār wuld Būnah, to the Almaami, and to many of the most accomplished scholars of the late eighteenth century.[16] Ruqayya and Mariama Niass, daughters of Shaykh Ibrāhīm, were widely respected as scholars. The former is a writer of Arabic poetry and prose promoting Islamic conceptions of the rights of women.[17] The latter is a famously efficacious teacher of Qurʾan who trained disciples from 1951 until the 2010s at the very western edge of the world in the capital city of Dakar.[18]

Someone must safeguard the Qurʾan and write it onto the children of Adam until the Hour arrives. Not being swept away by every new ruler or every new idea over a millennium takes work. And through their works and deeds, African Muslims have said that this way of knowing, teaching, and building human society is still relevant. In the *daara*, the house of the Qurʾan, we will keep building a sound foundation for the *umma* by shaping one lowly clay brick at a time.

Rituals of Incorporation II—Purification and Protection

If the Qurʾan school is a mirror for society's soul, the *taalibés* help clean and polish that mirror. They are a source of purification and protection at all of humanity's most fragile moments—from the cradle to the grave. Before the birth of my son in Ann Arbor, Michigan, in 2010, I received very specific instructions from religious scholars and laypeople back in Senegal about what to do after the *gente*, the naming ceremony or *ʿaqīqa* on the eighth day after birth. I was told to feed guests with the meat of a slaughtered animal sacrifice (preferably a lamb) and to distribute the remaining food to neighbors and *taalibés*. I was also told to give "white alms" to *taalibés* if I could find any in Michigan. This proved to be difficult, so instead I made a small donation to the local mosque and community center, which has a modern Islamic school.

I had been told to give "white alms" to *taalibés* a number of times before: when my daughter was born in Dakar during field research in 2001; earlier that year, when I moved my family from one house to another; and on other occasions. In fact, whenever there was the possibility of spiritual danger or an important outcome was hanging in the balance, I was instructed to give alms (preferably something white—*lu weex*) to *taalibés*. When I asked what "white alms" meant, I was told that it could be sugar, rice, a white garment, flour, or even "silver" (*xaalis*), the Wolof word for money. While I cannot say that I fully understand the significance, I have always assumed that giving charity in this way is a form of expiation and purification, since alms are understood in classical Islamic discourse as serving the soul in these ways. While *taalibés* might like money and sugar, the other white things seem (at least to me) almost useless to them and instead seem to represent purity and purification for the giver.

The other time for giving white alms is on ʿĀshūrāʾ, or Tamkharit, as it is called in local languages. The tenth day of the New Year is understood to be a time of profound spiritual danger. Amadu Bamba discusses ʿĀshūrāʾ in his magnum opus of the exoteric sciences, *Masālik al-Jinān*. His treatment captures the way it was understood by classically trained Sunni scholars: It was the day that Adam was forgiven of his sins, the day that Noah's ark came to rest on Mt. Jūdī, and the day that the waters parted for Moses and drowned Pharaoh. On this day, too, Jonah came out of the belly of the fish, Joseph escaped from the well, and Abraham was saved by God from being burned alive by Nimrod. It was the day that Idrīs (Enoch) and Jesus were raised to the heavens.[19] Bamba, like most Sunni scholars, accentuates the positive side of all of these events, but Adam's forgiveness is also the day he is cast out of the Garden. Obviously, this is a catalog of the trials and tribulations of the believing people. The specter of death lurks.

The holiday is best understood, at least in its Sunni form, as the feast of deliverance.[20] Danger lurks, but God intervenes and delivers the faithful. Bamba, following the majority of scholars, recommends fasting on this day. Many adults do so, though it is not required, and many (perhaps most) people eat the main meal of the day at sunset instead of at midday. The meal has symbolic importance. It must consist of millet couscous, the traditional daily bread of Senegambia, and people who can afford to slaughter a chicken, bull, ram, or goat do so. Some also eat *ñebbe* (black-eyed peas) the following day, a ritual that is also associated with New Year's celebrations in the African diaspora. People also greet one another with a ritual of mutual forgiveness. Each person prays that the other will live to see next year's feast, and then they ask one another for forgiveness of any wrongs. Finally, they ask God to forgive them together. Society is starting the new year with a clean slate.

DEATH AND DELIVERANCE, ALMS AND EXPIATION

But what is most striking about the holiday—and most relevant to this discussion—is what the *children* do. After sunset, nearly all children, not only *taalibés*, go out to collect "white alms." There are two major differences in the alms seeking practiced on this occasion and the habitual *yalwaan* of the *taalibés*. First, the children go out *in disguise, usually with boys dressed as girls and vice versa*. Second, they often carry drums and sing a particular song, Taajabóon:

Abdu Jambaar
Ñaari malaaka la,
Ci kow lay joge,
Daanu ci sa ruu,
Mu ni la, degg julli nga am?
Mu ni la, degg wor nga am?[21]

The song explains the reason for the masquerade. Though usually sung playfully and sometimes quite beautifully, the Taajabóon is a terrifying evocation of death. On Tamkharit, the children are in disguise so that death will not find them on the day of trials and tribulations.

Abdu Jambaar (Abdu the Soldier) is the Wolof name for ʿAzraīl, the Angel of Death. "He is two angels" conflates ʿAzraīl with two lesser (but still mighty) angels, Munkar and Nakīr, who conduct the interrogation of the grave until the Hour arrives. "He is coming down from on high, landing on your soul. He's saying to you, 'Have you prayed?' He's saying to you, 'Have you fasted'?" re-creates the Angel of Death taking a soul and the angels of the grave questioning the deceased. This interrogation will result in a spacious and comfortable grave for the righteous, but the two angels of the grave will impose harsh punishment on the sinful. This punishment is usually represented in hadith and other sources as unimaginably painful *physical* beatings. Only pious deeds—such as fasting, prayer, giving alms, and reciting the Qur'an—can protect the dead from these blows.[22]

According to Ponty student Demba Beye, on this dangerous occasion, the wash water from the Qur'an schools' slate boards was needed to provide protection: "During the 'Tamkharite' . . . each *talibé* must bring five francs to the marabout and receive in return a liter of '*sâfara*.' This '*sâfara*' is a holy liquid [*liquide sacrée*]: the water having washed Arabic writings."[23] Another Ponty student, Yousouf Sakho, noted that most alms were given to *gariibus* in Fuuta Tooro on Thursday at sunset because "Death is a spirit that roams the night around people's huts, and who speaks and has feelings. He eats only once a week, on Thursday evening, or, in other words, the night before Friday."[24]

"All will perish save His face" (Q 28:88). Death is inevitable for all but God. After the horn is blown to announce the Hour, death will come to every living thing. Even the Angel of Death must die before God brings the Resurrection. The giving of alms to *taalibés* or using the Qur'an school's *saafara* to drink, wash, or mix with food is best understood not as forestalling death as much as purifying the body and soul in case death should come. And when it does, the *taalibés* will be there to recite the Qur'an. A number of students recalled those living in their *daara* traveling en masse to recite the Qur'an at funerals.[25] They were there, I think, not only because they can recite the Book but because they are innocents; their recital is more noble before God, and their prayers are always answered. They also signal the community's piety and bring peace to the deceased in the grave and in the next world. Qayrawānī's *Risāla*, a widely taught Mālikī *fiqh* text, reports that "teaching young children the Book of God calms the Divine Wrath."[26] West African Muslims have protected the Qur'an school because they believe the Qur'an school is protecting them, from the cradle to the grave and on to the Hour, the Resurrection, and the Reckoning.

Islamic Knowledge, the Body, and the Health of the *Umma*

In word as in deed, West African Muslims have been saying for at least a thousand years that without *taalibés* and Qur'an schools, the community faces grave spiritual peril. What then, does the schools' embattled condition in—or even disappearance from—so many Muslim societies say about the spiritual health of the *umma*, the global community of Muslims? Is it too much to suggest that the absence of Qur'an schooling and its embodied approach to knowledge has alienated Muslims from classical ways of knowing?

For many people, Islamic knowledge is increasingly separated from its embodied bearers and accessed primarily through unmediated texts rather than directly from people. As we saw in chapter 1, "one of the greatest calamities is taking texts as shaykhs."

Reading in isolation, imprisoned, and with a heavy heart, worldly aspirations, and a background in Western totalitarianism, Sayyid Qutb wrote *Milestones*, developing a theory of aggressive jihad that mocks the Qurʾan and the Prophetic tradition.[27] This is exactly what the classical tradition sought to prevent. Reading with authorized teachers was meant to guide brilliant intellects such as Qutb to within reasonable bounds of interpretation. Nowadays, people without any training in even the basic elements of traditional scholarship—like Qutb—are looked at as authorities on interpreting Islam. Others are well versed in classical texts but read and understand them in ways that are alien to the scholarly tradition. Contemporary disciples of Qutb in al-Qaeda and other such organizations now wage an endless war on Islamic knowledge and Muslim society. This sickness is even now threatening to reach "the people of the West," for in Timbuktu in 2012–13, these terrorists sacked the tombs of the learned and burned priceless manuscripts. Like the worldly slaving kings of yesteryear, the terrorists entered cities of God, destroyed the books of the scholars, and desecrated the bodies of the Walking Qurʾan. While contemporary extremist Islamism is about power and ideology, it is also about *epistemology*. It is rooted in a relentlessly dehumanizing positivist approach to knowledge that takes disagreement for disbelief. It is no mere coincidence that Sayyid Qutb spent only one day in Qurʾan school and was disgusted by the practice of licking the slate boards. *A man without any bit of the Qurʾan in his belly is like a broken-down house.*

Similarly, Rashīd Riḍā did not care whether the practice of drinking the Qurʾan went back to the time of the Prophet or not. He wrote it off as excessive devotion because learning, for moderns, is about understanding, not memorization and drinking dirty water. His view is all tied up in modern notions of reason and agency. Many modern Muslims apparently no longer believe that God's Word is capable of healing or teaching the children of Adam from the inside out. With their deeds, they are saying that understanding through the intellect, *ʿaql* must always mediate knowledge, as if people "know" only with something called the mind. Has the Grand Tribunal of Reason become the god of modern Muslims?[28]

Aḥmad b. Idrīs (d. 1837), a North African scholar and Sufi, wrote of the problem of putting reason ahead of all else when it comes to knowing God: "The people of this persuasion believe in God according to what they understand, while the people of God are people who believe in God inasmuch as he makes himself known to them. And what a difference there is between the two persuasions, because he who believes inasmuch as God makes himself known to him places his intellect behind his belief, so that he believes whether his intellect accepts it or not. And he who has this kind of belief, God informs him of what he did not know before by means of revelation, not through the intellect. He who only believes in what he understands, he goes no further than the letters."[29] At the highest levels—or perhaps at the inner core—reason itself is only a veil that obscures truth. Some kinds of knowing must be experienced in unmediated fashion.

THE MIND AND THE BODY

All of this may be hard to accept—and I say this measuring the words—for those who make an idol of reason. Cartesian habits of mind, whether explicitly avowed or not, tend to do this. First they discretely separate the mind from the body; then they exalt the former and degrade the latter. The religion the Prophet learned and taught was free of this delusion. In the Qurʾan, perception, cognition, and understanding are intertwined and are intensely bodily. Limbs see, know, hear, and speak. Thinking like post-Enlightenment figures whose only god was human *reason* has left Muslims very uncomfortable with human *bodies*. For this reason, I suspect, Riḍā and Qutb were disgusted by the idea of ingesting the Qurʾan; this may also help explain why Salafi scholars usually deny that anyone ever drank the Prophet's blood.

This leads me to a question that I pose partly for rhetorical effect: Do modern Muslims really not love the Qurʾan enough to lick it off of the *alwāḥ*? In the first decades of Islam, it was taught that the "the mark of a man worthy of the name is that he be seen with ink on his lips from licking the revelation." Have Western notions of hygiene so thoroughly reprogrammed the *umma*? Catherine Mayeur-Jaouen has written cogently about how the colonial and postcolonial imposition of Western modernity has transformed Muslim ideas about the body since the late nineteenth century:

> Muslim reformism and its many followers profoundly changed the place accorded to the body and the relationship of the body to the sacred. Rationalization . . . of the religion . . . came to consist of rejecting whole sections of it, [supposedly] in the name of the Sunna but really as a consequence of the demands of a modernity that rejects the most directly bodily expressions of the religious and the sacred. . . . Alongside traditional notions of purity and impurity are introduced . . . Western notions of hygiene and

decency, conveying a secularized vision of the body. . . . The success of Muslim reformism is undoubtedly a "civilizing process": being modern while remaining Muslim becomes the new stakes in body politics.[30]

This modern alienation from the body is also driving the urban revulsion at the sight of *taalibés*. Their bodies are often more covered by dust than by clothing, neither of which conceals their scabs, scars, and sores. Seeing such a sight once sparked empathy and pity as well as intense pride. Now those things make moderns uncomfortable. It is striking that modern Muslim approaches to the body—the new body politics—are often about grooming it and covering it, not using it to transmit knowledge. Reformism, as Benkheira notes, is interested mainly in what Aḥmad b. Idrīs called the "*externalities* of the law" and the *surfaces* of the body, especially beards and veils: "Seeking to resist an often blind westernization, fundamentalism finds itself somehow confined to reducing Islamic normativity to its most visible face. . . . While it pretends to revive ancient Islamic culture, contemporary fundamentalism in fact turns its back on it, bringing to the surface only arbitrarily selected fragments."[31]

While I agree with Benkheira in broad terms, I do not think there is anything arbitrary at all about the fragments that are brought forward. They are mainly those that deny the body, reinforce individualism, and project social control over women. They are also those that most specifically project a visible outsider status in Western (and Westernized) societies. The surface appearance is what matters. All this is tied up in politicized displays of identity and performance of cultural resistance. Most West African Muslims do not get too caught up on beards and veils. Living Islam is about reshaping the person underneath. Draping the body with Islam is easy; the real challenge is to reshape the lowly flesh from which we were fashioned.

Embodied Knowledge

In the classical tradition of Islam—still alive in West Africa—true knowledge was seen as held in the human body. This complex form of understanding usually included (but was not limited to) the intellect. Muḥammad b. Yūsuf al-Sanūsī's (d. 1490) *ʿAqīda al-ṣughra*—a text widely read, taught, and commented on in West Africa—illustrates this. Sanūsī's recommendations for reciting the *shahāda* are particularly instructive: God's oneness and Muḥammad's message were to be affirmed with the tongue "while calling to mind that which it contains from the articles of faith until it, with its meaning, mingles with his flesh and blood. Then, if God wills, he will behold some of His boundless wonders."[32] *If Christianity's truth is the Word made Flesh, Islam's knowledge is the flesh made Word.*

When this moment of true knowledge—unveiling or gnosis—arrives, the body itself is filled with knowledge of God. In the words of Usman dan Fodio (ʿUthmān b. Fūdī), an accomplished scholar and mystic from what is now northern Nigeria,

> God removed the veil from my sight, and the dullness from my hearing and smell, and the thickness from my taste, and the cramp from my two hands, and the restraint from my two feet, and the heaviness from my body. And I was able to see the near like the far, and hear the far like the near, and smell the scent of him who worshipped God, sweeter than any sweetness; and the stink of the sinner more foul than any stench. And I could recognize what was lawful to eat by taste, before I swallowed it; and likewise what was unlawful to eat. I could pick up what was far away with my two hands while I was sitting in place; and I could travel on my two feet [a distance] that a fleet horse could not cover in the space of years. That was a favour from God that He gives to whom He will. And I knew my body, limb by limb, bone by bone, sinew by sinew, muscle by muscle, hair by hair, each one by its rank, and what was entrusted to it. Then I found written upon my fifth rib, on the right side, by the Pen of Power, "Praise be to God, Lord of the Created Worlds" ten times; and "O God, bless our Lord Muḥammad, and the family of Muḥammad, and give them peace" ten times; and "I beg forgiveness from the Glorious God" ten times: and I marveled greatly at that.[33]

Like many of the people in this book, ʿUthmān b. Fūdī was a traveler on the Sufi way. Sufism continues to preserve this original approach to Islamic knowledge. It is not the only place where it can still be found, of course, but the *corporate* structures of *ṭarīqa* have done much to protect the *corporeal* practices of education in Islam, especially in the past century and a half. In fact, Sufi orders have thrived during this period and are plainly expanding in Africa and in many other parts of the world. If Sufism is now erroneously seen as *the* tradition of embodiment in Islam, it is perhaps because the exoteric sciences have been more thoroughly colonized by modern sensibilities toward texts and disembodied knowledge. To survive the onslaught, the old ways of knowing have needed an institutional locus. It is no accident that in those places in West Africa where this spiritual discipline continues to thrive, people maintain a deep commitment to writing the Book on the bodies of the children of Adam.

QUR'ANIC KNOWLEDGE, BEING, AND THE COSMOS

The approach to *epistemology* traced in this book is deeply rooted in Muslim *ontology* and *cosmology*. That is to say it is tied to Muslim conceptions of the nature of being on the one hand and to the contents and ordering of the Islamic universe on the other. The implicit and explicit attention to the human body that I have explored in this study is not based on a belief that there is anything inherently noble about the dirt from which we are made. The Qur'an says that this was the mistake of Iblīs (Satan): he thought that he was made of noble stuff. The most infamous jinn in history refused to bow to Adam because he thought that the smokeless fire from which he was cast was better than Adam's lowly clay (Q 7:12). His pride caused him to forget his ultimate purpose in creation: "*And I did not create jinn or mankind except to serve me*" (Q 51:56). When he fell from grace, he refused to see his mistake and ask forgiveness. He was still too proud.

The Qur'an also says that like Iblīs—and with his misguidance—Adam and Eve also fell (Q 2:35–38). But as they became aware of their hunger, the weakness in their limbs, and the fatigue that was overcoming them, they asked immediately for forgiveness. "*They said, 'O Lord, we have wronged ourselves, and if You do not forgive us and have mercy on us, surely we will be lost!*" (Q 7:23). Unlike Iblīs, they were not too proud to repent.

The classical ontology and cosmology of Islam never encouraged people to see their bodies as a source of pride. Amadu Bamba explicitly writes about contemplating the body to *overcome* the sin of pride: "The cure is to know that your body was created the same way as all the others. You are not, dear brother, above anyone. You know neither when you will die nor what tomorrow may bring. The Book of God warns of stern punishment for those guilty of pride. It was this that brought low the cursed Iblīs—we seek refuge in our Lord from both [Satan and pride]. You were once but a fetid drop of sperm, now a carrier of filth, and you will end as a stinking corpse, odious and rotting. You are, without exception, the children of Adam, and it is from dust that you were created."[34]

We are frail, powerless creatures made from dirt. Each one of us begins as a drop of semen, lives life as a sack of feces, and ends as a rotting corpse. Don't get too full of yourself. The Qur'an says this in many ways. But it also says that God loves the children of Adam and Eve. In fact, nowhere does the Qur'an say clearly and explicitly say that God loves anything other than human beings. Each and every time the Qur'an says God loves (*Allāh yuḥib*) followed immediately by an object, that object is a collective noun referring to people. This is not because a thing made of dust is inherently noble. To the contrary, it is the struggle to overcome the limits of these fragile, tired, dying bodies by filling them with knowledge of God and busying them with good works that makes mankind beloved of God. In the Qur'an, God loves

al-muqsiṭīn—the just (60:8)
al-ṣābirīn—the patient (3:146)
al-ṭāwabīn—the repentant (2:222)
al-mutawakkilīn—those who trust in Him (3:159)
al-mutaṭahirīn and *al-muṭahirīn*—those who purify themselves (2:222, 9:108)
al-mutaqīn—the God-conscious (3:76, 9:4)
al-muḥsinīn—those who do what is beautiful (2:195, 3:134, 3:148)

■ The Qur'an says that God creates through speech. He has only to say unto a thing, "Be!," and it is. *Kūn fa Yakūn*. But this is not exactly how He created mankind. The Qur'an says that God shaped the human body with *His own two hands* (Q 38:75). Everything else in the world is made with speech, with *discourse*, an objectifying act external to the self. Speech separates the speaker from the spoken, with the speaker in a position of dominance. In contrast, the human body is lovingly crafted by hand. This body is lowly clay, but it is ennobled by God's love. Neither is the human being animated with a word. Instead, God breathes His spirit into the first body (Q 15:29). Humanity was made with a caress and animated with the kiss of life.

And this perspective on the special nature of the human being in the cosmos is the ultimate key to understanding classical *epistemology* and its privileging of bodily practices. In the Qur'an's view, bodies can be low and foul and dirty, but they can also be ennobled by *knowledge*. This lowly flesh can be raised to a status higher than that of the angels, who are told to bow to Adam, a creature made of mud, because he possessed *knowledge* of the names of all things (Q 2:31–33). The human being may have been made of lowly clay, but the mightiest angels bowed.

The offspring of Adam and Eve can be raised back up to the lofty station of their auspicious ancestors through knowledge and concrete service (*ʿibāda*). Perhaps there is something—if not noble then at least exceptional—in these bodies after all. For they can contain the Qur'an itself, a thing bearing enough of God's transcendent power that it would have split apart the Earth, leaving it broken and quivering, but that can be kept (*hifẓ*) and carried (*ḥaml*) in the human body: "*Had we brought this Qur'an down upon a moun-*

tain verily you would have seen it fall down, rent asunder by the fear of God!" (*Q 59:21*).

Preparing the children of Adam and Eve to bear this charge within their fragile bodies—and raising them to honor from a single common origin in lowly dust—is what the Qur'an school is all about. Perhaps this is why some in the African West remain committed to triumphantly teaching Truth by Truth until the Horn blows to announce that this part of the story has ended and that the Hour has arrived.

GLOSSARY

abjad (Arabic): the alphabet, especially arranged in numerological order
adab (Arabic): etiquette, manners, training, education
ʿajamī (Arabic): non-Arab; refers here to African languages written in Arabic script
ʿālim (Arabic) (pl. *ʿulamāʾ*): learned or knowledgeable person
almaami (Fula): Fula rendering of the Arabic *al-imām*, leader or guide
alwāḥ (Arabic): wooden boards for Qurʾan learning (Wolof, *àlluwa*)
baraka (Arabic): blessing, grace, benediction, divinely derived power (Wolof, *barke*)
basmala (Arabic): invocation of God's name, *bismillah*, usually upon beginning a task
bāṭin (Arabic): hidden or concealed, esoteric knowledge
bayḍān or *bīḍān* (Arabic): "white," racial designation, salient after 1600 in West Africa
ceddo (Wolof): enslaved warrior caste; from *ceɗɗo* (Fula, sing.; pl. *seɓɓe*)
ceerno (Fula): Qurʾan teacher, cleric; closely related etymologically to Wolof, *sëriñ*
daara (Wolof): Qurʾan School; from Arabic *dār al-Qurʾān*, house of the Qurʾan
daara tarbiya (Wolof): training school, a male Murid institution focused on work
dāʾira (Arabic): circle or group; in Wolof, a religious association, *daayira* or *kurél*
duʿāʾ (Arabic): supplication, call on God, prayer distinct from ritual *ṣalāt*
duɗal (Fula) (pl. *dude*): hearth, Qurʾan school, referring to firelight studies
école arabe (French): modern Arabic school; also *école franco-arabe, médérsa*
école française (French): school using French as the main medium for instruction
fiqh (Arabic): Islamic law as a discipline in the curriculum of Islamic study
Fuutanke (Fula) (pl. *Fuutankoobe*): inhabitant of Fuuta Tooro in Senegal River Valley
gariibu (Fula): young, beginning Qurʾan student; derived from verb meaning "to beg"
hadiyya (Arabic): gift, esp. the gifts given to Qurʾan teachers, clerics, and Sufi shaykhs
hāfiẓ (Arabic) (pl. *huffāẓ*): keeper or guardian; Wolof, *kàŋ*; (*ḥifẓ*) memorization
ḥubb (Arabic): love, especially affection and kindness to teachers as a social value
ʿilm (Arabic) (pl. *ʿulūm*): knowledge, discipline or field of study in Islamic curriculum
jaam (Wolof): slave or slaves; in Fula, *maccuɗo* and *rimayɓe*
janng (Fula): read, study, or learn; Wolof, *jàng* (learn), *jàngal* (teach)
julli (Wolof): Muslim ritual prayer; *jullit*: Muslim, Pious Person; from Fula, *juul*
khidma (Arabic): service, especially voluntary labor offered to a teacher or cleric
kuttāb (Arabic): writing place, Middle Eastern term for Qurʾan school
madhhab (Arabic) (pl. *madhāhib*): school of Islamic jurisprudence or legal rite

madrasa (Arabic): place of study, formal school, especially in medieval Middle East
maḥw (Arabic): erasure, "holy water" made by washing Qur'an verses from *alwāḥ*
majlis al-ʿilm (Arabic): knowledge session, classical format for advanced study
marabout (French): Muslim religious leader or notable; from Arabic *mrābiṭ*
médérsa (French): French colonial Islamic school; from Arabic *madrasa*
moodibo (Fula) (pl. *moodibaaɓe*): scholar, educator; from Arabic *mu'addib*
murīd (Arabic): spiritual aspirant, seeker of God, technical term in Sufism
ndongo (Wolof): Qur'an school student, equivalent of *taalibé*
njàngaan (Wolof): live-in Qur'an student, alms-seeking trip by Qur'an school
qāḍī (Arabic): judge, historically in West Africa, often nonstate arbitrators
saafara (Wolof): remedy, especially Qur'an water referred to as *kiis*; see also *maḥw*
ṣadaqa (Arabic): voluntary or expiatory alms, especially to *taalibés*; Wolof, *sarax*
sëriñ (Wolof): Qur'an teacher, cleric, evangelist; likely from Arabic *bashirīn*
sūdān (Arabic): blacks, dark-skinned Africans; *bilād al-sūdān*: lands of the blacks
sūdānī (Arabic) (adjectival form): black, from the *bilād al-sūdān*, African
sunna (Arabic): well-trod path, normative example, especially of the Prophet
taalibé (Wolof): Qur'an learner, disciple of religious leader; from Arabic *ṭālib*
taalibo (Fula): advanced Qur'an learner, student of religious sciences; from Arabic *ṭālib*
tafsīr (Arabic): Qur'an exegesis, among final fields broached in classical curriculum
takfīr (Arabic): to call a Muslim a nonbeliever, verbal excommunication
tamsiir (Fula) or *tafsiir*: Qur'an exegete, scholar, religious official; from Arabic *tafsīr*
ṭarīqa (Arabic) (pl. *ṭuruq*): path, way, method, technical term for a Sufi order
taṣawwuf (Arabic): the science (or discipline) of spiritual excellence, Sufism
téere (Wolof): book, but especially written talisman; Songhay, *tira*
yalwaan (Wolof): seeking alms, ritual mendicancy
yar (Wolof): lash, whip, switch; to raise or educate, moral education and discipline
ẓāhir (Arabic): manifest or apparent, exoteric knowledge

NOTES

Abbreviations

ANFOM Archives Nationales d'Outre-Mer, Aix-en-Provence
ANS Archives Nationales du Sénégal, Dakar
PRO British Public Records Office, Kew

Introduction

1. Katz, *Body of Text*, 99.

2. See al-Qābisī, *Al-Risāla al-mufaṣṣila*, 315–20.

3. Thanks to one of the manuscript's anonymous readers for this turn of phrase.

4. Mayeur-Jaouen, "Introduction." The special edition is titled *Le corps et le sacré en Orient musulman* Other essays in it include Gril, "Corps du prophète," and Fortier, "Mort vivante."

5. See Fortier, "Pedagogie coranique"; Fortier, "Memorisation et audition." On the body more broadly, see Fortier, "Lait, le sperme, le dos"; Fortier, "Mort vivante."

6. For Brenner's works alluding to the body, see his "Histories of Religion" and "Sufism in Africa."

7. Lambek, *Knowledge and Practice*, jacket; for a striking discussion of what could be read as embodied learning of Islam, see 149–56.

8. See Masquelier, *Prayer Has Spoiled Everything*; I. M. Lewis, al-Safi, and Hurreiz, *Women's Medicine*; Boddy, *Wombs and Alien Spirits*; Stoller, "Embodying Cultural Memory."

9. In Masquelier's *Prayer Has Spoiled Everything* on Niger, this is not restricted to subtext or even primary text. It is explicit even in the title. Niger is 98 percent Muslim.

10. Launay, "Invisible Religion?," 188. Launay's 1992 monograph, *Beyond the Stream*, set the standard for anthropological writing on African Muslim society, one met in recent works by Meunier, *Dynamique*, and Soares, *Islam and the Prayer Economy.*

11. Anthropologist Bertrand Hell's *Tourbillon des genies* situates the spirit possession cults of the Gnāwa in Morocco within the broader Islamic tradition while exploring embodiment, race, and the recent commercialization of their practices.

12. This point is also made, though in reference to divination rather than spirit possession, by Saul, "Islam and West African Anthropology," and Brenner, "Histories of Religion."

13. Writing in the early 1970s, Jacqueline Monfouga-Nicolas argued that recent *bori* practice bore no substantive historical relationship to traditional Hausa religion. See *Ambivalence et culte de possession*. See also the productive approach taken by O'Brien in the introduction to her dissertation, "Power and Paradox."

14. On the problems of thinking of indigenous African healing as "religion," see Feierman, "Colonists, Scholars, and the Creation of Invisible Histories," 202–4. Landau's "'Religion' and Christian Conversion" expands on this as well as the broader problem of "African traditional religion" as a fraught category.

15. On Asma' bint ʿUthman b. Fudi, see Mack and Boyd, *One Woman's Jihad*. For a lament on African women's Islam, see Hutson, "Development of Women's Authority," 43. These are also overarching themes in the wonderful study by sociolinguist Ousseina Alidou, *Engaging Modernity*, and Umar, "Mass Education." The essays in Badran's *Gender and Islam in Africa* offer an exemplary exploration of more mainstream struggles to create space for feminine authority.

16. Kugle, *Sufis and Saints' Bodies*, 14.

17. Which puts Jibrīl in the role of the teacher and Muḥammad the student. This is exactly how Jibrīl behaves in the famous hadith of Gabriel, wherein he appears as a stranger in an audience of the Prophet's companions and publicly tests the Prophet's knowledge of Islam. The master/disciple relationship in Qur'an learning thus starts with the first revelation and is enshrined in the Qurʾan schools, which likely functioned during the Prophet's lifetime and certainly existed during the caliphate of ʿUmar—a full century before the formative period of the legal schools or any institutionalized forms of Sufism.

18. To name only a few important works: Metcalf, *Moral Conduct and Authority*; Eickelman, "Art of Memory"; Chamberlain, "Production of Knowledge"; Messick, "Genealogies of Reading"; Graham, "Traditionalism in Islam."

19. Thanks to Amir Syed for help with this idea.

20. The phrase was suggested by distinguished African historian Joseph Miller.

21. For an excellent exploration of the role of the Prophet's body in Islamic thinking, see Gril, "Corps du Prophète."

22. Of course this is not true only of *Islamic* education but of *education*. See, for example, Geurts's insightful exploration of embodied knowledge practices in a non-Muslim region of Ghana, *Culture and the Senses*.

23. Many thanks to Pier Larson for suggesting this particular image in a presentation of earlier work from my dissertation.

24. Indeed, this is the precise sense of the colloquial expression Corrine Fortier notes for Mauritania, "*Hāfiẓu wa ḥāmilu Kitābi Allah al-ʿazīzi* [He keeps and carries the Book of Almighty God]" ("Pédagogie coranique," 253).

25. Hamet, *Chroniques*, 229.

26. Kamara, *Florilège*, 351.

27. There are a number of useful regional sketches from other parts of sub-Saharan Africa. For beginnings, see Seesemann, "Where East Meets West," for this kind of schooling in Sudan. See also Skinner, "Islam and Education"; Santerre, *Pédagogie musulmane*; Meunier, *Dynamique*; Mommersteeg, "Éducation coranique." For Gambia, see Sanneh, *Jakhanke Muslim Clerics*. For Burkina Faso, see Saul, "Qurʾanic School Farm and Child Labour."

28. This is the strong impression created by Salama, *Enseignement islamique*, which highlights, among many other important details, that many of the Qurʾan school teachers, especially though not exclusively in Upper Egypt, were Mālikīs from the Maghrib.

29. There are a total of 791 notebooks treating various topics. See Afanou and Pierre, *Catalogue*.

30. The notebooks consulted here are listed as unpublished sources in the bibliography.

31. I also conducted two formal group interviews involving a dozen students aged be-

tween six and eighteen. Although no sensitive information was communicated in these interviews, I chose not to make audio recordings and instead took notes.

32. Thanks to Gottfried Hagen for this image.

33. For an exploration of reformism that is insightful but too uncritical of reformist claims, see Miran, *Islam, histoire, et modernité*, esp. 443–66,.

34. See Rosander and Westerlund, *African Islam and Islam in Africa*, esp. the introductory essay.

35. This understanding owes much to conversations with Robert Launay. For related insights, see Ware and Launay, "Comment (ne pas) lire le Coran."

36. Cheikh Hamidou Kane, *Aventure ambigüe*, 188.

37. Among the fine studies that explore this process, see especially Gesink, *Islamic Reform and Conservatism*; Zaman, "Religious Education"; Fortna, *Imperial Classroom*; Eickelman, "Mass Higher Education."

38. Starrett, *Putting Islam to Work*, 26. For the political and economic context, see the introduction to Mitchell, *Rule of Experts*.

39. The most compelling statement of this perspective was expressed in a lengthy informal conversation with Boye Harouna, Boghé, Mauritania, December 2005.

40. Pew Research Center, *Future*. I have disaggregated the data that assimilate North Africa to the Middle East and have repositioned Sudan back in sub-Saharan Africa.

41. The CIA World Factbook (https://www.cia.gov/library/publications/the-world-factbook/) gives figures of thirty-one million for both places, whereas Pew estimates Ethiopia's Muslim population at just under twenty-nine million.

42. Insoll, *Archaeology of Islam*, 162–68, 177–82.

43. Marty, "Mourides," 123–24.

44. See Marty, *Études sur l'Islam maure*; Marty, *Études sur l'Islam au Sénégal*; Marty, *Études sur l'Islam et les tribus du Soudan français*; Marty, *Études sur l'Islam et les tribus maures*; Marty, *Études sur l'Islam en Côte d'Ivoire*; Marty, *L'Islam en Guinée: Fouta Diallon*; Marty, *Études sur l'Islam au Dahomey*. While he did not create Islam Noir, the central administrative and intellectual construct guiding French action, he was its most important author. For a deeper historical examination of French conceptions of African Muslims, see chap. 3.

45. ANS J86, "Rapport Marty à monsieur le gouverneur general sur les écoles coraniques," 33. Nearly all of this document was also published by the *Revue du Monde Musulman* under the misleading title, "Écoles maraboutiques du Sénégal: La Médersa de Saint-Louis."

46. Abdelkader Fall, "École coranique," 24.

47. Marty, *Études sur l'Islam au Sénégal*, 261.

48. See the "Avant-Propos" to Marty, "Mourides," 1.

49. Seesemann, *Divine Flood*, 11.

50. Robinson, *Muslim Societies*, 42.

51. The useful concept of "Islamic religious culture" was introduced by Brenner and most explicitly discussed in his "Histories of Religion."

52. As Feierman noted in an earlier draft, this argument is equivalent to the one made about Africa in relation to Europe by Mudimbe in *Invention of Africa*. Islamic Africa thus appears doubly peripheral.

53. See Soares, "Notes," for a brief and enlightening discussion of "islams" as well as an effort to situate the anthropology of Islamic Africa within the broader context of the anthropology of Islam, something that I do not do here.

54. See Hunwick, "Islamic Law and Polemics," 51.

55. Many thanks to Zachary Wright for bringing this mistranslation to my attention. For excellent discussion, see Wright, "Embodied Knowledge," 209–11.

56. See Said's scathing critique, "Impossible Histories."

57. See McDougall, "Discourse and Distortion"; Ware, "Slavery in Islamic Africa."

58. Hall's *History of Race* is a fine study.

59. The slave trade in French is still called *la traite nègriere*, and a slaver is a *nègrier*.

60. I treat these issues at length in Ware, "Slavery in Islamic Africa." Chap. 2 of this book demonstrates that jet-black African Muslim scholars were admired and honored teachers of Arab *shurafa*, and chap. 3 of this book contains an original contribution to the study of abolitionism.

61. Abdu-Salaam Lo, interview. The racial logic of pan-Arabism was an important topic raised by some of my interlocutors, especially Abdu-Salaam Lo, a traditionally trained scholar who also studied in the Middle East in the 1970s and 1980s.

62. The passages here on Bilal are inspired by too many sources to name. This telling incorporates many versions of the story I have heard in sermons and in texts, including Tabari and other Muslim historians in translation. The narrative account here also draws on an encyclopedia entry by ʿArafat, "Bilāl b. Rabāḥ."

63. See Ware, "Islam in Africa."

64. Launay, "Invisible Religion" 188 (emphasis added).

65. See Last, *Sokoto Caliphate*; Hiskett, *Sword of Truth*; Robinson, *Holy War.*

66. Feierman, "Colonizers, Scholars, and the Creation of Invisible Histories," 184.

67. Ibid., 185.

68. Schoenbrun, "Conjuring the Modern," 1403.

69. On Bamba, see Babou, *Fighting the Greater Jihad*. On Niass, see Seesemann, *Divine Flood*; Wright, "Embodied Knowledge."

70. At a December 2010 Institute for the Study of Islamic Thought in Africa workshop in Dakar on Sufism, prominent intellectuals from different branches of the Tijāniyya and the Murīdiyya were put in a context where they could read and examine the ideas of the other Sufi masters. Most had never done so and were excited to see common threads of experience and insight in the other orders.

71. See Hall, *History of Race*.

72. Farias promotes but does not systematically pursue this idea in his methodologically innovative deep time study, *Arabic Medieval Inscription*.

73. One interesting recent example of spatial analysis used in this way is Nast, *Concubines and Power.*

74. For example, the writings of Moodibo Muḥammad al-Kābarī—discussed in chap. 2—can still be found in manuscript form. His *Bustān al-fawāʾid wa-l-manāfiʿa fī ʿilm al-ṭibb wa-l-sirr,* written sometime in the first half of the fifteenth century, is possibly *the oldest surviving primary text written in any language by a West African*. What light might it shed on the early efflorescence of sub-Saharan Islamic scholarship, legal thought,

or history in the fifteenth century? A copy of this manuscript is kept in the Arabic Manuscripts Collection at Northwestern University's Melville Herskovits Africana Library.

Chapter 1

1. Human Rights Watch, "Off the Backs," 67–68.

2. Ibid., 90.

3. The data in the report can easily be used to read the document against itself. For example, the average self-reported sum required of *talibés* in daily mendicancy ranged from 228 FCFA(francs communauté financière d'Afrique) per day (less than fifty cents) in the northern urban center of Saint Louis to 463 FCFA per day (less than one dollar). When one understands that Qur'an teachers usually receive no financial support for live-in students from parents, such sums for maintaining students seem in fact quite low.

4. Human Rights Watch, "Off the Backs," 37.

5. Ibid., 51, 70–71.

6. Ibid., 37.

7. Ibid., 5.

8. I treated these topics at length in my doctoral dissertation: Ware, "Knowledge, Faith, and Power," chap. 5. And I treat the topic of ritual mendicancy in Ware, "Njàngaan." HRW refers to that article in three footnotes that indicate that the authors either did not read it or wished they had not. In one note, they mark my dissent from simplistic narratives of abuse. In another, they suggest that my historicization of colonial and precolonial practices of schooling instead constitutes documentation of prior centuries of "abuse." See Human Rights Watch, "Off the Backs," 17–18.

9. Zadeh, "Fire Cannot Harm It," 54.

10. Masamba Buso, interview: "Already, you are supposed to go to heaven when you memorize [*mokkal*] the Qur'an." Samb mocks this attitude in *Matraqué*, 49.

11. For thoughtful material on hardship as an educational value in Christian and animist regions, see Bledsoe, "No Success without Struggle." Traditional initiatory forms of education and socialization in Africa and elsewhere also include important elements of hardship and physical privations. For female non-Islamic forms of initiation in Mauritania, see Fortier, "Lait, le sperme, le dos."

12. In Beye, "Étude coranique," 39, he and his classmates plot to throw the master's lash in the river.

13. In the illustrations accompanying the Cahiers Ponty, the lash was the most prominently featured inanimate object, surpassed in its frequency of representation only by drawings of the teacher surrounded by students. For Sanneh, the cane symbolized the school (*Crown and the Turban*, 127).

14. Ware, "Njàngaan."

15. Abdourahmane Diop, "École coranique," 25–27.

16. Amadu Basiru Jeŋ, interview. See also Abdoulaye Bara Diop, *Famille Wolof*, 45: "The Wolof say that parents are weak [soft-hearted] toward their children, who are better educated by strangers [*jurut du yërëm*]."

17. For a thoughtful exploration of this paradox, see Brenner, *Controlling Knowledge*, 18–19.

18. Cheikh Hamidou Kane, *Ambiguous Adventure*, 4.

19. The Qur'an and study of the Qur'an were often described as "heavy" by students who grew up in the schools, especially when they were arguing for the importance of studying in hardship. Ibrahima Sey, interview: "The Qur'an is a heavy thing. And it is an important thing. . . . To build character, to remove character faults[, studying] it has to be difficult."

20. Beye, "Étude coranique," 42.

21. Shariif Sulaymaan Aydara, interview.

22. Médoune Fall, "École coranique," 7.

23. The term is borrowed from Sanneh, *Crown and the Turban*; Brenner, *Controlling Knowledge*.

24. Anta Njaay, interview. She was born in Tivaouane in 1971 and studied Qur'an for a short time in childhood before returning to memorize the Qur'an in her twenties.

25. Aliu Gay, interview. A farmer in the village of Ngabou also discussed the importance of menial tasks in shaping character. He was born in 1940 and entered the Qur'an school in a village not far from Louga when he was five years old.

26. Gueye, "École coranique," 16–17.

27. Francisco de Lemos Coelho cited in Mbaye, "Islam au Sénégal," 238. The identification of *sëriñ* with *bexerin*, *bischarÿns*, or *bushreen* is almost universally accepted in the literature on Islam in Senegal.

28. For useful comparative ethnographic material from what is now Burkina Faso, see Saul, "Qur'anic School Farm and Child Labour."

29. Ware, "Njàngaan." For a late eighteenth-century account, see Villeneuve, *Afrique*, 3:95.

30. Mansuur Caam, interview.

31. Abdelkader Fall, "École coranique," 14.

32. Bamany, "École coranique," 29.

33. Ibrahima Bàjjan, interview.

34. Xaliil Lo, interview; Mansuur Cuun, interview; Daan Buso, interview; Ibrahima Bàjjan, interview; Abdallah Juuf, interview.

35. Ibrahima Bàjjan, interview.

36. Ibrahima Sey, interview: "It takes a lot out of you, and puts a lot into you [*Dafay gene ci yow lu bare, def ci yow lu bare*]."

37. Colin, *Systèmes d'éducation*, 113–14.

38. Those who defend corporal punishment in Qur'an schools often refer to this injunction—found in the Risāla of Qayrawāni, among other places—that children may be struck by age ten if they neglect their prayers.

39. Malick Sèye Fall cited in Colin, *Systèmes d'éducation*, 114–15.

40. Abdourahmane Diop, "École coranique," 8.

41. Mokhtar Kebe, oral communication, Institute for the Study of Islamic Thought in Africa, Dakar, August 2007.

42. Amadu Basiru Jeŋ, interview.

43. "Vieux" Faal, interview.

44. Gueye, "École coranique," 11–12.

45. See Fortna, *Imperial Classroom*. In the late Ottoman period, before modernization obviated traditional Qur'an schooling through most of the empire, the spectacle of students rocking while reciting was seen as a sign of backwardness.

46. Abdelkader Fall, "École coranique," 21–22.

47. For a thoughtful discussion, see Graham, *Beyond the Written Word*, chap. 9.

48. Shaykhuna Lo, interview; Masamba Buso, interview.

49. Abdu-Salaam Lo, interview.

50. Shaykh Lo Njaay, interview.

51. Diané, "École coranique," 11–12.

52. See Colin, *Systèmes d'éducation*, 120.

53. Shariif Sulaymaan Aydara, interview: "*Ku la jàngal araf ci alxuraan, ku mu mënn doon, sa sang la.*" Though I have not verified it, I assume that this was a Wolof translation of an Arabic textual source, possibly a hadith report. Fortier, "Mémorisation et audition," 95, represents the saying, transcribed as "*man ʿallamaka harfan fa huwa mawlaka*," as a *dicton maure* (Moorish proverb).

54. See Colvin, "Shaykh's Men."

55. Babou, *Fighting the Greater Jihad*, 105–6.

56. Shaykh Lo Njaay, interview: "Being in front of the master with him educating me, you know *tarbiya* [*Dama nekkoon ci kanam Siin bi, tarbiya daal, waaw di ma yar*]." Njaay was born in 1968. His family came to Ngabou before he was born. He studied at the Qur'an school operated by Modu Siise there at age seven and left at age twelve or thirteen. He was not an internal student.

57. See Chamberlain, *Knowledge and Social Practice*, 116–25.

58. Amadu Basiru Jeng, interview. Jeng was born in Touba and began study in the Qur'an school at age five in 1973. In 1974, he was sent to a *daara tarbiya*, where he lived until 1980.

59. See Amadu Bamba Mbacké, *Nahj Qaḍāʾ al-Hāj*, lines 208–11. It also appears in his *Diwān fī ʿulūm al-dīnīyya*, 387.

60. This is a key point of emphasis in an interesting thesis by Wan Daud, "Concept of Knowledge," 124–93. See also Rosenthal, *Knowledge Triumphant*, 240–76.

61. For discussion of knowledge personified, see Ware and Launay, "Comment (ne pas) lire le Coran."

62. Graham, "Traditionalism in Islam," 507.

63. See Abdallah, "Malik's Concept," 170–83. For a broader though more polemical argument, see Dutton, *Origins of Islamic Law*. For a very similar portrait of embodied example in early Meccan teaching practice, see Motzki, *Origins of Islamic Jurisprudence*.

64. See Hallaq, *Law and Legal Theory*, esp. "Was al-Shafi'i, the Master Architect of Islamic Jurisprudence." For an argument that opposes mine here, see Melchert, "Traditionist-Jurisprudents."

65. Ibn al-Qāsim reports that Mālik said, "I do not know of this practice as far as obligatory prayers are concerned, but there is no harm in someone doing it in voluntary prayers, if he has been standing for a long time, in order to make things easier for himself." See Dutton, "ʿAmal v Hadith," 15.

66. Dutton, *Origins of Islamic Law*, 44; discussion of ʿamal versus hadith on pp. 41–52.

67. Ibāḍī Islam was present in the South Sahara earlier. See Savage, "Berbers and Blacks." The transition to Malikism in sub-Saharan Africa remains poorly documented. Intriguing questions persist. See, for example, Brett, "Islam and Trade."

68. Shiite scholars have been similarly interested in preserving the status of certain early Muslims, especially ʿAlī and the *ahl al-bayt*, as normative exemplars. Many thanks to Najam Haider for a thoughtful critique of this section on legal thinking.

69. Qayrawānī, *Al-Risāla*, 269–70. The page numbers here are from the most easily available European-language translation, the French edition by Fagnan. This is book 45:8 in any traditional Arabic presentation of the text or in the handful of English translations, none of which I find fully adequate for academic citation. For an excellent discussion of how this text was learned in traditional scholarly circles in early twentieth-century Mali, see Berndt, "Closer Than Your Jugular Vein," 88–98.

70. For an excellent illustration of this point in a Sufi context, see Hanretta, *Islam and Social Change*, 142. He notes that Senegalese Sufi Mālik Sy criticized fellow Tijānīs in a ritual matter "for following their own readings . . . rather than the teaching of reputable shaykhs . . . since it was impossible for a *walī* to lead a follower into error through his practice."

71. In Niger, the most common name for Qur'an school is *makarantar allo*, meaning "wooden-slate school." See Alidou, *Engaging Modernity*.

72. For a detailed description of this process, see Ware, "Knowledge, Faith, and Power," chap. 1.

73. Ibrahima Sey, interview, was among a number who were absolutely convinced of the practice's efficacy in this regard.

74. Sanneh, *Crown and the Turban*, 137.

75. El-Tom, "Drinking the Koran," 429.

76. For Arabic edition with French translation, see Qābisī, *Al-Risāla al-mufaṣṣila*. Throughout the text, the author refers to himself as ʿAlī b. Muḥammad al-Qābisī. For discussion of two of his rulings concerning trade with sub-Saharan Africa, see Brett, "Islam and Trade." For more detail on al-Qābisī as well as his contemporary, Ibn Abi Zaid al-Qayrawānī (922–96), see Idris, "Deux juristes kairouannais."

77. See Sarton, "*Al-tarbīya*." The *Mudawwana* is in some ways the most important legal book in the Mālikī school and is probably more widely taught than the *Muwaṭṭa*ʾ. See also Brockopp, "Contradictory Evidence."

78. And the shoulder blades of animals (*aktāf*).

79. Ahwānī, *Al-tarbīya fi al-Islam*, 317; Qābisī, *Al-Risāla al-mufaṣṣila*, 124.

80. Mohamed, "Devoir de vacances," 20–21.

81. Ahwānī, *Al-tarbīya fi al-Islam*, 317.

82. Amadou Wane, "Trois ans," 763. The practice of writing the Qur'an on sweets to be eaten was apparently endorsed by a number of medieval Shafi'i scholars. See Zadeh, "Touching and Ingesting," n. 150.

83. Baba Ndiaye, "Islam," 40.

84. Abdelkader Fall, "École coranique," 39–40.

85. I return to the questions of eating, shared sacrifice, and alms in the conclusion.

86. Sanneh, *Jakhanke Muslim Clerics*, 149.

87. Santerre, *Pédagogie musulmane*, 111.

88. Mommersteeg, "Éducation coranique."

89. Berkey, "Tradition, Innovation, and the Social Construction," 39.

90. Most notably in a number of hadiths from Bukhārī, *Ṣaḥīḥ*, book 71, wherein the Prophet's saliva, saliva from the recited *fatiha*, and the blowing of Qur'an verses are endorsed for healing purposes. For more on this phenomenon in African history, see Owusu-Ansah, "Prayer, Amulets, and Healing."

91. For the searchable database of Arabic manuscripts cataloged in West Africa, see http://westafricanmanuscripts.org. The database is now housed at Northwestern University and owes its existence to pioneering work by John Hunwick, Charles Stewart, Muḥammad Sani Umar, Bruce Hall, and many others. For a fine work that utilizes the database and literary sources to reconstruct the outlines of advanced study of religion for precolonial Islamic scholars in West Africa, see Hall and Stewart, "Historic 'Core Curriculum.'"

92. I am deeply indebted to Zachary Wright and Souleymane Bachir Diagne for alerting me to the existence of stories of the Prophet Muḥammad and Shaykh Aḥmad al-Tijānī having their cupped blood drunk by followers.

93. This compilation is drawn from the website Islam Q & A (http://islamqa.com/index.php?ref=81692&ln=eng). Thanks to an anonymous reader of this manuscript for providing an identification of Muḥammad Ṣāliḥ al-Munājjid.

94. Gril, "Corps du Prophète," 28.

95. Souleymane Bachir Diagne, "Shaykh Al-Hajj Abbass Sall," 173.

96. Masamba Buso, interview. Drinking the water from the Prophet's ablutions seems to have been an established practice. See Gril, "Corps du Prophète," n. 40.

97. Chamberlain, *Knowledge and Social Practice*, 122.

98. Messick, "Genealogies of Reading," 400. See also Messick, *Calligraphic State*, chap. 5.

99. Kamara, *Florilège*, 320.

100. The *Iḥyā'* exists in too many full and partial editions in Arabic, as well as numerous partial translations into European languages, for a conventional note to be of much use here. For a wonderful introduction to the man and his thought, see Moosa, *Poetics of Imagination* (the story of the thieves is on 93–94). See also Ormsby, *Ghazali*.

101. For the Arabic text and translation of one such text, see Alyrres, *A Muslim American Slave*. For a translation and analysis of another, see Law and Lovejoy, *Biography*. For a fuller discussion of enslaved African Muslims in the Americas, see Sylviane Diouf, *Servants of Allah*. See also Gomez, *Black Crescent*; Gomez, "Prayin' on Duh Bead: Islam in Early America," in *Exchanging Our Country Marks*. Highly useful as well are the final three essays in Lovejoy, *Slavery on the Frontiers of Islam*.

102. Pap Lamin Njaay, interview.

103. Chamberlain, *Knowledge and Social Practice*, 123–24.

104. Launay artfully referred to this phenomenon: reformers "are convinced of the transparency of signs." See Ware and Launay, "Comment (ne pas) lire le Coran," 139.

105. Afsuraddin, "Excellences of the Qur'an," 19.

106. Berkey, *Transmission of Knowledge*, 26.

107. For early oral transmission of the Qur'an, see Dutton, "Orality"; for general treatment of orality in Islam, see Graham, *Beyond the Written Word*, 79–116.

108. For a very detailed biographical account of the struggle over Islamic education in Qutb's village, see Qutb, *Child from the Village*, 15–25. My attention was drawn to Qutb by a wonderful undergraduate honors history thesis written by one of my Northwestern undergraduate students, George Brandes. My thinking here and this paragraph owe much to conversations with him and material from his thesis, "In Search of Sayyid Qutb."

109. Boullata, "Sayyid Qutb's Literary Appreciation," 367.

110. Qutb, *Child from the Village*, 19.

111. Mollien, *Travels*, 252.

112. Carruthers, *Book of Memory*.

113. Santerre, *Pédagogie musulmane*, 131.

114. Oral communication, Institute for the Study of Islamic Thought in Africa Conference, Islamic Institute of Dakar, August 2007. The volume of Ghazālī's production is well known. Niass has eighty-eight separate listings in the bibliography compiled by Hunwick (*Arabic Literature*). Bamba's entry cites two hundred works. Neither list should be considered exhaustive. Niass Tijānīs refer to him as "an ocean without shores," and Murids like to say that Bamba wrote "seven tons" of books. On Niass, see Seesemann, *Divine Flood*; Wright, "Embodied Knowledge." See also Ousmane Kane, "Shaykh al-Islam."

115. Amadu Bamba Mbacké, *Masālik al-Jinān*, verses 46–54; my translation. I rendered *atabāʿi mā aqūlu* as the familiar English expression "practice what I preach."

116. Asad, "Idea of an Anthropology of Islam."

Chapter 2

1. Park, *Travels*, 60.

2. These are the most common terms in Wolof, Fula, Soninke, and Mandingo, respectively.

3. For a detailed description by a French botanist of clerics use of herbal medicines, see Villeneuve, *Afrique*, 3:102–3.

4. Levtzion and Hopkins, *Corpus*, 82. For an account of the rain prayer, see Sakho, "Croyances religieuses," 42–43.

5. "Marabouts are perceived in Senegalese society as the principal witch hunters" (Moumar Coumba Diop, "Contribution," 17).

6. A great deal of evidence supports all of the points made here except for the last, which I have only seen once, in Christian Lelong's fascinating documentary on Qāḍī courts in twenty-first-century Niger, *Justice à Agadez*. It may be a novelty, but I suspect that the practice is ancient.

7. Abdelkader Fall, "École coranique," 39. This was—and still is—a common practice. Mor Faal, interview, mentions that on his first day in the *daara* (1965 in Khaïré), the *sëriñ* wrote a *téere-baat* (talisman worn around the neck) for him.

8. Gaby, *Relation de la Nigritie*, 53.

9. For essays on "caste" in West Africa and an interrogation of the notion itself, see Conrad and Frank, *Status and Identity*. For an expansive argument for the origins of West African caste systems in the empire of Mali in the thirteenth century (as well as possibly an independent origin among the Soninke and Wolof), see Tamari, "Development of Caste Systems." The arguments and evidence therein abridge Tamari, *Castes*.

10. See Brunschvig, "Métiers." See also Chamberlain, *Knowledge and Social Practice*,

127. Cuppers, dyers, money changers, and goldsmiths were thought ritually impure in the Middle East.

11. See Ware, "Longue Durée."

12. Shwaʿīb Mbakke, interview. According to this direct descendant of Amadu Bamba, "It was in my limbs [*Ci sama céer*]."

13. For similar interpretations, see Brenner, "Histories of Religion," 147–48; Colvin, "Islam and the State of Kajoor," 589; and Willis, "Torodbe Clerisy," 202.

14. For useful discussions of marriage and the constitution of the clerical classes, see Schmitz, "Souffle de la parenté"; Dramé, "Planting the Seeds."

15. Willis, "Torodbe Clerisy."

16. For a prominent instance of this sort of marriage in the twentieth century, see Seesemann, "'Shurafa' and the 'Blacksmith.'"

17. Villeneuve, *Afrique*, 3:107.

18. Levtzion and Hopkins, *Corpus*, 81.

19. McIntosh, *Ancient Middle Niger*, 187.

20. For a useful introduction to the topic, see Sanneh, "Origins of Clericalism."

21. Levtzion and Hopkins, *Corpus*, 79–80.

22. Pioneering archaeological work by Roderick McIntosh has shown that the roots of West Africa's famous "caste" systems of endogamous occupational specialization can be found in this kind of sociospatial organization. See McIntosh, "Pulse Model."

23. See, for example, Curtin, "Jihad in West Africa,"13.

24. Sanneh, "Origins of Clericalism," 50–52.

25. Hamdun and King, *Ibn Battuta in Black Africa*, 58–59. The boy understands Baṭūṭa's spoken Arabic.

26. Ibid., 41.

27. Sanneh, "Origins of Clericalism," is the source for the identification of Zagha with Jakha or Diakha-Masina. Sanneh's *Jakhanke Muslim Clerics* is the best monograph on the subject.

28. The best short introduction to the tenets of the Jakhanke scholarly tradition is Wilks, "Juula." For an excellent ethnography of a branch of the Juula/Jakhanke diaspora in Côte d'Ivoire, see Launay, *Beyond the Stream.*

29. Wilks, "Juula," 98.

30. For earlier such opinions by North African Mālikīs, see Brett, "Islam and Trade." A hadith widely cited by early Mālikī authorities recommended treating the Magians like people of the book, and refusal to accept any authority was the only political stance forbidden to Muslims. See also Ware, "Slavery in Islamic Africa," esp. the discussion of jihad.

31. I do not know the original textual source for this, though I have heard the story a number of times orally. It is also retold in Babou, *Fighting the Greater Jihad*, 219 (n. 35); Glover, *Sufism and Jihad*, 71.

32. For thoughtful analysis that connects with this discussion of clerical autonomy but that cannot be fully engaged here, see Hunwick, "Secular Power."

33. Kati, *Tarikh el Fettach*, 179; see 314 for the French translation. For the English, see Kati, *Ta'rīkh al-Fattāsh*, 301.

34. Kati, *Tarikh el Fettach*, 179, 314.

35. Saʿdī, *Tarikh es-Soudan*, 56–57; Hunwick,, *Timbuktu*, 81–82.

36. Quoted in Hunwick, *Timbuktu*, 69, though I have changed the final sentence for a more literal translation. The work referenced is *Al-Tahdīb fi ikhtisār al-Mudawwana*, by Khalaf b. Muḥammad b. al-Baradhi'i (d. 982–83). It is an advanced versification and commentary of the *Mudawwana*, the most important legal textbook studied in most Māliki scholarly circles. The West African Manuscript Database shows four extant manuscript copies of the text, in libraries in Boutilimit and Nouakchott, Mauritania. A contemporary publication of the text was published in Dubai in 1999.

37. www.arabicmanuscripts.org. At least one of the two surviving manuscripts that appears complete—in Boutilimit—may also hold al-Kābarī's commentaries in the margins of the text.

38. Kati, *Ta'rīkh al-Fattash*, 169. Al-Kaʿti mentions the tomb of ʿUthmān al-Kābarī as a place where supplications to God are more likely to be answered.

39. Levtzion, "Islam in the Bilad al-Sudan," 69.

40. Al-Saʿdī, *Ta'rīkh al-Sūdān*, 57–58; Hunwick, *Timbuktu*, 71.

41. Al-Saʿdī, *Ta'rīkh al-Sūdān*, 48; al-Saʿdi, *Tarikh es-Soudan*, 78; Hunwick, *Timbuktu*, 70.

42. Levtzion and Hopkins, *Corpus*, 77.

43. Researching place-names could be useful, as many eastern and southeastern Senegambian village names suggest possible Soninke and/or Mandingo clerical origins.

44. Oumar Kane, *Première hégémonie*, 336–37.

45. See Kossmann, "Berber Islamic Terminology." Many thanks to Fiona McLaughlin for bringing this to my attention.

46. Fisher and Masonen, "Almoravid Conquest of Ghana."

47. Al-Naqar, "Takrur," 367.

48. Al-Naqar, "Takrur," 370. These references appear to come from a period before "Takrūr" was used in a general way to refer to West Africa. On its use in the latter sense, see El-Hamel, *Vie Intellectuelle*. The term "permanent pilgrims" is borrowed from Yamba, *Permanent Pilgrims*, a fine study of West Africans who established themselves in the modern Sudan during the course of pilgrimage odysseys.

49. The history of Jolof is due for revision; all the major research on it took place in the 1960s. See Boulègue, *Grand Jolof*, as well as two fine unpublished dissertations that complement each other: Coifman, "History of the Wolof State"; Charles, "History of the Kingdom of Jolof."

50. See Mamadou Ndiaye, *Enseignement*. In Wolof, the names for the Arabic letters as well as the names involved in counting syllabic combinations in the Qur'an (*waññ*) to help speed memorization seem to come from Fula.

51. See Colvin, "Islam and the State of Kajoor," 592.

52. Crone, *Voyages of Cadamosto*, 40; for most of Cà da Mosto's material on Islam among the "Zilofi," see 30–41.

53. Almada, *Brief treatise*, 19–20 (emphasis added).

54. Dramé's masterful Ph.D. thesis, "Planting the Seeds of Islam," explores the creation of a Mandingo clerical center in seventeenth-century Casamance, south of the Gambia River.

55. Almada, *Brief Treatise*, 46.

56. I have not yet identified the first two settlements, but the third appears to be Sutukoba, a village not far from Medina Gounasse in Senegal.

57. "Letter of Padre Baltesar Barreira to the Padre Provincial, Serra Leoa 15 April 1608," in Department of History, University of Liverpool, "Jesuit Documents," document 29.

58. Kati, *Ta'rīkh al-Fattash*, 168–69.

59. See Ka, *École de Pir*. The conventional date is 1603. Other sources place it in the reign of Dammel Maaxuréja Kuli, who ruled in the last decade of the sixteenth century and first decade of the seventeenth. But Kajoor's king list is off by a decade in dating the Tubanaan movement, which it places in the 1680s.

60. James P. Johnson, "Almamate," 493.

61. See Bobboyi, "Relations."

62. See Brooks, *Landlords and Strangers*.

63. Clerics sometimes were forced to take up arms in defense of their hosts. See Robinson, *Muslim Societies*, 124–38.

64. Temporal rulers may have understood these scribal and talismanic services as substitutions for the military and material aid that patrons would otherwise expect from clients.

65. This idea borrows from Guyer and Belinga, "Wealth in People."

66. From the verb *toraade*. See Baila Wane, "Fuuta Tooro," 44.

67. See Colvin, "Shaykh's Men."

68. See Ka, *École de Pir*. See also Demba Lamine Diouf, *Khally Amar Fall*. The name is derived from the Wolof term for Qur'anic exegesis, *firi*, or in its nominal form, *pir*.

69. Demba Lamine Diouf, *Khally Amar Fall*, 9–10.

70. Robinson, *Holy War*, 128, contains a stylistically similar description not of the founding of Pir but of one of al-Ḥājj Umar's early settlements.

71. Iberian sources for the fifteenth through seventeenth centuries have still not been systematically explored by historians of Senegambia. They could revolutionize historiography of the early Atlantic period. See Boulègue and Pinto-Bull, "Relations du Cayor."

72. This is the claim of Nicolas del Castillo Mathieu cited in Sylviane Diouf, *Servants of Allah*, 20, which claims that in 1522, Wolof Muslims led the first African slave revolt in American history. See also Gomez, *Black Crescent*, 40–42.

73. Sandoval, *De Instauranda*, 589.

74. Cadamosto leaves an account of the use of agricultural slaves by the dammel of Kajoor as early as the middle of the fifteenth century.

75. Almada, *Brief Treatise*, 10.

76. Joseph C. Miller, *Way of Death*, 71.

77. Boilat, *Esquisses sénégalaises*, 346.

78. Searing, *West African Slavery*, 17. For more on Kocc, see Boilat, *Esquisses sénégalaises*, 345–54.

79. Barry, "Guerre des marabouts"; Curtin, "Jihad in West Africa."

80. Hamet, *Chroniques*, 173.

81. ANFOM, C 6/2. See also Ritchie, "Deux textes," 339.

82. See Lovejoy, "Islam, Slavery, and Political Transformations."

83. ANFOM, C 6/2. See also Ritchie, "Deux textes," 342.

84. Hair, Jones, and Law, *Barbot on Guinea*, 131, 107. Gorée Island, just off the coast of what is now Dakar, was, along with Saint-Louis, an important port of call for slavers.

85. ANFOM, C 6/2. See also Ritchie, "Deux textes," 352.

86. Amadou-Bamba Diop, "Lat Dior," 499–500.

87. Ibid.

88. ANFOM C 6/18, Anonymous, "Remarques état en apperçu des esclaves."

89. Inikori, "Import of Firearms," reports that at least 350,000–400,000 guns per year were imported into West Africa from 1750 to 1807.

90. Wolof oral sources credit Latsukaabe as the veritable founder of large mounted *ceddo* armies equipped with rifles. While he did not initiate this military form—its roots go back another 150 years—he nonetheless expanded them. He is also credited as the founder of the *seriñu lamb* (*sëriñs* of the drum), titled clerics of the borderlands of Kajoor (especially Njambuur province) whose symbol of office was the drum, means of communicating imminent attacks from abroad. The institutionalization of this office has been explained as an effort to invest clerics with some limited political authority in Kajoor as a means of preventing future rebellions. This approach may have worked in Latsukaabe's lifetime, but most of these titled clerics were placed in Njambuur, near the coast, a region that would produce many revolutionary movements in the nineteenth century.

91. André Bruë quoted in Searing, *West African Slavery*, 28. Latsukaabe's new royal matrilineage bore the name Géej, which means "ocean" in Wolof, revealing its Atlantic orientation.

92. French slaver Saugnier uses the title "saltiguet" as an ethnonym, clearly referring to the deposed Deeñanke princes in the period after the 1776 Fuuta revolution. See Saugnier, *Relations*, 194, 228. "Siratick" and "Siratique," which appear to be French corruptions of the same word, were commonly employed in French documents before the revolution.

93. Charles Becker and Martin, "Journal historique," 262.

94. See Oumar Kane, "Causes."

95. Moore, *Travels*, 30–33.

96. James P. Johnson, "Almamate," 69–70.

Chapter 3

1. Kamara, *Florilège*, 316–17.

2. Ibid., 317. According to Kamara, the song of Aali Mayram was still chanted before wrestling matches in Fuuta in the early twentieth century.

3. David Eltis, www.slavevoyages.org. This site is a wonderful and well-documented resource, though like Eltis's published work, it tends to assess the scale of the trade—and its impact on social life in Africa—conservatively.

4. Clarence-Smith, *Islam and the Abolition*, 16–17.

5. Müller, "Sklaven."

6. Leitner, *Muhammadanism*, 16.

7. See, for example, Bernard Lewis, *Race and Slavery*; Said, "Impossible Histories."

8. Clarence-Smith, "A Fragile Sunni Consensus," in *Islam and the Abolition*.

9. Muusa Kamara, among others, makes this claim. See Hilliard, "Zuhur al-Basatin."

10. Cited in Leitner, *Muḥammadanism*, 17.

11. Clarence-Smith, *Islam and the Abolition*, 26.

12. Hunwick, "Islamic Law and Polemics."

13. This is the title of a chapter in Clarence-Smith, *Islam and the Abolition*.

14. Ware, "Slavery in Islamic Africa." See also the best of Fisher's writings on this topic, "Of Slaves, and Souls of Men," and "A Muslim Wilberforce?"

15. Hunwick and Powell, *African Diaspora*, 181.

16. Bernard Lewis, *Race and Slavery*, 148.

17. Hilliard, "Zuhur al-Basatin," 179.

18. Ibrahima Thioub, personal communication.

19. My never-ending thanks to Rebecca Scott for alerting me to her discovery of a manuscript in French by Clarkson, "Lettres nouvelles," that seems to suggest that he had heard of the Almaami.

20. Clarkson, *Letters*, 80.

21. Ibid., 31.

22. Ibid., 32.

23. Ibid., 31.

24. Roger, *Kelédor*, 238. Roger gives a date of roughly 1775. It is entirely possible that this policy began with Sulaymaan Baal and not the Almaami. Further research may clarify this.

25. For some discussion of the context of the work by a contemporary of Roger, see Jomard, "Kelédor." The abolition is discussed in this review on page 681: "Every former slave became free, *once he learned to read*" (emphasis in original).

26. This is the argument of Martin-Granel, *Du Clef d'Or à Kelédor.*

27. Thornton, *Africa and Africans*.

28. For an introduction to such resistance, see Sylviane Diouf, *Fighting the Slave Trade*.

29. Thornton, "African Political Ethics," 38.

30. Thornton, a specialist on Kongo, continues to try to explain away the fact that Affonso I, king of the Kongo, wrote to the king of Portugal in 1526, clearly portraying this prisoner's dilemma and pleading for an end to the slave trade. For translations of the letters, see Davidson, *African Civilization Revisited*, 223–26. Originals are in Jordão, *História do Congo: Documentos*.

31. Thornton, "African Political Ethics," 38.

32. Rodney, *How Europe Underdeveloped Africa*, 81.

33. Clarkson, *Letters*, 79.

34. Joseph C. Miller, *Way of Death*, 71.

35. Inikori, "Import of Firearms."

36. Both were edited and/or translated in the first two decades of the twentieth century under French colonial rule. Soh's work was translated by Henri Gaden and published by Delafosse in 1913 in the *Revue du Monde Musulman* under the title, "Chroniques du Foûta sénégalais." Shaykh Muusa Kamara's text was also sponsored by Gaden and Delafosse, though its translation into a European language is still incomplete. It is a much longer—and extremely erudite—work.

37. The author of that manuscript was Tafsiir Boggel Amadu Samba Lih. According to Soh, "Chroniques," Tafsiir Amadu Samba died from injuries suffered in the fight against the Ḥasānī clan Awlad al-Nasser in 1190 A.H., the year of the death of Ceerno Sulaymaan Baal. The text was completed sometime in or before 1776.

38. Both Kamara and Soh suggest that he died in 1190 A.H. Only the last six weeks of the lunar year would have fallen in 1777, so here I use the very revolutionary year of 1776.

39. Kamara, *Florilège*, 322.

40. James P. Johnson, "Almamate," 75.

41. For many of the technical details of the beginnings of the movement, the best published account is Robinson, "Islamic Revolution." For additional detail as well as much of the texture of the oral accounts about the movement, see James P. Johnson, "Almamate," chap. 2.

42. Soh, "Chroniques," 38: a female jinn arose from the rushing waters of the stream that lay between the king's compound and cleric's camp. Upon seeing the jinn, Sulay Njaay fired his rifle, only to have it explode in his hands, wounding him mortally.

43. James P. Johnson, "Almamate," 80–81.

44. Ceerno Saydu Nuuru Bah, interview. Bah also claims that all of the key leaders of the movement studied with and/or visited his ancestor, Samba Njuga Bah (b. 1714), in the village of Ron Jawle. He claims that Abdel Kader Kan from Kobilo, Ceerno Sileyman Baal from Bode, Ceerno Baila Perejo Hawre, Ceerno Yero from Janjoli, Ceerno Alfa Modu from Nabajji, Ceerno Amadu Moxtar Silla, Ceerno Saydu Taal from Halwaar, Tafsir Umar Kelli from Ndormoss, Ceerno Aali Mammudu from Ciloñ, Ceerno Abdul Karim from Seno Palel, Ceerno Amadu from Fonddu, Ceerno Tafsir Amadu from Kobilo all studied the *Risāla* of Qayrawānī, consulted his written copy of the text, or studied Baatin with him. Many thanks to Mamoudou Sy, with whom I conducted the interview, for translating and transcribing the interview tapes from Fula.

45. Kamara, *Florilège*, 318.

46. ANFOM C 6/16, Lettre de Boniface, Gorée, 22 October 1773. This cryptic letter is the first external, contemporary documentation of the Fuuta revolution that I found. It has not been cited in any previous source. British PRO records from the period identify Boniface as the French governor of Gorée. See PRO SP 78/289, "Boynes to Aiguillon," 17 June 1773.

47. ANFOM C 6/18. An anonymous document written a decade later claims, "Until 1775 the Moors made only a few captives which they always employed. . . . Mr. O'Hara and le Brasseur made it known that it was in their interest to sell them, and they made several great ravages in the different kingdoms, especially in that of the Brack [Waalo] where they took more than 8000 captives in six months."

48. The existence of such aid is obliquely corroborated by a number of sources, but is explicitly discussed only in Lamiral, *Affrique*, 176: "Governor O'Hara agreed to furnish aid to Elikoury in order to ravage the kingdom of Brak."

49. ʿAlī al-Kāwrī offered his allegiance to a new British governor in July 1780 (PRO CO 267/19 Intelligence Report, 17 July 1780).

50. Governor Charles O'Hara to Lord Dartmouth, 18 August 1775, PRO, CO 267/16. A copy of this letter is in CO 268/4 (Letters to the Secretary of State).

51. PRO CO 267/1, "Petition Presented by the Inhabitants of Senegal," 22 August 1775: "Going in the continent taken the Blacks People for himself. Burnt all King Brack villages—Likewise on the River side coming down from Glam [*sic*]."

52. PRO CO 267/16, Lieutenant Governor Matthias McNamara to Lord Dartmouth, 26 January 1776.

53. PRO CO 268/4 (Letters to the Secretary of State), Lieutenant Governor Matthias McNamara to Lord Dartmouth, 1 July 1776.

54. PRO CO 268/4, Letter from Mr. Demarin 4 July 1777. The letter laments that the trade to Galam will have to be given up altogether following O'Hara's unwise policies.

55. PRO CO 267/29, "Answers to the Questions Proposed to the Lieutenant Colonel Maxwell," 1 January 1811, answer 111.

56. PRO CO 268/4, Letter from Clarke, 26 July 1777, notes the situation of continual war in the Senegal River Valley but seems not to know the details.

57. Kamara, *Florilège*, 323.

58. Ibid., 263.

59. Ibid., 325.

60. Institut Fondamental d'Afrique Noire, Dakar, Fonds Gaden, Capitaine Steff, MS 1, "Histoire du Fouta Toro," 56. This version, told to Steff, has Ceerno Sulaymaan Baal shot rather than slain with an arrow, as in Kamara's account.

61. Kamara, *Florilège*, 326 and folio 276. Ibn Mahīb's work is actually a *takhmīs* of the *ʿIshrīnyyāt* of ʿAbdul-Raḥmān b. Yakhlaftān b. Aḥmad al-Fāzāzī (d. 1230). The *Dalāʾil al-khayrāt* was written by Abū ʿAbdallah Muḥammad b. Sulaymān b. Abū Bakr al-Jazūlī al-Taghtīnī al-Simlālī (d. 1465).

62. PRO CO 267/19, Lieutenant Governor Wall's Report, 17 July 1780—Intelligence Report. This alliance was so close that ʿAlī al-Kawrī of Trārza offered his troops to help the British expel the French from Saint-Louis.

63. Robinson, "Islamic Revolution"; James P. Joḥnson, "Almamate."

64. Kamara, *Florilège*, 324.

65. Robinson, "Islamic Revolution," 199–200.

66. See ibid., 201, where Robinson claims, without any evidence, that the Almaami continued the practice of enslaving non-Muslims, which Islamic law supposedly automatically condones.

67. Ana Njinga in what is now Angola gave freedom to the slaves of the Portuguese in the late 1620s and armed them to fight its enemies. The Spanish offered freedom to the slaves of the British colonies in the 1710s. Most famously, in November 1775, Lord Dunmore offered freedom to the slaves who would leave the side of the American colonists and fight for Britain. See WGBH, *Africans in America*, 93–94, 163–68. Thousands fled to join the British, a tide that was a major factor in motivating the northern colonies to abolish slavery.

68. My thinking here owes a great deal to conversations with Sherwin Bryant, historian of Latin American slavery, on slavery as a mode of governance in the Atlantic world. See Bryant, *Rivers of Gold*.

69. Saugnier, *Relation*, 266.

70. French translation of the treaty is ANS 13 G 9, agreement, 31 March 1785.

71. Saugnier, *Relation*, 264.

72. Ibid., 281.

73. ANFOM C 6/18, 30 May 1785, indicates that the French are aware of an impending alliance between "Moctar roy des braknas" and "almami Roy des foutes." In fact, all indications are that the alliance was a decade old, but the plan to attack Trārza was new.

74. Golberry, *Travels*, 181: "Hamet Moktar . . . was sustained by the Chief of the Foulhas."

75. ANFOM C 6/16, Letter by Boniface, 1773: "Le frère de Çidi Moctar a embrassé son parti à cause des présents qu'il eu a reçu, et bientôt, à ce qu'on m'assure Le Marabou va faire la guerre a Sydy Moctar, au Roy Brac, et au Damel, qui contrarient Le Gouvernance du Senegal."

76. PRO CO 267/33, July 1809.

77. Robinson identifies ʿAlī al-Kowri as the great-grandson of Nasir al-Dīn's main enemy in the Tuubanaan ("Islamic Revolution," 203).

78. Lamiral, *Affrique*, 172–73.

79. Saugnier, *Relations*, 280.

80. For one of many examples, see Durand, *Voyage to Senegal*, 123–25. The brak is so drunk that he can be smelled at a distance, and he sells one of his top lieutenants after the man refused to give his share of liquor to the brak. In the nineteenth century, Faidherbe wrote of intentionally keeping the dammel drunk to facilitate colonial expansion. See Ba, *Penetration française*.

81. Clarkson, *Letters*, 79.

82. ANFOM C 6/17 (also CO 267/33). Among the goods listed as the per diem to Ali-Couri 20 July 1809 are eight quarts of wine. (There is also evidence of alcohol imports for AliCouri in PRO CO 267/33)

83. In chap. 2, the disciples of Njaay Saal assassinated Mafali Gey when they surprised him drinking *sangara* after he had promised to renounce it.

84. Lamiral, *Affrique*, 174 (emphasis added).

85. Durand, *Voyage to Senegal*, 126.

86. Kamara, *Florilège*, 330.

87. Marty, "Livre des lettrés," 319. Ghadīja was the sister and teacher of the prominent *zawāyā* scholar Aḥmad b. Muḥammad al-ʿĀqil (d. 1828). This work by Marty is a translation of a work by the latter. His sister was apparently one of the most reputed scholars of the generation and author of a well-known commentary on Muḥammad al-Sanūsī's *Umm al-Barāhīn.* The West African Arabic Manuscript database credits her with one extant text in six collections at Nouakchott, *Tawra ʿala-l-silm.* It is possible that this is the work mentioned by Marty. See also Leriche, "De l'enseignement."

88. Kamara, *Florilège*, 330. In Old Testament lore, Shem and Ham are the forefathers of Semites and blacks, respectively.

89. The Buurba Jolof had sworn an oath of allegiance, (*bayʿa*) to the Almaami. See also James P. Johnson, "Almamate," 173.

90. See Robinson, "Islamic Revolution," 202.

91. Pommegorge, *Description de la Nigritie*, 74.

92. Golberry, *Travels*, 184–85. "He insolently . . . announced some new and ridiculously exaggerated conditions. . . . We answered with contempt . . . and in 1787 the voyage to Galam was suspended."

93. ANFOM F 3/62, folio 255, Copy of the translation of the letter of Almamy Abdul Qadir to Blanchot, March 1789: "The marabout who taught them to read is named Umar Matel." It is striking that the children could be identified by the name of the teacher who taught them the Qur'an.

94. ANFOM C 6/20, Letter, 31 July 1790.

95. James P. Johnson, "Almamate."

96. Robinson, "Islamic Revolution," 216.

97. Amadou-Bamba Diop, "Lat Dior," 504.

98. Colvin, "Kajor," 168.

99. ANFOM C 6/2. Chambonneau mentions "Suran Marabou" as one of the main leaders of the fight against the brak of Waalo during the Tubanaan revolutions. See also Ritchie, "Deux texts," 351. The village of Suran was likely a clerical center that had also produced leaders of the revolutionary movement one hundred years earlier.

100. Kamara, *Florilège*, 338.

101. Colvin, "Islam and the State of Kajoor," 599.

102. Kamara, *Florilège*, 338.

103. Colvin, "Islam and the State of Kajoor," 600.

104. Roger, *Kelédor*, 15. See also Martin-Granel, *Clef d'Or*, which purports to identify the real-life Kelédor on whom Roger's fictional account was based.

105. Park, *Travels*, 236.

106. See Roger, *Kelédor*, 20; Christopher L. Miller, *French Atlantic Triangle* (which includes a chapter on *Kelédor*).

107. Ka, *École de Pir*, 129–30. The timing of this event is unclear. It is given as 1786, but it is also clearly identified as taking place during the rule of Amari Ngone, which did not begin until 1790. Furthermore, the oral sources on which this particular account is based are not terribly precise about dates. I am certain that Tafsiir Hamadi's murder occurred in 1796 rather than 1786, and given what we know from other sources about the sequence of events, I have chosen to place it after the knife episode noted by Park. See Soh, "Chroniques," 49.

108. Park, *Travels*, 342.

109. Amadou-Bamba Diop, "Lat Dior," 503. Kan would have been in his late sixties and he might not have actually fought in this battle, though he does appear to have ridden out at the head of his troops.

110. Park, *Travels*, 342.

111. Amadou-Bamba Diop, "Lat Dior," 504.

112. Park, *Travels*, 343.

113. Mamadou Lamine Diop, "Abreuvement," 6. According to the Wolofal poet Muusa Ka, himself an important transmitter of Mbakke family tradition, Maram Mbakke, ancestor of the famous Sufi shaykh Amadu Bamba, was directly involved in liberating the clerics held by Dammel Amari Ndella after the Battle of Suran.

114. Demba Lamine Diouf, *Khally Amar Fall*, 33.

115. For one example, see Kamara, *Florilège*, 338.

116. Roger, *Kelédor*, 68–69. Twentieth-century *taalibés* were also called on to write talismans. See Amadou Wane, "Trois ans," 772–73.

117. Amadou-Bamba Diop, "Lat Dior," 504.

118. Different oral traditions hold that the Almaami's imprisonment lasted between nine months and four years. The long estimates are certainly incorrect, as Park heard of the story in May 1797, a few months after the Battle of Bunguye, at which point ʿAbdul-Qādir had already returned to Fuuta.

119. Ka, *École de Pir*, 13.

120. See also Norris, "Znâga Islam," 506. In an account related by the *bayḍān* Zawāyā, who held ʿAbdul-Qādir Kan in high esteem during his lifetime, they lay claim to his miraculous survival. They say that his most famous Zawāyā contemporary, Muḥam-

mad al-Yadālī b. al-Mukhtār b. Maḥam Saʿīd al-Daymānī (d. 1753), appeared to Almaami ʿAbdul-Qādir in a vision and wrote him a talisman that remained in his possession after he awoke.

121. Soh, "Chroniques," 52–53.

122. See Robinson, "Islamic Revolution."

123. Roger, *Kelédor*, 66. The dammel's supposed speech on the occasion of the Almaami's capture (65) is clearly Roger's effort to portray the goals of Almaami's revolution as territorial and worldly.

124. Ṣaḥiḥ Muslim Book 17, *Kitāb al-Ḥudūd*, hadiths 4187–90. The quotation here is based on the wording in hadith 4187.

125. On Bundu, see Gomez, *Pragmatism*.

126. Park, *Travels*, 60.

127. See Coifman, "History of the Wolof State"; Charles, "History of the Kingdom."

128. Hunwick, *Timbuktu*, 111–13.

129. Soh, "Chroniques," 46.

130. Gray, *Travels in Western Africa*, 195.

131. In another version of the story, he is sentenced to exile in Fuuta before one of ʿAbdul-Qādir's men shoots him. See Robinson, "Islamic Revolution," 212.

132. Soh, "Chroniques," 46.

133. ANFOM C 6/20, "Plan d'administration," 60: "The Island of Saint-Louis will employ all the means at their disposal to oblige the leader of this nation to make the reparations required of him, This will not be difficult either with hostages, or if in returning from Galam one has been able to seize one of their principal marabouts."

134. ANFOM C 6/21, "Proclamation à tous les habitans du Sénégal."

135. Ibid.

136. James P. Johnson, "Almamate," 202–4.

137. Soh, "Chroniques," 55.

138. Kamara, *Florilège*, 347.

139. His identity is uncertain. According to Kamara (*Florilège*, 351), the burial shroud came from Fullu Dagaagu of Seno Palel, who was called by the nickname *Dīnullahi wa ʿimāmatuhu* (God's religion and his turban). According to Soh ("Chroniques," 59), the Almaami was buried in a turban and shroud belonging to a *bayḍān* cleric, "a wise man from the tribe of 'Ulād-Deymān called Dinullāhi-ed-Deymāni." Both Soh and Kamara are clearly basing their accounts on the document picture in BNF Arabe 5474, folios 127–28.

140. BNF Arabe 5474, folios 127a–128b.

141. Bukhārī, *Ṣaḥīḥ*, book 23, hadith 434.

142. Kamara, *Florilège*, 351.

143. Ibid., 352.

144. PRO CO 267/29, "Answers to the Questions Proposed to the Lieutenant Colonel Maxwell," 1 January 1811, answer 36.

145. Roger, *Kelédor*, 238.

146. Kamara, *Florilège*, 357–58.

147. Soh, "Chroniques," 56. Two are mentioned by name in accounts: Demba Hawa and Njaga Issa Jóob. This was undoubtedly a very small circle.

148. Amadou-Bamba Diop, "Lat Dior," 504.

149. The date is disputed, but 1798 is correct according to Mollien, *Voyage*, 141; Mamadou Diouf, *Kajoor*, 101–2.

150. Mollien, *Voyage*, 138–39.

151. Ibid., 338.

152. Ibid., 109–10.

153. Colvin, "Kajor," 179.

154. For excellent detail, see Colvin, "Kajor," 181–84. Her reconstruction is based largely on interviews with Bunaama's descendants in Kajoor. See also Mamadou Diouf, *Kajoor*, 137.

155. "Bu leen fab alalu jàmbur, bu leen dem ci jabaru jàmbur" (Abdoulaye Bara Diop, *Société Wolof*, 190).

156. The term "masters of the sea" is from *boroom geej*, an archaic Wolof name for Europeans. For capable discussions of this transition, see Colvin, "Kajor"; Mamadou Diouf, *Kajoor*.

157. Governor Faidherbe to the Min., 11 April 1855, cited in Colvin, "Kajor," 332.

158. Monserrat, "Mémoire inédit," 7.

159. Colvin, "Kajor," 231.

160. This particular symbol went back at least to the Tuubanaan movement, as it was mentioned by Chambonneau.

161. Committee of Commerce, 8 March 1830, cited in Colvin, "Kajor," 231.

162. For the French paper trail, see Colvin "Kajor," 232n.

163. Monserrat, "Mémoire inédit," 10.

164. Colvin, "Kajor," 233.

165. These are cardinal colors in Wolof, Fula, and most West African languages. When referring to people, this means white, black, or Arab.

166. Monserrat, "Mémoire inédit," 11.

167. For Ba's story, see Klein, *Islam and Imperialism*.

168. Ka, *École de Pir*, 167.

169. ANS 13 G318, Ma Ba to Pinet-Laprade, 29 August 1865, document 46.

170. Roger, *Kelédor*, 42.

171. Kamara, *Florilège*, 376–80.

172. Ibid., 375.

173. Babou, *Fighting the Greater Jihad*, 54.

174. Ibid., 155.

175. Mamadou Lamine Diop, "Abreuvement," 8.

176. For the most recent, thoughtful accounts of Majaxate Kala and Amadu Bamba's confrontation, see Glover, in *Sufism and Jihad*; Babou, *Fighting the Greater Jihad*. My account owes much to their work as well as to the Murid sources they explore.

177. Glover, *Sufism and Jihad*, 67.

178. See Babou, *Fighting the Greater Jihad*, 59; Glover, *Sufism and Jihad*, 69; Bachir Mbacké, "Bienfaits," 107.

179. Gerresch, "Livre de métrique," 743.

180. Mamadou Lamine Diop, "Abreuvement," 18.

181. Amadou-Bamba Diop, "Lat Dior," 525.

182. Mamadou Lamine Diop, "Abreuvement," 18.

183. Amadou-Bamba Diop, "Lat Dior," 525.

184. Bachir Mbacké, *Bienfaits*, 107.

185. Mamadou Lamine Diop, "Abreuvement," 9. This story is retold by Murid oral historians as well as in Ane, *Vie de Cheikh Amadou Bamba*, 7. Bamba was drawing on a strain of Sufi teaching that emphasized distance from earthly rulers.

186. Mamadou Lamine Diop, "Abreuvement," 18.

187. Ibid., 19.

188. Gerresch, "Livre de métrique," 748.

189. Mamadou Lamine Diop, "Abreuvement," 20.

190. Babou, *Fighting the Greater Jihad*, 58.

191. Ibid., 42.

192. Gerresch, "Livre de métrique," 753.

193. Ibid., 748.

194. Ibid., 769.

195. Robinson, *Holy War*, 114. See also Jah, "Case Study."

Chapter 4

1. For a useful introduction, see Manning, *Francophone Sub-Saharan Africa*. For context regarding Islam and colonial policy, see Robinson, *Paths of Accommodation*.

2. See Klein's insightful "A Question of Honor," in *Slavery and Colonial Rule*, esp. 245–47.

3. Institut Fondamental d'Afrique Noire, Dakar, Fonds Musa Kamara, Cahier 19, offers a clear statement to this effect. This was the general position of Shaykh Muusa Kamara in his correspondence with the French administrator Henri Gaden, and a number of late nineteenth-century and early twentieth-century sources affirm this view. See also Willis, "Torodbe Clerisy."

4. See Touati, "Héritiers," 67. Touati does not focus on embodiment, but he discusses the ease with which heirs of a clerical tradition in North Africa acquired and deployed Islamic knowledge. The inheritors (or heirs), he explains, "are doubly advantaged by the ease with which they accumulate knowledge on the one hand, and their propensity to acquire it on the other." This is represented as a gift of *baraka* in the hagiographical tradition, which depicts "the ease with which the heirs learn, their precocious intelligence, the speed with which they familiarize themselves with the most complex problems, [and] their eloquence. Dramatized, these 'family traits' are put in place as so many signs of election. For it is only natural that cultural heredity would take the appearance of grace."

5. Presentation, El-Hajj Ndiaye Ndindy, "Les Hadiths de Amadou Bamba," Institute for the Study of Islamic Thought in Africa Workshop, Dakar, December 2010. The full quote in Wolof is, "Soo ko moome, yaa ma moom. Ndax maa ak moom ñoo bokk borom."

6. This theme is stressed in much recent work on the Murīdiyya, especially Searing, *God Alone Is King*; Babou, *Fighting the Greater Jihad*; Glover, *Sufism and Jihad*.

7. This is an extension of an argument first put forth in Brenner, "Concepts of Tariqa."

8. ANS J86, "Rapport Marty à monsieur le gouverneur general sur les écoles coraniques," 21.

9. For a thorough exploration of colonial Islamic policy, see Harrison, *France and Islam*.

10. Rousseau, "Sénégal." In the most precise semantic terms, the statement fused two ostensibly separate categories of birth, *géer* and *gor*. *Géer* forms an oppositional pair with

ñeeño, the "casted" lineages of endogamous occupational specialists. *Gor* status is defined in opposition to *jaam*, a slave. However, Yoro Jaw's statement makes it clear that the categories of *gor* and *géer* were conflated for many purposes. On the life of this key colonial interlocutor, see Tamsir Oumar Sall, "Yoro Dyao"; Boulègue, "À la naissance."

11. Following Yoro Jaw and Abdoulaye Bara Diop, the *géer* are usually further broken into three distinct categories, those eligible for royalty (*garmi*), those ineligible for royalty with significant wealth and/or power (*jambur*), and free peasant farmers with little or no political or economic power (*baadolo*). In both Wolof and Fula, the term itself means "lacking strength." The line between *jambur* and *baadolo* is, properly speaking, a distinction of class, not caste. See Abdoulaye Bara Diop's analysis of "castes" and "orders" in *Société Wolof*, 33–215.

12. In Manding, the "casted" are called *ñamakala(w)*. In Fula, the singular is *ñeeño* and the plural is *ñeeñBe*. See Conrad and Frank, *Status and Identity*; Tamari, "Development of Caste Systems"; Tamari, *Castes*.

13. I discuss this in some detail in chap. 3. See also Abdoulaye Bara Diop, *Socété Wolof*, 36. In fact, given the absence of any discernible reference to Wolof as a language or ethnic group before the founding of Jolof in the thirteenth century, it is tempting to conclude that Wolof as a coherent ethnolinguistic identity emerged relatively late, in a context already shaped by medieval imperial slavery, "caste" structures, and the presence of Islam.

14. Abdoulaye Bara Diop, *Société Wolof*, 157–62.

15. Gamble, *Wolof of Senegambia*, 45.

16. Raffenel, *Voyage*, 19.

17. See Brunschvig, "Métiers."

18. I return briefly to sorcery in the conclusion. See also Ware, "Knowledge, Faith, and Power," chap. 4.

19. Heath, "Politics of Appropriateness."

20. Abdoulaye Bara Diop, *Société Wolof*, 40.

21. Ibid., 43–44.

22. See Klein, "Servitude among the Wolof." See also Searing, "Aristocrats, Slaves, and Peasants"; Searing, *God Alone Is King*. See also Moitt, "Slavery and Emancipation."

23. This was still the case in the 1970s in Senegal, and it likely persists. See Venema, *Wolof of Saloum*, 126–27. For comparable material from Mali, see Soares, "Notes."

24. Irvine, "Caste and Communication," is a rich source of documentation on the social stigma against the *jaam* and their descendants. On slavery and marriage taboos, see Ames, "Plural Marriage."

25. Abdoulaye Bara Diop, *Société Wolof*, 178 (emphasis added).

26. For an excellent initial exploration, see Thioub, "Stigmas and Memory."

27. Mbaye, "Islam au Sénégal," 263.

28. Almamy, "Système d'éducation," 17.

29. Roch, "Mourides," 41.

30. Abdoulaye Bara Diop, *Société Wolof*, 201.

31. For useful discussion of the *umm walad* as a category in early legal practice, see Brockopp, *Early Mālikī Law*, 192–204.

32. See Irvine, "Caste and Communication," chap. 2. For Fuuta, see Yaya Wane, *Toucouleur*, 76.

33. Crown slaves were the major partial exception here.

34. See, for example, Sanneh, *Jakhanke Muslim Clerics*, chap. 9.

35. Klein, *Slavery and Colonial Rule*, 25.

36. Ibid., 245–47.

37. Ames, "Plural Marriage," 98.

38. ANS J86, "Rapport Marty à monsieur le gouverneur general sur les écoles coraniques," 19–20.

39. Abdourahmane Diop, "École coranique," 20.

40. Bamany, "École coranique," 14.

41. See Alidou, *Engaging Modernity*, chap. 2, esp. 75–84.

42. Djibo, *Participation des femmes africaines*, 79. Indeed, I have often regretted the fact that there were no girls at the École Ponty, for even a single account from the early twentieth century written by a female student would have offered precious insight.

43. Abdourahmane Diop, "École coranique," 9.

44. Diallo, "Contribution," 40–42.

45. Abdel Kader Fall, "École coranique," 11.

46. Abdourahmane Diop, "École coranique," 12.

47. This is doubtless still the case today in a general sense, though most observers—including myself—would affirm that it is changing. Ethnographic research from the 1950s and 1960s certainly confirms that it was the case as Senegal moved to independence. Fadé, "Women of Dakar," 219, observed that in the early 1960s, Qur'an schooling for girls usually remained a short-term commitment: "During [childhood to early adolescence], she will have been to the Koranic school; but for girls, attendance is less strict and lasts for a shorter time."

48. Abdelkader Fall, "École coranique," 12.

49. Ibid., 11.

50. Anta Njaay, interview.

51. Abdelkader Fall, "École coranique," 11.

52. Shaykhuna Lo, interview, and informal conversations; Masamba Buso, interview. This pattern held true throughout the subregion, in what is now northern Nigeria. Both Usman dan Fodio's mother and his daughter were highly educated. The latter was a prolific writer and trained cadres of female teachers in the early nineteenth century. See Mack and Boyd, *One Woman's Jihad*; Boyd, *Caliph's Sister*.

53. Ruqayya Niass, interview.

54. Ruqayya Niass, "Taysir al-Fahm," my translation into English from the French translation by Ka, *École de Pir*, 246 (emphasis added).

55. Yaya Wane, *Toucouleur*, 102.

56. See Searing, *God Alone Is King*, 238–48.

57. Colvin, "Shaykh's Men," 64.

58. Brenner, "Concepts of Tariqa," 35.

59. See Ernst, *Shambhala Guide to Sufism*, esp. chap. 5.

60. For a continental overview of the Sufi orders, see Vikør, "Sufi Brotherhoods." For a useful introductory overview to the position of Islam in West Africa in the eighteenth century that pays some attention paid to Sufi orders, see Levtzion, "Eighteenth Century."

61. For an introductory history of the Tijāniyya, see Wright, *On the Path of the Prophet*.

62. See Batran, *Qādiriyya Brotherhood*; Stewart, *Islam and Social Order*; Brenner, "Concepts of Tariqa."

63. See Robinson, *Holy War*; Willis, *In the Path of Allah*.

64. See Ibrahima Abou Sall, "Diffusion de la Tijāniyya," 386. Sall argues that the Tijāniyya Umariyya survived colonial conquest by using the Qur'an schools to help spread the order's influence in spite of the fact that it was no longer associated with the ruling classes of the state: "Religious instruction remains one of the aspects of Muslim practice that is most strongly rooted in fuutanke society. . . . This is why the first undertaking of the intellectual class of the Tijāniyya vanquished by the French colonizer was to take over the centers of religious instruction to make them into instruments of diffusion. . . . The dudé [Fula plural for Qur'an school] played a primordial role in the formation of cadres . . . of propagators of the brotherhood."

65. On al-Ḥājj Mālik Sy, see Mbaye, *Pensée et action*. See also Robinson, *Paths of Accommodation*, chap. 10.

66. The failure of the smaller but no less dramatic jihads of Ma Ba Jaaxu Ba, Shaykh Amadu Ba (and the Maadiyanke), and Mamadu Lamin doubtless affected the clerics as well, but they cannot be considered here. For good, concise, though somewhat dated looks at the jihads of Umar and Ma Ba situated in a deep historical context, see Klein, "Moslem Revolution in Nineteenth-Century Senegambia"; Klein, "Social and Economic Factors." On the Maadiyanke, see Charles, "Shaykh Amadu Ba." On Mamadu Lamin, see Fisher, "Early Life and Pilgrimage."

67. Neither man publicly contemplated a jihad of the sword. Between 1910 and 1912, both men appear to have issued fatwas (written legal opinions) condemning jihad against the French based on the manifest inequities of force and the fact that the French did not inhibit religious observance. See Robinson, *Paths of Accommodation*, 56. Some observers have challenged the authenticity of the fatwas, particularly the one attributed to Bamba.

68. Babou, *Fighting the Greater Jihad*, 236.

69. Robinson, *Paths of Accommodation*, 196.

70. Mamadou Ndiaye, interview.

71. Marty, *Études sur l'Islam au Sénégal*, 186.

72. According to different traditions and his own biographies, these appear to have included Shadhili and Tijānī initiations. Reports of the Tijānī initiation are mildly controversial in Senegambia in that the ordinary doctrinal position of Tijānīs is that all who take the Tijānī *wird* are supposed to practice it for life and to the exclusion of any other.

73. Babou, "Educating the Murid," 313.

74. Chap. 3 of Searing's *God Alone Is King* is the best published account of the reasons for Bamba's deportation. In short, Wolof chiefs, who feared and resented his growing influence, conspired against him and manufactured unfounded charges that he was planning a jihad of the sword.

75. For some poetic discussion of this visionary experience, see Ware, "In Praise of the Intercessor," my versified and annotated translation of one of his most famous postexile pieces of *madḥa* poetry, *Mawāhib al-nāfiʿ fī madāʾiḥ al-shāfiʿ*.

76. Bachir Mbacké, *Bienfaits*, 107.

77. Mamadou Lamine Diop, *Abreuvement*, 9.

78. See Babou, *Fighting the Greater Jihad*, 60–64.

79. Babou, "Educating the Murid," 316.

80. A grandson of Amadu Bamba expressed this preoccupation to me: "There are basic elements [of *taṣawwuf*] you can study in books, but you must live it. It is a comportment" (Abdulaay Mbakke, interview). But this sentiment should not be narrowly associated with the Murīdiyya.

81. ANS 2D 14-6, Cercle de Tivaouane, Correspondence, 1914, "Rapport du tournée dans le M'Baouar," 3 March–3 April 1914, cited in Searing, *God Alone Is King*, 248–49.

82. See Babou, *Fighting the Greater Jihad*, chap. 7.

83. Shaykhuna Lo, interview.

84. Masamba Buso, interview. See also Babou, *Fighting the Greater Jihad*, 190.

85. An early article on the Tijāniyya, Marone, "Tidjanisme," 151, suggests this point: "By creating the first contacts among young classmates, then consecrating them with the blood of circumcision and finally by preparing them for religious obligations, the Qur'ānic school shows itself to be the basic cell of the brotherhood."

86. Similarly, the Sufi shaykh's role as a guide was an extension of the village Qur'an teacher's role as a counselor and arbitrator. Sufi teachings stressed the *murīd*'s obligation to follow the teachings of a shaykh, but Senegalese Muslims accepted the injunction because it was an extension of an earlier model. The term used to mean the directive of a Sufi shaykh in Wolof is *ndigal*. It is derived from a verb, *digal*, or perhaps *digle*, both of which mean "to counsel."

87. On the Wednesday field, see Cruise O'Brien, *Mourides*, 210–12. For discussion of Wolof agriculture and religious patronage networks, see Copans, *Marabouts de l'arachide*, 127–56.

88. Amsaata Jéy (Amsata Dieye) quoted in Couty, "Entretiens," 59.

89. More materialist historians could develop a story here about the struggles to control the agriculture output of the Wednesday field. The clerisy with their students, the shaykhs with their disciples, and finally the developmentalist state would be the protagonists, each vying for control over the surplus labor used on the Wednesday field. Mamadou Dia, Senegal's deposed and long imprisoned first prime minister, attributed his imprisonment mainly to resistance to his program of *animation rurale*, especially "the appearance of collective fields which were making the 'so-called Wednesday fields' disappear" (*Mémoires*, 121).

90. Babou, *Fighting the Greater Jihad*, 176.

91. According to Colvin, "Shaykh's Men," 60, "The children of royalty received their education in religion and literature without humiliating recourse to total dependence, hard labor and begging." See also Colvin, "Islam and the State of Kajoor," 595.

92. Mamadou Ndiaye, *Enseignement*, 31. See also Abdoulaye Bara Diop, *Société Wolof*, 303: "The students who did not live with him [worked for the *sëriñ*] in general, once a week: Wednesday which is a day of inactivity in Islamic instruction. Thus the fields [of the *sëriñ*] bore the name toolu-àllarba (Wednesday field)."

93. Ibrahim Bàjjan, interview.

94. Abdelkader Fall, "École coranique," 48.

95. Campistron, "Oulof Custom in Cayor," 10.

96. Baba Ndiaye, "Islam," 41.

97. Médoune Fall, "École coranique," 26.

98. Abdourahmane Diop, "École coranique," 15–16.

99. Baba Ndiaye, "Islam," 41.

100. Médoune Fall, "École coranique," 37.

101. Baba Ndiaye, "Islam," 41.

102. Abdelkader Fall, "École coranique," 16.

103. Médoune Fall, "École coranique," 5.

104. Ibid., 16–17.

105. Bamany, "École coranique," 13.

106. Abdelkader Fall, "École coranique," 16.

107. Cited in Bouche, "École française," 222. This article is a short and clear statement of material that is presented in greater detail in her doctoral thesis, *Enseignement dans les territoires français*. This thesis is the most thorough source on educational policy in the AOF colonies until the 1920s. See also David Gardinier, "The French Impact on Education in Africa," in *Double Impact*, ed. G. Wesley Johnson, 333–44; A. Y. Yansané, "The Impact of France on Education in West Africa," in *Double Impact*, ed. G. Wesley Johnson, 345–62.

108. Crowder, *Senegal*, 2 (emphasis added).

109. Harrison reminds us that such labels were irrelevant on the ground; they were for metropolitan consumption (*France and Islam*, 182).

110. For detailed analysis of the substance of legislative efforts to control Qur'an schooling and promote French schools, see Ware, "Knowledge, Faith, and Power," chap. 5. See also Mamadou Ndiaye, *Enseignement*, chap. 3; Bouche, "École française."

111. Conseil general, 2eme séance de la session ordinaire, 5 December 1896, "Lecture d'une petition addressée a l'Assemblée: Comptes rendus imprimés," cited in Bouche, *Enseignement dans les territoires*, 316.

112. Abdu-Salaam Lo, interview: "When the *tubaabs* [whites] came, they fought the *daaras*. It was in that struggle that the people came to see that they were not fighting the *daara*, they were fighting Islam."

113. ANS J86, "Rapport Destaing," document 111.

114. Bamany, "École coranique," 55.

115. Gueye, "École coranique," 52.

116. See Bouche, "École française," 231.

117. Médoune Fall, "École coranique," 16–17. Children who went to French school were exempted from chores, attending French school during the day and Qur'an school at night.

118. Beye, "Étude coranique," 43.

119. This retreat was facilitated by a 1922 decree on confessional neutrality in educational institutions. See Brenner, *Controlling Knowledge*, 61; Mamadou Ndiaye, *Enseignement*, 133.

120. The political economy of Sufi shaykhs and state authorities is the subject of a voluminous literature, the best of which is Villalón, *Islamic Society and State Power.*

121. Bouche, *Enseignement dans les territoires*.

122. Médoune Fall, "École coranique," 36–37.

123. Ibid., 30.

124. Almamy, "Système d'éducation," 18.

125. Médoune Fall, "École coranique," 18.

126. Sakho, "Croyances religieuses," 42.

127. Ibid., 57.

128. Bamany, "École coranique," 56–57.

129. For only one example among many, see Delafosse, "État actuel."

130. Marty, *Études sur l'Islam au Sénégal*, 280–81.

131. See *Revue du Monde Musulman*, "Politique indigène." The article was written to commemorate Ponty's death on 13 June 1915.

132. Bouche, *Enseignement dans les territoires*, 783.

133. See Mbengue, "Enseignement de l'arabe."

134. ANS J92, document 52.

135. The Médersa of Jenne in what is now Mali was founded in 1906. For more on the Médersas, see Bouche, *Enseignement dans les territoires*, chap. 7. See also Brenner, "Médersas au Mali"; Mbengue, "Enseignement de l'arabe."

136. ANS J86, Inspector of Public Instruction and Muslim Education to Governor-General of the AOF, Dakar, 2 April 1910.

137. Mbengue, "Enseignement de l'Arabe," 72.

138. Mariani, "Écoles coraniques," 92.

139. Ibid., 93.

140. Mbengue, "Enseignement de l'arabe," 77–81.

141. Bouche, *Enseignement dans les territoires*, 355–56, notes that Edward Wilmot Blyden, one of the founders of Pan-Africanist thought, then head of Muslim education in Sierra Leone, had met Souleymane Seck while he was teaching Arabic at the School of Chief's Sons and had been extremely impressed with him.

142. ANS J92, document 119.

143. Mbengue, "Enseignement de l'arabe," 81.

144. Marty, "Les écoles maraboutiques," unnumbered second page of the "Avant-Propos."

145. Brenner, *Controlling Knowledge*, 43–45.

146. The reports were on Qur'an schools, the Murīdiyya, Mauritanian conquest, and Muslim amulets in Senegal. The confluence of *bayḍān* and French racism during the colonial period is an underexamined factor in the development of Islam Noir as well as in the history of race relations between Mauritania and Senegal.

147. André, *Islam et les races*, 2:159.

148. ANS J86, "Rapport Marty à monsieur le gouverneur general sur les écoles coraniques," 15.

149. ANS J 94, "Note de Marty sur la médersa de Djenné," Dakar, 16 June 1917.

150. For a translation of al-Ḥājj Umar Taal's writings to justify jihad against Masina, and for erudite and nuanced discussion of the theological and historical issues, see Mahibou and Triaud, *Voilà ce qui est arrivé*.

151. Trouillot, *Silencing the Past*, 72.

152. See Khadim Mbacké, *Pelerinage*.

153. Eickelman, *Knowledge and Power*.

154. Gomez-Perez, "Histoire," chap. 2.

155. For *Al-Manar*, see Dudoignon, Komatsu, and Kosugi, *Intellectuals in the Modern Islamic World*. For *Al-Manar* in East Africa, see Bang, *Sufis and Scholars*, 140, 231.

Chapter 5

1. The portrait here is drawn from Mouhamed Kane, "Vie et œuvre."

2. See Khadim Mbacké, *Pélerinage.*

3. This is my exuberant phrasing. For a more sober and detailed explication of this process, see Lauzière, "Evolution of the Salafiyya," esp. chap. 3.

4. ANFOM, DFC XVI Senegal, Dossier 19 G 25, "Controle des livres en arabes," 1924–26. The notes about the fatwas begin in the dossier after 17 October 1924.

5. This movement aroused a great deal of suspicion from colonial authorities. See Mouhamed Kane, "Vie et œuvre."

6. Brenner, *Controlling Knowledge*, 8.

7. Bang, *Sufis and Scholars*, 62. See Mitchell, *Rule of Experts*, 9, for additional context.

8. Hunwick, *Sharīʿa in Songhay.*

9. Fisher and Blum, "Love for Three Oranges," 79.

10. See Loimeier, "Islam Ne Se Vend Plus"; Loimeier, "Cheikh Touré." See also Khadim Mbacké, "Rôle du mouvement réformiste." See also Gomez-Perez, "Mouvement culturel"; Piga, *Dakar et les ordres soufis*, 444–56.

11. El Ayadi, "Acteurs religieux."

12. For a discussion of ʿAbduh's fascination with English Darwinist philosopher Herbert Spencer and especially his views on education, see Sedgwick, *Muhammad Abduh.*

13. See Masud, "Growth and Development," 8.

14. Lia, *Society of Muslim Brothers*, 25; see also 37: "When by the age of twelve Hasan had still not memorized the whole of the Qurʾan, his father had wanted him to continue at the mosque school or with a Qurʾan memorizer [*hāfiẓ al-Qurʾan*]. But Hasan opposed his father's wish and was enrolled in the middle school instead."

15. Ibid., 56 (emphasis added). The quotation is from the first issue of the *Jaridat al-Ikhwan al-Muslimun*, 3.

16. See Qutb, *Milestones.*

17. Riḍā, *Tafsīr al-Qurʾān*, 26–27. Thanks to Andrea Brigaglia for bringing this quotation to my attention and sharing his translation, which is the basis for mine here.

18. The best treatment of this process of rapprochement is Lauzière, "Evolution of the Salafiyya"; for a work that will revolutionize understanding of Salafism as a whole, see Lauzière, "Construction of Salafiyya."

19. Quoted in O'Fahey, *Enigmatic Saint*, 74.

20. For a biography, see Loimeier, "Cheikh Touré."

21. Loimeier, "Islam Ne Se Vend Plus," 172–74.

22. Ibid., 175.

23. For the tone of the anticolonial discussion, see Ly, *Où va l'Afrique?*

24. See Gomez-Perez, "Mouvement culturel."

25. Ly, *Où va l'Afrique?*, 85; drawn from "En depit des tempêtes et des marées," *Vers l'Islam*, 5 April 1955.

26. For some discussion of the purely local impetus behind educational reform, see Loimeier, "Cheikh Touré"; Brenner, *Controlling Knowledge*, 75.

27. Gomez-Perez, "Mouvement culturel," 537.

28. See Ware and Launay, "Comment (ne pas) lire le Coran."

29. See Kaba, *Wahabiyya.*

30. Triaud, "Crepuscule," 518. For a concise English-language summary of some of the arguments in this article, see also Triaud, "Islam in Africa," esp. 176–78. For the surveillance and repression of educational reform in French Soudan (Mali), see Brenner, *Controlling Knowledge*.

31. See Brenner, "Médersas au Mali," esp. 68–75.

32. Loimeier, "Islam Ne Se Vend Plus," 174–75.

33. Dia, *Mémoires*, 130–31.

34. Loimeier, "Islam Ne Se Vend Plus," 176.

35. See Mamadou Ndiaye, *Enseignement*, 138. See also Shariif Sulaymaan Aydara, interview; Masamba Buso, interview; Abdu Salaam Lo, interview.

36. Syndicat National, untitled document, 5–6.

37. Loimeier, "Islam Ne Se Vend Plus," 177.

38. I have been unable to locate a copy of this report in any archive. Some of the results of the research can be gleaned from Comité National, "Rapport de synthèse." Diallo, "Contribution," also draws data from the report.

39. The CNAS was under the authority of the *ministre de la santé et des affaires sociales* (minister of health and social affairs).

40. Comité National, "Rapport de synthèse."

41. A few years earlier, M. J. Traoré, who had been educated in metropolitan France, had released *Njangaan*, centered on the supposedly brutal exploitation of children. The film is discussed in Ware, "Njàngaan." For the director's reflections on the film, see Traoré, "Islam Noir."

42. Mamadou Ndiaye, *Enseignement*, 164–65.

43. See Collignon, "Lutte des pouvoirs." See also Piga, *Dakar et les ordres soufis*, 413–26.

44. Cissé, "Rapport d'orientation générale," 24: "One must take account of the fact that there exists, among Muslims, the need to practice charity. . . . This is why it would not be bad that this mendicancy [of genuine Qur'an school students], which is very different from the vagabondage of '*talibés*,' be tolerated beginning at certain times."

45. Piga, *Dakar et les ordres soufis*, 418.

46. Abd El Kader Fall, "Allocution d'ouverture."

47. Mane, "Discours de cloture."

48. Malick Diop, "Extraits," 5.

49. Syndicat National, untitled document, 7.

50. Cissé, "Rapport d'orientation générale," 21.

51. See Mamadou Ndiaye, *Enseignement*, chap. 8.

52. See Loimeier, "Islam Ne Se Vend Plus."

53. Piga, *Dakar et les ordres soufis*, 449.

54. Loimeier, "Islam Ne Se Vend Plus," 183.

55. See Reenders, "Ambiguous Adventure."

56. Institute for the Study of Islamic Thought, "Catalogue."

57. Loimeier, "Je Veux Étudier," 125–26.

58. For more on this, see Khadim Mbacké, *Daara et droits de l'enfant*.

59. Le Soleil/Wal Fadjri, 8.4.1992, 14, cited in Loimeier, "Je Veux Étudier," 118.

60. Ibid., 133.

61. See UNESCO, "Hope for the Taalibés."

62. Khadim Mbacké, interview.

63. Reenders, "Ambiguous Adventure," 67.

64. Ibid., 70.

65. Loimeier, "Islam Ne Se Vend Plus," 175.

66. Ibid., 171.

67. Loimeier, "Je Veux Étudier," 126.

68. Khadim Mbacké, "Impact de l'Islam," 540.

69. See Eickelman, "Art of Memory."

70. See Seesemann, *Divine Flood*; Wright, "Embodied Knowledge."

71. Ousmane Kane and Villalón, "Entre confrérisme, réformisme, et islamisme."

72. Mbaye Diop Fary, "Du problème de l'éducation religieuse des masses musulmanes," *L'Islam Éternel: Bulletin Mensuel de l'Association Éducative Islamique*, no. 2, October 1957, 3. Several issues of this bilingual Arabic and French newspaper are available at the library of the Institut Fondamental d'Afrique Noire, Dakar.

73. I presume, though I have not been able to verify, that this is the man sometimes referred to as Abdul Aziz Sy Jr., the son of Shaykh Tijaan Sy, not Abdul Aziz Sy, the Tijāniyya-Mālikiyya's second caliph. For intelligent discussion of Sy family politics (and a partial genealogy), see Villalón, "Moustarchidine."

74. El-Hadji Oumar Dia, "L'action culturelle et éducative de la fédération," *L'Afrique Musulmane: Organe de la Féderation Nationale des Associations Culturelles Musulmanes du Sénegal*, no. 2, November 1965, 19.

75. See Villalón, "Moustarchidine." See also Ousmane Kane and Villalón, "Entre confrérisme, réformisme, et islamisme."

76. Khadim Mbacké, *Soufisme*, 93–94.

77. Villalón, *Islamic Society and State Power*, 238.

78. Shaykhuna Lo, interview; Masamba Buso, interview; Abdu-Salaam Lo, interview.

79. These descriptions of schools are based on personal observations from several visits to each between August 2001 and May 2002. They are also based on Shaykhuna Lo, interview; Xaliil Lo, interview; Ibrahima Bàjjan, interview; and Amadu Faal, interview, as well as a September 2001 interview with a group of six of the advanced students in Ibrahima Bàjjan's *daara* in Tivaouane.

80. Shaykhuna Lo, interview.

81. Xalil Lo, interview.

82. Shaykhuna Lo, interview.

83. The information regarding the sources of financial support for this *daara* is from an unrecorded conversation with Amadu Faal in Tivaouane.

84. Ibrahima Bàjjan, interview.

85. Diané, "École coranique," 17. A Guinean Ponty student used the same expression referring to his Qur'an teacher: "He teaches and educates at the same time [*Il instruit et éduque à la fois*]."

86. Xaliil Lo, interview.

87. Mansuur Caam, interview. To drive home the point, he crafted a capable Wolof paraphrase of the famous saying attributed to Mālik b. Anas, the eponym of the Mālikī school: "One who studies *fiqh* without *Sufism* becomes a debauched degenerate [*fāsiq*]."

88. Anta Njaay, interview.

89. The catalog of the library in BokiDiawe was part of a project to catalog libraries in Fuuta Tooro. It was the only explicitly "reformist" library among roughly twenty libraries surveyed. See Institute for the Study of Islamic Thought, "Catalogue."

90. Shaykhuna Lo, interview. Lo expressed a part of this idea when he denied a hard-and-fast distinction between the two schools. "Between the *daara* and the *école arabe*," he said, "there is no difference. The *daara* evolved to bring about the Arabic schools. It's only an evolution in the *daara*; it's not a question of the one being one way and the *daara* being another."

91. Many of the Cahiers Ponty were decorated with elaborate drawings of these tablets. The only other inanimate object receiving equal artistic attention was the lash.

92. Abdelkader Fall, "École coranique," 4.

93. This comment was made during an unrecorded 17 July 2001 conversation between Ibrahima Bàjjan and Amadu Faal prior to Ibrahima Bàjjan, interview.

94. Ibid.

95. Shaykhuna Mbakke, a young member of a prominent Murid family, was the Qur'an teacher who taught my children in Dakar in November and December 2010. I witnessed his preparation of the pens.

96. Sidi Mohamed, "Devoir de vacances, l'école coranique," 9.

97. Médoune Fall, "École coranique," 10.

98. This was the case in a number of places, but it was particularly noticeable in the Qur'an schools in Medina Baye Kaolack, tied to the Niass Branch of the Tijāniyya.

99. Ngañ Jomg was the one person I formally interviewed who had never been a Qur'an school student. He studied in one of the Muridiyya's modern Arabic schools—École Falel—in Mbacké. He was not alone, however, in beginning his response to questions about the difference between the *daara* and the *école arabe* by talking about clean bodies and clean clothes: "In this one you shower until you're clean, put on a nice shirt, and don't have any problems. Those other ones, the *daaras* like that, you go and *sometimes* you shower. Sometimes you don't have decent clothes. On top of that, you go out to beg."

Conclusion

1. Almamy, "Système d'éducation," 13–14.

2. Bamany, "École coranique," 11–12.

3. This is the title of Claire Robertson's wonderful social history of women in Ghana.

4. Mommersteeg noted this in Jenné as well; see "Éducation coranique," 58.

5. Du Bois, *Souls of Black Folk*, 3.

6. See Amadu Bamba Mbacké, *Masālik al-Jinān*, verses 580–85.

7. Bukhārī, *Ṣaḥīḥ*, book 61, hadith 545, narrated by the Caliph Uthman.

8. Copans, "Entretiens," 41, interview no. 3, "Un maitre d'école coranique: Omar N'gom 28 juin 1967."

9. Hunwick, *Timbuktu*, 69.

10. This is the title of a chapter in the novel *Fire and Clay* by Kaaronica Evans-Ware.

11. Faye, "L'efficacité externe des daara," 6.

12. Loimeier, "Je Veux Étudier," 127. Loimeier's data here are drawn primarily from Wiegelmann, "Alphabetisierung."

13. This is one of the many lasting contributions of Feierman, *Peasant Intellectuals*.

14. Soh, "Chroniques," 46.

15. See Hunwick, *Arabic Literature*, entries for Bamba and Niass.

16. Khadīja bint Muḥammad is discussed in more detail in chapter 3.

17. See Niass, *Ḥuqūq al-nisāʾ*.

18. For an amazing interview with the shaykha, see Sāmī Kalīb, "Maryam Niasse, nashr al-islām wa taʿlīm al-qur'ān," *al-Jazīra*, 24 October 2009, http://aljazeera.net/NR/exeres/7CEC0193-D1A2-4B01-A554-0CBF0C035DF4.htm. Dr. Joseph Hill translated the article for his website: "Translation of Sayyidah Maryam's Al-Jazeera Interview," http://medinabaay.org/en/news/310-translation-of-sayyidah-maryams-al-jazeera-interview. For more on both sisters, see Wright, "Embodied Knowledge," chap. 5.

19. See Amadu Bamba Mbacké, *Masālik al-Jinān*, verses 246–54.

20. For Shīʿa perspectives, see Leichtman, "Africanisation of ʿAshura."

21. The song has been immortalized in a beautiful ballad by Ismaël Lo, "Tajabone."

22. The summary here is not drawn from any particular source but rather general knowledge among Muslims; for discussion, see Smith and Haddad, *Islamic Understanding*.

23. Beye, "Étude coranique," 37.

24. Sakho, "Croyances religieuses," 38.

25. Abdourahmane Diop, "École coranique,"11. Fortier's brilliant article, "Mort vivante," contains an exceptional discussion of death and the body in Islam, including the presence of Qur'an school students at funerals in Mauritania.

26. Al-Qayrawānī, *Risāla*, cited in Ka, *École de Pir*, 282.

27. See particularly the chapter "Jihad" in Qutb, *Milestones*. The overall argument for the Muslim world as in a state of pre-Islamic *jahiliyya* is typical totalitarian "the ends justify the means" sort of thinking.

28. Sakho, "Croyances religieuses," 57.

29. O'Fahey, *Enigmatic Saint*, 74.

30. Mayeur-Jaouen, "Introduction," 28.

31. Benkheira, *Amour de la loi*, 13.

32. Sanusi, *Aqida al-sughra*, cited in Brenner, "Sufism," 344–45.

33. Hiskett, *Sword of Truth*, 64–65.

34. Amadu Bamba Mbacké, *Masālik al-Jinān*, verses 926–32.

BIBLIOGRAPHY

Archives

Archives Nationales de France, Paris
Archives Nationales d'Outre-Mer, Aix-en-Provence
Archives Nationales du Sénégal, Dakar
British Public Records Office, Kew
Institut Fondamental d'Afrique Noire, Dakar
    Cahiers William Ponty
    Collection Amar Samb
    Fonds Gaden

Interviews

Shariif Sulaymaan Aydara, Touba, April 2002
Ceerno Saydu Nuuru Bah, Ndioum, 9 December 2005
Ibrahima Bàjjan, Tivaouane, 17 July 2001, August 2001
Daan Buso, Touba, May 2002
Masamba Buso, Mbacké, 30 May 2002
Mansuur Caam, Tivaouane, August 2001
Mansuur Cuun, Tivaouane, 17 July 2001
Ceerno Abdoulaye Daff, Séno Palel, July 2007
Ahmad Faal, Mbacké, May 2002
Amadu Faal, Tivaouane, 13 September 2001
Mor Faal, Mbacké, 29 May 2002
"Vieux" Faal, Ngabou, May 2002
Bassiru Fey, Tivaouane, September 2001
Aliu Gay, Ngabou, May 2002
Shaykh Gey, Tivaouane, July 2001
Commandant Boy Haruna, Boghé, 10 December 2005
Amadu Basiru Jeŋ, Touba, 29 May 2002
Amadu Lamin Jiggo, Demett, 10 December 2005
Sada Musa Jiggo, Cewel Halaybe, 10 December 2005
Abdu Majid Joob, Dara Birahim Joop, Saint-Louis, 5 December 2005
Ngañ Jomg, Mbacké, 29 May 2002
Abdallah Juuf, Tivaouane 18 July 2001
Abdul-Xadir Jeylani Kamara, Ganguel Sulé, 4 July 2007
Amadu Bayla Kan, Bokijjawe, July 2007
Abdu-Salaam Lo, Ngabou, April 2002
Ibrahima Lo, Ngabou, May 2002
Shaykh Mbakke Lo, Touba, February 2002
Shaykhuna Lo, Ngabou, 8 March 2002, 28 May 2002
Xaliil Lo, Ngabou, 28 May 2002

Khadim Mbacké, Dakar, 17 May 2002
Abdulaay Mbakke, Touba, 7 March 2002
Bara Mbakke, Touba, March 2002
Shaykh Abdu-Rahman Mbakke, Touba, 7 March 2002
Shwaʿīb Mbakke, Touba, March 2002
Aliun Ndaw, Tivaouane, 9 February 2002
Ruqayya Niass, Kaolack, December 2010
Mamadou Ndiaye, Dakar, June 2002
Anta Njaay, Tivaouane, 9 February 2002
Pap Lamin Njaay, Tivaouane, August 2001
Shaykh Lo Njaay, Touba, May 2002
Sidi Njaay, Tivaouane, August 2001
Uztaz Aliun Saar, Saint-Louis, 5 December 2005
Abdu-Ali Sekk, Tivaouane, August 2001
Shaykh Lo Sekk, Touba, 30 May 2002
Ibrahima Sey, Touba, May 2002
Mamadu Musa Sih and Cerno Usman Sih, Fanay, 7 December 2005
Adama Sow, Gaya, 6 December 2005
Muhamadu Moxtar Sow, Dagana, 6 December 2005
Omar Issa Sow, Gamadji Saré, December 2005
Aliu Taal, Gëm Yalla, 7 December 2005
Cerno Hachiru Madani Taal, Njum, 9 December 2005
Mamadu Lamin Talla, Sincu Bamambe, July 2007

Newspapers

L'Afrique Musulmane (Tivaouane)
L'Islam Éternel (Tivaouane)
Reveil Islamique (Dakar)
Vers l'Islam (Dakar)

Published Sources

Abdalla, Ismail Hussein. "Diffusion of Islamic Medicine into Hausaland." In *Social Basis of Health and Healing in Africa*, ed. Steven Feierman and John M. Janzen. Berkeley: University of California Press, 1992.

Afanou, François, and Raymond Togbe Pierre. *Catalogue des "Cahiers William Ponty": extrait Sénégal.* Dakar: Institut Fondamental d'Afrique Noire, 1967.

Afsuraddin, Asma. "Excellences of the Qur'an: Textual Sacrality and the Organization of Early Islamic Society." *Journal of the American Oriental Society* 122, no. 1 (2002).

Ahwānī, Aḥmad Fu'ād. *Al-tarbīya fī-l-Islām aw Al-ta'līm fī ray al-Qābisī.* Cairo: Dār al-Kutub al-'Arabiya, 1955.

ʿAlī, Abdullah Yūsuf. *The Meaning of the Holy Qur'ān.* 6th ed. Beltsville: Amana, 1995.

Alidou, Ousseina. *Engaging Modernity: Muslim Women and the Politics of Agency in Postcolonial Niger.* Madison: University of Wisconsin Press, 2005.

Almada, André Alvares d'. *Brief Treatise on the Rivers of Guinea: Being an English*

Translation of a Variorum Text of Tratado Breve dos Rios de Guiné (c. 1594). Liverpool: Department of History, University of Liverpool, 1984.

Alyrres, Ala. *A Muslim American Slave: The Life of Omar Ibn Said*. Madison: University of Wisconsin, 2011.

André, Pierre J. *L'Islam et les races: tome seconde les rameaux*. 2 vols. Paris: Guethner, 1922.

Ane, Mouhamed Moustapha. *La vie de Cheikh Amadou Bamba*. Trans. Amar Samb. Dakar: Institut Fondamental d'Afrique Noire, 1974.

ʿArafat, W. "Bilāl b. Rabāḥ." In *Encyclopaedia of Islam*, 2d ed., ed. P. Bearman, Th. Bianquis, C. E. Bosworth, E. van Donzel, and W. P. Heinrichs. http://referenceworks.brillonline.com.proxy.lib.umich.edu/entries/encyclopaedia-of-islam-2/bilal-b-rabah-SIM_1412.

Asad, Talal. "The Idea of an Anthropology of Islam." *Qui Parle* 17, no. 2 (2009): 1–30.

Ba, Oumar. *La Penetration française au Cayor: documents recueillis*. Dakar: Archives Nationales du Sénégal, 1976.

Babou, Cheikh Anta Mbacké. "Educating the Murid: Theory and Practices of Education in Amadu Bamba's Thought." *Journal of Religion in Africa* 33, no. 3 (2003): 310–27.

———. *Fighting the Greater Jihad: Amadu Bamba and the Founding of the Muridiyya of Senegal, 1853–1913*. Athens: Ohio University Press, 2007.

Badran, Margot, ed. *Gender and Islam in Africa: Rights, Sexuality, and Law*. Stanford: Stanford University Press, 2011.

Bang, Anne. *Sufis and Scholars of the Sea: Family Networks in East Africa, 1860–1925*. London: Routledge, 2003.

Baradhiʿi, Khalaf ibn Muhammad. *Al-Tahdīb fī ikhtisār al-Mudawwana*. Dubai: Dar al-Buhuth, 2002.

Barry, Boubacar. "La guerre des marabouts dans la région du Fleuve Sénégal de 1673 à 1677." *Bulletin de l'Institut Fondamental d'Afrique Noire*, ser. B, 32 (1971).

———. *Senegambia and the Atlantic Slave Trade*. Cambridge: Cambridge University Press, 1998.

Bashir, Shahzad. *Sufi Bodies: Religion and Society in Medieval Islam*. New York: Columbia University Press, 2011.

Batran, Aziz. *The Qadiriyya Brotherhood in West Africa and the Western Sahara: The Life and Times of Shaykh al-Mukhtar al-Kunti*. Rabat: Institut des Études Africaines, 2001.

Becker, Charles, and Victor Martin. "Journal historique et suitte du Journal Historique (1729–31): Documents inédits." *Bulletin de l'Institut Fondamental d'Afrique Noire*, ser. B, 39, no. 2 (1977): 223–89.

Becker, Felicitas. *Becoming Muslim in Mainland Tanzania, 1890–2000*. Oxford: Oxford University Press, 2008.

Behrman, Lucy. *Muslim Brotherhoods and Politics in Senegal*. Cambridge: Harvard University Press, 1970.

Benkheira, Mohammed H. *Amour de la loi: essai sur la normativité en Islam*. Paris: Presses Universitaires de France, 1997.

Berkey, Jonathan. "Tradition, Innovation, and the Social Construction of Knowledge in the Medieval Islamic Near East." *Past and Present* 146 (1995): 38–65.

———. *Transmission of Knowledge in Medieval Cairo: A Social History of Islamic Education*. Princeton: Princeton University Press, 1992.
Bledsoe, Caroline. "No Success without Struggle: Social Mobility and Hardship for Foster Children in Sierra Leone." *Man* 25, no. 1 (1990): 70–88.
Bledsoe, Caroline, and Kenneth M. Robey. "Arabic Literacy and Secrecy among the Mende of Sierra Leone." *Man* 21, no. 2 (1986): 202–26.
Bobboyi, Hamidu. "Relations of the Borno 'Ulamā' with the Sayfawa Rulers: The Role of the Maḥrams." *Sudanic Africa* 4 (1993): 175–204.
Boddy, Janice. *Wombs and Alien Spirits: Women, Men, and the Zar Cult in the Northern Sudan*. Madison: University of Wisconsin Press, 1990.
Boilat, David. *Esquisses sénégalaises: physionomie du pays, peuplades, commerce, religions, passé et avenir, récits et legends*. Paris: P. Bertrand, 1853.
Bouche, Denise. "L'école française et les musulmans au Sénégal." *Revue Française d'Histoire d'Outre-Mer* 61, no. 223 (1974): 218–35.
———. *L'enseignement dans les territoires français de l'Afrique occidentale de 1817 à 1920: mission civilisatrice ou formation d'une elite?* Lille: Atelier Reproduction des Thèses, 1975.
Boulègue, Jean. "À la naissance de l'histoire écrite sénégalaise: Yoro Dyao et ses modèles." *History in Africa* 15 (1988): 395–405.
———. *Le grand Jolof, XIIIe–XVIe siècle*. Paris: Karthala, 1987.
———. "La participation possible des centres de Pir et de Ndogal à la revolution islamique sénégambienne de 1673." In *Contributions à l'histoire du Sénégal*, ed. Jean Boulègue. Paris: Afera, 1987.
Boulègue, Jean, and Benjamin Pinto-Bull. "Les relations du Cayor avec le Portugal dans la première moitiés du XVIe siècle, d'après deux documents nouveaux." *Bulletin de l'Institut Fondamental d'Afrique Noire*, ser. B, 28 (1966).
Boullata, Issa. "Sayyid Qutb's Literary Appreciation of the Qur'an." In *Literary Structures of Religious Meaning in the Qur'an*, ed. Issa Boullata. Richmond: Curzon, 2000.
Boyd, Jean. *The Caliph's Sister: Nana Asma'u, 1793–1865, Teacher, Poet, and Islamic Leader*. London: Frank Cass, 1989.
Brenner, Louis. "Concepts of Tariqa in West Africa: The Case of the Qadiriyya." In *Charisma and Brotherhood in African Islam*, ed. Donal Cruise O'Brien and Christian Coulon. Oxford: Clarendon, 1988.
———. *Controlling Knowledge: Religion, Power, and Schooling in a West African Muslim Society*. Bloomington: Indiana University Press, 2001.
———. "Histories of Religion in Africa." *Journal of Religion in Africa* 30, no. 2 (2000): 143–67.
———. "Médersas au Mali: transformation d'une institution islamique." In *L'enseignement islamique au Mali*, ed. Bintou Sanankoua and Louis Brenner. Bamako: Jamana, 1991.
———. "Sufism in Africa." In *African Spirituality: Forms, Meanings, Expressions*, ed. Jacob Olupona, 324–49. New York: Crossroad, 2000.
Brett, Michael. "Islam and Trade in the Bilād al-Sūdān, Tenth–Eleventh Century A.D." *Journal of African History* 35, no. 2 (1983): 431–40.

Brigaglia, Andrea. "Two Published Hausa Translations of the Qurʾan and Their Doctrinal Background." *Journal of Religion in Africa* 35, no. 4 (2005): 424–49.

Brockopp, Jonathan. "Contradictory Evidence and the Exemplary Scholar: The Lives of Sahnun b. Sa'id (d. 854)." *International Journal of Middle East Studies* 43, no. 1 (2011): 115–32.

———. *Early Mālikī Law: Ibn ʿAbd al-Hakam and His Major Compendium of Jurisprudence*. Leiden: Brill, 2000.

Brooks, George E. *Landlords and Strangers: Ecology, Society, and Trade in Western Africa, 1000–1630*. Boulder: Westview, 1993.

Bryant, Sherwin K. *Rivers of Gold: Governing through Slavery in Colonial Quito*. Chapel Hill: University of North Carolina Press, 2014.

Bukhārī, Muḥammad b. Ismāʿīl. *Ṣaḥīḥ al-Bukhārī*. Būlāq: Dār al-Ṭibāʿah al-ʿĀmirah, 1869-70.

Campistron, M. "Oulof Custom in Cayor." *Publications du Comité d'Études Historiques et Scientifiques de l'Afrique Occidentale Française*, ser. A, no. 3, p. 10. Computer file in New Haven: Human Relations Area Files, 1999.

Carruthers, Mary. *The Book of Memory: A Study of Memory in Medieval Culture*. Cambridge: Cambridge University Press, 1990.

Chamberlain, Michael. *Knowledge and Social Practice in Medieval Damascus, 1190–1350*. Cambridge: Cambridge University Press, 1994.

———. "The Production of Knowledge and the Reproduction of the A'yān in Medieval Damascus." In *Madrasa: La transmission du savoir dans le monde musulman*, ed. Nicole Grandin and Marc Goborieau. Paris: Arguments, 1997.

Charles, Eunice A. "Shaykh Amadu Ba and Jihad in Jolof." *International Journal of African Historical Studies* 8, no. 3 (1975): 367–82.

Clarence-Smith, William G. *Islam and the Abolition of Slavery*. New York: Oxford University Press, 2006.

Clarkson, Thomas. *Letters on the Slave Trade, and the State of the Natives in Those Parts of Africa, Which Are Contiguous to Fort St. Lewis and Goree*. London: Phillips, 1791.

Colin, Roland. *Systèmes d'éducation et mutations sociales: continuité et discontinuité dans les dynamiques socio-éducatives: le cas du Sénégal*. Lille: Atelier Reproduction des Theses, 1980.

Collignon, René. "La lutte des pouvoirs publics contre les 'encombrements humains' à Dakar." *Canadian Journal of African Studies* 18 (1984): 573–82.

Colvin, Lucie G. "Islam and the State of Kajoor: A Case of Successful Resistance to Jihad." *Journal of African History* 15 (1974): 587–606.

———. "The Shaykh's Men: Religion and Power in Senegambian Islam." In *Rural and Urban Islam in West Africa*, ed. Nehemia Levtzion and Humphrey Fisher. Boulder: Rienner, 1987.

Conrad, David, and Barbara Frank, eds. *Status and Identity in West Africa: The Nyamakalaw of Mande*. Bloomington: Indiana University Press, 1995.

Copans, Jean. *Les marabouts de l'arachide: la confrérie mouride et les paysans du Sénégal*. Paris: Harmattan, 1988.

Coulon, Christian. *Le marabout et le prince: Islam et pouvoir au Sénégal*. Paris: Pedone, 1981.

Crone, G. R. *The Voyages of Cadamosto and Other Documents on Western Africa in the Second Half of the Fifteenth Century*. London: Hakluyt, 1937.
Crowder, Michael. *Senegal: A Case Study in French Assimilation Policy*. London: Methuen, 1967.
Cruise O'Brien, Donal. *The Mourides of Senegal: The Political and Economic Organization of an Islamic Brotherhood*. Oxford: Clarendon, 1971.
———. *Saints and Politicians: Essays in the Organization of a Senegalese Peasant Society*. London: Cambridge University Press, 1975.
Cruise O'Brien, Donal, and Christian Coulon, eds. *Charisma and Brotherhood in African Islam*. Oxford: Clarendon, 1988.
Curtin, Phillip. "Jihad in West Africa: Early Phases and Inter-Relations in Mauritania and Senegal." *Journal of African History* 12 (1971): 11–24.
Davidson, Basil, ed. *African Civilization Revisited: From Antiquity to Modern Times*. Trenton: Africa World, 1991.
Delafosse, Maurice. "L'état actuel de l'Islam dans l'Afrique Occidentale Française." *Revue du Monde Musulman* 11 (1910): 32–53.
Dia, Mamadou. *Mémoires d'un militant du Tiers-Monde*. Paris: Publisud, 1985.
Diagne, Souleymane Bachir. "Shaykh Al-Hajj Abbass Sall: In Praise of the Tijaniyya Order" (translation of the Wolofal of Seriñ Abbas Sall). In *Tales of God's Friends: Islamic Hagiography in Translation*, ed. John Renard. Berkeley: University of California Press, 2009.
Diallo, Cheikh Amalla. "Contribution à une étude de l'enseignement privé coranique au Sénégal." *Revue Française d'Études Politiques Africaines* (April 1972): 34–48.
Diop, Abdoulaye Bara. *La famille wolof: tradition et changement*. Paris: Karthala, 1985.
———. *La société wolof: tradition et changement: les systèmes d'inégalité et de domination*. Paris: Karthala, 1981.
Diop, Amadou-Bamba. "Lat Dior et le problème musulman." *Bulletin de l'Institut Fondamental d'Afrique Noire. Série B: Sciences humaines* 38 (1966).
Diouf, Demba Lamine. *Khally Amar Fall, fondateur de l'Université de Pire*. Dakar: Centre d'Étude des Civilizations, 1988.
Diouf, Mamadou. *Le Kajoor au XIXe siècle: pouvoir ceddo et conquête coloniale*. Paris: Karthala, 1990.
Diouf, Sylviane. *Servants of Allah: African Muslims Enslaved in the Americas*. New York: New York University Press, 1998.
———, ed. *Fighting the Slave Trade: West African Strategies*. Athens: Ohio University Press, 2003.
Djibo, Hadiza. *Participation des femmes africaines à la vie politique*. Paris: Harmattan, 2001.
Du Bois, W. E. B. *Souls of Black Folk: Essays and Sketches*. Chicago: McClurg, 1903.
Dudoignon, Stéphane Hair, Hisao Komatsu, and Yasushi Kosugi, eds. *Intellectuals in the Modern Islamic World: Transmission, Transformation, Communication*. London: Routledge, 2006.
Durand, Jean Baptiste Léon. *Voyage to Senegal*. Paris: Agass, 1806.
Dutton, Yasin. "'Amal v Hadith in Islamic Law: The Case of Sadl al-Yadayn (Holding

One's Hands by One's Sides) When Doing the Prayer." *Islamic Law and Society* 3, no. 1 (1996).
———. "Orality, Literacy and the 'Seven *Ahruf' Hadith*." *Journal of Islamic Studies* 23, no. 1 (2012): 1–49.
———. *The Origins of Islamic Law: The Qur'an, the Muwatta', and Madinan 'Amal*. London: Surrey, 1999.
Eickelman, Dale. "The Art of Memory: Islamic Education and Its Social Reproduction." *Comparative Studies in Society and History* 20, no. 4 (1978): 485–516.
———. *Knowledge and Power in Morocco: The Education of a Twentieth-Century Notable*. Princeton: Princeton University Press, 1985.
———. "Mass Higher Education and the Religious Imagination in Contemporary Arab Societies." *American Ethnologist* 19, no. 4 (1992): 643–55.
El-Hamel, Chouki. *La vie intellectuelle islamique dans le Sahel ouest-africain, XVI–XIX siècles: une étude sociale de l'enseignement islamique en Mauritanie et au nord du Mali (XVI–XIX siècles) et traduction annotée de Fatḥ ash-shakūr d'al-Bartilī al-Walātī (mort en 1805)*. Paris: Harmattan, 2002.
El-Tom, Abdullahi Osman. "Drinking the Koran: The Meaning of Koranic Verses in Berti Erasure." *Africa* 55, no. 4 (1985): 414–31.
Ernst, Carl. *The Shambhala Guide to Sufism: An Essential Introduction to the Philosophy and Practice of the Mystical Tradition of Islam*. Boston: Shambhala, 1997.
Evans-Ware, Kaaronica. *Fire and Clay: Book One*. Ann Arbor: Sashakira, 2013.
Faladé, Solange. "Women of Dakar and the Surrounding Area." In *Women in Tropical Africa*, ed. Denise Paulme, 217–29. London: Routledge, 1963.
Farias, Paulo F. M. *Arabic Medieval Inscription from the Republic of Mali: Epigraphy, Chronicles, and Songhay-Tuareg History*. Oxford: Oxford University Press, 2003.
———. "Models of the World and Categorial Models: The 'Enslavable Barbarian' as a Mobile Classificatory Label." In *Slaves and Slavery in Muslim Africa*, ed. J. R. Willis, 1:27–46. London: Cass, 1985.
Feierman, Steven. "Colonizers, Scholars, and the Creation of Invisible Histories." In *Beyond the Cultural Turn: New Directions in the Study of Society and Culture*, ed. Victoria Bonnell, Lynn Hunt, and Richard Biernacki. Berkeley: University of California Press, 1999.
———. *Peasant Intellectuals: Anthropology and History in Tanzania*. Madison: University of Wisconsin Press, 1990.
———. "Struggles for Control: Social Roots of Health and Healing in Modern Africa." *African Studies Review* 28 (1985): 73–147.
Feierman, Steven, and John M. Janzen, eds. *Social Basis of Health and Healing in Africa*. Berkeley: University of California Press, 1992.
Fisher, Humphrey. "The Early Life and Pilgrimage of Al-Hajj Muhammad Al-Amin the Soninke (d. 1887)." *Journal of African History* 11 (1970).
———. "A Muslim Wilberforce?: The Sokoto Jihad as Anti-Slavery Crusade: An Enquiry into Historical Causes." In *De la traite à l'ésclavage du Ve au XIXe siècle: actes du colloque international sur la traite des noirs, Nantes 1985*, ed. Serge Daget. Nantes: Centre de Recherche sur l'Histoire du Monde Atlantique, 1988.
———. "Of Slaves, and Souls of Men." *Journal of African History* 28 (1987): 141–49.

Fisher, Humphrey, and Charlotte Blum. "Love for Three Oranges; or, The Askiya's Dilemma: The Askiya, al-Maghili, and Timbuktu c. 1500 A.D." *Journal of African History* 34, no. 1 (1993): 65–91.

Fisher, Humphrey, and Pekka Masonen. "Not Quite Venus from the Waves: The Almoravid Conquest of Ghana in the Modern Historiography of Western Africa." *History in Africa* 23 (1996): 197–232.

Fortier, Corrine. "Le lait, le sperme, le dos. Et le sang?" *Cahiers d'Études Africaines* 161 (2001): 97–138.

———. "Mémorisation et audition: l'enseignement coranique chez les Maures." *Islam et Sociétés au Sud du Sahara* 11 (1997): 85–105.

———. "La mort vivante ou le corps intercesseur (société maure-islam malekite)." *Revue des Mondes Musulmans et de la Méditerranée* 113–14 (2006): 229–45.

———. "Une pédagogie coranique: modes de transmission des saviors islamiques (Mauritanie)." *Cahier d'Études Africaines* 43 (2003).

Fortna, Benjamin. *Imperial Classroom: Islam, the State, and Education in the Late Ottoman Empire*. Oxford: Oxford University Press, 2002.

Gaby, Jean Baptiste. *Relation de la Nigritie*. Paris: Couterot, 1689.

Gamble, David. *The Wolof of Senegambia: Together with Notes on the Lebu and the Serer*. London: International African Institute, 1957.

Gerresch, Claudine. "Le livre de métrique *Mubayyin al-ishkāl* du Cadi Madiakhaté Kala." *Bulletin de l'Institut Fondamental d'Afrique Noire* 36 (1974): 714–832.

Gesink, Indira. *Islamic Reform and Conservatism: Al-Azhar and the Evolution of Modern Sunni Islam*. London: Tauris, 2010.

Geurts, Kathryn. *Culture and the Senses: Bodily Ways of Knowing in an African Community*. Berkeley: University of California Press, 2002.

Glover, John. *Sufism and Jihad in Modern Senegal*. Rochester: University of Rochester Press, 2007.

Golberry, Sylvain. *Travels in Africa, Performed during the Years 1785, 1786, and 1787*. London: Jones, 1803.

Gomez, Michael. *Black Crescent: The Experience and Legacy of African Muslims in the Americas*. Cambridge: Cambridge University Press, 2005.

———. *Exchanging Our Country Marks*. Chapel Hill: University of North Carolina Press, 1998.

———. *Pragmatism in the Age of Jihad: The Precolonial State of Bundu*. Cambridge: Cambridge University Press, 1992.

Gomez-Perez, Muriel. "Un mouvement culturel vers l'indépendance: le réformisme musulman au Sénégal (1956–1960)." In *Le temps des marabouts: itinéraires et strategies islamiques en Afrique occidentale française*, ed. David Robinson and Jean-Louis Triaud. Paris: Karthala, 1997.

Goody, Jack. *Literacy in Traditional Societies*. Cambridge: Cambridge University Press, 1968.

Graham, William A. *Beyond the Written Word: Oral Aspects of Scripture in the History of Religion*. Cambridge: Cambridge University Press, 1987.

———. "Traditionalism in Islam: An Essay in Interpretation." *Journal of Interdisciplinary History* (1993).

Grandin, Nicole, and Marc Goborieau, eds. *Madrasa: la transmission du savoir dans le monde musulman*. Paris: Arguments, 1997.
Gray, William. *Travels in Western Africa: In the years 1818, 19, 20, and 21*. London: Murray, 1825.
Gril, Denis. "Le corps du prophète." *Revue des Mondes Musulmans et de la Méditerranée* 113–14 (2006): 37–57.
Hair, P. E. H, Adam Jones, and Robin Law, eds. *Barbot on Guinea: The Writings of Jean Barbot on West Africa, 1678–1712*. London: Hakluyt Society, 1992.
Haj, Samira. *Reconfiguring Islamic Tradition: Reform, Rationality, and Modernity.* Stanford: Stanford University Press, 2009.
Hall, Bruce. *A History of Race in Muslim West Africa, 1600–1960*. Cambridge: Cambridge University Press, 2011.
Hall, Bruce, and Charles C. Stewart. "The Historic 'Core Curriculum' and the Book Market in Islamic West Africa." In *The Trans-Saharan Book Trade: Manuscript Culture, Arabic Literacy, and Intellectual History in Muslim Africa*, ed. Graziano Krätli and Ghislaine Lydon, 109–74. Leiden: Brill, 2011.
Hallaq, Wael b. *Law and Legal Theory in Classical and Medieval Islam*. Aldershot: Varorium, 1994.
Hamdun, Saïd, and Noel King, eds. and trans. *Ibn Battuta in Black Africa*. Princeton: Wiener, 1994.
Hamès, Constant. "Entre recette magique d'Al-Būnī et prière Islamique d-Al-Ghazāli: textes talismaniques d'Afrique occidentale." In *Fétiches II: Puissance des Objets, Charme des Mots, Systèmes de Pensée en Afrique Noire* 12 (1993).
Hamet, Ismaël. *Chroniques de la Mauritanie sénégalaise: Nacer Eddine: texte arabe, traduction, et notice.* Paris: Leroux, 1911.
Hamza, Feras, trans. *Tafsir al-Jalalayn.* Louisville: Fons Vitae, 2008.
Hanretta, Sean. *Islam and Social Change in French West Africa.* Cambridge: Cambridge University Press, 2010.
Harrison, Christopher. *France and Islam in West Africa, 1860–1960*. Cambridge: Cambridge University Press, 1988.
Heath, Deborah. "The Politics of Appropriateness and Appropriation: Recontextualizing Women's Dance in Urban Senegal." *American Ethnologist* 21, no. 1 (1994): 88–103.
Hell, Bertrand. *Le tourbillon des genies: au Maroc avec les Gnāwa*. Paris: Flammarion, 2002.
Hilliard, Constance. "Zuhur al-Basatin and Ta'rikh al-Turubbe: Some Legal and Ethical Aspects of Slavery in the Sudan as Seen in the Works of Shaykh Musa Kamara." In *Slaves and Slavery in Muslim Africa*, ed. J. R. Willis, 1:160–81. London: Cass, 1985.
Hiskett, Mervyn. *The Sword of Truth: The Life and Times of the Shehu Usuman dan Fodio*. New York: Oxford University Press, 1973.
Human Rights Watch. *Off the Backs of the Children: Forced Begging and Other Abuses against Talibés in Senegal*. New York: Human Rights Watch, 2010.
Hunwick, John, comp. *Arabic Literature of Africa: The Writings of Western Sudanic Africa.* Leiden: Brill, 2003.
———. "Islamic Law and Polemics over Race and Slavery in North and West Africa

(16th–19th Century)." In *Slavery in the Islamic Middle East*, ed. Shaun E. Marmon, 43–68. Princeton: Wiener, 1999.

———. "Secular Power and Religious Authority in Muslim Society: The Case of Songhay." *Journal of African History* 37, no. 2 (1996): 175–94.

———. *Sharīʿa in Songhay: The Replies of al-Maghīlī to the Questions of Askia al-Ḥājj Muḥammad*. Oxford: Oxford University Press, 1985.

———. *Timbuktu and the Songhay Empire: Al-Saʿdī's Taʾrīkh al-Sūdān down to 1613, and Other Contemporary Documents*. Leiden: Brill, 1999.

Hunwick, John, and Eve Trout Powell, eds. *African Diaspora in the Mediterranean Lands of Islam*. Princeton: Wiener, 2002.

Hutson, Alaine. "The Development of Women's Authority in the Kano Tijaniyya, 1894–1963." *Africa Today* 46, nos. 3–4 (1999): 43–64.

Idris, H. R. "Deux juristes kairouannais de l'époque ziride: Ibn Abî Zayd et al-Qâbisî." *Annales de l'Institut des Etudes Orientales* (Alger) 12 (1954): 122–98.

Inikori, Joseph. "Import of Firearms into West Africa, 1750–1807." *Journal of African History* 18, no. 3 (1977): 339–68.

Insoll, Timothy. *The Archaeology of Islam in Sub-Saharan Africa*. Cambridge: Cambridge University Press, 2003.

Johnson, G. Wesley, ed. *Double Impact: France and Africa in the Age of Imperialism*. Westport: Greenwood, 1985.

Jomard. "Kelédor, histoire africaine, publiée par M. Roger." In *Révue Encyclopédique: ou analyse raisonnée des productions les plus remarquables* 37 (1828): 673–87.

Jordão, Levy M. *Historia do Congo*. Lisbon: Academia, 1877.

Ka, Thierno. *École de Pir Saniokhor: histoire, enseignement, et culture arabo-islamiques au Sénégal du XVIIIe au XXe siècle*. Dakar: Institut Fondamental d'Afrique Noire, 2002.

Ka, Thierno, and Alassane Diop. *École de Ndiaye-Ndiaye Wolof: histoire, enseignement, et culture arabo-islamiques au Sénégal, 1890–1990*. Dakar: Institut Fondamental d'Afrique Noire, 2009.

Kaba, Lansiné. "The Pen, the Sword, and the Crown: Islam and Revolution in Songhay Reconsidered, 1464–1493." *Journal of African History* 25, no. 3 (1984): 241–56.

———. "The Politics of Quranic Education among Muslim Traders in the Western Sudan." *Canadian Journal of African Studies* 10 (1976): 409–21.

———. *The Wahabiyya: Islamic Reform and Politics in French West Africa*. Evanston: Northwestern University Press, 1974.

Kamara, Muusa. *Florilège au jardin de l'histoire des noirs, Zuhūr al-Basātīn: l'aristocraties peule et la révolution des clercs musulmans, vallée du Sénégal*. Ed. Jean Schmitz. Trans. Saïd Bousbina. Paris: Centre National de Recherche Scientifique, 1998.

Kane, Cheikh Hamidou. *Ambiguous Adventure*. Trans. Katherine Woods. New York: Walker, 1963.

———. *L'aventure ambigüe: récit*. Paris: Julliard, 1961.

Kane, Mouhamed Moustapha. "La vie et œuvre d'Al-Hajj Mahmoud Ba Diowol (1905–1978)." In *Le temps des marabouts: itinéraires et strategies islamiques en Afrique occidentale française*, ed. David Robinson and Jean-Louis Triaud, 431–63. Paris: Karthala, 1997.

Kane, Oumar. "Les causes de la révolution musulmane de 1776 dans le Fuuta-Tooro." In *Contributions à l'histoire du Sénégal*, ed. Jean Boulègue. Paris: Afera, 1987.

———. *La première hégémonie peule: le Fuuta Tooro de Koli Teŋella à Almaami Abdul*. Paris: Karthala, 2004.

Kane, Ousmane. "Shaykh al-Islam Al-Hajj Ibrahim Niasse." In *Le temps des marabouts: itinéraires et strategies islamiques en Afrique occidentale française*, ed. David Robinson and Jean-Louis Triaud, 299–316. Paris: Karthala, 1997.

Kane, Ousmane, and Jean-Louis Triaud, eds. *Islam et islamismes au sud du Sahara*. Paris: Karthala, 1998.

Kane, Ousmane, and Leonardo Villalón. "Entre confrérisme, réformisme, et islamisme: les mustarshidin du Sénégal." In *Islam et islamismes au sud du Sahara*, ed. Ousmane Kane and Jean-Louis Triaud, 263–327. Paris: Karthala, 1998.

Kati, Maḥmūd. *Ta'rīkh al-Fattash: The Timbuktu Chronicles, 1493–1599*. Ed. and trans. Christopher Wise. Trenton: Africa World, 2011.

———. *Tarikh el-Fettach: chronique du chercheur*. Ed. and trans. Octave Houdas and Maurice Delafosse. Paris: Leroux, 1913.

Katz, Marion. *Body of Text: The Emergence of the Sunni Law of Ritual Purity*. Albany: State University of New York Press, 2002.

Klein, Martin. *Islam and Imperialism: Sine Saloum, 1847–1914*. Stanford: Stanford University Press, 1968.

———. "Ma Ba." In *Les Africains*, ed. Charles Julien. Paris: Éditions J. A., 1977.

———. "Moslem Revolution in Nineteenth-Century Senegambia." In D. McCall, N. Bennett, and J. Butler, eds., *Boston University Papers on Africa IV: Western African History*. New York: Praeger, 1969.

———. "Servitude among the Wolof and Sereer of Senegambia." In *Slavery in Africa: Historical and Anthropological Perspectives*, ed. Suzanne Miers and Igor Kopytoff. Madison: University of Wisconsin Press, 1977.

———. *Slavery and Colonial Rule in French West Africa*. Cambridge: Cambridge University Press, 1998.

———. "Social and Economic Factors in the Muslim Revolution in Senegambia." *Journal of African History* 13 (1972): 419–41.

Kugle, Scott. *Sufis and Saints' Bodies: Mysticism, Corporeality, and Sacred Power in Islam*. Chapel Hill: University of North Carolina Press, 2007.

Lambek, Michael. *Knowledge and Practice in Mayotte: Local Discourses of Islam, Sorcery, and Spirit Possession*. Toronto: University of Toronto Press, 1993.

Lamiral, Dominique. *L'Affrique et le peuple affriquaine considérés sous tous leurs rapports avec notre commerce et nos colonies*. Paris: Dessenne, 1789.

Landau, Paul. "'Religion' and Christian Conversion in African History: A New Model." *Journal of Religious History* 23, no. 1 (1999): 8–30.

Last, Murray. *The Sokoto Caliphate*. London: Longman, 1977.

Launay, Robert. *Beyond the Stream: Islam and Society in a West African Town*. Berkeley: University of California Press, 1992.

———. "An Invisible Religion?: Anthropology's Avoidance of Islam in Africa." In *African Anthropologies: History, Critique, and Practice*., ed. Mwenda Ntarangwa, David Mills, and Mustafa Babiker, 188–203. London: Zed, 2006.

Lauzière, Henri. "The Construction of Salafiyya: Reconsidering Salafism from the Perspective of Conceptual History." In *International Journal of Middle East Studies* 42, no. 3 (2010): 369–89.

Law, Robin, and Paul Lovejoy. *The Biography of Mahommah Gardo Baquaqua: His Passage from Slavery to Freedom in Africa and America*. Princeton: Wiener, 2001.

Leichtman, Mara. "The Africanisation of ʿAshura in Senegal." In *Shiʿi Islam and Identity: Religion, Politics and Change in the Global Muslim Community*. London: I. B. Tauris, 2012.

Leitner, G. W. *Muhammadanism*. Woking: Oriental Nobility Institute, 1889.

Lelong, Christian. *Justice à Agadez* (video). New York: Cinédoc, 2006.

Leriche, Albert. "De l'enseignement arabe feminin en Mauritanie." *Bulletin de l'Institut Français d'Afrique Noire* 14 (1952): 975–83.

Levtzion, Nehemia. "The Eighteenth Century: Background to Islamic Revolutions in West Africa." In *Eighteenth Century Renewal and Reform in Islam*, ed. Nehemia Levtzion and John Voll. Syracuse: Syracuse University Press, 1987.

———. "Islam in the Bilad al-Sudan." In Nehemia Levtzion and Randall Pouwels, eds., *History of Islam in Africa*. Athens: Ohio University Press, 2000.

———. *Islam in West Africa: Religion, Society, and Politics to 1800*. Norfolk: Variorum, 1994.

Levtzion, Nehemia, and Humphrey J. Fisher, eds. *Rural and Urban Islam in West Africa*. Boulder: Rienner, 1987.

Levtzion, Nehemia, and J. F. P. Hopkins, eds. *Corpus of Early Arabic Sources for West African History*. Trans. J. F. P. Hopkins. Princeton: Wiener, 2000.

Levtzion, Nehemia, and Randall Pouwels, eds. *History of Islam in Africa*. Athens: Ohio University Press, 2000.

Levtzion, Nehemia, and John Voll, eds. *Eighteenth Century Renewal and Reform in Islam*. Syracuse: Syracuse University Press, 1987.

Lewis, Bernard. *Race and Slavery in Middle East: An Historical Enquiry*. New York: Oxford University Press, 1990.

Lewis, I. M., Ahmed El-Safi, and Sayed Hamid A. Hurreiz, eds. *Women's Medicine: The Zar-Bori Cult in Africa and Beyond*. Edinburgh: Edinburgh University Press for the International African Institute, 1991.

Lia, Brynjar. *The Society of Muslim Brothers in Egypt: The Rise of an Islamic Mass Movement*. Reading: Ithaca, 1998.

Loimeier, Roman. *Between Social Skills and Marketable Skills: The Politics of Islamic Education in 20th Century Zanzibar*. Leiden: Brill, 2009.

———. "Cheikh Touré: du reformisme a l'islamisme un musulman sénégalais dans le siècle." In *Islam et islamismes au sud du Sahara*, ed. Ousmane Kane and Jean-Louis Triaud, 55–66. Paris: Karthala, 1998.

———. "L'Islam Ne Se Vend Plus: The Islamic Reform Movement and the State in Senegal." *Journal of Religion in Africa* 30, no. 2 (2000): 168–90.

———. "Je Veux Étudier sans Mendier: The Campaign against the Qur'ānic Schools in Senegal." In *Social Welfare in Muslim Societies in Africa*, ed. Holger Weiss, 118–37. Stockholm: Elanders Gotab, 2002.

Lory, Pierre. "Verbe coranique et magie en terre d'Islam." In *Fétiches II: Puissance des Objets, Charme des Mots, Systèmes de Pensée en Afrique Noire*, 12 (1993).
Lovejoy, Paul. "Islam, Slavery, and Political Transformation in West Africa: Constraints on the Atlantic Slave Trade." *Outre-Mers: Revue d'Histoire* 336–37 (2002): 247–82.
———, ed. *Slavery on the Frontiers of Islam*. Princeton: Wiener, 2004.
Ly, Ciré. *Où va l'Afrique?* Dakar: n.p., n.d.
Mack, Beverly, and Jean Boyd. *One Woman's Jihad: Nana Asma'u, Scholar and Scribe.* Bloomington: Indiana University Press, 2000.
Mahibou, Sidi Mohamed, and J. L. Triaud, eds. and trans. *Voilà ce qui est arrivé: Bayân mâ waqa'a d'al-Hâgg 'Umar al-Fûtî: plaidoyer pour une guerre sainte en Afrique de l'Ouest au XIXe siècle*. Paris: Centre National de Recherche Scientifique, 1983.
Manning, Patrick. *Francophone Sub-Saharan Africa, 1880–1985*. Cambridge: Cambridge University Press, 1988.
Mariani, Jules Antoine François. "Les écoles coraniques de Saint-Louis." *Revue du Monde Musulman* 7 (1909).
Marone, Ibrahima. "Le Tidjanisme au Sénégal." *Bulletin de l'Institut Fondamental d'Afrique Noire, Série B: Sciences Humaines* 32, no. 1 (1970): 136–215.
Martin, Bradford G. *Muslim Brotherhoods in Nineteenth Century Africa.* Cambridge: Cambridge University Press, 1976.
Martin-Granel, P. *Du Clef d'Or à Kelédor: genèse du premier roman antiesclavagiste de l'histoire*. Arles: Catimini, 2009.
Marty, Paul, trans. "Les amulettes musulmanes au Sénégal." *Revue du Monde Musulman* 27 (1914): 318–43.
———. "Les écoles maraboutiques du Sénégal: La Médersa de Saint-Louis." Paris: Leroux, 1914.
———. *Études sur l'Islam au Dahomey*. Paris: Leroux, 1926.
———. *Études sur l'Islam au Sénégal*. Paris: Leroux, 1917.
———. *Études sur l'Islam en Côte d'Ivoire*. Paris: Leroux, 1922.
———. *Études sur l'Islam et les tribus du Soudan français*. Paris: Leroux, 1920–21.
———. *Études sur l'Islam et les tribus maures*. Paris: Leroux, 1921.
———. *Études sur l'Islam maure*. Paris: Leroux, 1916.
———. *L'Islam en Guinée: Fouta Diallon*. Paris: Leroux, 1921.
———. "Le livre des lettrés renseignés sur l'histoire des puits." *Bulletin du Comité des Études Historiques et Scientifiques* 3 (1920).
———. "Les Mourides du Sénégal." *Revue du Monde Musulman* 25 (1913): 1–164.
Masquelier, Adeline. *Prayer Has Spoiled Everything: Possession, Power, and Identity in an Islamic Town of Niger.* Durham: Duke University Press, 2001.
Masud, Muhammad Khalid. "The Growth and Development of the Tablighi Jamaʿat in India." In *Travellers in Faith: Studies of the Tablīghī Jamāʿat as a Transnational Islamic Movement for Faith Renewal*, ed. Muhammad Khalid Masud. Leiden: Brill, 2000.
Mayeur-Jaouen, Catherine. "Introduction." *Revue des Mondes Musulmans et de la Méditerranée* 113–14 (2006): 9–33.
Mbacké, Amadu Bamba. *Diwān fī ʿulūm al-dīnīyya*. Ed. and trans. Sam Mbaye. Casablanca: Dar el Kitab, 1989.

———. *Diwān fī amdāḥ khayr al-mursalīn*. Ed. and trans. Sam Mbaye. Casablanca: Dar el Kitab, 1989.
———. *Masālik al-Jinān*. Ed. and trans. Sam Mbaye. Casablanca: Dar el Kitab, 1989.
Mbacké, Bachir. *Les bienfaits de l'éternel: Ou la biographie de Cheikh Amadou Bamba Mbacké*. Trans. Khadim Mbacké. Dakar: Institut Fondamental d'Afrique Noire, 1995.
Mbacké, Khadim. *Daara et droits de l'enfant*. Dakar: Institut Fondamental d'Afrique Noire, 1994.
———. "Impact de l'Islam sur la société sénégalaise." *Africa* 53, no. 4 (1998): 530–56.
———. *Le pélerinage aux lieux saints de l'Islam: participation sénégalaise, 1886–1986*. Dakar: Presses universitaires de Dakar, 2004.
———. "Le rôle du mouvement réformiste dans le developpement du Sénégal au XXème siècle." *Africa* 57 (2002): 87–101.
———. *Soufisme et confréries religieuses au Sénégal*. Dakar: Imprimerie Saint-Paul, 1995.
Mbaye, Ravane. *Pensée et action: le grand savant El Hadji Malick Sy*. Ozoir-la-Férrière: Al-Bouraq, 2003.
McDougall, E. Ann. "Discourse and Distortion: Critical Reflections on the Historiography of the Saharan Slave Trade." *Outre-Mers: Revue d'Histoire* 336–37 (2002): 195–227.
McIntosh, Roderick. *Ancient Middle Niger: Urbanism and the Self-Organizing Landscape*. Cambridge: Cambridge University Press, 2005.
———. "The Pulse Model: Genesis and Accommodation of Specialization in the Middle Niger." *Journal of African History* 34 (1993): 181–220.
McLaughlin, Fiona. "Halpulaar Identity as a Response to Wolofization." *African Languages and Cultures* 8 (1995): 153–68.
Melchert, Christopher. "Traditionist-Jurisprudents and the Framing of Islamic Law." *Islamic Law and Society* 8, no. 3, Hadith and Fiqh (2001): 383–406.
Messick, Brinkley. *The Calligraphic State: Textual Domination and History in a Muslim Society*. Berkeley: University of California Press, 1993.
———. "Genealogies of Reading and the Scholarly Cultures of Islam." In *Cultures of Scholarship*, ed. S. C. Humphreys. Ann Arbor: University of Michigan Press, 1997.
Metcalf, Barbara, ed. *Moral Conduct and Authority: The Place of Adab in South Asian Islam*. Berkeley: University of California Press, 1984.
Meunier, Olivier. *Dynamique de l'enseignement islamique au Niger: le cas de la ville de Maradi*. Paris: Harmattan, 1997.
Miers, Suzanne, and Igor Kopytoff, eds. *Slavery in Africa: Historical and Anthropological Perspectives*. Madison: University of Wisconsin Press, 1977.
Miller, Christopher L. *French Atlantic Triangle: Literature and the Culture of the Slave Trade*. Durham: Duke University Press, 2008.
Miller, Joseph C. *Way of Death: Merchant Capitalism and the Angolan Slave Trade, 1730–1830*. Madison: University of Wisconsin Press, 1988.
Miran, Marie. *Islam, histoire, et modernité en Côte d'Ivoire*. Paris: Karthala, 2006.
Mitchell, Timothy. *Rule of Experts: Egypt, Techno-Politics, Modernity*. Berkeley: University of California Press, 2002.
Moitt, Bernard. "Slavery and Emancipation in Senegal's Peanut Basin: The Nineteenth

and Twentieth Centuries." *International Journal of African Historical Studies* 22, no. 1 (1989): 27–50.
Mollien, Gaspard. *Travels in the Interior of Africa, to the Sources of the Senegal and Gambia: Performed by the Command of the French Government, in the Year 1818.* London: Colburn, 1820.
———. *Voyage dans l'intérieur de l'Afrique, aux sources du Sénégal et de la Gambie.* Paris: Bertrand, 1822.
Mommersteeg, Geert. "L'éducation coranique au Mali: le pouvoir des mots sacrés." In *L'enseignement islamique au Mali*, ed. Bintou Sanankoua and Louis Brenner. Bamako: Jamana, 1991.
Monfouga-Nicolas, Jacqueline. *Ambivalence et culte de possession: contribution à l'étude du Bori hausa*. Paris: Anthropos, 1972.
Monserrat. "Un mémoire inédit de Monserrat sur l'histoire du nord du Sénégal." *Bulletin de l'Institut Fondamental d'Afrique Noire*, ser. B, 32 (1970).
Moore, Francis. *Travels into the Inland Parts of Africa*. London: Cave, 1738.
Moosa, Ebrahim. *Ghazālī and the Poetics of Imagination*. Chapel Hill: University of North Carolina Press, 2005.
Motzki, Harald. *Origins of Islamic Jurisprudence: Meccan Fiqh before the Classical Schools*. Leiden: Brill, 2002.
Mudimbe, Valentin Y. *The Invention of Africa: Gnosis, Philosophy, and the Order of Knowledge*. Bloomington: Indiana University Press, 1988.
Müller, Hans. "Sklaven." In *Handbuch der Orientalistik*, ed. B. Spuler. Leiden: Brill, 1977.
Naqar, 'Umar al-. "Takrur: The History of a Name." *Journal of African History* 10 (1969): 365–74.
Nast, Heidi. *Concubines and Power: Five Hundred Years in a Nigerian Palace*. Minneapolis: University of Minnesota Press, 2005.
Ndiaye, Mamadou. *L'enseignement arabo-islamique au Sénégal*. Istanbul: Centre de Recherches sur l'Histoire, l'Art, et la Culture Islamiques, 1985.
Niasse, Ruqiyya. *Ḥuqūq al-nisā' fī al-islām* [*The Rights of Women in Islam*]. New Jersey, 2006.
Norris, H. T. "Znâga Islam during the Seventeenth and Eighteenth Centuries." *Bulletin of the School of Oriental and African Studies* 32, no. 3 (1969): 496–526.
O'Fahey, Rex Sean. *Enigmatic Saint: Ahmad ibn Idris and the Idrisi Tradition*. Evanston: Northwestern University Press, 1990.
Ormsby, Eric. *Ghazali: The Revival of Islam*. Oxford: Oneworld, 2008.
Owusu-Ansah, David. "Prayer, Amulets, and Healing." In *The History of Islam in Africa*, ed. Nehemia Levtzion and Randall Pouwels, 477–88. Athens: Ohio University Press, 2000.
Park, Mungo. *Travels in the Interior Districts of Africa: Performed under the Direction and Patronage of the African Association, in the Years 1795, 1796, and 1797*. London: Bulmer, 1799.
Pew Research Center. *The Future of the Global Muslim Population*. January 2011.
Piga, Adriana. *Dakar et les ordres soufis: processus socioculturels et developpement urbain au Sénégal contemporain*. Paris: Harmattan, 2002.
Pommegorge, Antoine Pruneau. *Description de la Nigritie*. Amsterdam: Maradan, 1789.

Qābisī, ʿAlī b. Muḥammad al-. *Al-Risāla al-mufaṣṣila li-aḥwāl al-mutaʿallimīn wa-aḥkām al-muʿallimīn wa-al-mutaʿallimīn*. Ed. Ahmed Khaled. Tunis: Al-Sharika al-Tūnisīya lil-Tawzī, 1986.
Qayrawānī, Ibn Abī Zayd. *Al-Risāla*. Cairo: Dār al-Kutub al-Islāmīyah, 1980.
———. *Risala*. Trans. Edmond Fagnan. Paris: Geuthner, 1914.
Qutb, Sayyid. *A Child from the Village*. Ed. and trans. John Calvert and William Shepard. Syracuse and Cairo: Syracuse University Press and American University in Cairo Press, 2005.
———. *Milestones*. Damascus: Dar al Ilm, 2003.
Raffenel, Anne. *Voyage dans l'Afrique Occidentale*. Paris: Bertrand, 1846.
Reenders, Marlene. "An Ambiguous Adventure: Muslim Organizations and the Discourse of 'Development' in Senegal." *Journal of Religion in Africa* 32, no. 1 (2002): 61–82.
Revue du Monde Musulman. "La politique indigène du Gouverneur General Ponty en Afrique Occidentale française." *Revue du Monde Musulman* 31 (1915).
Riḍā, Muḥammad Rashīd. *Tafsīr al-Qur'ān al-ḥakīm al-shahīr bi-tafsīr al-manār*. Beirut: Dar al-Ma'rifa, 1970.
Ritchie, Carson. "Deux texts sur le Sénégal (1673–1677)." *Bulletin de l'Institut Fondamental d'Afrique Noire* 30, no. 1 (1968): 289–353.
Robinson, David. "French Islamic Policy and Practice in Late 19th Century Senegal." *Journal of African History* 29 (1988): 415–35.
———. *The Holy War of Umar Tall: The Western Sudan in the Mid-Nineteenth Century*. Oxford: Clarendon, 1985.
———. "The Islamic Revolution of Futa Toro." *International Journal of African Historical Studies* 8 (1975): 185–221.
———. *Muslim Societies in African History*. Cambridge: Cambridge University Press, 2004.
———. *Paths of Accommodation: Muslim Societies and French Colonial Authorities in Senegal and Mauritania, 1880–1920*. Athens: Ohio University Press, 2000.
Rodney, Walter. *How Europe Underdeveloped Africa*. Washington, D.C.: Howard University Press, 1981.
Roger, Jacques F. *Kelédor: histoire africaine*. Paris: Nepveu, 1828.
Rosander, Eva, and David Westerlund. *African Islam and Islam in Africa: Encounters between Sufis and Islamists*. Athens: Ohio University Press, 1997.
Rosenthal, Franz. *Knowledge Triumphant: The Concept of Knowledge in Medieval Islam*. Leiden: Brill, 2007.
Rousseau, R. "Le Sénégal d'autrefois: les cahiers de Yoro Dyâo." *Bulletin du Comité d'Études Historiques et Scientifiques de l'Afrique Occidentale Française* 12 (1929): 133–211.
Saʿdī, ʿAbd al-Raḥmān ibn ʿAbdallāh. *Tarikh es-Soudan*. Ed. and trans. Octave Houdas and Edmund Benoist. Paris: Leroux, 1898.
Said, Edward. "Impossible Histories: Why the Many Islams Cannot Be Simplified." *Harpers*, July 2002, 69–74.
Salama, Ibrahim. *Enseignement islamique en Égypte: son evolution, son influence sur les programmes modernes*. Cairo: Imprimérie Nationale, 1938.

Sall, Ibrahima Abou. "La diffusion de la Tijāniyya au Fuuta Tooro (Mauritanie-Sénégal)." In *La Tijāniyya: une confrérie musulmane à la conquête de l'Afrique*, ed. Jean-Louis Triaud and David Robinson. Paris: Karthala, 2000.

Sall, Tamsir Oumar. "Yoro Dyao, un aristocrate Waalo-Waalo dans le système colonial." In *Contributions à l'histoire du Sénégal*, ed. Jean Boulègue. Paris: Afera, 1987.

Samb, Amar. *Matraqué par le destin; ou, La vie d'un tālibé*. Dakar: Nouvelles Éditions Africaines, 1973.

Sanankoua, Bintou, and Louis Brenner, eds. *L'enseignement Islamique au Mali*. Bamako: Jamana, 1991.

Sandoval, Alonso. *De instauranda aethiopum satlute; el mundo de la esclavitud negra en América*. Bogota: Empresa Nacional de Publicaciones, 1956.

Sanneh, Lamin. *The Crown and the Turban: Muslims and West African Pluralism*. Boulder: Westview, 1997.

———. *The Jakhanke Muslim Clerics: A Religious and Historical Study of Islam in Senegambia*. Lanham: University Press of America, 1989.

———. "The Origins of Clericalism in West African Islam." *Journal of African History* 17 (1976): 49–72.

Santerre, Renaud. *Pédagogie musulmane d'Afrique noire: l'école coranique peule du Cameroun*. Montreal: Presses de l'Université de Montréal, 1973.

Sartain, Elizabeth. *Jalal al-Din al-Suyuti: Biography and Background*. Cambridge: Cambridge University Press, 1975.

Sarton, George. "*Al-tarbīya fī-1 -Islām aw Al-ta'līm fī ray al-Qābisī* by Aḥmad Fu'ād al-Ahwānī." *Journal of the American Oriental Society* 76, no. 1 (1956): 46–48.

Saugnier. *Relation des voyages de Saugnier à la côte d'Afrique, à Maroc, au Sénégal, à Gorée, à Galam, etc. avec les détails intéressans pour ceux qui se destinent au commerce, de l'or, de l'ivoire, et autre productions de ces pays, en 1784, 1785, et 1786*. Paris: Lamy, 1799.

Saul, Mahir. "Islam and West African Anthropology." *Africa Today* 53, no. 1 (2006): 3–33.

———. "The Qur'anic School Farm and Child Labour in Upper Volta." *Africa: Journal of the International African Institute* 54, no. 2 (1984): 71–87.

Savage, Elizabeth. "Berbers and Blacks: Ibadi Slave Traffic in Eighth-Century North Africa." *Journal of African History* 18, no. 2 (1992): 351–68.

Schmitz, Jean. "Un politologue chez les marabouts." *Cahiers d'Études Africaines* 91 (1983): 329–51.

———. "Le souffle de la parenté: marriage et transmission de la baraka chez des clercs musulmans de la vallée du Sénégal." *L'Homme* 154 (2000): 241–78.

Schoenbrun, David. "Conjuring the Modern in Africa: Durability and Rupture in Histories of Public Healing between the Great Lakes of East Africa." *American Historical Review* 111, no. 5 (2006): 1403–39.

Searing, James F. "Aristocrats, Slaves, and Peasants: Power and Dependency in the Wolof States, 1700–1850." *International Journal of African Historical Studies* 21, no. 3 (1988): 475–503.

———. *"God Alone Is King": Islam and Emancipation in Senegal: The Wolof Kingdoms of Kajoor and Bawol, 1859–1914*. Portsmouth: Heinemann, 2002.

———. *West African Slavery and Atlantic Commerce: The Senegal River Valley.* Cambridge: Cambridge University Press, 1993.
Sedgwick, Mark. *Muhammad Abduh*. Oxford: Oneworld, 2010.
Seesemann, Rüdiger. *The Divine Flood: Ibrāhīm Niasse and the Roots of a Twentieth-Century Sufi Revival.* Oxford: Oxford University Press, 2011.
———. "The 'Shurafa' and the 'Blacksmith': The Role of the Idaw Ali of Mauritania in the Career of the Senegalese Shaykh Ibrahim Niasse (1900–1975)." In *Transmission of Learning in Islamic Africa*, ed. Scott Reese, 72–98. Leiden: Brill, 2004.
———. "Where East Meets West: The Development of Qur'anic Education in Darfur." *Islam et Sociétés au Sud du Sahara* 13 (1999): 41–61.
Skinner, David E. "Islam and Education in the Colony and Hinterland of Sierra Leone (1750–1914)." *Canadian Journal of African Studies* 10, no. 3 (1976): 499–520.
Smith, Jane I., and Yvonne Haddad. *The Islamic Understanding of Death and Resurrection*. Albany: State University of New York Press, 1980.
Soares, Benjamin. *Islam and the Prayer Economy: History and Authority in a Malian Town*. Ann Arbor: University of Michigan Press, 2005.
———. "Notes on the Anthropological Study of Islam and Muslim Societies in Africa." *Culture and Religion* 1–2 (2000): 277–85.
Soh, Siré Abbas. "Chroniques du Foûta sénégalais." *Revue du Monde Musulman* 25 (1913).
Stambach, Amy. "Education, Religion, and Anthropology in Africa." *Annual Review of Anthropology* 39 (2010): 361–79.
Starrett, Gregory, *Putting Islam to Work: Education, Politics, and Religious Transformation in Egypt*. Berkeley: University of California Press, 1998.
Stewart, Charles Cameron. *Islam and Social Order in Mauritania: A Case Study from the Nineteenth Century.* Oxford: Clarendon, 1973.
Stoller, Paul. "Embodying Cultural Memory in Songhay Spirit Possession." *Archive de Sciences Sociales des Religions* 79 (1992): 53–68.
Sy, Cheikh Tidiane. "Ahmadou Bamba et l'islamisation des Wolof." *Bulletin de l'Institut Fondamental d'Afrique Noire*, ser. B, 32, no. 2 (1970): 412–33.
———. *La confrérie sénégalaise des Mourides*. Paris: Presence Africaine, 1969.
Sylla, Assane. *La philosophie morale des Wolof.* Dakar: Sankore, 1978.
Tamari, Tal. *Les castes de l'Afrique occidentale: artisans et musicians endogames.* Nanterre: Société d'Ethnologie, 1997.
———. "The Development of Caste Systems in West Africa." *Journal of African History* 32 (1991): 221–50.
———. "Islamic Higher Education in West Africa: Some Examples from Mali." In *Islam in Africa*, ed. George Stauth and Thomas Bierschenk. London: Lit, 2003.
———. "The Role of National Languages in Mali's Modernising Islamic Schools (*Madrasa*)." In *Languages and Education in Africa*, ed. Birgit Brock-Utne and Ingse Skattum. Oxford: Symposium, 2009.
Thilmans, G. "Le Sénégal dans l'oeuvre d'Olfried Dapper." *Bulletin de l'Institut Fondamental d'Afrique Noire*, ser. B, 33 (1971).
Thioub, Ibrahima. "Stigmas and Memory of Slavery in West Africa: Skin Color and Blood as Social Fracture Lines." *New Global Studies* 6, no. 3 (2012): 1–18.

Thornton, John K. *Africa and Africans in the Making of the Atlantic World, 1400–1800*. Cambridge: Cambridge University Press, 1998.
———. "African Political Ethics and the Slave Trade." In *Abolitionism and Imperialism in Britain, Africa, and the Atlantic*, ed. Derek R. Peterson, 38–62. Athens: Ohio University Press, 2010.
Touati, Henri. "Les héritiers: anthropologie des maisons de science maghrébines au XIe/XVIIe et XIIe/XVIIIe siècles." In *Modes de transmission de la culture religieuse en Islam*, ed. Hassan Elboudrari. Cairo: Institut Français d'Archéologie Orientale, 1993.
Traoré, Mahama J. "L'Islam Noir n'est pas violent: entretien avec Mahama Johnson Traoré." *Africultures* 47 (2002).
Triaud, Jean-Louis. "Le crepuscule des affaires musulmanes en AOF, 1950–1956." In *Le temps des marabouts: itinéraires et strategies islamiques en Afrique occidentale française*, ed. David Robinson and Jean-Louis Triaud. Paris: Karthala, 1997.
———. "Islam in Africa under French Colonial Rule." In *The History of Islam in Africa*, ed. Nehemia Levtzion and Randall Pouwels. Athens: Ohio University Press, 2000.
Triaud, Jean-Louis, and David Robinson., eds. *Le temps des marabouts: itinéraires et strategies islamiques en Afrique occidentale française*. Paris: Karthala, 1997.
———. *La Tijāniyya: une confrérie musulmane à la conquête de l'Afrique*. Paris: Karthala, 2000.
Trouillot, Michel-Rolph. *Silencing the Past: Power and the Production of History*. Boston: Beacon, 1995.
Umar, Muhammad Sani. "Mass Education and the Emergence of Female Ulama in Northern Nigeria." In *Transmission of Learning in Islamic Africa*, ed. Scott S. Reese, 99–120. Leiden: Brill, 2004.
UNESCO. "Hope for the Taalibés: The DAARA Association of Malika, Senegal." In *Working with Street Children: Selected Case Studies from Africa, Asia, and Latin America*. Paris: UNESCO, 1995.
Venema, L. B. *The Wolof of Saloum: Social Structure and Rural Development in Senegal*. Wageningen: Centre for Agricultural Publishing and Documentation, 1978.
Vikør, Knut. *Sufi and Scholar on the Desert Edge: Muhammad b. ʿAli al-Sanusi and His Brotherhood*. Evanston: Northwestern University Press, 1995.
———. "Sufi Brotherhoods in Africa." In *The History of Islam in Africa*, ed. Nehemia Levtzion and Randall Pouwels, 441–76. Athens: Ohio University Press, 2000.
Villalón, Leonardo. *Islamic Society and State Power in Senegal: Disciples and Citizens in Fatick*. Cambridge: Cambridge University Press, 1995.
———. "The Moustarchidine of Senegal: The Family Politics of a Contemporary Tijan Movement." In *La Tijāniyya: une confrérie musulmane à la conquête de l'Afrique*, ed. Jean-Louis Triaud and David Robinson. Paris: Karthala, 2000.
Villeneuve, Réné Geoffroy. *L'Afrique; Ou histoire, moeurs, usages, et coutumes des africains: le Sénégal*. Vols. 1–4. Paris: Nepveu, 1814.
Wane, Baila. "Le Fuuta Tooro de Ceerno Suleymaan Baal à la fin de l'almamiyat (1770–1880)." *Revue Sénégalaise d'Histoire* 1, no. 1 (1981): 38–50.
Wane, Yaya. *Les Toucouleur du Fouta Tooro (Sénégal): stratification sociale et structure familiale*. Dakar: Institut Fondamental d'Afrique Noire, 1969.

Ware, Rudolph. "In Praise of the Intercessor: A Verse Translation of *Mawāhib al-Nāfiʿ fī Madāʾiḥ al-Shāfiʿi* by Amadu Bamba Mbacké." *Islamic Africa* 4, no. 2 (2013).
———. "Islam in Africa." In *Princeton Companion to Atlantic History*, ed. Joseph Miller. Princeton: Princeton University Press, 2013.
———. "The Longue Durée of Qur'an Schooling, Society, and State in Senegambia, c. 1600-2000." In *New Perspectives on Islam in Senegal: Conversion, Migration, Wealth, Power, and Femininity*, ed. Mamadou Diouf and Mara Leichtman, 21–50. Basingstoke: Palgrave Macmillan, 2009.
———. "Njàngaan: The Daily Regime of Qur'anic Students in 20th Century Senegal." *International Journal of African Historical Studies* 37, no. 3 (2004): 515–38.
———. "Slavery in Islamic Africa, 1400–1800." In *Cambridge World History of Slavery*, ed. Stanley Engerman and David Eltis, 3:47–80. Cambridge: Cambridge University Press, 2011.
Ware, Rudolph, and Robert Launay. "Comment (ne pas) lire le Coran: logiques de l'enseignement religieux au Sénégal et en Côte d'Ivoire." In *L'Islam: nouvel espace publique en Afrique*, ed. Gilles Holder, 127–45. Paris: Karthala, 2009.
Werbner, Pnina, and Helene Basu, eds. *Embodying Charisma: Modernity, Locality, and Performance of Emotion in Sufi Cults.* London: Routledge, 1998.
WGBH Educational Foundation. *Africans in America: America's Journey through Slavery.* New York: Harcourt Brace, 1998.
Wilks, Ivor. "The Juula and the Expansion of Islam into the Forest." In *The History of Islam in Africa*, ed. Nehemia Levtzion and Randall Pouwels. Athens: Ohio University Press, 2000.
———. "The Transmission of Islamic Learning in the Western Sudan." In *Literacy in Traditional Societies*, ed. Jack Goody. Cambridge: Cambridge University Press, 1968.
Willis, John Ralph. *In the Path of Allah: The Passion of al-Hajj ʿUmar: An Essay into the Nature of Charisma in Islam*. London: Frank Cass, 1989.
———. "The Torodbe Clerisy: A Social View." *Journal of African History* 19 (1978): 195–212.
Wright, Zachary. *On the Path of the Prophet: Shaykh Ahmad Tijani and the Tariqa Muhammadiyya*. Atlanta: African American Islamic Institute, 2005.
Yamba, C. B. *On Permanent Pilgrims: The Role of Pilgrimage in the Lives of West African Muslims in Sudan*. Edinburgh: Edinburgh University Press, 1995.
Zadeh, Travis. "Fire Cannot Harm It: Mediation, Temptation, and the Charismatic Power of the Qurʾan." *Journal of Qurʾanic Studies* 10 (2008): 50–72.
———. "Touching and Ingesting: Early Debates over the Material Qurʾan." *Journal of the American Oriental Society* 129, no. 3 (2009): 443–66.
Zaman, Muhammad Q. "Religious Education and the Rhetoric of Reform: The Madrasa in British India and Pakistan." *Comparative Studies in Society and History* 41, no. 2 (1999): 294–323.

Unpublished Sources

Abdallah, Umar Faruq. "Malik's Concept of ʿAmal in the Light of Maliki Legal Theory." Ph.D. diss.,University of Chicago, 1978.

Almamy. "Système d'éducation traditionnelle des Torobés." Cahier William Ponty, XV-Se-10, Institut Fondamental d'Afrique Noire, Dakar, 1949.
Ames, David. "Plural Marriage among the Wolof in the Gambia." Ph.D. diss., Northwestern University, 1953.
Bamany, Modibo. "L'école coranique que vous avez fréquentée et que vous connaissez bien: mon école." Cahier William Ponty, Institut Fondamental d'Afrique Noire, Dakar, n.d.
Berndt, Jeremy. "Closer Than Your Jugular Vein: Muslim Intellectuals in a Malian Village, 1900 to the 1960s." Ph.D. diss., Northwestern University, 2008.
Beye, Demba. "Étude coranique de Gassama." Cahier William Ponty VII-Se-3, Institut Fondamental d'Afrique Noire, Dakar, [ca. 1941–44].
Brandes, George. "In Search of Sayyid Qutb: Reconceptualizing the Father of Islamic Fundamentalism." Undergraduate honors thesis, Northwestern University, 2007.
Charles, Eunice A. "A History of the Kingdom of Jolof (Senegal), 1800–1890." Ph.D. diss., Boston University, 1973.
Cissé, Moustapha. "Rapport d'orientation générale." Federation Nationale des Associations Culturelles Musulmanes du Sénégal, Congress, 7–9 March 1975.
Clarkson, Thomas. "Lettres nouvelles sur le commerce de la Côte de Guinée, 1789–1790." William L. Clements Library, University of Michigan, Ann Arbor.
Coifman, Victoria. "History of the Wolof State of Jolof until 1860." Ph.D. diss., University of Wisconsin, Madison, 1969.
Colvin, Lucie G. "Kajor and Its Diplomatic Relations with Saint-Louis du Senegal, 1763–1861." Ph.D. diss., Columbia University, 1972.
Comité National pour l'Action Sociale. "Rapport de synthèse du groupe de travail pour la participation des associations religieuses à l'action sociale: l'école coranique." Archives Nationales du Sénégal Library, Dakar, 11 June 1969.
Copans, Jean. "Entretiens avec des marabouts et des paysans du Baol." Vol. 2, Office de la Recherche Scientifique et Technique Outre-Mer, Dakar-Hann, October 1968.
Couty, Phillipe. "Entretiens avec des marabouts et des paysans du Baol." Vol. 1, Office de la Recherche Scientifique et Technique Outre-Mer, Dakar-Hann, February 1968.
Department of History, University of Liverpool. "Jesuit Documents on the Guinea of Cape Verde and the Cape Verde Islands, 1585–1617: In English Translation." 1989.
Diagne, Mody. "La religion, celle de votre famille, la vôtre." Cahier William Ponty VII-Se-4, Institut Fondamental d'Afrique Noire, Dakar, 1940–41.
Diané, Lansana. "Une école coranique que vous avez fréquentée." Cahier William Ponty VII-G-1, Institut Fondamental d'Afrique Noire, Dakar, n.d.
Diop, Abdourahmane. "Une école coranique que vous avez frequentée et que vous connaissez bien." Cahier William Ponty VII-Se-7, Institut Fondamental d'Afrique Noire, Dakar, [ca. 1941–44].
Diop, Malick. "Extraits de l'étude presentée par M. El Hadji Serigne Malick Diop, sur l'école Malekite Mohsinite de Saint-Louis." Seminar on Teaching the Qur'an in Senegal, Islamic Institute of Dakar, Department of Education, 17–18 May 1978.
Diop, Mamadou Lamine. "L'abreuvement du commensal: traité historique et biographique sur Cheikh Amadou Bamba." http://www.daarayweb.org.

Diop, Moumar Coumba. "Contribution a l'étude du Mouridisme: la relation taalibé—marabout." Memoire de Maitrise de Philosophie, University of Dakar, 1976.
Dramé, Aly. "Planting the Seeds of Islam: Karantaba, a Mandinka Muslim Center in the Casamance, Senegal." Ph.D. diss., University of Illinois at Chicago, 2006.
El Ayadi, Mohamed. "Les acteurs religieux dans le champ politique marocain." Placing the Maghrib at the Center of the Twentieth Century, University of Michigan, 7 April 2009.
Fall, Abd El Kader. "Allocution d'ouverture du seminaire sur l'enseignement du Coran au Sénégal." Seminar on Teaching the Qur'an in Senegal, Islamic Institute of Dakar, Department of Education, 17–18 May 1978.
Fall, Abdelkader. "Une école coranique que vous avez fréquentée et que vous connaissez bien." Cahier William Ponty VII-Se-6, Institut Fondamental d'Afrique Noire, Dakar, [ca. 1941–44].
Fall, Cheikh. "L'école coranique." Cahier William Ponty XV-Se-6, Institut Fondamental d'Afrique Noire, Dakar, 1946–48.
Fall, Médoune. "L'école coranique." Cahier William Ponty VII-Se-8, Institut Fondamental d'Afrique Noire, Dakar, [ca. 1941–44].
Faye, Sokhna Diouf. "L'efficacité externe des daara comme contribution à la stratégie educative au Sénégal: L'exemple du daara rural murid." Seminar on Islamic Education in Senegal, Institute for the Study of Islamic Thought in Africa, Dakar, August 2007.
Gomez-Perez, Muriel. "Une histoire des associations islamiques sénégalaises (Saint-Louis, Dakar, Thiès): itineraries, strategies, et prises de parole (1930–1993)." Ph.D. diss., Université de Paris VII Denis Diderot, 1997.
Gueye, Sega. "L'école coranique." Cahier William Ponty VII-Se-9, Institut Fondamental d'Afrique Noire, Dakar, [ca. 1941–44].
Institute for the Study of Islamic Thought in Africa. "Catalogue des bibliothèques de Fouta." Northwestern University Arabic Manuscript Library.
Irvine, Judith T. "Caste and Communication in a Wolof Village." Ph.D. diss., University of Pennsylvania, 1973.
Jah, Omar. "A Case Study of al-Haj Umar al-Futi's Philosophy of Jihad and Its Sufi Basis." Ph.D. diss., McGill University, 1973.
Johnson, James P. "The Almamate of Futa Toro, 1770–1836: A Political History." Ph.D. diss., University of Wisconsin, Madison, 1974.
Kābarī, Moddibo Muḥammad. *Bustān al-fawā'id wa al-manāfi'a fī 'ilm al-ṭibb wa al-sirr.* Partial copy at Herskovits Library, Northwestern University. Paden/161/MS. [Before 1450].
Kossmann, Martaan. 2007. "Berber Islamic Terminology in Wolof." Paper presented at "The Atlantic Languages: Typological or Genetic Unit?" University of Hamburg, 17–18 February 2007.
Lauzière, Henri. "Evolution of the Salafiyya in the Twentieth Century through the Life and Thought of Taqi al-Din al-Hilali." Ph.D. diss., Georgetown University, 2008.
Mane, Mamadou Marena. "Discours de cloture." Seminar on Teaching the Qur'an in Senegal, Islamic Institute of Dakar, Department of Education, 17–18 May 1978.

Mbaye, Ravane. "L'Islam au Sénégal." Thèse de Doctorat de Troisième Cycle, Université de Dakar, 1975–76.
Mbengue, Babacar. "L'enseignement de l'Arabe dans le système scolaire colonial du Sénégal."Master's thesis, Université Cheikh Anta Diop de Dakar, 1992–93.
Mohamed, Sidi. "Devoir de vacances, l'école coranique." Cahier William Ponty VII-M-I, Institut Fondamental d'Afrique Noire, Dakar, n.d.
Ndiaye, Baba. "L'Islam en pays noir, l'école coranique" ("L'Islam au Sénégal, l'école coranique"). Cahier William Ponty VII-Se-I, [ca. 1941–44].
Ndiaye, Mamadou. "Communication de l'Institut Islamique de Dakar." Seminar on Teaching the Qur'an in Senegal, Islamic Institute of Dakar, Department of Education, 17–18 May 1978.
O'Brien, Susan M. "Power and Paradox in Hausa Bori: Discourses of Gender, Healing, and Islamic Tradition in Northern Nigeria." Ph.D. diss., University of Wisconsin, Madison, 2000.
Roch, Jean. "Les Mourides du vieux bassin arachidier sénégalais: entretiens recueillis dans la region du Baol." ORSTOM, Dakar-Hann, March 1971.
Sakho, Youssouf. "Les croyances religieuses au Sénégal: principalement dans le Fouta-Toro, théâtre et source de grandes séditions islamiques, pays de fanatisme, foyer ardent du mahométisme." Cahier William Ponty XI-Se-1, Institut Fondamental d'Afrique Noire, Dakar, n.d.
Sy, Mamoudou. "Le DIMAR aux XVIIIe et XIX e siècles: trajectoire d'un état théocratique sénégambien." Thèse de Doctorat de Troisième Cycle, Université Cheikh Anta Diop de, Dakar, 2004.
Syndicat National des Enseignants en Langue Arabe au Sénégal. Untitled document, [after 1991]. In possession of the author.
Touré, Abd al-Aziz Muhammad al-Hadi. "Sur l'exèmple de l'école coranique de Fas Touré." Seminar on Teaching the Qur'an in Senegal, Islamic Institute of Dakar, Department of Education, 17–18 May 1978.
Wan Daud, Wan Mohd Nor. "The Concept of Knowledge in Islam and Its Implications on the National System of Education in the Malaysian Context." Ph.D. diss., University of Chicago, 1988.
Wane, Amadou. "Trois ans d'école coranique." Cahier William Ponty VII-Se-2, Institut Fondamental d'Afrique Noire, Dakar, 1943–44.
Ware, Rudolph. "Knowledge, Faith, and Power: A History of Qur'anic Schooling in Twentieth Century Senegal." Ph.D. diss., University of Pennsylvania, 2004.
Wiegelmann, Ulrike. "Alphabetisierung und Grundbildung in Senegal: Ein empirischer Vergleich zwishen modernen und traditionellen Bildungsgängen und Schulen." Ph.D. diss., University of Münster, 1998.
Wright, Zachary. "Embodied Knowledge in West African Islam: Continuity and Change in the Gnostic Community of Shaykh Ibrāhīm Niasse." Ph.D. diss., Northwestern University, 2010.

INDEX

Abbas Saal, 66
ʿAbduh, Muḥammad, 202, 208, 289 (n. 12)
ʿAbdul-Wahhāb, Muḥammad b., 13, 204, 210. *See also* Wahhabism
Abjad, xv, 20–21
Ablution, 3, 66–67, 73, 175, 229, 256
Abolitionism: Islamic and African forms, 37, 104, 110–17, 126–27, 131, 143–45, 161, 274 (nn. 8, 14), 277 (n. 67); as justification for European colonialism, 112, 244; French forms, 143–44, 148–49, 162–64, 171–72; British and American forms, 143–44, 277 (n. 67). *See also* Almaami ʿAbdul-Qādir; Clarkson, Reverend Thomas; Slavery or slaves
Abraham (Prophet), 248
Abū Bakr al-Ṣiddīq, 27, 59
Adab (good conduct), 54, 58–60, 72
Adam (Prophet), 239, 248, 255–57
African-American Islamic Institute, 246
Aḥmad b. Idrīs, 210, 251, 253
ʿĀʾisha (wife of Prophet), 7
ʿ*Ajamī* writing, 31, 35, 45, 66, 174, 245
Alcohol (eau de vie or *sangara*), 100–102, 105, 108, 122, 128, 148, 151, 278 (nn. 80, 82)
Algeria, 10, 41, 197, 199
ʿAlī b. Abū Ṭālib, 59, 71, 268 (n. 68)
Alidou, Ousseina, 173
Almaami ʿAbdul-Qādir, 111, 114–17, 125–46 passim, 149–50, 153–54, 161–62, 247
Almada, André Alvares, 96, 101, 272 (nn. 53, 55)
Almamy (Ponty student), 283 (n. 28), 287 (n. 124), 292 (n. 1)
Almoravids, 94–95, 272 (n. 46)
Alms: and *taalibés*, 3, 39–40, 43, 46–48, 76, 188–89, 217, 229, 237, 249; *ṣadaqa*, 3, 40, 43, 46–48, 61, 76, 97–98, 106, 174, 187, 189, 204, 217–18, 222, 229, 237–41, 248–50; associated with clerics, 47, 97–98; offerings of food, 61, 187, 239; modern unease with, 204, 217–19, 222, 238, 241; giving as cultural value, 218, 239–40, 290 (n. 44); *zakāt*, 237–38; white alms, 248; as expiation, 249–50
Alphabet: teaching of, 3, 20–21, 173, 195. See also *Abjad*; Literacy skills
Alwāḥ or *àlluwa* (boards or tablets), 2, 9–10, 21, 32, 43, 47, 50, 52, 57–61, 66, 68, 72, 78–79, 83–84, 97, 103, 182, 208–9, 227, 233–36, 240–41, 244, 250–52. See also *Maḥw* or *miḥāya*
Amadu Shehu, 156–57, 162
ʿ*Amal* (deeds), 8, 12, 55–56, 267 (n. 66)
André, P. J. (alias Pierre Rédan), 200, 288 (n. 147)
Angels: Jibrīl, 1, 9, 25, 70, 262 (n. 17); recording deeds, 90, 158; of death and grave, 249–50, bowing to Adam, 256
Antislavery. *See* Abolitionism
ʿ*Aqīqa* (naming ceremony), 136, 248
Asad, Talal, 76, 270 (n. 116)
ʿĀshūrāʾ, 94, 248–50, 293 (n. 20)
Askiya Muḥammad Turé, 206
Atlantic slave trade. *See* Euro-American slave trade
Aurality and orality, 1, 6, 25–28, 50, 52, 71, 73, 231, 252–54
Al-Azhar (Egypt), 202, 205, 207–8, 214, 224
Al-Azhar Institute (Touba), 227–28
Averroes (Muḥammad Ibn Rushd), 205

Ba, Maḥmūd, 203–4, 207, 211, 213–14, 221, 230
Ba, Tafsiir Hamadi, 134–35, 144, 279 (n. 107)
Baal, Ceerno Sulaymaan, 110–11, 119, 122–23, 125–26, 128–29, 154, 275 (n. 24), 276 (n. 44), 277 (n. 60)

Babou, Cheikh Anta Mbacké, 159, 183
Badibu (in Rip region), 120, 152
Bah, Ceerno Saydu Nuuru, 276 (n. 44)
Bàjjan, Ibrahima, 48–49, 227–30, 234–35
Al-Bakrī, Abū ʿUbayd, 86, 93–94
Bamany, Modibo (Ponty student), 48, 173, 191, 193, 239–40, 288 (n. 128)
Bamba, Amadu: and racial attitudes, 24–25, 75; educational ethics, 53–54; bodily reverence of his disciples, 66; *Masālik al-Jinān*, 75, 248, 255; resisting enslavement of Muslims, 154–62, 164; scholarship of daughters, 160, 174; Sufism and educational innovation, 180–87; scholarly productivity, 247; on ʿĀshūrāʾ, 248; on pride and body, 255; *Nahj Qaḍāʾ al-Hāj* (on *adab*), 267 (n. 59)
Bambara, 132–33, 139–42, 154, 160
Bang, Anne, 205, 288 (n. 155), 289 (n. 7)
Banī Ḥasān, 103, 110–11, 119–26, 128, 133–34, 150, 275 (n. 37). See also *Bayḍān*; Brākna; Trārza
Banjul, 12
Al-Bannā, Ḥasan, 208. *See also* Islamism; Qutb, Sayyid
Baraka or *barke*), 53, 67, 164, 179, 184, 186, 189, 234, 282 (n. 4)
Barbot, Jean, 104
Barry, Boubacar, 103, 273 (n. 79)
Bashir, Shahzad, 6
Bashirīn, *bixirin*, or *bushreen*, 79, 96, 101, 266 (n. 27). *See also* Clerisy or clerics; *Sëriñs*; Toorobbe
Bāṭin. *See* Esoteric knowledge
Bayḍān, 24, 34, 82–84, 90–92, 105–7, 110, 119, 126, 128–31, 140, 148, 183, 200, 247
Berbers, 19, 34, 87, 91, 93–95, 103, 108. See also *Bayḍān*
Berkey, Jonathan, 62
Beye, Demba (Ponty student), 45, 193, 250, 265 (n. 12)
Bilāl the Muezzin, 1, 13, 25–29, 264 (n. 62)
Blood: as metaphor for kinship, 26, 82–84, 104, 109; of Prophet, 64–67, 252; and ink, 66–67, 109, 119, 130, 145, 179; of martyrs, 77–78, 109; sanctity of, 97, 132–33, 137, 156; carrying impurity, 166–67; and ritual, 286 (n. 85)
Bodies: limbs of, 1, 6, 8, 42, 49–50, 54, 66–67, 110, 113–15, 144, 252–55, 271 (n. 12); and Cartesian division, 5, 67, 252; as flesh, 8, 42, 49, 118, 239, 243–44, 253–54, 256; and alleged impurity, 37, 163–72, 270 (n. 10), 283 (nn. 24, 26); capable of sanctifying space, 65–66, 96–97, 142–43, 251, 272 (n. 38); as knowing and sentient, 253. *See also* Embodiment; Walking Qurʾan
Bokidiawé, 230–32
Bousbina, Saïd, 304
Brak, 104, 128, 278 (n. 80). *See also* Waalo
Brākna, 128, 131, 141, 277 (n. 73)
Brenner, Louis, 4, 178, 204–7, 263 (n. 51)
Brigaglia, Andrea, 289 (n. 17)
Bryant, Sherwin, 277 (n. 68)
Bunaama (Abū Naʿam), 148
Bundu, 125, 139–40, 152
Burkina Faso, 266 (n. 28)
Buurba Jolof, 95, 278 (n. 89)

Caam, Jilé, 150–52
Caam, Mansuur, 230
Cà da Mosto, Alvise, 95–96, 100
Cahiers Ponty: as source, 11, 194; illustrations in, 43; representations of discipline, 48–49; and remuneration of teachers, 189; and colonial indoctrination, 194–95
Caliphs or caliphates, 2, 24, 27, 29, 69–70, 90, 112–15, 158, 179, 225–26, 246, 262 (n. 17)
Cantor (Kantora), 88, 96
Carruthers, Mary, 270 (n. 112)
Caste (*ñeeño*), 82–83, 108, 163–69, 176–77, 188–90, 241, 270 (n. 9), 271 (n. 22), 283 (n. 11). *See also* Bodies: and alleged impurity
Ceddo, 98, 100–108, 119–22, 126–28, 147–48, 151, 153–54, 168, 184

Chamberlain, Michael, 70
Chambonneau, Louis Mareau de, 104, 124, 147
Cissé, Shaykh Hassan, 246
Clarkson, Reverend Thomas, 114–18, 126–31, 143, 244, 275 (n. 19)
Clerisy or clerics: and social hierarchies, 9, 17, 34, 36, 47, 82–85, 96–99, 107–9, 164–65, 203, 213; and spatial organization, 16, 86, 90, 95, 96–99, 107–8, 176–77, 181–85; embracing politics, 31, 37, 95, 111–14, 119–22, 125, 139, 146–62 passim, 206, 210; rooted in teaching, 34, 59, 77–80, 82–83, 89, 100, 165, 178, 224; shunning politics, 37, 89–90, 97–99, 112, 145, 157–58, 162; as internal diaspora, 61, 78–80, 89, 96, 100, 181–82; emergence and definitions of, 77–81, 86–87, 93–94; multiethnic composition, 79, 81, 84, 91, 108, 144–45; and critique of Atlantic economy, 101–8, 243; and Sufism, 178–88, 216; and memories of colonial repression, 193; colonial approaches to, 196–201, 214; of Saudi regime, 204, 210; mediating educational change, 207, 223–33 passim. *See also* Blood: and ink; Marabouts; *Sëriñs*; Sufism; Tooroɓɓe; Walking Qur'an: as synonym for *hāfiẓ* or *huffāẓ*
Coifman, Victoria, 272 (n. 49)
Colvin, Lucie, 133, 147, 151, 176
Concubines, 119, 140, 152–54, 170–71, 283 (n. 31)
Corporal punishment, 1, 3, 8, 39–44, 51–52, 66, 222, 228

Daara. See Qur'an schooling
Daara tarbiya, 184–85
Dakar (Ndakaaru), 2, 10–12, 50, 63, 146, 152, 172–73, 175, 177, 192, 200, 204, 212, 216–17, 221–22, 237–38, 243–44, 247–48
Dammels: of Kajoor, 95, 100–101, 103, 147–52, 243–44; Maaxuréja Kuuli, 99; Deccefu Njoogu, 100; Amari Ngóone Sobel, 100, 243; assassination of Fali Géy, 105; Bira Mbanga, 105; Dao Semba, 105; Latsukaabe, 106; Biram Fatim Penda, 128; Amari Ngóone Ndella Kumba, 133–37, 142, 145–48, 243; Birima Fatma Cubb, 147–50; Maissa Tenda Joor, 152, 160; Lat Joor Jóob, 154–59, 183
Deeñanke, 98, 107, 111, 119–27, 132–33, 137–39, 142, 145, 154
Dia, Mamadou, 215, 286 (n. 89)
Diagne, Souleymane Bachir, 269
Diané, Lansana (Ponty student), 52, 291 (n. 85)
Diop, Abdourahmane (Ponty student), 172–73, 189, 287 (n. 98), 293 (n. 25)
Diouf, Demba Lamine, 99
Diouf, Sylviane, 269 (n. 101), 275 (n. 28)
Divination, Islamic, 14, 79, 261 (n. 12)
Duʿā. See Prayers: supplication
Dudal. See Qur'an schooling
Durand, Jean, 278 (n. 80)
Dutton, Yasin, 55, 269 (n. 107)

Écoles arabes (modern Arabic schools), 3, 15–17, 38, 63, 67–68, 198, 200, 202, 204–7, 213–16, 220–36
Écoles françaises (French schools), 48, 165, 188, 191–95, 212–13
Écoles franco-arabes. See *Écoles arabes*
Egypt, 10, 16, 18, 62, 72, 85, 94, 202, 205, 207–11, 214, 221, 224, 231, 262 (n. 28)
Eickelman, Dale, 202
El-Tom, Abdullahi Osman, 58, 62–63
Embodiment: and Islamic studies, 1–10; and mastery or masters, 6, 53–55, 66, 68–75, 84, 98, 178, 185–88, 194, 211, 231, 233, 262 (n. 17); as internalization, 8, 50, 54, 68–69, 72, 111, 164, 213; as posture or disposition, 9, 16, 45, 50, 60, 108, 234–35; as incorporation, 36, 61, 203, 209–10, 239–41, 247–51; as practical example or mimesis, 37, 55–56, 84, 96, 103, 205, 268 (n. 68); and epistemology, 49–57; as personification,

54–56, 205, 210, 267 (n. 61). *See also* Bodies; Walking Qur'an
Epistemology, 3–4, 7, 9–10, 14–15, 23, 31–38, 41–42, 49–57, 67–76, 82, 98, 111, 164–66, 195–96, 202–14 passim, 227–36, 245–57 passim
Eschatology (death and end of days), 129, 142, 150, 237, 243–44, 247–50, 257
Esoteric knowledge, 4, 14, 79, 92, 130, 183, 204–5, 211, 247. *See also* Talismans
Ethiopia, 17–18, 26–29
Ethnicity, xvi, 24–25, 29, 33–34, 79, 81, 84, 91, 95, 108, 138, 144–45, 196–97, 218, 241. *See also* Banī Ḥasān; Berbers; Fula; Mandingo; Race; Sereer; Soninke; Wolof
Euro-American slave trade, 31, 36–37, 69, 80–82, 84, 99–101, 103, 106, 110–18, 123–24, 135–36, 141–43, 148, 161–62, 269 (n. 59), 275 (n. 28)

Faidherbe, Louis, 149, 191–92, 278 (n. 80)
Fall, Abdelkader (Ponty student), 47, 52, 61, 173–74, 190–91, 234, 263 (n. 46), 270 (n. 7), 286 (n. 94)
Fall, Amar Jégi (Qāḍī Amar Fall), 99
Fall, Malick Seye (Ponty student), 266 (n. 39)
Fall, Médoune (Ponty student), 189–91, 194, 235, 266 (n. 22)
Fasting, 139, 229, 249–50
Fatima (daughter of Prophet), 139
Faye, Sokhna Diouf, 244–45
Feierman, Steven, 32–33, 35, 246, 263 (n. 52)
Fiqh, 68, 125, 140, 178, 199, 229, 231, 250, 267 (n. 63), 291 (n. 87). *See also* Islamic law; Mālikī *madhhab*; *Qāḍīs*; Sharia
Fortier, Corinne, 4, 261 (n. 5), 262 (n. 24), 265 (n. 11), 293 (n. 25)
Ft. James, 80, 120
Fula (Pulaar or Fulfulde), xvi–xvii, 45, 48, 83, 93, 95, 98, 100, 125, 135, 166, 190, 231, 241, 270 (n. 2)
Fulɓe (Toucouleur, Peul, Fulani), xvi, 51, 53, 73, 91, 93, 95, 98, 100, 107–10, 119, 123, 139, 146, 148, 150, 169, 172, 179, 203
Fuuta Tooro: Qur'an schools in, 12, 44, 50, 51, 93; and ISITA research, 12, 50, 221, 290 (n. 56), 292 (n. 89); photos of, 44, 51, 130, 232; and Tuubanaan movement, 104–7; theater for 1770s revolution, 110–11, 115–17, 119–45 passim, 150, 153–54; homeland of nineteenth-century clerics, 179–80; and twentieth-century scholars, 204, 221, 231, 246. *See also* Almaami ʿAbdul-Qādir; Bokidiawé; Fula; Fulɓe; Takrūr; Tooroɓɓe

Gambia, 9, 12, 80, 96, 107, 132, 136, 147, 152, 262 (n. 27). *See also* Jakhanke
Gariibu, 48, 250. See also *Taalibés*
Géer. *See* Caste
Gender: and spirit possession, 4–5; female scholars, 5, 9, 81, 130, 160, 247, 262 (n. 15), 284 (n. 52); education of girls, 5, 45–46, 160, 172–76, 284 (nn. 42, 47); Qur'anic conception of gender difference, 25; gendered socialization, 44–46, 48, 173–74, 191; covering female bodies, 45–46, 87, 206, 253; and notions of honor, 46, 119, 124, 126, 152–54, 160, 169; marriage and kinship, 83–84, 98, 105, 109, 133, 149, 152, 154, 163, 168, 170, 185, 271 (n. 14), 274 (n. 91), 283 (n. 24); and gendered political violence, 124, 139–40, 147–48, 152–54, 160; and low status groups, 168–70, 176; mothers of *daaras*, 240; and Islamic feminism, 247; gender reversal on ʿĀshūrāʾ, 249. *See also* Khadīja bint Muḥammad al-ʿĀqil; Niass, Mariama
Gente. See *ʿAqīqa*
Gerresch, Claudine, 156
Géwël. See Griots
Ghana Empire, 84–88, 90, 93–95
Ghazālī, Abū Ḥamid b. Muḥammad, 69, 75, 269 (n. 100)
Glover, John, 157

263 (n. 33). See also *Écoles arabes*; Islamism; Salafism; Wahhabism

84, 193, 200–201, 204, 211–13, 216, 219, 224–25, 227–30, 233
Pilgrimages, 85, 91, 94, 96–97, 150, 168, 181, 202–4, 210–11, 224, 272 (n. 48)
Pir, 97–99, 109, 119, 125, 134, 136, 145, 149
Ponty, William, 20, 197–200
Prayers: *ṣalāt* daily ritual, 1–3, 9, 27, 43, 50, 55–56, 91, 93–94, 145, 147, 175–76, 190, 229–31, 235, 250; Friday congregational, 2, 86, 91; *adhān* call to, 28–29, 240; supplication, 61, 79–80, 84, 97, 130, 136, 145, 149, 152, 230, 250, 272 (n. 38); for protection, 79; for rain, 79, 195, 270 (n. 4); litanies, 179–82. *See also* God; *Qabḍ*; *Sadl*; *Wird*

Qabḍ, 55–56, 230, 267 (n. 65)
Al-Qābisī, 58–63, 268 (n. 76)
Qāḍīs, 60, 87, 90, 99, 105, 125, 154–60. *See also* Islamic law
Qādiriyya, 24, 148, 178–82, 185. *See also* Murīdiyya; Sufism; Tijāniyya
Qalam. See *Xalima* or *qalam*
Al-Qayrawānī, 56, 231, 250, 266 (n. 38), 268 (nn. 69, 76), 276 (n. 44)
Qurʾan or God's Word: transmission and reproduction of, 1, 6, 14, 55, 63, 71, 76; revelation of, 1, 7, 25–26, 45, 70, 234, 262 (n. 17); recitation of, 1–2, 7–9, 14, 21, 27, 44, 47, 51–53, 62, 71, 76, 95, 110, 114–15, 125, 139, 154, 187, 194, 209, 227, 231, 233–34, 237, 243, 250; language of, 3, 207, 214–15, 234–35; and jinn, 5, 167, 209, 255, 292 (n. 10); keepers and bearers of, 8, 36, 49, 54, 70, 79, 111, 122, 133, 137, 139, 163, 171, 257; written on flesh, 8, 39–42, 49, 254; quotations and citations from, 10, 25–26, 61, 69, 78, 234, 250, 255–57; agency or power of, 14, 51, 57, 60–63, 66, 79–80, 122, 126, 143, 209, 214, 235, 251, 256; as *muṣḥaf* (written copy), 14, 71, 239; communities of, 17, 80–84, 90, 95–99, 105–8, 148–50, 184, 186, 239–41; creation stories, 25–26, 234, 239, 248, 255–57; deserving respect, 43–44, 59–60, 110, 229, 235; love and affection for, 44, 72, 209, 252; requiring preparation for, 49, 61, 235, 257; as social critique, 239. *See also* Embodiment; *Maḥw* or *miḥāya*; Qurʾan schooling; Walking Qurʾan
Qurʾan schooling: corporeal discipline, 1, 3, 8, 41–44; basic aims and origins, 1–3, 5, 7–9; contemporary perceptions of, 1–3, 39–41, 213, 216–20, 222–23; alms seeking and mendicancy, 1–3, 46–48; Western perceptions of, 2–3, 39–41, 212–13; materials of instruction, 9–10, 57–60, 233–36, 244; regional distribution of, 10, 77–80, 89, 100; and Sufism, 11, 37, 48, 162–65, 176–88 passim, 244–46; as public symbol of Muslim identity, 16–17, 43–44, 84, 87, 192, 240; first days of school, 21, 50–52, 60–62, 233–34, 239, 270 (n. 7); chores and labor, 39–40, 45–46; pleasures of learning, 51–52; veneration of teachers, 53–54; spreading Islam in West Africa, 77–89 passim, 219; and social status, 83, 163–66, 168–72, 176–78, 184, 188–91, 241; recent transformations in, 207, 227–36. See also *Abjad*; Alphabet; Embodiment; Gender: gendered socialization; Literacy skills; Memorization; Pedagogy; Qurʾan or God's Word
Quraysh, 26–29, 65, 138, 239
Qutb, Sayyid, 71–72, 208, 251–52, 270 (n. 108), 293 (n. 27). *See also* Islamism

Race, 10, 13–14, 16, 19–30 passim, 34, 36–37, 41, 63, 75, 78, 82–83, 87, 90–92, 105, 123, 126, 140, 152, 180, 192–93, 195–202, 215, 224, 241, 247, 278 (n. 88). See also *Bayḍān*; Euro-American slave trade; Islam Noir; Slavery or slaves
Reason or rationalization, 5, 15, 43, 71–75, 143, 194–96, 202, 205, 216, 219, 251–54
Riḍā, Rashīd, 202, 209, 251

Society for the Abolition of the Slave Trade, 113–14, 143. *See also* Abolitionism: British and American forms
Somalis, 18–19
Songhay Empire, 85, 90, 206
Soninke, 83, 85, 87, 91, 93–95, 148, 166. *See also* Ghana Empire; Jakhanke
Sow, Aḥmad, 230–31. *See also* Ḥarakat al-Falāḥ
Spirit possession, 4–6, 14, 167. *See also* Qur'an or God's Word: and jinn
Starrett, Gregory, 16, 197
Stewart, Charles, 269 (n. 91)
Sudan, 10, 17, 58–59, 225, 262 (n. 27)
Sufism: part of religious sciences curricula, 6, 68, 165, 291 (n. 87); as embodiment, 6, 254; and Qur'an schooling, 11, 37, 48, 162–65, 176–88 passim, 244–46; as "African Islam," 14, 34, 66, 196; social expansion of, 37, 165–66, 176–88 passim; and Salafism, 38, 66–67, 207, 220–21, 223–27; as *jihād al-nafs*, 155; and pedagogy, 155; and colonial administration, 194, 212; and postcolonial state, 213–16, 219–20, 233, 287 (n. 120); and statutory associations, 218, 225–27; safeguarding classical epistemology, 253–54. *See also* God: experiential knowledge of; Murīdiyya; *Tarbiya*; Qādiriyya; Tijāniyya
Ṣuḥba (companionship), 53–54
Sunjaata Keita, 95
Sunna, 7, 12–13, 56, 113, 212, 252
Suwarī, Al-Ḥājj Salīm (Cissé), 89. *See also* Jakhanke
Al-Suyuṭī, Jalāl al-Dīn. See *Tafsīr*: Jalālayn
Sy, al-Ḥājj Mālik, 165, 180–82, 184–86, 225–26, 229, 268 (n. 70), 285 (n. 65). *See also* Tijāniyya
Sy, Mamoudou, 276 (n. 44)
Syed, Amir, 262 (n. 19)
Sylla, Mañaaw, 187
Syncretism, 4–5, 14, 20–22, 31, 57–58, 63, 66, 161, 196–98, 206, 210
Syria, 17–18, 66, 70, 210
Taal, Al-Ḥājj ʿUmar, 31, 161–62, 179–80, 185, 201, 273 (n. 70), 285 (n. 64), 288 (n. 150)
Taalibés, 3, 39–40, 45–47, 53, 110, 136, 143, 170, 174, 178, 181, 185–89, 190, 200–201, 215, 217–19, 222, 229, 235, 236–42, 245–50, 253, 265 (n. 8), 286 (n. 89), 290 (n. 44)
Taʿalīm, 184, 230, 244
Tafsīr: embodied exegesis, 12, 263 (n. 32); classical genre, 26, 72; Jalālayn, 89, as honorific in Fula, 135; Lo family, 185; at Médersa of St. Louis, 199–200; al-Manār, 209; of Adam's creation, 239; *firi* or Pir in Wolof, 273 (n. 68). *See also* Ba, Tafsiir Hamadi; Pir
Tahdhīb of al-Barādhʿī, 91–92, 272 (n. 36)
Takfir, 161, 210
Takrūr, 93–95, 243, 272 (n. 48). *See also* Fuuta Tooro
Talismans (*ṭilāsim*), 96, 126, 269 (n. 90), 279 (n. 120), 288 (n. 146)
Al-Tamāsīnī, Sīdī ʿAlī, 66
Tamkharit. *See* ʿĀshūrā'
Tarbiya (spiritual training), 48, 72, 183–85, 230, 244, 267 (nn. 56, 58)
Ta'rīkh al-Fattāsh, 90, 271
Ta'rīkh al-Sūdān, 90–91, 139, 243
Tarqiyya (ascension), 183–84
Taṣawwuf. *See* Sufism
Tawḥīd. *See* God: oneness of; Theology
Theology (study of *tawḥīd*), 130, 178, 199
Thioub, Ibrahima, 275 (n. 18), 283 (n. 26)
Thornton, John, 117–18
Al-Tijānī, Aḥmad, 66, 181–82, 269 (n. 92)
Tijāniyya, 11, 24, 48, 66, 174–77, 179–82, 187, 211, 223–29, 246, 268 (n. 70), 270 (n. 114), 284 (n. 61), 285 (n. 64), 286 (n. 85). *See also* Niass, Al-Ḥājj ʿAbdullahi; Niass, Shaykh Ibrāhīm; Sy, al-Ḥājj Mālik; Taal, Al-Ḥājj ʿUmar; Al-Tijānī, Aḥmad
Timbuktu, 77, 88, 90–93, 97, 113, 148, 200, 206, 247, 251. See also Ta'rīkh al-Fattāsh; Ta'rīkh al-Sūdān

Tivaouane, 11, 45, 47–48, 177, 181–82, 225–29
Toorobbe, 98, 122, 132, 139, 144–45, 164, 179, 195, 203
Touati, Henri, 282 (n. 4)
Touba, 11, 51–53, 177, 193, 227–29, 242, 244
Touré, Cheikh, 211, 220, 223
Trārza, 123–24, 126–29, 131, 135, 150. *See also* Banī Ḥasān; *Bayḍān*
Triaud, Jean-Louis, 214
Trimingham, J. Spencer, 22
Tunisia, 10, 58
Tuubanaan, 103–9, 114, 119, 123

ʿUmar b. al-Khaṭṭāb, 2, 59, 115, 262 (n. 17)
Umm walad. *See* Concubines
ʿUthmān b. ʿAffān, 27, 59, 292 (n. 7)
ʿUthmān b. Fūdī (Usman dan Fodio), 31, 161–62, 254

Villalon, Leonardo, 227, 287 (n. 120)
Villeneuve, Réné Geoffroy de, 115–17, 266 (n. 29), 270 (n. 3)

Waalo, 95, 104, 107, 124, 128–31, 146, 149–52, 163, 166, 276 (nn. 47, 48, 51), 279 (n. 99). *See also* Brak
Wahhabism, 6, 12–16, 62–64, 203–4, 210–14, 221–25, 230–32
Walking Qurʾan: as actualized knowledge, 4, 8, 14, 36, 54–55, 95, 114, 183, 245; as synonym for *ḥāfiẓ* or *huffāẓ*, 7, 37, 69, 84, 95, 109, 203; as reference to Prophet, 7–8, 10, 12, 25–29, 36, 49, 66–67, 79; as textual embodiment, 7–8, 36–37, 42, 49–52, 69, 96, 165, 237, 251; and mobile knowledge, 32, 83–84, 110, 203, 237; enslavement and murder of, 110–15, 129, 133–56 passim
Wane, Amadou (Ponty student), 60–61, 279 (n. 116)
Al-Wansharīsī, 114–15
Warsh, ʿUthmān b. Saʿīd al-Miṣrī, 21, 231
Wiegelmann, Ulrike, 245
Wilks, Ivor, 89
Wird (*awrād*). *See* Prayers: litanies
Witches (*dëmm*), 79, 167–68, 239–40
Wolof: language, 8, 11–12, 25, 42, 51, 53, 57–58, 76, 79, 83, 93, 99, 103, 115, 128, 133, 137, 152, 160, 186, 199, 234, 238, 241, 243, 248–49; ethnicity, 95–98, 100–109, 135, 137, 146–47, 149, 163, 166, 170, 172, 179–80, 187, 241
Wolofal. See *ʿAjamī* writing
Wright, Zachary, 23, 284 (n. 61), 291 (n. 70)

Xalima or *qalam* (Pen), 9–10, 26, 32, 57, 78, 234–35, 244, 254

Yalwaan. *See* Alms: and *taalibés*
Yasin Buubu (*lingeer*), 105, 149
Yemen, 68
Yūsuf b. Tāshfīn, 94

Zadeh, Travis, 265 (n. 9), 268 (n. 82)
Ẓāhir. *See* Esoteric knowledge
Zakāt. *See* Alms
Zawāyā, 103
Zāwiya, 181–82, 225

Rudolph T. Ware III, *The Walking Qur'an: Islamic Education, Embodied Knowledge, and History in West Africa* (2014).

Sa'diyya Shaikh, *Sufi Narratives of Intimacy: Ibn 'Arabī, Gender, and Sexuality* (2012).

Karen G. Ruffle, *Gender, Sainthood, and Everyday Practice in South Asian Shi'ism* (2011).

Jonah Steinberg, *Isma'ili Modern: Globalization and Identity in a Muslim Community* (2011).

Iftikhar Dadi, *Modernism and the Art of Muslim South Asia* (2010).

Gary R. Bunt, *iMuslims: Rewiring the House of Islam* (2009).

Fatemeh Keshavarz, *Jasmine and Stars: Reading More than "Lolita" in Tehran* (2007).

Scott A. Kugle, *Sufis and Saints' Bodies: Mysticism, Corporeality, and Sacred Power in Islam* (2007).

Roxani Eleni Margariti, *Aden and the Indian Ocean Trade: 150 Years in the Life of a Medieval Arabian Port* (2007).

Sufia M. Uddin, *Constructing Bangladesh: Religion, Ethnicity, and Language in an Islamic Nation* (2006).

Omid Safi, *The Politics of Knowledge in Premodern Islam: Negotiating Ideology and Religious Inquiry* (2006).

Ebrahim Moosa, *Ghazālī and the Poetics of Imagination* (2005).

miriam cooke and Bruce B. Lawrence, eds., *Muslim Networks from Hajj to Hip Hop* (2005).

Carl W. Ernst, *Following Muhammad: Rethinking Islam in the Contemporary World* (2003).

Made in the USA
Columbia, SC
29 January 2020

87273724R00212